PUBLICATIONS
OF THE
AMERICAN ASSOCIATION
FOR
NETHERLANDIC STUDIES

PAPERS FROM
THE THIRD
INTERDISCIPLINARY
CONFERENCE ON
NETHERLANDIC STUDIES

held at
The University of Michigan
Ann Arbor
12-14 June 1986

Edited by
Ton J. Broos

Copyright © 1988 by

The American Association for Netherlandic Studies

University Press of America,® Inc.

4720 Boston Way
Lanham, MD 20706

3 Henrietta Street
London WC2E 8LU England

All rights reserved

Printed in the United States of America

British Cataloging in Publication Information Available

Co-published by arrangement with
The American Association for Netherlandic Studies, Inc.

ISBN 0–8191–7056–9 (alk. paper)

All University Press of America books are produced on acid-free paper which exceeds the minimum standards set by the National Historical Publications and Records Commission.

Foreword

This volume marks the first issue of the *Publications of the American Association of Netherlandic Studies* (PAANS), which, as the name suggests, is the official publication of the five-year old American Association of Netherlandic Studies (AANS). Though still in its formative stage of development, AANS has already had a remarkable growth. With a membership of over two hundred, AANS consists mainly of American academics engaged in the teaching or research of Dutch language, literature, history, art history, music, and other areas in the fields of Dutch culture, including the humanities, the social sciences, and sometimes even the physical and mathematical sciences.

Because our organization represents so many diverse disciplines whose focus is the Netherlands and the Dutch language areas of Belgium, we encourage an interdisciplinary approach to Dutch studies, often producing interesting results not encountered in most specialized organizations. Though primarily an American body, AANS has also attracted a considerable number of foreign members who are making valuable contributions. Besides scholars from the Netherlands and Belgium, our membership includes participants from Canada, Great Britain, Australia, and Indonesia.

During the first five years of its existence, AANS organized three conferences, the so-called bi-annual Interdisciplinary Conference on Netherlandic Studies (ICNS), held in 1982 (University of Maryland), 1984 (Georgetown University) and 1986 (University of Michigan). We also publish two Newsletters per year which have been expanded to include book reviews.

The Association is governed by a Board of Directors, of which the five-member Executive Council takes care of the practical operations. Under the auspices of the Board Proceedings of the first two ICNS conferences have been published, with generous contributions from the Dutch Ministry of Education and Sciences and the Taalunie, which in turn is supported by the governments of The Netherlands and Belgium.

But the Board has decided to discontinue the *Proceedings* format and initiate a new venture. Beginning with the present issue, *PAANS* will represent the official journal of the Association (besides the Newsletter) and publish not only a selected number of the papers presented at the ICNS conferences, but gradually include other articles and reviews as well. The journal will appear irregularly at first, and we will not solicit subscriptions. We expect that in the not too distance future *PAANS* will in effect become a Yearbook, featuring interdisciplinary articles on Dutch culture primarily--but not exclusively--by American scholars. Judging from the response of ICNSparticipants, the Board believes there should be plenty of material for a highly respectable journal.

The editorial Board of *PAANS* will consist of the Executive Council of AANS, which may appoint a Special Editor for any given issue. Appropriately, the Special Editor of the first volume is Ton Broos, who does not only serve as Officer at Large on the Executive Council, but who also organized the successful Third Interdisciplinary Conference on Netherlandic Studies, where the articles in this volume were first presented as papers.

The Editorial Board of PAANS consists of

>Ton Broos, University of Michigan (Ann Arbor);
>Margriet Lacey, North Dakota State University (Fargo);
>Walter Lagerwey, Calvin College (Grand Rapids);
>Johan Snapper, University of California (Berkeley);
>Ray Wakefield, University of Minnesota (Minneapolis).

The editorial address is

>Dutch Studies Program
>Department of German
>University of California
>Berkeley, California 94720

I urge you as readers of this new publication to share your suggestions and reactions to *PAANS* and, in due time, submit your articles. I look forward to your response.

Johan P. Snapper
President, AANS

Introduction

From the enthusiastic reactions and observations, further confirmed in correspondence from participants and invited speakers, it can be concluded that the Third Interdisciplinary Conference on Netherlandic Studies was a successful event. It was my privilege to organize this conference and to build on and expand the laudable initiatives of Dr. William H. Fletcher, organizer of the two previous conferences.

The organizers and the A.A.N.S. again chose an interdisciplinary format, which proved to be a successful one. Many academics, Netherlandic, Netherlandish or Dutch, found their way to Ann Arbor. Because the scholar in the field of the Low Countries often feels him/herself in a minority position, it is important to meet colleagues to exchange ideas or to revitalize the energy cells. A conference like this makes the lonely rower in his or her own pond, who so often has to be knowledgeable on all aspects of The Netherlands and Belgium, aware of specific problems, new trends and fields of interest.

Another aspect is the viability of Netherlandic Studies in The United States and Canada towards our European colleagues, who are not always aware of the vivid interest and the quality of the research which exists outside of Europe.

Also, the general public in both The Netherlands and Belgium, albeit sometimes only through their representatives in the respective ministries of Education and Culture, will come to realize, not seldom to their surprise. that their history and culture is being appreciated and often studied with great enthusiasm. The publication of these papers again show that the people of the Low Countries can and should be proud of their past and present culture.

CONFERENCE PROGRAM

Art of the Low Countries

Chair: Carol Janson, University of Missouri, St.Louis

1. *The Image of the Craftsman in Early Netherlandish Art.*
   George Szabo, Metropolitan Museum, New York

2. *The Art of Paradox in the Christian North: 1400-1700.*
   Robert Baldwin, Connecticut College, New London

3. *Barent Fabritius' Three Paintings of Parables for the Lutheran Church in Leiden.*
   Barbara Haeger, Ohio State University, Columbus

Enlightenment in The Netherlands

Chair: Ton Broos, The University of Michigan

1. *Rhetoric and Reality in the Patriot Revolution.*
   W.Ph.te Brake, State University, Purchase, New York

2. *Enlightenment in Dutch Freemasonry 1805-1825.*
   André J.Hanou, University of Amsterdam

3. *The Picture of the Enlightenment in The Netherlands brought into Focus through Betje Wolff & Aagje Deken.*
   Piet J.Buijnsters, Catholic University, Nijmegen

Perspectives on Seventeenth Century Dutch Culture

Chair: Margriet Bruijn Lacy, University of North Dakota, Fargo

1. *Little Blue Books and Political Life in the Early Dutch Republic.*
   Craig Harline, Rutgers University, New Brunswick, N.J.

2. *A Pub Crawl (kroegentocht) through Seventeenth Century The Hague: Shady lights on Friends of John Donne in The Netherlands.*
   Paul Sellin, University of California, Los Angeles & A.Veenendaal, Rijkscommissie Vaderlandse Geschiedenis

3. *Musical life in Seventeenth Century Holland.*
   Jaap Schröder, Sweelinck Conservatory, Amsterdam

The Modern Dutch Literary Landscape Theatre Poetry

Chair: Arie van den Berg, University of Michigan

1. *Dutch Theater 1960 - 1985 : from Political Engagement to Innocent Beauty.*
   Kester Freriks, University of Minnesota, Minneapolis

2. *Dutc Modernist Poetry of the Fifties and the Cobra Movement in Painting.*
   Hugo Brems, Catholic University, Leuven

3. *Genitives Left and Right in Vroman's Poetry.*
   Wim G.Klooster, University of Amsterdam

History of the Dutch Language

Chair: Robert S.Kirsner, University of California, Los Angeles

1. *Mistress of Many: How Dutch was Grammatically Stripped.*
   Tom L. Markey, University of Michigan

2. *The Origin of the Middle Dutch Suffix -ster.*
   Garry Davis, University of Michigan

3. *Some Remarks on the Origin of the 'ie' Preterits stierf, wierf, wierp, zwierf, bedierf in Dutch.*
   Robert Howell, University of Wisconsin, Madison

Language and Politics

Chair: Ray Wakefield University of Minnesota. Minneapolis

1. *Dutch on the Edge, Peripheral Vocabulary in General Dictionaries.*
   Roland Willemyns, Free University Brussels

2. *Crisis, Instability, Continuity in the Dutch Political System*: *the Cruise Missiles and the 1986 Elections*
   Samuel J. Eldersveld, University of Michigan

The Nineteenth Century and Beyond

Chair: Herbert Rowen, Rutgers University, New Brunswick, N.J.

1. *Prolegomena for a Biography of Jan Rudolf Thorbecke (1798-1872)*
   Frits L. van Holthoon, University of Michigan & Groningen

2. *The Dutch Sources of Vincent van Gogh.*
   Petra ten Doesschate Chu, Seton Hall University, N.J.

3. *Self-stylization and Narrative Strategies in Frederik van Eeden's roman à thèse: De Nachtbruid.*
   Augustinus P. Dierick. University of Toronto

The Dutch in America

Chair: Herbert Rowen, Rutgers University

1. *Images of Dutch Immigrant Women in the Late Nineteenth and Early Twentieth Century.*
   Suzanne Sinke, University of Minnesota. Minneapolis

2. *Dutch Investments in American Railroads.*
   Augustus Veenendaal, Rijkscommissie Vad. Geschiedenis

3. *A Liberal Protestant Congregation in Grand Rapids, Seat of Orthodoxy.*
   Walter Lagerwey, Calvin College, Grand Rapids

Literature of the Low Countries in Modern Times

Chair: E.M. Beekman, University of Massachusetts, Amherst

1. *Gerard Reve's Window of Vulnerability.*
   Johan Snapper, University of California, Berkeley

2. *Conflicting Cultures. Edgar Du Perron; an Unusual Temper Towards the End of the Dutch Colonial Era.*
   Kees Snoek, University of Djakarta, Indonesia

3. *The Islands by A. Alberts Viewed as an Exemplification of Contemporary Literary Technique.*
   Adrian van den Hoven, University of Windsor

Perspectives on 17th Century Dutch Culture II

Chair: Johan Snapper, University of California, Berkeley.

1. *Vondel and Christian Tragedy.*
   James A. Parente, Princeton University, Princeton, N.J.

2. *Self-reflexivity and the Dream of Time in Huygens.*
   Fred Nichols, Graduate Center, New York

The Dutch Language Today

    Chair: Robert L.Kyes, University of Michigan

    1.   *Word Order in the Dutch Inner Field.*
         Jeanne van Oosten, University of California, Berkeley

    2.   *Relational Grammar, Passives and Dummies in Dutch or What's a Dummy Like You Doing as a Subject?*
         Thomas Shannon, University of California, Berkeley

    3.   *Indirect Objects With and Without 'aan' in Written Dutch.*
         Robert S.Kirsner, University of California, Los Angeles

Exporting the Dutch Language

    Chair: Robert S. Kirsner University of California, Los Angeles

    1.   *Nederlands - Afrikaans Diglossis at Cape of Good Hope.*
         Paul T.Roberge, University of North Carolina, Chapel Hill

    2.   *Dutch Immigrants in the U.S.: Dialect Museum or Laboratory for Dialect Loss.*
         Henriëtte Schatz, P.J.Meertens Institute Amsterdam

    3.   *Problems of Code Switching.*
         Jo Daan, Barchem, The Netherlands

ON TRANSLATING DUTCH LITERATURE a panel discussion on the intricacies, delicacies and difficulties of translating Dutch literature.

    E.M.Beekman, University of Massachusetts, Amherst (chair)
    H.C. ten Berge, Zutphen, The Netherlands
    Arie van den Berg, The University of Michigan
    Johanna H.Prins, Princeton University, Princeton, N.J.
    Hendrika Ruger, Netherlandic Press Windsor
    Henrietta ten Harmsel, Calvin College Grand Rapids

The following cultural events and exhibitions took place:

I [love] $ (1985) a film by Johan van der Keuken
Concert by Jaap Schröder & Elaine Thornburgh, violin and harpsichord;
Exhibition 'Animation Films in The Netherlands'
Exhibition 'Dutch Literature in translation'
Exhibition 'The Dutch in Michigan'
Exhibition 'Patriots and Orangists : Revolutionary Pamphlets and Caricatures in The Netherlands 1780-1800'

Acknowledgments

Our thanks go to the Ministries of Education and Culture of The Netherlands, the Belgian National Fund for Scientific Research, and The University of Michigan, whose financial support was the foundation on which this conference was built. The conference Department of The University of Michigan and its staff, especially Glenda Radine, deserve the highest marks for their organizational assistance.

Special thanks go to those outstanding musicians Jaap Schröder and Elaine Thornburgh. To Mary Arnheim, Arie van den Berg, Robert Starring and Karla Vandersypen for organizing the exhibitions and poet H.C. ten Berge for his last minute decision to join us in the translation session.

The section chairs deserve many thanks for their help in introducing and selecting the papers and presentations. I am especially grateful to Sue Crawford, Alice Norberry and my wife Janet for so carefully preparing and processing the manuscripts.

Finally, I would like to thank the people who made it all possible: the speaker and the listener, the typist and the reader, the giver and the receiver, the entertainer and the bore, the cheese and crackers maker and the eater, the video technician and the viewer, the nervous and the confident, the questioner and the answerer...who all came together for this conference on Netherlandic Studies.

Ton Broos
The University of Michigan
Ann Arbor

Table of Contents

Foreward — iii

Introduction — v

Conference Program — vii

Literature of the Low Countries

Self-reflexivity and the Dream of Time in Huygens — 3
    Fred Nichols, Graduate Center, New York

Een kroegentocht door oud den Haag: Shady lights on Friends of John Donne in The Netherlands — 13
    Paul Sellin, University of California, Los Angeles & A.Veenendaal, Rijkscommissie Vaderlandse Geschiedenis

Wolff & Deken and the Dutch Enlightenment — 25
    Piet J.Buijnsters, Catholic University, Nijmegen

The Heritage of Enlightenment: The Struggle in Dutch Masonry: 1780-1825 — 37
    André J.Hanou, University of Amsterdam

Self-stylization and Narrative Strategies in Frederik van Eeden's roman à thèse: De Nachtbruid — 45
    Augustinus P. Dierick. University of Toronto

Conflicting Cultures: Edgar Du Perron; an Unusual Temper Towards the End of the Dutch Colonial Era — 55
    Kees Snoek, University of Djakarta, Indonesia

Dutch Poetry of the Fifties and the Cobra-Movement — 61
    Hugo Brems, Catholic University, Leuven

Gerard Reve's Window of Vulnerability — 75
    Johan Snapper, University of California, Berkeley

A. Alberts' The Island *as an Exemplification of Contemporary Novelistic Techniques* — 83
    A. van den Hoven, University of Windsor

Genitives Left and Right in Vroman's Poetry   93
    W. G. Klooster, University of Amsterdam

The Dutch in America

The Huisvrouw and the Farmer's Daughter: Images of   109
Dutch Immigrant Women in the Late Nineteenth and
Early Twentieth Century
    Suzanne Sinke, University of Minnesota.
    Minneapolis

Voices from the Free Congregation at Grand Rapids,   125
Michigan: An Introduction to the Holland Unitarian
Church 1885-1918
    Walter Lagerwey, Calvin College, Grand
    Rapids

Risky Rails: Dutch Investments in American   139
Railroads
    Augustus Veenendaal, Rijkscommissie Vad.
    Geschiedenis

Problems of Code Switching: Dialect Loss of   149
Immigrants of Dutch Descent
    Jo Daan, Barchem, The Netherlands

The Language of Dutch Immigrants: Dialect Museum   157
or Laboratory for Dialect Loss
    Henriëtte Schatz, P.J.Meertens Institute
    Amsterdam

History and Politics of the Low Countries

Blue Little Books and Political Life in the Dutch   169
Republic
    Craig Harline, Rutgers University, New
    Brunswick, N.J.

Prolegomena for a Biography of Jan Rudolf Thorbecke   177
Part I
    Frits L. van Holthoon, University of
    Michigan & Groningen

Crisis, Instability, Continuity in the Dutch Political   183
System: the Cruise Missiles and the 1986 Elections
    Samuel J. Eldersveld, University of Michigan

History and Structure of the Dutch Language

Mistress of Many: How Dutch was Grammatically   203
Stripped

Tom L. Markey, University of Michigan

The Origin of the Middle Dutch Suffix -ster   231
    Garry Davis, University of Michigan

Relational Grammar, Passives and Dummies in Dutch?   237
    Thomas Shannon, University of California, Berkeley

Remarks on the Origin of the ie Preterits stierf, wierf, wierp, zwierf, bedierf in Dutch   269
    Robert Howell, University of Wisconsin, Madison

Prepositional Versus 'Bare' Indirect Objects in the Written Dutch of Novels and Newspapers   279
    Robert S.Kirsner, University of California, Los Angeles

Word Order in the Dutch Inner Field   297
    Jeanne van Oosten, University of California, Berkeley

Dutch on the Edge, the Lexicographical Treatment of Peripheral Vocabulary   309
    Roland Willemyns, Free University Brussels

**Literature
of the
Low
Countries**

SELF-REFLEXIVITY AND THE DREAM OF TIME IN HUYGENS

Fred J. Nichols
Graduate Center, City University of New York

Dutch poets often live to a ripe old age, and the poet Constantijn Huygens was no exception. A central feature of this long life was his happy marriage to Suzanna van Baerle, but that marriage lasted for only ten of the poet's ninety-one years. What I am here concerned with are the literary consequences, the textual consequences, one might say, of that biographical fact.

Huygens as a poet has an especial interest because he is at once immersed in the literary conventions of his time and is yet in a sharp state of reaction against them. His time is that extension of the literary Renaissance we now think of as the Baroque period. The chief characteristics of that period in literature are an obsessive concern with form for its own sake, and a tendency for language to acquire a kind of autonomous status, for words to become things. Both of these tendencies are evident in sixteenth century European literature, but at the end of the century they become curiously accentuated. Form seems to detach itself from meaning, and words seem to detach themselves from what they express, or - as we might say - the signifier detaches itself from the signified. A consequence of this development is the existence of texts which significantly draw our attention to their own textuality, to the fact that they are essentially constructs of language, and also to the ways that as texts they have come into being. Baroque texts are then particularly self-reflective, and tend to meditate on their own beginnings.

The dominant set of poetic conventions in Huygens' time for expressing erotic relationships is that of Petrarchan love poetry. The persona in such a rhetoric is always aware of himself both as a poet and as a lover. He endows the lady who is the object of his desire with a name that will bear the weight of a network of complex literary associations. It is Huygens' greatest peculiarity, in terms of this literary convention, that in the poems we will be considering he is addressing not a lady who remains distant and unattainable, but the wife he is happily married to. In his poetry he calls her Sterre, star.

What I want to do here is to examine the way in which Huygens deals with questions of presence and absence in certain selected poems in terms of the ideas of self-reflexivity, of dreaming, and of time. The pattern that I will trace begins with the presence of both the poet and of the lady, of his language and her language, in his poetic discourse. When her voice is silenced by death, there is a radical dislocation between the poet who is still a presence and the lady who is now an absence. The ideal solution to recreate the perfect union between the poet and the lady will be for him to become an absence as well.

I would also stress here that what I am concerned with in this discussion is not necessarily the actual person named Constantijn Huygens who lived and died in seventeenth century Holland, but with the person who speaks in the first person in the poems I am going to analyze. That persona - and this too is part of the convention of the period - is an artifact, a creation of the poet's art, which may or may not coincide with the actual historical personality of the poet. This raises complex questions about an age which tended to see all human activity as a more or less conscious performance, but we cannot deal with those questions here. Let me merely indicate that from this point I will use the words "persona" and "poet" to indicate the first person speaker who is the creation of the poet's art.

Huygens begins his *Dagwerk*, a versified account of a day's activities, with an address to his wife in which he gives a curious account of the poem's origin, describing it in metaphoric terms as a birth. If the poem begins in a rather conventional way by addressing his wife as *Sterre* and by complimenting her on the way in which she shines out uniquely among other brilliant objects in the sky, the poet develops a more original conceit when he implicates her language with his:

Sterre...
Die mij eens met Ia verheugden
Noyt bedroeven sult met Neen
Tegen 'tja-woord van de Re'en. (III, 49)[1]

The original word ja is the source of his joy, and in a sense is the source of this text, and her word ja is associated with reason (re'en or reden), and therefore never will be answered by the word neen, no. The word reden is repeated in the lines that follow:

Sterre, regel van mijn' reden,
Al van doe mij mijn gebeden,
Voor uw' reden stelde veil...

The alliteration of regel and reden reinforces the sense of the way in which she provides a rule and a pattern for his texts. (Note the two senses of regel, "rule" and "line of verse.") His speech has been dependent on hers since that time when her reden answered his gebeden, when she answered his prayer with the reasonable word ja.

The two are now linguistically entwined: Dat Ick Gij en t'eener tijd / Ghij tot ick geworden zijt" (III, 50). The Ick and the Gij have become interchangeable and their pleasures and their wills merge in a state of peace and rest:

Nu mijn' lusten zijn' uw willen,
All uw willen al mijn lust,
Yeders vrede elkanders rust. (III, 50).

But the poem does not pause at this point of harmonious stasis. Now that the lady has answered the poet's prayers with "yes", now that their union has been consummated linguistically, we are prepared for the account of the poem's birth.

The injunction "Luystert" begins a description of the labor pain of "de overslagen, / Die mijn Siele, lang gedragen, Nu voldragen, barens-ree..." The soul of the poet is now ready to give birth - to give form - to his reflections which he presents to her "Als een' droppel in uw' Zee / Van bescheidenheit..." The striking image of the drop of water in the sea of her wisdom (an older meaning of bescheidenheit) suggests a kind of reverse impregnation. It is the force of her reason ("uw krachtiger bedencken") that will help him in the pain of the childbed: "'tkinder-kraem / Daar sij gaern te bedd af quaem". The birth of a poem has rarely been so clinically plotted out.

That the birth of the poem has been successful we know because we have already gotten forty lines into it. This child will curiously be called "Ernst van voorraed", voorraed here having a more etymological sense of preliminary consideration. The seriousness of preliminaries again hints back to genesis, understood as an origin that had been thought out beforehand. But the lady, the "gij", must continue to help the poet with his process of creation:

Helpt mij door den arbeid sweeten,
Daer Ghij Ick zijt en Ick Ghij
Moet de moeder heeten: Wij. (III,50)

Again the first and second persons merge, the distinction between them is collapsed, with the curious result that they both can be called the "mother" of the text. The obliteration of grammatical and sexual distinctions is striking here.

The poet goes on to detail specific problems of poetic composition. Is he writing too fast or too slow, is there a perfect consonance between rijm and reden, between form and meaning, is his tone too harsh or too sweet? Again it is the fact that their two souls have been exchanged, "Ziel is tegen ziel geruylt", that makes possible the solution of even these technical problems. The perfectly achieved form of the poet is thus a sign of, is literally engendered by, their harmony understood in linguistic and in sexual terms.

Here we might step back a moment and reflect upon how striking this text would be to a sixteenth-century reader familiar with the dominant Petrarchan tradition of love poetry. The Petrarchan lover is by definition a rejected one: he creates the poetic text to compensate for the lady's absence. One might say that she generates the text by not being physically present and the text is an attempt to fill that gap with language. Here the lady contributes to the generation of the text by her presence and specifically by her physical presence in bed, the consequence of her saying yes to the poet's proposal. The two thus form a tight closed system where first person singular and second person singular discourses (Ik-Gij) merge in first person plural discourse. The text itself terms their closed system "dese kleine wereld", and describes it with more precision ("om nauwer te beschrijven" - note how this text constantly draws our attention to what it is doing with language) as "Beddgemeente van twee Lijven, / Van twee lieven, segg ick best..." (III,51). This little world is a community of two bed-mates whose bodies and - putting it better - loves are joined. Note that the persona, still refining his text, has slipped back into first person discourse here (segg ick) but this section of Dagwerk will conclude with the persona enacting the fusion of his language and her language. All of this self-contained linguistic-sexual construct with its pleasures, "Hebb ick, hebben ick en ghij / Dus beregelt, seggen wij." Her discourse, beginning with that simple "ja-word", empowers his linguistic creation, and leads to wij as the concluding and triumphant word.

We should also observe what this intensely self-reflexive text serves to introduce us to. It is a prelude to temporality, to a lengthy text in which the day's routine will be recreated in language. It will reproduce the persona's world as that world is experienced in time.

The lady, the "gij", is both the source and the hearer of the piece of text we have just examined. We readers are in some sense eavesdroppers. What will happen when the lady's discourse is removed?

Huygens had not yet completed Dagwerk when his wife died. The text responds to this event with one of Huygens' most original effects, one which reflects the breakdown of discourse when her voice has been silenced. He evokes her voice in the seven syllable line that he has used in Dagwerk until now. "Spreeckt ghij, Sterre, neffens mij" (III, 105). But she cannot answer. He has only his own discourse now and the poem abruptly shifts into longer and more solemn alexandrine lines: "Maar wie staet neffens mij? wat spreeck ick, en waer henen?" He is alone now. What is the point of his speaking? "Mijn Lezer valt in slaep...," he says simply. The striking reference to the lady as his lezer underlines his double loss. The source and the reader of his poetic discourse is absent.

Temporality has now become a problem as well: "Sy strijckt ten Tyden uijt". She wafts herself out of time which now isolates him, still in time, from her: "Wij spreecken veel te laet, / Mijn Hert..." (III, 107). The problem of time will become an ever more pressing one as the years without her will go on.

His discourse about her is confused, as he shifts from the third person to the second person in referring to her, but in her absence second person discourse tends to lose its meaning. "Ei, Sterre, noch," he cries out, repeating a phrase he used as the beginning of a line earlier, but here he must break off: "Wat noch? Sy is geen Sterre meer, / Sij treedt op sterren." His own poetic name for her has now become mere inaccurate rhetoric. In heaven she seems to be beyond the reach of his language.

At this point the persona abruptly becomes aware of the fact that we are reading the poem, that there are other readers: "Troost, troost, vrienden..." That the text is being read by sympathetic hearers enables him to continue: "Kent, wat ick lyd' en troost." In some curious way we substitute for the absent beloved, but the consolation, the <u>troost</u>, is still tenuous, and he calls on us for our voices: "Spreeckt, vrienden ik besw...!" He breaks off in mid-word, perhaps <u>bezwijk</u> (succumb) or <u>bezwijm</u> (swoon), leaving the line unfinished. The next line begins with a more measured and distant tone: "Daer ligt mijn plompe Penn..." (III, 108). We are abruptly aware that he is not speaking, but writing; this text is a literary construct after all. The rhyme scheme changes here too. The poem has been in couplets but will end now with an ABAB quatrain. And we have formally taken over the role of <u>lezer</u>: "Maar, Leser, 'tkan bestaen, veel minder waer genoegh." The broken text ends itself with references to its own imperfection, its length, its excess of words over matter: "Waer 't kind volmaeckt ten sou syn' vader niet gelijcken." <u>Dagwerk</u> began as we saw that the persona and the lady were together the mother of a text where <u>reden</u> and <u>regel</u> were the principles of the text's carefully worked out formal perfection. At its imperfect end the persona is an impaired and isolated father who has engendered a defective child.

Huygens also responded to Sterre's death more formally in a sonnet, elaborately entitled "Cupio Dissolvi. Op de dood van Sterre." Here the perfection of form that the sonnet imposes upon the poet's grief leads to a certain kind of consolation. He invokes the heavens, begging them to speak in a language that he can understand: "O Hemelen... / Spreeckt menschen-tael en seght, waer is mijn' Sterre henen" (III, 46). It is striking that heaven does answer, and at once, and indeed in human language:

Den Hemel slaet geluyd, ick hoor hem door mijn stenen,
En seght: mijn' Sterre staet in 't heilighe gebied....

The poet, through his moaning, hears an answer that his prayer has provoked. This is another tribute to the force of the poet's language and a repetition of the prayer and answer response pattern that is characteristic of Huygens. He is told that she is in heaven, where she and the deity ("de Godheid") are contemplating each other: "Daer sij de Godheid, daar de Godheid haar besiet." Chiasmus, the rhetorical figure this she-God-God-she pattern creates, was the rhetorical patterning that the persona once used to describe his relationship with her: <u>Gij-Ik-Ik-Gij</u>. God has replaced him, and furthermore she is laughing at his useless weeping, "belacht mijn ijdel weenen". It should be observed that although the rhetorical structure posits God as the persona's rival, he will resist this view of things. He cannot replace God in turn, but he and God and she can become a kind of triangle, the idea which concludes the sonnet: "Mijn Heil, mijn Lief, mijn Lijf, mijn' God, mijn' Sterr, en mij."

The problem however remains the same as in the previous text we have considered: that the poet is still in the world of time while the lady - and God - are out of it. The way for the poet to join them will be through death. He invokes death twice, at the beginning of each tercet, in this sonnet. "Komt, dood, en maeckt mij korts van deze Cortsen vrij," he says the second time. He plays on the temporal word <u>korts</u> (quickly) and the word <u>Corts</u>

(koorts) in the sense of fever. To be on earth, to be plunged into earthly temporal life is to be ill, and a death that comes quickly is the ultimate cure. The Latin part of the poem's title, *Cupio dissolvi*, in fact means "I long to be dissolved." The problem that the persona in Huygens' poetry will have however is that death will not come quickly.

A recurring theme in the poetry that will be written in the fifty years that Huygens will still have to live is the passage of time and the problem of his continued existence in it. He is ready to be removed from the world of time, but that does not happen. He is left in the world of time - and of language. He waits for these texts to become frozen traces in language of the absent poet, but he remains a presence, and responds by creating new texts that mark the passage of that problematic time. He must work his way through time to get to death, and to silence.

We should note that our poet has been thrust into the conventional situation of the Petrarchan lover. The lady is now an absence. But Huygens characteristically refuses to adopt a Petrarchan stance. Whereas Petrarch in his cycle of poems had celebrated the anniversary of his first seeing his beloved Laura, Huygens will write poems celebrating his own birthday. And whereas Petrarch recreates the lady in language, evokes her as a fiction shaped by his own language, Huygens declines to use language in this way. For him, this use of language to compensate for an absence is a kind of dream, and he finds dreams problematic.

Let us look back briefly. In the imperfect text concluding Dagwerk we might expect to find the poet attempting to reconstruct the absent Sterre in language, but he does not. His idea is that with her gone, he is speaking too late. He goes on to say, "hopeloose wenschen / Zijn droomen bij schoon dagh van vaeckeloose menschen" (III, 107). These daylight dreams of men with no proper occupation are no consolation to him now.

The sonnet, on the other hand, where the very form implies a Petrarchan frame of reference, is more hospitable to dreaming, since Petrarch's sonnets are often concise visions of the absent beloved, and the sonnet on the death of Sterre has some of this quality. It begins, in fact, by suggesting that this may be all a dream: "Of droom ick, en is 't nacht, of is mijn' Sterr verdwenen?" (III, 46). Note here that he does not dream of her, but thinks - hopes - that her disappearance is a dream. But in the next line he wakes, "'t is hoogh dagh," it is broad daylight, and he does not see her. Dreams still provide no consolation.

This is a theme the poet returns to again and again in the epigrams, the sneldichten, that he occupied himself with for the rest of his life. At times it seems hard to distinguish dream from reality. In a short poem entitled "Ontwaeck", he plays with the typically baroque idea that waking life itself may be indistinguishable from dreaming. Upon awakening he asks, "Welck is de waerheit, dit of dat... Welck is het sekerste van tween?" (VIII, 20). The idea is developed in a more complex way in one of several short poems entitled "Dromen". It begins with a characteristic alliterating play on words: "Twee werre-Werelden bewoon ick over hands..." (VII, 139). These two worlds in which he lives are both confused, but there is a difference explained this way: "Dese sie 'ck, die droom ick dat ick sie." The distinction between seeing and dreaming that one sees is clear enough, but it can blur nevertheless: "In arbeid en in ernst gelijcken sij malkander." Both worlds can seem to have the same kind of force, and having made the distinction we have seen, the poet wonders of actual life, "Of is dees' mogelick soo wel een droom als die?

This as I've observed is the conventional idea of Huygens' immediate literary context. But in more reflective poems, the poet is disturbed by the dreams he has. Again the vital importance of form should be emphasized. In sonnets one may have pleasant visions, but in epigrams dreams are likely to be less satisfying. Another one of the poems entitled "Dromen" begins with the characteristic question and response: "Wat haest heb ick na Bedd? daer moet ick liggen dromen..." (VIII, 113). We should note that the now isolated persona, alone in his bed, has nothing else but dreaming. The period of the bed-gemeente is long past. Doesn't he ever dream of anything pleasant? He does. Sometimes he dreams "wat soets en swemm ick in vermaeck." The problem with swimming in the pleasure of such dreams is the final sense that they are only, after all, dreams, a kind of shadow-life: "Hoe verr zijn hebben en niet hebben van malkand'ren / Hoe droevigh sietmen 'tlyf in schaduwe verandren." Dreams are a kind of non-being, or - more precisely - a kind of non-having, bodies that turn into shadows. There is no consolation in this vision. On the other hand, he sometimes dreams of horrors, of death and hunger and anguish, and so concludes with the words the poem began with: "wat haest heb ick na Bedd?" The circularity of this short text underlines the problematic relationship between dreaming and time. What one does in time is dream, life in time is like a dream. To escape from time would be to escape from dreaming as well. And so it is certainly not helpful to reconstruct - or construct - dreams in language.

The idea of death as an escape from dreaming is developed in a poem called "Tegen 'tdroomen". Night is for rest "en ick heb all' mijn' Rust in onrust doorgebracht" (VIII, 39). This restlessness leads the poet to disagree with another commonplace, the resemblance between sleep and death. The poet's answer is succinct: "Die doodt wil zijn, moet sterven." What sleep deprives of life is thought. It kills thought, and so in sleep the poet has only dreamt senselessness, "dat rijm noch reden heeft." In this reasoned rhyme, the poet is playing on words in saying this, but the wordplay draws our attention to a profound defect of dreams, their formlessness. To the seventeenth century mind, this is to imply their meaninglessness. What kind of death is the mere death of ordering thought? The poet concludes, "'kheb mijn selven overleeft."

This sense of having outlived himself is expressed again and again in the numerous epigrams Huygens wrote on the subject of his own aging as he celebrated various points in time during the long years he lived. In a poem entitled "Niew jaar" he again links dreaming with being in time. This poem is being written on New Year's Day of his seventy-ninth year, and as the persona contemplates his eightieth birthday which will come in the following September, he wonders where all those years have gone:

Als niewe droomen elck verschenen en verdwenen,
En na de volle som maar eenen ouden droom. (VIII, 132)

Each year itself is like a dream; time is a dream. The poet compares himself to an old tree with tough roots which still stands while thousands of others have fallen around it.

We might ask who the reader of this poem is, since it is a firm part of the tradition of the epigram that the poem may be addressed to one specific person. The reader of this poem is the Lord. When asking himself how many more years he will have, he responds, "Ghij weet het, Heer, alleen, en houdt het mij verborgen", and the poem ends with an invocation to the "goedertieren God". The problem that the persona now has is that his continued presence in time, the length of his being in time, depends upon the reader to whom these poems are often addressed, God.

A gathering sense that the poet's being in time is becoming a burden to himself can be gathered from the poem entitled "Op mijnen geboortdagh". Another September fourth has come. The poem is a kind of conversation with the Lord, who is addressed four times in twenty-six lines. The persona now wishes for no more time: "Ick bidd om geen verlang" (VII, 89). He has had enough. His plea gathers strength as the poem goes on: "Mij, Heere, laet vrij gaen. / Mijn' roll is afgespeelt..." Life is thought of now as shadows and play-acting and the poet finally balances his resignation and his desire to cease to be a presence: "'K wacht, heer, dat ghij 'tgebiedt." The whole poem is in fact a prayer, in several senses. And it implies a paradoxical answer. If the Lord grants the speaker his wish, the voice will cease, and there will be no more poems as the persona is removed from the world of time and with it the world of language.

But the Lord waits, and so more texts are produced, each text a paradox also in that there is a sense in which each text regrets that it has come into being. The state of perfection would imply absence of text, silence. A poem called "Overlang Leven" plays with the idea that old people who want to live still longer are like children who want to stay up past their bedtime. The persona views all of this amusedly as a kind of pleasant human foolishness, but separates himself from such an attitude. Again human life is a kind of play-acting: "Mijn Rol is afgedaen, / God roep' als 't hem gevalt, 'kwil te bedde gaan" (VIII, 57). The idea of childish play leads to a witty conclusion on a serious matter. The aged persona has no wish to stay up late, and the sleep that follows implies no dreams.

The idea is expressed in terms of a different kind of imagery in a poem entitled "Ouderdom". Here the lives of old men are compared to dry leaves still clinging to a branch in the winter. Although they tenaciously cling to the branch, it doesn't take much to carry them off: "Een windje, een rijpje van een Coortsje" (VIII, 171). The last line has the unexpected bite that is characteristic of the end of an epigram: "En dan wie min or meer gewaeckt hebt, goeden nacht." The unexpected change of reference here expresses the inevitability of what lies at the end of the process of time, but the existence of the poem indicates that it has not yet come for the speaker.

Still the Lord does not answer. The exasperation that the poet feels is expressed in a poem on the fact that he has reached eighty-nine. "Op twaelf na hondert jaer," he exclaims at the beginning which is significantly addressed to his children, themselves now aged, "ghij al selver Oud'ren / en Overoudren zijt" (VIII, 344). The poet asks another of his questions: "Gaet alle ding verandren / op mij naer?" In the manuscript of the poem the poet wrote "mensch" over the word "ding" and "een" over the word "mij", providing the alternate reading, "Gaet alle mensch verandren / op een naer?" For a fleeting moment it is as if the poet may be caught in time forever. But the temporal flow that discourse is a part of will bring even this long life to a close. With a little patience, "een kort geduld", he tells his children, the time will come "dat gh' u ontvadert sult". Thus "unfathered" they can get on with their aging unencumbered, and repeat the words that the poem concludes with: "Komt, Heere, "tis genoegh".

There is no textual ending to this pattern because, as we have seen, there can be none. The ending is absence of further texts. A writer of autobiographical texts in any form can only imagine the concluding of the text prospectively, never describe it as it happens. As a matter of historical fact we know that the poet Constantijn Huygens finally died at the age of ninety-one, fifty years after the death of his wife Suzanna van Baerle. Thus the discourse ceased, and the texts became what at a deeper level of intentionality they had always wished to be: words fixed permanently in time spoken by a voice now absent, traces of that absence.

NOTE

[1] I have followed the text as given in the standard edition, *De Gedichten van Constantijn Huygens*, edited by J.A. Worp, 9 vols. (Groningen: Wolters, 1892-99). The references give volume and page number.

EEN KROEGENTOCHT DOOR OUD DEN HAAG: SHADY LIGHT ON ENGLISH FRIENDS OF JOHN DONNE IN THE NETHERLANDS

Paul R. Sellin and Augustus J. Veenendaal, Jr.

Among the so-called Conway Papers, a collection generally described as "early seventeenth-century" manuscripts in the British Library, there reposes a Dutch poem of ten stanzas entitled "Een Geestelijk Liedeken."[1] Neatly copied in a competent, albeit amateur secretary hand, the work is anonymous, undated, and one wonders at its inclusion. That is, the Conway papers are especially interesting to English literature because they contain copies and fragments of some eleven poems and six verse epistles by the famous English metaphysical poet John Donne. The collection derives chiefly from Viscount Sir Edward Conway (Secretary of State and Ambassador to Bohemia under King James I, and Privy Councillor after the accession of King Charles I in 1625) and from his son Edward, second Viscount Conway. Sir Edward the elder was a lifelong friend of Donne and known to the poet personally, while Sir Edward the younger was a man of literary interests. The presence of a Dutch poem among the Conway papers is especially intriguing, for it points directly to Conway interests and involvements in the Low Countries. Indeed, Sir Edward's father, Sir John Conway, had served with Leicester during the latter's governor-generalship in the Netherlands. Sir Edward himself served in the Vere regiment during Prince Maurits' campaigns of the 1590's and ultimately succeeded his father as Lieutenant Governor of the Brill, then an English cautionary town. Although Donne biographers ignore the point, Sir Edward spent much of his early career - that is, from 1598 up through the return of the Cautionary Towns to Dutch authority in 1616 - residing in the Netherlands. Indeed, Donne's relationship with the family during these very years was such that he is known to have entrusted Sir Edward with manuscript copies of at least two of his works.[2]

To some extent, as befits friends of the intense author of some of the greatest religious lyrics in English, the Conways were famous for their piety. Indeed, back in 1570 and 1571, Sir John had authored a set of pious meditations and prayers, and these were reissued, presumably with Sir Edward the elder's blessing, in 1611 under the title of *Poesie of Floured Praiers*.[3] One would expect, thus, that a poem entitled "Een Geestelijk Liedeken" preserved among the papers of Englishmen championing the Reformed faith abroad would reflect tastes faithful to their ancestor's. Yet instead of a Psalm, here is what we find:

> De Kasewaeris is een juweel
> dat is de capeteyn
> van alle dees bordelen veel
> hier in dit Haechse Plein.

5   Moer Tyssen kent haer pollen wel
die geern speelen het minnespel
ghij moet U toonne niet reebel
maer kompt daer slechs alleyn.

ii.

op't midden
vannet Kerkhof
10   daer is een groot bordeel
't Geschildert Huys isset genampt
daer vint ghij hoeren veel.
De weerdin is schoon Heleennae genampt
den roffiaen vrij onbeschampt
15   hebt ghij slechs gelt soo't wel betampt
soo valt daer geen krackeel.

iii.

Sint Jooris is ons wel bekant
'tis een snoot roffiaen
daer vint ghij se oock aldermeest
20   seer net ende bey naam.
Is uwen buydel wel gestoffeert
soo krijcht ghij al wat ghij begeert
maar als dat geldeken is verteert
schampa[r] soo moet ghij gaen.

iv.

25   De Pellekaen op de Graft seer schoon
siet men seer veer en wijt
men kander ome een Franse kroon
speelen in Veennus krijt
in Veennus boogert met genucht
30   't geschiet daer al op eer en ducht
doe slechs maer soo wel als ghij muecht
al sonder haet en nijt.

v.

Al in de Gaepert oppet Spuy
siet men een soet gesicht
35   De man die is van a[ ]den luy
de vrou van neersen licht
Mameerken met haer gaut geel haer
die sal wel speelen mijn soete kaer
als ghij slech wilt betoonen haer
40   dat ghij sult wesen dicht.

vi.

Op't Spuy al tot moer Oolevier
compt daer een braef soldaet
dan sechtse ick en heb wijn noch bier
omdat se de broeders haet.
45 Maer kompt daer dan een rijken boer
die hael men straek een floxe hoer
soo geeft men dan den lompen loer
al'tgeen daer hij nae staet.

vii.

De Clock dat is een eerlijk huys
50 men tapt daer wijn en bier
kompt daer slechs stillekens als een muys
vracht nae [e]en veennu[s] dier.
Ariaenken weet soo go[e]de raet
een getrout vrouken delekaet
55 terwijl soo geeft haer dochter een praet
en mackt doch geen getier.

viii.

In't Achterom in de Oranienstam
daer hebt ghij goet loogys
Maykens die hou[t] veel duyfkens aen
60 al voor dees man proopys.
Kompt daer vrij in ter middernacht
men salder op u wel neemen acht
hebt ghij slechs gelt daer sij nae tracht
maer stelt daer niet den [di]ef.

ix.

65 De Groene Pellekaen is een goet huys
men heeft daer g[oet] quartier
kompt daer al v[ry] sonder abuys
vracht nae een prooper dier.
Maer wilt ghij dan speelen den beyerman
70 de weert die weet der oock wel van
hij sal wel doen al wat hij kan
ghij en hebt daer geen dansier.

x.

Het Patmoes is t[e] veel bekant
daer wont te vee[l] gespuys.
75 Van hier soo ghaen wij oock ontrent
al nae dat Roode Cruys
brengt daer een hoer seven of tien

> 80 de weert en salder niet op sien
> jae de weerdin sal self misschien
> oock speelen metter sluys.
>
> Finis is goet voor een erm bloet
> die tot den hals toe in de stront is.[4]

What can we infer from this bit of Dutch martial swagger? First, there are the questions of dating the poem and determining the extent to which it actually reflects life in The Hague at the beginning of the Thirty Years' War. Strictly speaking, of course, The Hague was no city but then, as now, only an open village with no defensive works. Yet this relatively small community was the center of the Dutch republic, for here was where the administrative bodies of the central government were established when the Dutch attained factual independence from Spain. As a consequence, all kinds of people flocked to the city, nobles and commoners, lawyers and burgomasters, artisans and tramps, strict Calvinists and libertines, who were sometimes glad to escape the stifling discipline of the church in their home towns. Above all, the garrison, swelled to large proportions during the winter, added an international dimension to this already cosmopolitan mixture. Officers of every conceivable nation and fortune, ranging from Swedes and Germans to French Hugenots and English Cavaliers, were always seeking excuses for not having to serve in one of the dreary frontier towns, to which they greatly preferred the comforts of The Hague.

Small wonder, then, that a large number of inns, hotels, public houses, cabarets, and the like sprang up in The Hague, ranging from high-class facilities for wealthy and important visitors down to the most sordid drinking-houses for the dregs of society. Not all inns were to be identified with brothels, but while ostensibly catering to the needs of the ordinary traveler, many an innkeeper was known to keep doves in his loft, as the saying went. So far as the contents of this poem are concerned, there was little taboo regarding sexuality in the first half of the seventeenth century. Dutch literature and the stage were very outspoken, and in this the work is no exception. On the other hand, the official attitude of the Calvinist churches regarding prostitution and adultery was strictly disapproving. Prostitution was a sin and ostensibly prohibited by the authorities. Yet there were ways of escaping the penalties by coming to composition with the authorities and buying them off. In short, The Hague was widely known for its many bordellos and the like, and it was considered second only to Amsterdam in this respect, far surpassing all other Dutch towns.[5]

With respect to the trustworthiness of the poem and the dates it reflects, it is in fact possible to identify some of the houses mentioned in the text. The first of them, the Kasewaeris, was of course named after the cassowary, an ostrich-like bird from Australia and New Guinea, the first specimen of which had been introduced into Europe in 1597. The inn named after this exotic fowl was situated strategically just north of the Binnenhof, the government center, on a corner of the large square called the Plein, which had originally been the cabbage patch of the stadholders. The garden was finally parceled out in building lots in 1633, but the first houses surrounding it, one of them the Kasewaeris, had been built earlier. The neighborhood quickly became fashionable in the higher social circles in The Hague. In fact, the house stood on the corner of the Houtstraat and the Sterlincxstraat, where our "moer Tyssen", together with her husband Francois Potharst van Hoxteren (or Oxteren) bought a house and garden in 1617. In the notarial records of The Hague, her name appears as Willemtje Thyssen van Breen, and her husband's occupation as no less than the chief supervisor of all fortifications of the Dutch republic![6] The couple was evidently well-to-do, and during the next few years they kept adding to the property. That they used the house as a hotel or inn during this period is improbable, and it is nowhere mentioned as such. But when Francois died in 1625 or 1626, the widow probably had to turn her home into an inn or a high class bordello to maintain a living. At the time of the census in 1627, her property was assessed at fl. 4000, not rich, but solidly middle class, and she must have done a thriving business as her house was situated in a neighborhood just coming into vogue. Thereafter we lose trace of the proprietress, but in 1635, the house is referred to as "formerly named the Casewaris."[7] Obviously, the establishment had lost its name by then, and it is probable that Moer Willemtje was no longer in business.

Some of the other houses alluded to by the mock soldier-speaker in the poem have also turned up, but identification is less certain. There was an inn called the Sint Joris on the Nieuwe Turfmarkt in 1618, and this could be the "Saint George" listed in the poem.[8] Houses on the Spui have not been traced, but the area was renowned for its brothels and cabarets. It was the place from which barges left for other Dutch towns, and this traffic made it a busy but shabby place where every need of weary travelers was catered to. The "Bell" must have been quite a bit more respectable. Assessed in 1627 at fl. 12,000, the property stood on the old Warmoesmarkt.[9] The "Patmos" was located in a notoriously disreputable section of town. It was known as the Scottish quarter because many Scottish soldiers serving in the Army of the States lived there.

None of the other houses can be identified with certainty. All the streets, however, recur on any modern map of The Hague, with the exception of the Graft, where the famous "Pelican" was evidently located. "Graft" (or "Gracht") means "canal", and it is difficult to say which of several possibilities is intended, although the Lange Gracht between the Spui and Wagenstraat is the most probable. The Kerckhof, where the suggestively named "Painted House" stood, is the square surrounding the great St. Jacobskerk, the largest church in The Hague, then mostly an area occupied by small shopkeepers and artisans. A brothel there must have been very conspicuous indeed, certainly if it dared to sport such a sign under the very nose of the main Reformed congregation in the city.

Given the historical evidence, therefore, "Een Geestelijk Liedeken" is not a product of pure fancy but reflects real life and society in The Hague during the first quarter of the seventeenth century. In all likelihood, it dates from the late twenties or early thirties of the seventeenth century, with 1627 and 1635 as the terminal extremes. Unless the poet composed his verses from memory, the text is actually contemporaneous with Donne's last years.

Its presence among the Conway papers suggests considerable interest in and familiarity with both the language and things Dutch on the part of Sir Edward the elder and his sons, and that at a time when they all enjoyed high place either at court in England or in the Army of the State.

Upon first encountering the poem, the initial inclination certainly of an English-speaking reader is to dismiss it as nothing more than trifling soldier's doggerel in an inartistic tongue, not worth serious attention. Yet, the stanzaic pattern that the verse employs is an uncommon one with a remarkable history.[10] Indeed, the complicated rhyme scheme and meter invest it in more subtlety than we would look for if the sole purpose were but to elicit cheap laughs through bawdy content. The origin of this unusual pattern is apparently rooted in medieval musical traditions, whether in the Low Countries, England, or elsewhere. In the oldest extant version of the Dutch *Geuzenliedboek*, there is a song entitled "Hoe salich sijn die Landen" by Willem van Haecht, factor of the Antwerp rederijker Chamber der Violieren. However, this text is earlier than 1581, for the content is thought at least to predate the outbreak of the Dutch revolt, and as for the rhyme scheme, an instance of it occurs in the famous psalm settings of the *Souterliedekens*, which pushes the date back to around 1640. During the late sixteenth century and the first decennia of the seventeenth in both the free and Spanish Netherlands, the rhyme pattern occurs again and again in various applications. Early versions entail serious ethical, military, political, and religious contexts, but in Bredero it recurs as a drinking song ("Haarlemsche drooghe harten nu") and Vondel uses it in the chorus closing the *Leeuwendalers*. Not surprisingly, there was a closely related poem circulating in England during the late sixteenth century and beginning of the seventeenth too. "King Cophetua and the Beggar Maid," a popular ballad well known to Shakespeare and Ben Jonson, was probably familiar to the Conways and their friends.[11] Although the English poem uses a twelve line stanza rather than an eight, the first eight lines of the English song duplicate the Antwerp rhyme scheme.

The common denominator in all these texts, whether Dutch or English, was music, apparently, and it thus seems likely that "Een Geestelijk Liedeken" was meant to be sung, probably to an existing melody, one so familiar that it did not need to be specified. However, unlike the rhyme scheme, whatever tune "Een Geestelijk Liedeken" employed could not possibly have derived from the *Geuzenliedboek* or anything like the Dutch music it uses. Whereas the rhythm of Haecht's stanza essentially resembles hymnodic Short Meter doubled, the pattern used in "Een Geestelijk Liedeken" is Common Meter, oscillating between tetrameter lines and trimeter. In this respect the Conway text differs radically from Haecht's poem, and the words simply cannot be sung to that rhythm. But although there seems to be no Dutch ancestor of the metrical pattern in "Een Geestelijk Liedeken" that springs readily to mind, the same is not true of English. For in the first eight lines of "King Cophetua," remarkably enough, one finds not only that the rhyme scheme is the same as that in the Dutch poem, but that the meters are the same, too. It is as though "Een Geestelijk Liedeken" had been written to fit an old Dutch rhyme scheme and an

English melody, and the Conway document seems truly to be an Anglo-Dutch poem in more than one sense.

A second reason for subjecting "Een Geestelijk Liedeken" to more serious scrutiny than at first seems warranted is the relation it bears to contemporary Dutch genre painting. It reminds us of paintings depicting not so much low life as a more fashionable monde of cavaliers that masters like Willem Buytewech, Adriaen van de Venne, Anthonie Palamedesz, Dirk Hals, Pieter Codde, Hendrik Pot, Willem Duyster, and many others began to put on canvas in the seventeenth century. Think, for example, of Jacob Duck's *Interior with Girl and Soldiers*, with its suggestive interior (a backroom of a kitchen?) and maid of seemingly stealthy gesture; Adriaen Brouwer's *Tabakskroeg met soldaten en vrouwen*; Pieter Quast's *A Girl and a Soldier Playing Cards* (is she dropping cards out of inebriety or to cheat?); and Duck's *A Street Scene*, which perhaps suggests a milieu like those surrounding establishments like the Patmos.[12]

Ultimately, the bawdy realism of such poems as "Een Geestelijk Liedeken" and Dutch genre paintings like these is a bit puzzling. Just what is the point, if there is one? The Conway manuscript serves to remind us that certain coarser elements in Donne's own poetry, particularly the love elegies *Songs and Sonets*, and are not far removed from Netherlandish work in this vein. Indeed, compared with Donne's, even Dutch frankness pales, and the effects go far beyond the simply prurient or amusing. That is, in addition to the clever indecencies touching fornication, adultery, inconstancy, and blind passion on which much of the charm in the *Songs and Sonets* rests, Donne's muse also indulged, especially in his love elegies, in harshly realistic sexual references little softened by clever play of tasteful wit.[13] Even for the most liberated sensibilities, whether of Donne's contemporaries or modern university students, parts of some of these poems are hard to take because at points they spill over into the tasteless and repulsive. Donne was himself an ex-soldier, into whose sensual character as a young swashbuckler the Lothian portrait gives striking insight.[14] He too had fought as an English volunteer serving with veteran units of the States' Army against the king of Spain at Cadiz, the Azores, and perhaps in the Low Countries themselves. Like the Conways, he too must have known the rough world of camp and court depicted in "Een Geestelijk Liedeken." Why did a manifestly devout poet like Donne write and distribute such lines among a large coterie of highly respectable friends and patrons? And what is a poem like "Een Geestelijk Liedeken" doing among the papers of a Conway? There is no certain answer, but surely such tough, satirical poetry drives vividly home, if not what to choose, then certainly what to avoid. For Protestants schooled in the doctrine of original sin like Donne and his military friends, confessing things in the fallen world to be what they are was perhaps a first step toward salvation.

NOTES

[1]British Library, London, Additional MS 23229, fol. 169^{r-v} (of 170). Cf. Peter Beal, *Index of English Literary Manuscripts*, I: 1450-1625 (New York and London, 1980), pp. 247-248, 254-55; Alan MacColl, "The Circulation of Donne's Poems in Manuscript," *John Donne: Essays in Celebration*, ed. A.J. Smith (London, 1972), pp. 35-36.

[2]*Biathanatos* and *Problems*. Regarding the former, see R. C. Bald, *John Donne: A Life* (New York and Oxford, 1970), p. 201; John Donne, *Letters to Severall Persons of Honour (1651)*, ed. M. Thomas Hester (New York, 1977), pp. 34-35; E.W. Sullivan II, "The Genesis and Transmission of Donne's *Biathanatos*," *The Library*, Ser. 5, Vol. 31 (1976), pp. 52-53; and Sullivan, *Biathantos by John Donne* (Newark, 1984), pp. xxxiv-xxxv. Regarding the latter, see Helen Peters, ed., *John Donne: Paradoxes and Problems* (Oxford, 1980), pp. 139-40. As the correspondence between Sir John Throckmorton, Lieutenant Governor of the sister garrison at the Cautionary Town of Flushing, and his commandant Sir Robert Sidney the elder suggests, superior officers spent much of their time in The Hague or London while the Lieutenant Governors tended shop sur les lieux for their absentee chiefs. See *Letters and Memorials of State*, ed. A. Collins (London, 1746), passim, and F. J. G. ten Raa and F. de Bas, *Het Staatsche Leger 1568-1795* (Breda, 1911--), I, 249, II, 275, 281, 301; III, 46, 178, 274.

[3]A.W. Pollard and G.R. Redgrave, *A Short-title Catalogue of Books Printed in England, Scotland, and Ireland and of English Books Printed Abroad 1475-1640*, rev. by W. A. Jackson, F. S. Ferguson, and Katharine F. Pantzer, Vol. I (2nd. ed; London, 1986), nos. 5651-53.

[4]The following translation attempts roughly to preserve the meter but makes no effort to imitate the rhyme scheme:

i.

> The Cassowary is a jewel,
> It is the commandant
> Of all of these bordellos fair
> Here in this *Haagse Plein*.
> 5 Ma Thyssen knows her clients well,
> Who're glad to play the game of love.
> You must not look like holding back,
> But just show up alone.

ii.

> In the middle of the *Kerkhof*,
> 10 There is a brothel huge.
> The Painted House is its true name,
> You'll find there plenty whores.
> Beauteous Helen's the Madam's name,
> The Pandar's almost without shame.
> 15 If you've but money, as is right,
> No argument at all.

iii.

          Saint George's familiar to everyone,
          Nefarious is the bawd.
          You'll find the girls there by and large
20   Quite classy, and with names.
          If you've a wallet well stuffed out,
          You will get all that you desire.
          But once that precious money's gone,
          In scorn they'll turn you out.

iv.

25   The Pelican on the Graft so fine
          One sees from far and wide.
          One can there for a Gallic crown
          Go duel in Venus' field,
          In Venus' orchard with delight,
30   In honor bright and virtue right,
          Do only that which you best like,
          From rancor free, and spite.

v.

          There in the Gaper on the Spuy
          One sees a pretty sight.
          The man is slack [from everything],
          The woman light of rump.
          [Mameerken] with her bright gold hair,
          She'll gladly go and play my sweet
          If you but only let her see
40   That you'll stay tightly shut.

vi.

          A' th' Spuy, to Mother Oliver,
          There comes a soldier brave.
          O then she says, "I've wine nor beer,"
          She hates us merry men.
45   But if a wealthy farmer comes,
          For him they'll fetch a spicy whore
          And quickly give the loutish knave
          All that his heart desires.

vii.

          The Bell, O that's an honest house.
50   They serve there wine and beer.
          But come there stealthy as a mouse,
          Ask for a Venus jade.
          [Ariaenken] knows good counsel straight,
          A married lady delicate.
55   She'll drop her daughter but a word,
          And never make a fuss.

viii.

  I' th' Orange Tree on the *Achterom*,
  You'll find the lodging good.
  Sweet Maykens keeps there many a dove
60 But for this man alone.
  Though late at night, just come on in,
  They'll take good care of you indeed.
  If you've but money that they want,
  No thief will rob you there.

ix.

65 The Verdant Pelican's a house,
  Where lodging good is yours.
  Be there at ease, without a doubt,
  Pick out a jade you like.
  If you prefer to play the bells,
70 Mine host knows much of that line too.
  He's sure to do what 'eer he can,
  He doesn't just only dance.

x.

  The Patmos' name is too well known,
  There's too much riffraff there,
75 And so from here we'll turn around
  And find the Red Cross Inn.
  Bring there a whore, or seven or ten,
  The keeper will not raise an eye
  The madam shall herself perhaps
80 Put her own sluice in play.
  Ending is good for a down-and-out-er
  who's up to his neck in shit.

[5]See H. E. van Gelder, *'s-Gravenhage in Zeven Eeuwen* (Amsterdam, 1937), p. 117; P. L. Muller, *Onze Gouden Eeuw: De Republiek der Vereenigde Nederlanden in haar bloeitijd geschetst* (Leiden, [1896]), III. 275-81; J. S. Poelhekke, *Frederik Hendrik, Prins van Oranje: Een biografisch drieluik* (Zutphen, 1978), pp. 72-74; B. H. D. Hermesdorf, *De herberg in de Nederlanden: Een blik in de beschavingsgeschiedenis* (Assen, 1957), pp. 251 ff.; J. H. Bose, *Had de mensch met een vrou niet connen leven:...Prostitutie in de literatuur van de zeventiende eeuw* (Zutphen, 1985), p. 32 et passim; Arie van Deursen, *Het kopergeld van de Gouden Eeuw*, II: Volkskultuur (Assen/Amsterdam), 1978, 32-57.

[6]Gemeente Archief, The Hague (=G.A.H.), Transportregisters 1610-1619, no. 1376; Transportregisters 1620-1629, nos. 978, 1000, 1143; H. E. van Gelder, "Haagsche Cohieren, I, 1627," *Jaarboek Die Haghe* (1913), p. 53. Dr. Veenendaal is most indebted to the staff of the Gemeente Archief, The Hague, for generous cooperation.

[7]G.A.H., Transportregisters 1630-1639, nr. 1007.

[8]G.A.H., Notarieel Archief, 6, fol. 341.

[9]G.A.H., Transportregisters 1610-1619, no. 629; Transportregisters 1640-1649, no 2358; Van Gelder, p. 34.

[10]Cf. L. Strengholt, "De strofevrom van Bloems 'Koning Cophetua en het bedelmeisje'," *De Nieuwe Taalgids*, 76 (1983), p. 251. Professor Sellin is indebted to Professor Strengholt, Department of Netherlands Language and Literature, Free University, Amsterdam, for bringing the rhyme scheme to his attention and generously sharing his research.

[11]Thomas Percy, *Reliques of Ancient English Poetry* (London, 1765), I, 166-171. In Shakespeare, Mercutio (*Romeo and Juliet*, II. i. 14), Falstaff (*2 Henry IV*, V. iii), Don Armado (*Loves Labours Lost*, I. ii. 108-118; IV. i. 67) and Bolingbroke (*Richard II*, V. iii. 80) all allude to it; in Ben Jonson, Oliver Cob the water bearer (*Every Man in His Humor*, III. iv. 75). Marston seems to refer to it in *The Scourge of Villany* (1598), ed. A. H.Bullen, John Marston, *Works* (london, 1887), III. 302: "Go buy some ballad of the Fairy King,/ And of the Beggar-wench, some roguy thing./ Which thou mays't chant unto the chamber-maid / To some vile Tune."

[12]Respectively, Jacob Duck, *Interior with Girl and Soldiers*, The J. Paul Getty Museum, Malibu, California, No. 70. PB 19 (Dr. Sellin is most indebted to Ms. Christiane Ramirez, Curatorial Secretary, Painting Department, for providing slides, prints, and information about this painting); Adriaen Brouwer, *Tabakskroeg met soldaten en vrouwen*, Frans Hals Museum, Haarlem; Pieter Quast, *A Girl and Soldier Playing Cards*, Los Angeles County Art Museum, Gift of Arnold S. Kirkeby, Los Angeles, California, No. 54.137.3 (Dr. Sellin is indebted to Ms. Pamela Tippman, Photographic Services, for providing reproductions and information about this and the following painting; Jacob Duck, *A Street Scene*, Los Angeles County Art Museum, Gift of John Wayne, Los Angeles, California, No. 58.50.1. As Duck stems from Utrecht, of course, the scene is not likely to derive from the Hague.

[13]E.g., "The Anagram", "The Comparison", "Sapho to Philaenis", "Love's Progress", "The Autumnal", "On His Mistris", "Going to Bed", "The Apparition", "The Dreame", "Loves Alchymie", "Farewell to Love", "The Dampe", "Selfe Love", "Satyre I", Satyre II", "The Jughler", and *Metempsychosis*, *The Complete Poetry of John Donne*, ed. John T. Shawcross (Garden City, New York, 1967), passim.

[14]See frontispiece, Shawcross.

WOLFF & DEKEN AND THE DUTCH ENLIGHTENMENT

P.J. Buijnsters
Catholic University, Nijangen

I.

Not so terribly long ago, every Dutch history of literature, as soon as the eighteenth century came in sight, began to make excuses in advance. Its spirits sank, its tone became gloomy, if not apprehensive. There usually followed a comparison with the literature of our seventeenth, or 'golden' century, with which the eighteenth century, now dealt with, contrasted unfavourably as a period of stagnation and decline.

This disapproval was, by the way, not only (and not even in the first place) directed against literature. It included the whole cultural pattern, society as a whole, and with it, as the main culprit the eighteenth century Dutchman himself.

He was supposed (in contrast with his robust predecessor of the time of Piet Hein) to have become a vegetating rentier, a frenchified decadent, no longer capable of making an original contribution to European culture. In matters of literature he began by slavishly imitating French classicism, which resulted in the sterile mannerisms of the Nil Volentibus Arduum society and writers like Huydecoper and Feitama. And when finally there comes a change round about 1770, it comes through yet another outside influence and by no means from within. Our literary innovators of the second half of the century (Hieronymus van Alphen, Rhijnvis Feith, Jacobus Bellamy) were also nothing but imitators, in this case, of German or English models. A similar development can be traced in politics. It was the French revolutionists who prepared the way for the Batavian Republic of 1795. The Dutch Patriots were no more than puppets manipulated by foreign hands.

This picture (admittedly slightly overdrawn) has long determined opinions about our eighteenth century. I would not have evoked it, if it had completely disappeared. Meanwhile the decadence aspect has long been corrected by scholarly research. And after the publications of the last twenty years by, among others, Cor de Wit, Leonard Leeb and Simon Schama,[1] nobody would want to deny the originality of the Dutch political revolution of the eighteenth century any longer. But how about the literary imagemaking of this period?

It can, of course, never be my intention here to reverse the image, like some kind of business promoter of eighteenth century Dutch literature. I am not going to maintain that the period of the Enlightenment produced more interesting writers and literary texts than our golden age. What is important is to realize that a work of literature does not possess a clear value established for all times. All one can talk about are potentials of meaning.

Which of its qualities at a given moment appeal to the reader depends among other things upon his receptivity. This holds even more true for a whole period of literature. There is then no Dutch eighteenth century literature as an objectively knowable and for ever constant phenomenon. What there is, is a series of ever-changing appreciations of that literature.

In the Netherlands eighteenth century literature received renewed attention around 1930 through the work of Jacobus Wille and Leendert Brummel. Their interest focussed on two figures, who rightly or wrongly, were presented as precursors of romanticism: these were Rijklof Michäel van Goens (1748-1810) and the philosopher Frans Hemsterhuis (1722-1790). Professor Wille dedicated practically his whole scholarly career to Van Goens: a precocious, but whimsical genius, who after an unsuccessful career as professor and politician, left the Republic in 1786 for Germany and Switzerland, where (under the name of Cunninghame) he established close contacts with the pietists Lavater and Jung Stilling[2]. Brummel for his part chose as the subject for his dissertation another equally un-Dutch outsider in Frans Hemsterhuis, who published exclusively in French, but who exerted considerable influence through his philosophical essays.[3] First on the pietistic circle around Fürstenberg and Amalia, princess Von Gallitzin at Münster, and later on various German romantics, as for instance Herder, Friedrich Schlegel, Jacobi and Novalis.

The studies by Wille and Brummel are still as valuable in 1987 as when the were first published. But they did not significantly change the image of Dutch eighteenth century literature. In order to explain that, I have to go back shortly to the negative stock-image of the eighteenth century mentioned in the beginning.

All its inherent criticism of the matter-of-fact rationalism, the cheap optimism and the moral decadence of eighteenth century Dutch culture originated chiefly with the spokesmen of the reaction: the writers of the so-called Reveil, Bilderdijk for instance, and with early nineteenth century romantics like Potgieter. The sharpest criticism is to be found in Da Costa's well-known Objections against the Spirit of the Age (Bezwaren tegen de geest der Eeuw) of 1823. In the eyes of these anti-evolutionary critics, the 'impious scoffer and superficial ink-spiller' Voltaire represented everything that made the Enlightenment a period of spiritual decadence. There was no room left for poetic inspiration.

Nor did the aesthetically-minded critics of the eighteen-eighties have any use for the allegedly prosaic literature of the enlightenment. Kloos and Verwey accorded some value to the best work of a poet like Rhijnvis Feith, in whom they believed to see a faint precursor of their own ideal in art. But in the final analysis Wille, Brummel and other pioneers of the history of eighteenth century Dutch literature before the Second World War were just as impercipient. They felt already very little affinity with the age of Voltaire. Their interest for the eighteenth century was not so much selective as metaphoric. They tried as it were to unearth from under the dominant cultural pattern of the enlightenment the hidden tendencies that pointed the direction of either romanticism (Brummel) or the Reveil (Wille). Thus Van

Goens and Hemsterhuis were celebrated as figures who had triumphed over the limitations of the idea of the enlightenment.

I hurry to add that until the nineteen-fifties a similar selective interest in certain eighteenth century authors can be noticed also outside the Netherlands. Especially the so-called pre-romantic transitional writers like Edward Young, Thomas Gray, Bernardin de Saint-Pierre and the young Goethe of Werther, found acceptance in the eyes of Paul van Thieghem and his school. Moreover, the whole pre-romantic movement was seen as an emotional reaction to the rationalism of Voltaire, and as such was placed under the banner of Rousseau. It was Rousseau who also inaugurated the literary aggiornamento.

Directly after the Second World War, it was especially Jan C. Brandt-Corstius, who gave new impulses to eighteenth century Dutch studies in the Netherlands. Until 1960 he was our leading dix-huitiemist.

Up to a point Brandt-Corstius continued the pre-romantic line of Van Tieghem. With a naturally more specialized knowledge of affairs, he brought the latter's vast, generalizing, views to bear on a more detailed Dutch context. Thus he produced several publications on Dutch writers halfway between classic and romantic: on Elizabeth Maria Post, Rhijnvis Feith and -- again --on Rijklof Michäel van Goens. Programmatical to the very title was his article of 1957, entitled Rhijnvis Feith as a transitional writer.[4] All these studies were concerned with 'Phenomena in our literature at the end of the eighteenth century in connection with changing views on religion and nature.'[5] As you may have noticed, I just quoted another of Brandt-Corstius's essay-titles. Students who had to study this article for their exam, sometimes inadvertently referred to it as 'Phenomena ...(etc.) in connection with changed views ..' but that was not what Brandt-Corstius meant. What he was concerned with was just the fact that there was a development still in progress, a conflict with as yet undetermined outcome between romantic sensibility and classical sense of form. This dualism could be seen in many Dutch writers, male and female, around the turn of the nineteenth century. It was most obvious in third-class authors like the poet and novelist Elizabeth Maria Post.

One has to admit that Brandt-Corstius did not overvalue the authors he dealt with. As a comparative-literature scholar, he placed our eighteenth century in an international context. Simultaneously he introduced and popularized what were then innovative studies on eighteenth century history of ideas by foreigners, such as Arthur P. Lovejoy's *Great Chain of Being*. Yet one might have expected a stronger affinity with the Dutch enlightenment from a scholar of his humanistic stamp. But his sympathies were limited to Betje Wolff. Thus Brandt-Corstius' research concentrated on what he alternately referred to as 'the emotional enlightenment' or 'pre-romanticism'.

In the meantime, round about 1960, the tide with regard to the eighteenth century began to turn dramatically on the international level. The romantic notions about life which had also inspired the dix-huitiemistes for so long seemed suddenly discredited. A secularized, anti-authoritarian and cosmopolitically orientated society, as that of the nineteen-sixties, recognized itself in the writings of Voltaire, Diderot, Rousseau, Hume and Lessing. This opened the way for a revaluation of those elements that till then had found only little understanding: namely the ideology of the enlightenment.

However, in order to get true insight into enlightenment thought, it was necessary to study its sources. This was the reason behind the intensive activities since the fifties that went into the editing of correspondences and other primary texts. The high point of these original researches was the publication in more than one hundred volumes of the Correspondence of Voltaire by Theodore Besterman.

The text-editions were followed by interpretations and, finally, by organizations. No synthesis gained so much authority as Peter Gay's *The Enlightenment* (1967-1969) with the subtitle *An Interpretation*. The contents-page referred almost ostentatiously to 'The Rise of Modern Paganism' and 'The Science of Freedom'. The same autonomous thinking about humanity which several decades ago had seemed diametrically opposed to the post-romantic view of life, was now recognized an valued as the most precious product of the whole eighteenth century. The enlightenment, that was the eighteenth century!

The same explicit interest in the ideas of the enlightenment was also manifest in the organizations and periodicals which were founded everywhere during the sixties. The Dutch-Belgium Society for Eighteenth century Studies, founded in 1968, followed in the footsteps of this international trend. Through its yearly symposia and its own periodical publication, the *Dokumentatieblad Werkgroeùp 18e Eeuw*, it stimulated the study of the specifically Dutch contribution to eighteenth century culture. This was by no means a superfluous endeavour with a view to the fact that Peter Gay's synthesis had not even mentioned the Dutch enlightenment. Did it exist at all, one might ask oneself. Or was the Republic solely to be viewed as a service-hatch, a place where new ideas took shape and were published exclusively by and for foreign philosophers? One thing had in the meantime become quite clear: An answer to this pressing question could only come from Dutch-speaking eighteenth century scholars.

I myself have already once tried to sketch the specific character of the Dutch enlightenment; that was in 1971 at the Third International Congress of the Enlightenment, held at Nancy, where I reacted to Peter Gay's book with a paper on Les lumiéres Hollandaises.[6] Seven years later, in 1978, the French periodical *Le Dix-huitieme siècle* devoted a good part of its tenth number to the problem, hitherto totally neglected of a possible differentiation within that complex whole, which one called light-heartedly -- and as if they were synonymous -- the enlightenment, les lumiéres, Aufklaérung, or verlichting. Where formerly one tacitly tended to identify the enlightenment with the French philosophes (Voltaire, Rousseau, Diderot, d'Alembert, Holbach, La Mettrie), the accent has shifted slowly in the past fifteen years to investigations of the various modifications, the regional manifestations; and within these to chronological differences or the different phases of the enlightenment.

At the moment the simple term 'enlightenment' already begs the question: which enlightenment are we talking about? The Scottish enlightenment, or the Catholic enlightenment? the tempered Newtonian enlightenment or the Radical enlightenment, to which Margaret C. Jacob drew attention in 1981?

In view of so much differentiation it does not seem surprising that Roland Mortier thought it necessary to emphasize the fundamental unity of the Enlightenment; first in an essay, which has already become a classic, entitled "Unité ou scission du siécle des Lumiéres? and more recently in a paper given at Budapest with the title Lumiéres, Pré-romantisme, Romantisme."[7]

Bearing this view of a single enlightenment in mind, we can still say that it has actually always had two faces: an international and a national one. These two aspects of it should not be confused. Every consideration should therefore take the relation between these two poles into account. For the Republic such a consideration boils down to the following subject: The Enlightenment in the Netherlands and the Dutch Enlightenment. The value of any study about the Netherlands and the enlightenment can thus be gauged among other things by the amount of attention paid to this double aspect. Let me illustrate this point with a negative and a positive example.

In 1972, there appeared a book with the promising title *The Netherlands and the Enlightenment*[8] by the historian Haijo Zwager. However well written it may be, it is basically a depressing book. After all, the author himself hardly believes in the importance of his subject. Right from the start he is on the defensive in the way I referred to at the beginning of my paper. "The enlightenment in the Netherlands or Dutch enlightenment writers...the result will be -- so he fears (I quote him literally) -- 'a portrait gallery of the forgotten, about as useful as a treatise on winegrowing north of the Moerdijk.' The point actually is that Zwager has a fixation on the French model of the enlightenment which he subsequently uses as a measure for the Dutch representatives of the enlightenment.

Quite a different approach was used by Professor Hans Bots and Jan de Vet in their joint contribution to the tenth issue of *Le Dix-huitieme Siècle*, already mentioned. Their article, entitled 'Les Provinces-Unies et les Lumiéres' fits in closely with my paper of 1971.[9] It constitutes in a way an elaboration on my point of view. In both papers attention is being drawn to the fact that enlightenment thought in the Netherlands knows its own native tradition which goes back to such sixteenth-century tolerant thinkers and christian humanists as for instance Coornhert, Spiegel and Erasmus. What has always characterized the enlightenment in the Netherlands is its conscious aim to view reason and the Revelation not as opposites but as complementary to each other. This aim sometimes produced a precarious balance, but it never let the Dutch enlightenment become anti-christian (except for a few marginal figures). Such a thing was also hardly possible, because so many of the exponents of enlightenment ideology in our country were theologians and ministers. In this connection, Professor Ferdinand

Sassen has introduced the term Reformatory Enlightenment, in order to indicate this search for a model of harmony.[10]

There is no denying the fact then, that the last fifteen years have sharpened our eyes for the native character and the specific role of the Dutch enlightenment. This development is not in the last instance due to a series of publications under the auspices of the Nijmegen Institute of Intellectual Relations directed by Professor Hans Bots. These studies however focused mainly on the booktrade, the publishing business and the French periodical press around the beginning of the eighteenth century, as did the monumental five-volume standard-work of Mrs. Isabella H. van Eeghen, which deals with the Amsterdam booktrade from 1690 to 1725.[11] In other words: even nowadays more attention is still being paid to Holland as a free-port for enlightenment scholarship than to our native Dutch enlightenment literature. It is always the historians, like W.W. Mijnhjardt to name a recent example, who are leading the discussion.[12] The literary critics on the other hand do not quite seem to know what to do with the concept of the enlightenment, which is, or course, more easily applicable to the history of ideas than to the history of literary forms.

However that may be, it is a notable fact that the last great standard companion to Dutch literature, written by Gerard Knuvelder, while giving ample space to the discussion of the currents of the renaissance, the baroque and the romantic period, hardly talks about the enlightenment at all, not even as a term.[13] As a typical representative of the Dutch enlightenment, and without saying exactly what he means by enlightenment, Knuvelder mentions among others Betje Wolff (1738-1804), a poet, controversialist, and author (together with her friend Aagje Deken) of the epistolary novel *Sara Burgerhart*, published in 1782. This novel, which also was translated into French and German, constitutes for many people the high point of Dutch eighteenth century literature. In any case, Wolff and Deken are generally held to be our most important representatives of the enlightenment, so that the general question about the specific character of the Dutch enlightenment, may perhaps be best answered by using their case as an illustration.

By now a whole library can be filled with the books and articles that have been written about Wolff and Deken;[14] yet all this writing has not resulted in any clear definition of their position as spokeswomen of the enlightenment. On the contrary, there is a lot of misunderstanding and confusion about this crucial point. Therefore I should like to devote the rest of the time allotted to me here to a discussion of Wolff and Deken and the Dutch enlightenment.

II.

Whoever reads the novel *Sara Burgerhart*[15] will easily discover in it all sorts of enlightenment opinions, as for example a defense of religious tolerance, sociability and public spirit, advocacy of sensible education which begins with a mother breastfeeding her own children, as well as advocacy of marriage in which man and wife are equal partners to each other. What, on the other hand, one will discover them to be against are: idleness, bigotry and useless erudition. But I had better stop, before I give you the impression that the novel consists of nothing but messages that are as boring as they are true. Nor am I going to talk about the literary value of *Sara Burgerhart*. What I am concerned about here is solely its ideological content. However, from a purely ideological point of view this enlightenment novel contains passages which make the authors look just the opposite of enlightened. In letters seventy-two and ninety-four for instance we get the literal account of a discussion between Sara's future husband, Hendrik Edeling, and the Voltairean free-thinker Cornelia Hartog. The conversation is about the sufficiency of virtue and about the problem of human freedom versus determinism. In Sara Burgerhart's presence the detestable Miss Hartog -- for whom the Bible, as she herself says, is not more than 'a pretty fairytale' -- is totally defeated. Of the same libertine mettle is the aristocratic villain R., who unsuccessfully tries to rape Sara, after first having abducted her.

Also in the other novels of Wolff and Deken, like *Willem Leevend* (1784-85) and *Cornelia Wildschut* (1793-96) we meet free-thinkers, esprits forts who only too gladly have exchanged the Bible for d'Holbach's Systéme de la Nature. They all come to a bad end! The somber libertine Jambres in *Willem Leevend* bears the sign of Cain on his forehead. Hein van Arkel, the amoral hedonist in *Cornelia Wildschut* perishes finally in a duel. Again the conventionally christian tendency seems to have won an easy victory over a caricatured enlightenment philosophy. But is that so?

The study of Wolff and Deken in the Netherlands was made respectable and has long been dominated by Mrs. Hendrika Ghijsen. In her dissertation on Betje Wolff in relation to the intellectual life of her time (1919)[16] she immediately touched upon our problem: namely Betje Wolff's position as enlightenment philosopher. According to Mrs. Ghijsen, the end of Betje's marriage to the Reverend Wolff in 1777 and her subsequent moving in with Aagje Deken, also marked the end of her development as an enlightened eighteenth century thinker. Her being enlightened in this case simply meant: familiarity with and acceptance of the first, moderate era of the enlightenment up to roughly 1750. Wolff completely agreed with rational christians like Leibnitz, Pope, Marmontel, Gellert. But the most radical second phase of the enlightenment with its philosophical materialism, I mean the philosophy of Holbach, Bolingbroke and Lessing, was quite alien to her. Not to mention Kant, whom she abhorred.

In the light of this train of thought, Betje Wolff looks more like a reargard figure than an innovative thinker. In Dutch terms she may have been enlightened, but internationally speaking she was out of step. And this picture seems to agree quite well with the way in which certain enlightenment philosophers, be they French, German or English, are discussed in the novels of Wolff and Deken. Especially Voltaire later on becomes the butt of criticism.

Let me first remark here that Mrs. Ghijsen revised her point of view in her Wolff and Deken biography of 1954.[17] She then found that there was no such thing as an intellectual stagnation after 1777.

Another point of consideration concerns the political development of Wolff and Deken. with regard to that, there never has been any mention of a growing conservatism. On the contrary, in this respect Wolff and Deken were comparatively late developers. Until 1787 they belonged to the pro-stadhouder majority; only after that date they publicly joined the democratic bourgeois Patriots. Their living in revolutionary France for almost ten years (1788-1797) did not cool their enthusiasm for freedom, although they always disassociated themselves from populism and street-fighting. Having returned to their native country, they support in 1798 the radical government of Pieter Vrede as ghost-writers. With the overthrow of this short-lived government by a conservative coup d'etat, the political role of Wolff and Deken also comes to and end. But in their collection of *Poems and Songs for the Fatherland*, published in that crucial year of 1798, they defended the Batavian revolution with unbroken enthusiasm. As far as that was concerned, they could truly say: je ne regrette rien,

This political awakening and their radical position alone make it quite improbable that Wolff and Deken should at the same time have abandoned their own enlightened philosophy. It is another matter that Betje Wolff, through and in her cooperation with Aagje Deken, should have developed a more socially orientated writing urge. Up to then she had always waged her own private little war against everything that appeared to her ridiculous. But as her verse-satires and pamphlets were mainly directed against orthodox ministers and their circles, she made the impression to be more free-thinking than she actually was. A recent study by Pieter van der Vliet[18] has, however, sufficiently demonstrated that Betje Wolff was not the deist or Spinozist she was thought to be by her contemporary enemies as well as by her admirers of a later date. Wolff as well as Deken essentially believed in all the truths of revealed religion. Their heterodoxy was just a pose, (almost) to the point of anti-clericalism. That is the reason why in 1779 Betje Wolff and Aagje Deken left the church: henceforth they were chretiéns sans église.

All this, however, fits in exactly with the tradition of the Dutch enlightenment. It links up with the libertinism of Coornhert and Spiegel, with Erasmian tolerance and with the political freedom of Hugo de Groot. It was not for nothing that in her study Betje Wolff had the portraits of Erasmus and Grotius flanking that of Rousseau. Consequently also with respect to religion Wolff and Deken never had to relinquish their enlightened position. There never was anything like a breach with the past (as one finds it with Van Goens, for instance, who from Dutch reformed switched to Voltairianism and from Voltairianism back to pietism). With great enthusiasm Wolff and Deken urge Dutch mothers to take the education of their children as of today into their own hands. Equally optimistic they employ their pen for the enlightenment of the man in the street. This they did even before the Society for Public Welfare, founded in 1784 (and still in existence), was to devote its activities especially to just this 'man in the street'.

It was in order to further the enlightenment of the common people that Wolff and Deken in 1781 published their *Economic Songs* (re-edited six times), just as in their novels and essays they addressed themselves specifically to the bourgeoisie. Down to their last joint venture, the *Writings of an Aged Women* in 1802, they appear to us always the same convinced, militant advocates of the christian enlightenment.

Where then does the intellectual stagnation first presumed by Ghijsen come from? Whence the growing criticism in their novels of so-called 'esprits forts' and free-thinkers? It seems to me important to understand that we are not only concerned here with the incidental case of Wolff and Deken, but with the problem of the Dutch enlightenment as such.

Round about 1790, as the eighteenth century is speeding towards its close, one notices everywhere in the Netherlands the need to take stock of the results and the range of the enlightenment. For some people, as for instance for the poet Rhijnvis Feith, this leads to a complete reckoning with the century of the enlightenment, to wit his didactic poem The Grave of 1792. Others, like Hieronymus van Alphen, feel driven into a corner and begin to draw a clear line between a true and a false, a christian and a pagan enlightenment. The great number of programmatical poems and treatises point to the fact that by 1790 the time had come to regauge the term as well as the concept of the enlightenment. These discussions get louder around the turn of the century; a fact which proves that Da Costa's Protests against the Spirit of the Age of 1823 did not come out of the blue.

I must admit that much in the battle about the enlightenment still seems unclear to me. We do not quite know yet how things were related and where the dividing line lay. But it does seem as if among the sworn advocates of enlightenment thought -- and especially among these -- the thought of imminent decay took hold. First we get the decline of belief in the christian revelation not through rational arguments but through the loss of moral standards under the guise of free-thinking. On the basis of this, perhaps false assessment, Wolff and Deken with their novel *Willem Leevend*, and more explicitly with *Cornelia Wildshut*, publicly enter the debate about the credibility of the Gospels which, towards the end of the century, was to be waged with great vehemence all over Europe. However, when these two Dutch women-writers make critical remarks about the German theologican Gotthilf Samuel Steinbart, about Lessing and about Holbach, it does not necessarily follow that this means farewell to the enlightenment. they did not cross over into the reactionary camp of Willem Bilderdijk or Hieronymus van Alphen. One rather ought to say that they caught the signal of their time and, just as engaged as ever, reacted to it. It was not they who had changed. It was the conditions that had in their eyes become less favorable to the enlightenment. And they were not the only ones who felt this.

Thus in 1794, the former preacher and leader of the Patriots, Jacobus Kantelaar, gave a remarkable lecture for the Society of Public Welfare about the influence of true enlightenment on the lot of women and their happiness in marriage.[19] The argumentation could not be more enlightened! Starting from the premise that man is a social being by nature, Kantelaar considers marriage everybody's vocation. But marriage only in the sense that man and wife are equal partners to one another. This happy natural state, hélas, is not free from dangers. Source of all evil is man's deviation from nature.

Formerly this deviation expressed itself -- as it still does today among primitive peoples -- in the form of brutality. Nowadays, however, unnatural behaviour manifests itself in decadence and luxury. 'It is the duty of true enlightenment (according to Kantelaar) to set bounds to these bad effects of civilization'. Kantelaar makes a fundamental distinction between enlightenment and civilization. The latter is no more than a veneer. It consist in acquired manners. Civilization degrades women to luxury dolls, or (as we would say now) to sex objects. Enlightenment on the other hand leads to their intellectual and moral development.

And who was supposed to spread this infectious love of luxury at the end of the eighteenth century? Who else, the answer must be, but the French-orientated drawing-room aristocracy. A certain part of the Dutch bourgeoisie seemed very susceptible to this influence and slowly became alienated from the good old Dutch solidity. Mundane libertinism and moral decadence then formed a greater danger for true enlightenment than strict orthodoxy.

So much for the train of thoughts of Jacobus Kantelaar which is the same (to give you another example) as that of Ijsbrand van Hamelsveld in his book published in 1791 with the title *The moral state of the Dutch nation at the end of the eighteenth century*.[20] It is remarkable that this point of view was not held by orthodox diehards but by representatives of the Dutch enlightenment who played a leading part in the Batavian revolution, which had just begun.

Exactly the same was the case with Wolff and Deken. Their novels, poems, essays and letters express a continual concern for the true enlightenment of the people which is firmly based on patriotic feeling. In her younger years Betje Wolff had still tried to get the laugh on her side with a satire like *The Minuet and the Minister's Whig* (1772): a narrative poem about an elder who was threatened with suspension by the church council because he had dared to dance a minuet at his daughter's wedding. At the end of the seventeen-eighties such an attack would have been hardly suitable. At that stage the enlightenment ideal in the Netherlands was less threatened by intolerant orthodoxy than by libertine free-thinkers, who at the same time undermined the strength of the nation.

Ghijsen was certainly right in pointing out Betje Wolff's lessing interest in the philosophy of her time. Only her explanation for it missed the point. It was by no means a question of intellectual inertia, nor was it a farewell to enlightenment. Just as their great example Justus van Effen, Betje Wolff and Aagje Deken with their novels and poems simply wanted to give the Dutch of all classes concrete models of enlightened and unenlightened behaviour: blueprints for an enlightened society along patriotic lines.

A possible lack of speculative thought in their work is certainly compensated by an unexpected richness of observation in their benevolently critical and humorous picture of the Dutch bourgeoisie of the second half of the eighteenth century.

NOTES

[1] C.H.E. de Wit, *De Nederlandse revolutie van de achttiende eeuw 1770-1787.* Oirsbeek 1974; I. Leonard Leeb, *The Ideological Origins of the Batavian revolution.* the Hague 1973; Simon Schama, *Patriots and Liberators. Revolution in the Netherlands 1780-1813.* New York 1977.

[2] J. Wille, *De literator R.M. van Goens en zijn kring* I (all published). Zutphen 1937.

[3] L. Brummel, *Frans Hemsterhuis, een philosofenleven.* Haarlem 1925.

[4] J.C. Brandt Corstius, 'Rhijnvis Feith als overgangsfiguur', in: *De Nieuwe Taalgids* L (1957), p. 241-247.

[5] J.C. Brandt Corstius, 'Verschijnselen in onze literatuur aan het einde van de 18de eeuw in verband met veranderende opvattingen omtrent geloof en natuur', in: *De Nieuwe Taalgids* XLIV (1951), 241-253.

[6] P.J. Buijnsters, 'Les lumières hollandaises', in: *Studies on Voltaire and the Eighteenth Century* LXXXVII (Geneve 1972), p. 197-215.

[7] Roland Mortier, *Clartès et Ombres du Siècle des Lumières.* Geneve 1969; Actes du VIIe Congres de L'Association Internationale de Littérature Comparée. Budapest 1985, p. 105-107.

[8] H.H. Zwager, *Nederland en de Verlichting.* Bussum 1972.

[9] Hans Bots and Jan de Vet, 'Les provinces-Unies et Les Lumières', in: *Dix-Huitième Siecle* 10 (1978), p. 101-122.

[10] Ferdinand Sassen, *Johan Lulofs (1711-1768) en de Reformatorische Verlichting in de Nederlanden.* Amsterdam 1965.

[11] I.H. van Eeghen, *De Amsterdamse Boekhandel 1680-1725.* Amsterdam 1960-1978. 6 vols.

[12] W.W. Mijnhardt, 'De Nederlandse Verlichting in europees perspectief', in: *Theoretische geschiedenis* 10 (1983), p. 335-347.

[13] G.P.M. Knuvelder, *Handboek tot de geschiedenis der Nederlandse letterkunde* II-III. 's-Hertogenbosch 1971-1973.

[14] P.J. Buijnsters, *Bibliografie der geschriften van en over Betje Wolff en Aagje Deken.* Utrecht 1979; idem, *Wolff & Deken, een biografie.* Leiden 1984; idem *Briefwisseling van Betje Wolff en Aagje Deken.* Utrecht 1987, 2 vols.

[15] E. Bekker - wed. ds. Wolff, en A. Deken, *Historie van Mejuffrouw Sara Burgerhart.* Naar de eerste druk van 1782 uitgegeven door P.J. Buijnsters. Den Haag 1980, 2 vols.

[16] H.C.M. Ghijsen, *Betje Wolff in verband met het geestelijk leven van haar tijd.* Rotterdam 1929,

[17] H.C.M. Ghijsen, *Dapper vrouwenleven.* Assen 1954.

[18] P. van der Vliet, *Wolff & Deken's Brieven van Abraham Blankaart*. Een bijdrage tot de kennis van de Reformatorische Verlichting. Utrect 1982.

[19] Jacobus Kantelaar, "Over den invloed der ware Verlichting op het lot der vrouwen en het huwelijksgeluk', in: *Redevoeringen en Dichtstukken van Jacobus Kantelaar*, ed. M. Siegenbeek. Haarlem 1826.

[20] Ijsbrand van Hamelsveld, *De zedelijke toestand der Nederlandsche Natie op het einde der achttiende eeuw*. Amsterdam 1791.

Translation of this paper: Mrs. Dr. Uta Janssens-Knorsch. For a general survey of this period in Dutch literature see: P.J. Buijnsters, Nederlandse literatuur van de achttiende eeuw. Veertien verkenningen. Utrecht 1984.

THE HERITAGE OF ENLIGHTMENT
The Struggle in Dutch Masonry 1780-1825

André J. Hanou
University of Amsterdam

The fact that in 1782 (26th of February) the province of Friesland (one of the 'states' of the Dutch Republic) was the first nation of the world to decide to recognize the U.S.A., should not exactly be seen as a token of undivided harmony of opinion in the Netherlands. We should rather regard it as an indication of the division of the Dutch nation. As matters stood, the Republic as such was not at liberty to make such a gesture.

Indeed, partly owing to the American War of Independence, a division of opinion began to prevail between a more progressive and enlightened section of the population, and a more conservative group on which the political ideas of the Enlightenment had failed to gain a hold. It is this contrast which was to govern life in the Republic for the last two decades of the eighteenth century. This very struggle for and against the Enlightenment was to bring the Netherlands on the verge of ruin; sometimes even beyond that stage, at least from a political point of view. The Republic's involvement with America resulted in the fourth English war (1780-84), piteously lost. This caused feelings of antipathy against the inefficient government of the stadtholder, which led up to civil war and a revolution in 1787: two years before the swelling sound of the Carmagnole was heard in the streets of Paris. A counter-reaction, still in 1787, restored the power of the stadtholder, but drove thousands of democrats out of the country. In 1793 these came back, and again the tables were turned. The Republic threw in her lot with France. Virtually it was this alliance which was to bring about the financial - and in the end the political - annihilation of the Republic. The maritime nation found her trade-routes blockaded; the nation which until recently had been the strongest economic power in the world, was once and for all relegated to a second place.

At home coups followed each other in close succession; emotionally the population was torn by party strife. Towards the end of the century the Republic was not unlike a Central American banana-republic. Therefore we need not be surprised that towards the year 1800 we see a tendency to revert to the values of former times. Christendom appeared as a new alternative, offering support to the entangled soul. In a way the Netherlands would prefer to be allowed retreat from the European political turmoil. After 1813, this will happen indeed; all through the nineteenth century the country will be retreating into 'splendid isolation', drowsily watching the events in the rest of the world.

But about the year 1800 the ideals of the Enlightenment had not entirely been quenched here. The cat was not completely cured of her curiosity. In the field of science the Netherlands still kept their front rank.

The Amsterdam school of chemists (most important member: Deiman) was famous throughout Europe. And in a great number of cultural societies the results of science, the latest anthropological, sociological etc. ideas were discussed every week. A self-conscious man who wished to keep abreast of the times was a member of at least one of these societies. To mention just two of them: *Concordia et Libertate, Felix Meritis*. In 1800 a new society was founded: the Batavian Society for the Fine Arts and Sciences. This society, which, later on, had important dependencies in several towns, clearly aimed at keeping the Netherlands at virtually the same level as the rest of the world in the fields of literature, philosophy and science. At the same time, a group of the Dutch intelligentsia spared no efforts to raise the lower population groups to a higher level of education. With this goal in mind the *Maatschappij tot nut van 't algemeen* (Society for the Common Weal). founded in 1784, succeeded in forming branches all over the country.

At the same time, however, we must admit that a wave of reaction and conservatism swept over the Netherlands. If, in the beginning of the 19th century, we are to connect one person with this movement, we ought to mention Willem Bilderdijk (1756-1831). Doubtlessly he was the greatest Dutch man of letters of his day (and for a long time to come); a man, endowed with unusual gifts, but also one who was chaotic and given to subjectivism. Not only did he assume to have the profoundest understanding of literature, he also felt to be well-versed in philosophy and linguistics; indeed, there was hardly any field on which he didn't feel entitled to speak the final word. After his banishment to England and Germany (which had been forced upon him by the revolutionary government of 1793) Bilderdijk lapsed into a most melancholy reaction. He dreamt of the return of the nation to an orthodox (and rather inflexible) christianity; he longed to see back the old Republic governed by the House of Orange, as this state had always enjoyed the special care of the God of the Netherlands. And not seldom did he praise the spirit of the Middle Ages, which was rather unusual in his days (to the enlightened mind the medieval era was an age of barbarity and gothic superstitions). Those who were dissatisfied, who saw the Enlightenment as the source of all evil which had swept over the Netherlands, rallied round Bilderdijk. Within the framework of this article it is also important to know that he translated and published a pamphlet on freemasonry with an anti-masonic tenor, Mac Benac. For Bilderdijk freemasonry was clearly one of the evil influences of his day: an organization which seduced people to wander away from the straight path to Christianity.

With reference to this particular opinion on Dutch freemasonry a few observations may be made. On close observation of the situation around 1800, I find that in some respects Dutch freemasonry is far from being what you might call 'liberal'. The Dutch organization (rather: two organizations, amassing some 6000 freemasons to a population of 1.1/2 or 2 millions - showed, as far as progressiveness and conservatism are concerned, rather close resemblance to similar societies in the rest of Europe, at least on the continent. It is true that on the continent the masonic movement of the end of the 18th and beginning of the 19th century was the organization in which a great part of the more tolerant intelligentsia or middle class came together. But outside the Anglo-Saxon world the structure and aims of freemasonry were not always very clear. As a rule, the three-degree system of symbolic masonry was recognized. But apart from that (or, as some of the adepts would have it: above that) a great many systems of 'high' degrees were in common use. These systems were often invented 'at random', and not seldom they were endowed with an imaginary historical past. Often these systems of degrees attracted people with a greater susceptibility to the exotic rites here pursued, and who found pleasure in esoteric, mysterious performance. This is what was also known in the Netherlands. We may say that we can speak of a 'left' wing in freemasonry, with a preference for the three-degrees system, and a 'right' wing. Besides, in several rituals of the high degrees Christian themes and symbols were not infrequently used. Those freemasons who still (or again) regarded Christianism as a superior form of religion often found shelter in the organization of the high degrees. The text of the highest degree (that could be reached in the Netherlands, the text belonging to the degree of 'Prince of the Rosy Cross' (as established in 1803), betrays this tendency. In this text Christ is held up as the pattern of the true freemason, and Christianism is presented as the doctrine to whose principles other professors of the world-religions (Judaism, Islam) should convert, if they wished to be freemasons in the true sense. In order to avoid any misunderstanding, I must stress the fact that this opinion is nowhere to be found in the common, symbolic freemasonry with its three-degrees system.

Now I have given you an epitome of a certain division in the society of the Netherlands, as well as in Dutch freemasonry. From 1805 onwards, we may say that Dutch freemasonry shows signs of an attempt at reformation, and a wish for reorganization in a more enlightened sense.

Here I must mention the name of Jan (Johannes) Kinker (1764-1845). In his youth Kinker was an admirer and even a friend of Bilderdijk's. He even worked in Bilderdijk's law firm. At the time of Bilderdijk's banishment he acted as his representative in court. When Bilderdijk became increasingly more conservative, they gradually drifted apart. Kinker himself appeared to be a man of great literary accomplishments. In several magazines he brilliantly commented on cultural and political developments in the Netherlands. His ironic prose still makes very readable matter (whereas Bilderdijk was not good at debating in prose; he pontificated too much). In Kinker we will never look in vain for a certain degree of humanitarian idealism. Moreover, Kinker developed into one of the most outstanding scholars of his period. As a philosopher he was also a great man. As evidence of this I will only mention that it was his summarizing view on Kant's philosophical theses which made the Konigsberger's works, and German idealism in general, known in France. Stendhal for instance, only read Kant via Kinker. For a man as Bilderdijk, however, Kant remained a modernist, an irreligious man. His system was simply reprehensible. For Kinker Kant and his critical philosophy was a source of inspiration. From a moral point of view he was a support for mankind, by means of his doctrine of doing good without reward (as every individual human being had to respond to the moral, categorical imperative of his own heart). At the same time Kant's idea of a developing history, towards a better society, necessarily so, but maintaining individual freedom, was a great support to Kinker. Kinker was a bit of an utopian, and with his whole heart he longed for a better society in which everyone would be given a chance to realize his own potentials. Thus Kinker and Bilderdijk become specimens of the polarity in Dutch society.

Kinker was not the only Kantian in the Netherlands, though. At the end of the 18th century there is clearly a group of enthusiastics, inspired by the new light from Germany. A person I mentioned before, Deiman, Amsterdam's leading man of science, was a Kantian. Falck, the friend of Kinker's boyhood, restoration minister of state since 1813, was also a Kantian. The best-known of them was Paulus van Hemert; he became the editor of their magazine, the *Magazine of Critical Philosophy*, in which this group popularized their ideas.

Strangely enough the 'clout' of this group of Kantians, their influence, has never been examined. Here historiography has left an important field untouched. But it is clear that their positions were constantly and heavily attacked, especially by philosophers and theologians with orthodox christian leanings. It is no use here to explain the logic behind their opposition: whoever studies Kantianism will immediately understand why Christianism felt little sympathy for the Aufklärungs-philosopher Kant, who rejected all metaphysical speculation so drastically, and who described the foundations of a moral life (without any need for Christendom) and of a society evolving itself (also without any mediation of Christianity).

In 1805 something strange happens. It is described by Kinker's first biographer, Van Hall. Almost the whole group of Kantians suddenly turns to masonry. From a cultural-historical point of view this is an interesting step. According to Van Hall, Kinker became a freemason in order to propagate his philosophical fundamental propositions, with the intention to disseminate the 'ideal of a cosmopolitan situation' outside the narrow circle of philosophers and scholars. Almost all these people join the Amsterdam lodge 'La Charite in 1805 and 1806. Among this group were, apart from Kinker, Paulus van Hemert, Deiman; also Klijn and Helmers, both men of letters of considerable reputation at the time; Kinker's later biographer, Van Hall; and the theorist of art, Le Fevre, who translated Kinker's work on Kant into French.

The reason why this group opted for La Charite is unknown to me. Probably this may have been due to the ideas of the presiding master, Willem Holtrop, a well-known publisher.

Naturally the entry of this group was a great acquisition and reinforcement for Dutch masonry. But it might be anticipated that the aspirations of this group could lead to clashes of opinion. Of course, masonry in general did aim at world fraternity, but this was no more than a vague ideal; and as an organization they certainly didn't mean actively to promote a world-state ruled by Kantian, or rather: Enlightened principles. Moreover, as I told you before, for a large part the brotherhood consisted of people who liked to be occupied with the rite; especially in the high degrees. From now onwards I will discuss a few moments chosen from the following fifteen years, which throw a light on the aims and aspirations of the Kinker-group (as I will call them for the sake of convenience; Kinker being the one who appears to be the most active). Here I discuss these things from an administrative point of view; describing the ideas of Kinker c.s. about all kinds of masonic symbols, allegories etc. is no use in this case; though there are a great number of masonic poems by Kinker, which are most captivating, and we also have many masonic orations or instructive speeches, which he held as a functionary of his lodge. For the greater part these speeches are concerned with the duty of advancing world brotherhood and with its manifestations as they become apparent in European politics.

In 1806 Kinker c.s. were for the first time confronted with ideas among the followers of the high degrees, which, till then, had been unknown to them. Kinker - who then only held the first three degrees, as is usual in common symbolic freemasonry - introduced as a new member of La Charite a man of jewish origin. The majority of the lodge-council rejected this proposal. Kinker didn't understand the reason for this refusal. He couldn't help thinking that this was a case of discrimination, which was incompatible with the spirit and fundamental law of the brotherhood. Indignantly he and Van Hemert started writing letters to the Grand Lodge of the Dutch society - at the time a rather inefficient and archaic lot - in which they underlined the principle of tolerance with respect to whatever philosophy of life, and similar principles. He had every reason to be surprised, for in the 18th century it had been far from unusual to admit jews. Finally, in order to explain the nature of the objection to Kinker, the highest degree (outside of the symbolic masonry; the degree of 'Prince of the Rosy Cross') was imparted to him by way of 'communication'. Those who had objected, namely, appeared to hold this degree; and they were convinced that, owing to its christian oriented contents, and owing to the text of the ritual (then) clearly stipulating the superiority of the christian doctrine of salvation, the degree could never permit people with a jewish philosophy of life to be admitted. Once received in the first degree, anyone could, theoretically, acquire the highest degree in the end; so...

When this had been explained to him, we do not immediately see a direct action on Kinker's part. But from all his succeeding steps it appears that he has not accepted this form of intolerance, nor this idea with its explanation. The end result of his actions will be that finally, in 1819, a new organization is devised, in which there was to be no room for the old high degrees, and much less for the degree of Prince of the Rosy Cross.

After 1806, the next five years are devoted to finding supporters and to transforming the various Amsterdam lodges into a body which would be ready for the fray. Amsterdam gets a council consisting of representatives of the local lodges, empowered to take decisions and to give stringent instructions to the deputies who are to go to the yearly national assembly (a kind of freemason parliament). Such a council (its very existence) will surprise nobody; but it was a novelty in the masonic world, where every lodge gloried in its independence and uniquity. It will be unnecessary to tell you that the Kinker-group, who in the meantime had gained a foothold in the councils of the individual Amsterdam lodges, pulled the ropes in this Amsterdam General Council. From this platform all kinds of interesting things will happen. The freemason's catechism is newly formulated in a

Kantian sense. And year after year propositions are sent to the national assembly, each aiming at: reinforcement of the masonic organization, and the overthrow of the separate Council of the high degrees. This second aim is not formulated in so many words; it seems as if only is meant to bring about a fusion. Therefore it takes some time before the Kinker-opposition understands what exactly is happening. At any rate, for a time the Amsterdam bid for a merger is not very successful. There were other, more imminent problems. In 1810 the Netherlands are annexed by France; French lodges arise everywhere, which do not recognize the authority of the old (Dutch) Grand Lodge; and, according to their usual practice, the almighty French also try to absorb Dutch masonry. The Kinker-group, who had no use at all for such methods, energetically opposed this attempt.

I wish to mention two other Amsterdam initiatives. The first is a proposal to move the Grand Lodge of freemasonry from The Hague (where the Dutch Government had always resided) to Amsterdam. Amsterdam being more centrally situated, as the Kinker-group stated. Of course this would have enforced the group enormously; up till then the Grand Lodge had been ruled by a rather indolent set of people from The Hague. The attempt, however, was unsuccessful. More interesting is a proposal from Amsterdam to found an international correspondence bureau. This bureau was to keep up a correspondence with foreign masonic organizations and to start a kind of international annual or magazine. Via this medium the secretariat was to discuss all kinds of national arrangements and points of view, in order to advance internationalization; thus forwarding world fraternity among people, with freemasonry as a guide. I do not wish to exaggerate, but I do perceive here the possibility of a kind of first International, in which Holland as guiding country should show the straight path to other peoples of the world.

As a result of the new political relations after Bonaparte's definite downfall, a new situation arose, which concerned freemasonry as well. Various regions were added to the territory of the old Republic: the whole region of present day Belgium and Luxemburg. The country as a whole was now the Kingdom of the Netherlands, under a king from the old House of Orange: William I. The question is: what did this all mean for freemasonry? The ordinary masonry in the south (Belgium) had up till then been subordinate to Paris; but we also find a great many organizations of the high degrees in the south, which are of various natures. It is clear that the Kinker-group must have looked upon this chance of reorganization as being at the same time a chance of transformations in an ideal sense. In this case, however, they obviously needed a person who would be recognized as leader by all these organizations. And that is the reason why we see Kinker's friend Falck pleading with the King to make his second son, Frederick, Grand Master. An Orange as Grand Master could hardly be refused by the masons; as to the king, this would also be advantageous for the political unity in the entire Kingdom. During these negotiations the Kinker-group remains in the background; most probably in order to avoid the danger that the antipathy to the House of Orange - which in certain quarters of Dutch society and masonry had never subsided - would be revived by too much propaganda. To make a long story short: in 1816 the Dutch freemasonry forms an interim-council -with Kinker - to offer Frederick the office of Grand Master. He accepts; towards the end of 1816 follows his installation as Grand Master of symbolic freemasonry. Now negotiations start in order to get him accepted in 'Belgium' as well. Kinker has a hand in the negotiations in the south. This is also successful. Step by step now the group-Kinker tries to transform freemasonry, to shape it into the enlightened organization which from the beginning they meant it to be. But, did the new Grand Master himself, Frederick, have no views of his own? No policy? On reading his correspondence with a view on these developments, it becomes gradually clear that Kinker acted more or less as a mentor to the young Grand Master. Only recently did I find even more letters which bear witness to this statement. Also the very fact that as Grand Master of the high degrees Frederick was not installed before the end of 1817; and not in The Hague, but in Amsterdam, is an indication that such was the case. Frederick's view of the high degrees, and the importance of the first degrees, was shaped by Kinker. Mid-1817 he expresses his approval of the Amsterdam declaration "Fiat Lux" (composed by Kinker), in which all lodges are invited to unite in the spirit of the Enlightenment, into an organization which would better be able to assert itself.

The Kinker-policy of Enlightenment becomes still more clear. In a letter to Falck, dated August 15, 1817, Kinker mentions a visit to Frederick, in the course of which he suggested that the Grand Master would 'create' a new degree, over and above the three ordinary degrees, but at the same time as a substitute for whatever high degrees which might still be in use in the kingdom. A gigantic step: for in this way all rite-adepts were to lose any possibility whatsoever to organize things in their own circles; they would lost their mental foothold.

There's a catch to such an attempt, of course. Why should masons with beliefs in their old degrees accept such a new degree instead? And a degree in an enlightened jacket at that?

Good question. But - surprise! In the beginning of 1818 Frederick informs the lodges that via an anonym he has received various old, unknown minutes and documents. The most important document was the so-called 'Charter of Cologne'. This Charter contained the account of a masonic assembly in 1535 at Cologne, at which the most important European lodges were present. In this document they explained the actual nature, origin and organization of freemasonry, or what it should be. Without any doubt, and according to all historical criterions nowadays, this document must have been forged. Remarkably, it confirms all the beliefs of the group-Kinker. On translation it appears to contain the following basic tenets: masonry in its proper sense consists of the first three degrees (the rest: fabrications) except that the masters knew an additional elaboration to their degree (which is exactly what Kinker had proposed to Frederick); for the rest the first aim of the order had to be: the stimulating of morality present in every human being (a rather Kantish idea); there was no need to embrace Christendom: this was sometimes required only to avoid (medieval!) persecution. Indeed, all masonic mysteriousness was wrong; it was only needed sometimes, due to external circumstances. Obviously this document caused much commotion.

Here the (so far) oldest documents on freemasonry had been unearthed! But the consequence was that if the historical value of this charter should be accepted, the very reason of existence of the high degrees was denied at the same time; while a more enlightened form of masonry was validated. In the next few years we find Frederick trying to set up a new organization, following the lines of the Charter of Cologne. It is the system of the so-called 'bouw-hutten'. The result: bitter debates with the adherents of the high degrees, who at a certain moment withdraw from his organization. Thus a kind of schism follows. A schism which has existed till the present day, in Holland: the high degrees still have separate organizations.

With this schism, however, I must end my narration. The division could partly come about because in the twenties of the 19th century, Kinker could no longer pull the ropes of events. He had accepted a professorial chair in Liege, which forced him to keep away from the storm-centre of events. This attempt of his group, to create a masonic organization of Kantian liberals, the attractive power of which should have an impact on the rest of the masonic world (and via that on the world), must be seen as a failure around the year 1825. Therefore I'm sorry to be obliged to tell you that this story ends without any consequences. But I hope that what I told you in this brief space will still induce you to follow the curious events in Dutch freemasonry between 1800 and 1825; they are, as it were, a reflection of the problems in Dutch (and even in European) culture.

SELF-STYLIZATION AND NARRATIVE STRATEGIES IN FREDERICK VAN EEDEN'S ROMAN A THESE DE NACHTBRUID

Augustinus P. Dierick
Victoria College, University of Toronto

In a diary entry of June 22, 1905, Frederik Van Eeden noted among the various projects he wanted to undertake in the near future "het boek Waarnemingen in den slaap." This, according to H.W. Van Tricht, is the first reference to what was to become the novel *De nachtbruid*.[1] The rather summary fashion in which the project is announced stands in stark contrast to the entry of January ll, 1909, in which Van Eeden reports the conclusion of this novel, for it contains the following comment: "Het boek is een soort noodgebouw, waarin ik het kostbaarste onderbracht. Maar het heeft toch een goede architectuur en een innerlijke soliditeit gekregen, doordat de figuur van Muralto leeft." Obviously, *De nachtbruid* had become something other than a book about observations on sleep; moreover, since the main character in the book now appeared to be crucial to his enterprise, Van Eeden clearly had shifted emphasis from a scientific or quasi-scientific treatise to a full-fledged novel. The fact is that a profound ambivalence of purpose could be argued, were it not that the link between Van Eeden's ideas on the nature and significance of dreams and between certain other fundamental thought-complexes is established in and through the figure of Muralto.

Two important intentions are merged in *De nachtbruid*, both related to the particular situation in which Van Eeden found himself in the years between 1905 and 1909. There is first the author's original intention to report on his strange ability to dream clearly ("helder droomen"). But since the world of dreams is interpreted by Van Eeden as the "antechamber of the beyond,"[2] these dreams are linked to other important themes and ideas with which the author was struggling at this time. Van Eeden's second intention is to redefine his dual role as social reformer and philosopher-artist in the light of two recent failures: to establish a social utopia in the colony Walden, and to secure the continued existence of the co-operative De Eendracht, which was intended to employ railway workers locked out in the labour dispute of 1903. Both enterprises had collapsed because Van Eeden clearly was not practical enough, and had overestimated the power of good will alone.[3] But both from actions taken following the catastrophe of 1907, and from the writings of that period it becomes clear that - though the events created resentment against Holland, a country too small for prophets[4] - they merely forced Van Eeden to shift grounds, without sacrificing his belief in the essential correctness of his mission, and in his spiritual and social leadership. On May 17, 1906, before the collapse of his projects, Van Eeden had written in his diary: "Ik verlang naar een groote sfeer en vrijheid tot groote gedachten." The year 1907 still finds him very much in the same frame of mind: "Ik ben veel afgekomen van mijn aanvankelijke hoogheid, maar nu is het genoeg. Ik ben nu oud genoeg om te kunnen spreken zoals ik 't meen...ik ga nu niet meer links of rechts, om slechte verstaanders te gerieven of te ontwijken."

The immediate effect of the recent disasters was his attempt to find more congenial souls outside of Holland, primarily in Germany and in America. Two trips to America were undertaken, in 1908 and 1909, with essentially negative results; these experiences are incorporated in *De nachtbruid*. In the longer term, these additional failures had the effect of strengthening Van Eeden's tendency to see himself as a misunderstood genius. His "krasse zelfgevoel,"[5] an integral part of Van Eeden's character, became still more extreme. Always ready to point, as he did in 1906, to the "verschrikkelijke grootte van mijn taak,"[6] he could even after 1908 not acknowledge anything other than "misinterpretations" of his intentions. The retreat into isolation, which he grants his hero Muralto at the end of his life, he could never accept for himself. And even Muralto is not really willing to admit defeat, he merely acknowledges a temporary setback. *De nachtbruid* becomes in fact yet another forum in which Van Eeden explores the nature of the message he would like to impart to mankind, the form this message would have to take in order to be effective, and the kind of thinker who would be trusted by mankind and given the role of leader with a view to the future.

Van Eeden's preoccupation with the figure of Muralto is indeed inspired by his concern to have him meet the criteria governing the "true" prophet. This is so important because, in contrast to the scientist, the personal integrity and authority of the thinker or poet is a conditio sine qua non for the acceptance of his claims. In a diary entry of July 15, 1908 Van Eeden writes: "...voor wetenschappelijk werk... is geen kentering van algemeene opinies zoo nodig, en geen persoonlijk prestige, geen geloof. Maar de kunstenaar, de dichter heeft noodig dat zijn persoon geeerbiedigd en vertrouwd wordt." In emphasizing the importance of the personal authority and integrity of the non-scientific propagator of a theory, Van Eeden points to the crucial difference between the work of a scientist and that of a creative writer, and between science and art as cognitive instruments. Van Eeden believed that the subjectivity of literature allows poets to formulate important insights which science, with its objective and logical un-emotional methods need to phrase in quite different forms, and which may take very long to verify. In the opening sections of *De nachtbruid* it is argued that while scientific verification is always the final criterion, such verification might have to wait, while crucial discoveries need to be uttered immediately, even if only in tentative form - in the case of *De nachtbruid*, in pseudo-biographical form. This tentative form of formulation is in fact seen in a positive light by Van Eeden:"...de hoofdfout aller groote denkers was deze: dat ze met hun noodzakelijke denkfouten geen rekening hielden en hun waarheden als ééns-vooral en voor goed opstelden... ik geef mijn gedachten als schuchtere hypothesen, wachtend op bevestiging. en daardoor zullen ze langer duren."[7] Thus Muralto's character and "lijdensweg" are important precisely because the theories advanced by him are not strictly scientific.

There is of course a second reason behind Van Eeden's emphasis on Muralto as an exceptional figure: Muralto is made "transparent", in order to reveal Van Eeden's own message and to emphasize his own status. On April 25, 1908 he wrote in his diary: "In dezen vorm, de eerste persoon, in de fictie van een auto-biographisch gedenkschrift, meen ik het meest vrij te zijn om alle waarheid die ik voorhanden heb te uiten." The fictional autobiography of Muralto is intended to be an exemplary Bildungsroman, providing the foundation for the authority of the fictional philosopher; but since the resulting portrait is also a thinly-disguised self-portrait of Van Eeden, the novel's hero becomes the object of self-stylization, even self-indulgence. The emphasis on credibility explains at least to some extent the fact that for long periods of time Muralto is subjected to almost painful scrutiny. On the other hand, the intellectual opacity of the novel, which at times runs counter to the more purely novelistic aspects of the work, can be justified by referring to the book's thrust as that of a roman à thèse demonstrating Van Eeden's own thinking, though *De nachtbruid* is far from being only, or even primarily, a book about dreams, as Ilse N. Bulhoff (who provides the comments to a modern edition of the novel) argues.[8]

If there is talk about dreams in the early part of Muralto's life, it is about hollow ones, of faded opulence, of once splendid Italian palaces now in decay - dreams which obscure the tensions between aristocratic claims and democratic realities. Young Vico Muralto, son of an Italian count, experiences these tensions, and those between his father - an anti-philistine, anti-religious misanthrope - and his long-suffering, intensely religious mother, as anticipations of important constituent elements of his own future life. As a somewhat exalted youth, his early years are filled with disappointing male friendships, though he is attracted and attractive to women. Muralto cannot cope with the opposing forces of platonic and erotic love, which becomes obvious when he meets Emmy Tenders during a sojourn in London. Faced with insoluble dualisms, he insists on conversations about religion, the antinomy body-soul, and the meaning of nature. Emmy is soon tempted by a more practical rival, and this stage of Vico's life ends in mental and physical torment.

After this disastrous love-affair, a stay in Holland at first seems to hold out promises of relief, but when Vico is reunited with his mother, now accompanied by a beautiful young woman, Lucia del Bono, Vico's father fears that his son has once again come under the spell of religion, and a violent scene of confrontation takes place during a sailing trip along the Dutch coast. The elder Muralto is swept overboard and drowns, Vico survives but is in severe shock. Soon he returns with his mother to Rome, where he tries to understand religion by seeking instruction from Catholic priests, but is appalled by their ignorance and cynicism. He marries Lucia, though he does not really love her, and settles down to a career as a diplomat. It is at this stage of his life that Emmy Tenders appears to him in his dreams. Having died a few months earlier, she now offers Muralto access to the beyond, and leads him into an ever expanding dream world. Much of the subsequent sections of the novel are concerned with the exact nature of dreams, how to control them, and what sources of revelation are afforded through them.

During one of the dreams, a girl appears whom he calls "Elsje". Soon afterwards he meets this girl in real life, falls in love with her and makes her his "true wife". Separated from Lucia, he begins to lead a life of modest means, yet his aspirations grow in strength. Because of the privileged information he has gathered in his dreams, because he "has seen the future", he feels called upon to act as a social reformer and, like Van Eeden himself, he embarks on a journey to America in the company of Elsje. Though he meets with some sympathy, the journey is not a success, and when Elsje dies giving birth to a child (which only lives one day), he decides to return to Holland. In the solitude and tranquillity of a small Dutch fishing village he devotes himself to the writing of his memoirs, until one day he drowns trying to save his sailing companion during a storm. The announcement of Muralto's death, a notice in the local newspaper, is attached (by whom it is not specified) to his papers.

The fictitious autobiography has many advantages: it can make visible certain lines of development which are hidden to the immediate participants; the material is shaped to give a meaningful progression rather than an arbitrary collection of facts. The organization of the multiplicity of events, characters and circumstances also accounts for a certain amount of aesthetic manipulation, which is important in view of Van Eeden's final intention to write a novel, not a treatise. More important, of course, is the fact that this autobiography allows Van Eeden to expound on his own theories. Muralto's life can be seen to be guided by three principles, each during a specific stage of his life: religion, dreams, utopia - ideas and concepts to which Van Eeden was also drawn at this time. They are all interrelated, as the author is at pains to demonstrate, and all three hinge on the prime philosophical question: What we can know?

To arrive at any kind of knowledge, Van Eeden argues, there are two main sources: "revealed" knowledge, by which is meant philosophy and especially religion; and "intuition". At the time of writing of *De nachtbruid* Van Eeden's hostility towards religion had been overcome,[9] and although religion appears as tyranny in the eyes of Vico's father, while Vico's mother, Emmy Tenders and Lucia del Bono simply accept it without question, Muralto's own questioning attitude denotes primarily his refusal to give up his independent intellectual stance. In addition, behind these probing efforts stands Van Eeden's conviction that religion is still more valuable than mere ratio, which he had already attacked in *De kleine Johannes*.[10] Philosophy of the intuitive kind of Plato, Spinoza or even Nietzsche may provide some answers, ratio provides none. True, ratio creates order, but there exists a gap between ratio and reality, just as there exists a gap between our ideas about God and God himself (whatever God may be). In fact, it is only when ratio is suspended, in death, that true understanding becomes possible.

No wonder then that Muralto's musings on death are central to the novel. Van Eeden himself was throughout his life preoccupied with the problem of death, a rather hypochondriac obsession with it gradually making way for a more fundamental probing.[11] It becomes clear that Van Eeden did not consider death an absolute end, but the beginning of a mysterious, more or less indefinable "other existence".[12] Life is not only a constant progression towards death, it now also becomes the education for death. but how can this education become effective, and what can we learn about death to prepare for it properly?

What is absolutely crucial for *De nachtbruid* as well as for the whole thinking of Van Eeden in his later life, is that access to death, and consequently to the kind of truth it reveals, already exists here in life, namely in dreams. From early on in life, Van Eeden had been fascinated with parapsychological phenomena, with magnetism, spiritualism and hypnotism, and he was one of the first in Holland to write about these subjects.[13] A diary entry of 9 February, 1909 claims: "Dood is dis-integratie. Anders niets. Maar ook slaap is dis-integratie, en daar in zijn droomen partiele reintegratie." "Heldere droomen" thus have a significance going far beyond any conventional views on the wisdom of dreams. They are a springboard to a higher dimension: "...de oplossing van het geheim onzes levens ligt in de droom." (p. 95)

The emphasis on intuition over revelation, and the belief that in dreams there is access to truths which supersede those formulated in philosophy and religion has very important consequences. Van Eeden's rejection of traditional religion as well as ratio not only leads him to reject a definition of God, but also suggests to him a modification of the concept of Christ. In a passage from his diary which stems from the period of writing of *De nachtbruid*, Van Eeden writes: "De Christus-idee is de verpersoonlijking van de menschensoort" (31 January, 1907); and in *De nachtbruid* itself he suggests: "als de mensen nu van Christus spreken dan geloof ik...dat de meesten en de besten, die werkelijk iets menen by dat woord, iets echts, dat ze gevoeld hebben, - dat zij iets bedoelen wat overeenkomt met de mensheid." (p. 170) This explains why Muralto rejects indignantly the equation of Christ with Jesus of Nazareth. Christ cannot be a historical figure, since he is a symbol; he is beyond the historically fixed moment, and cannot be incorporated in a single figure.

Muralto's Nietzschean analysis of Jesus, and his attack on St. Paul for distorting "een echt kunstwerk", (p. 77) prepare the ground for the final major theme of *De nachtbuid*, namely its concern with the utopia here on earth, and the role Muralto is to play in its propagation. For just as the individual progresses towards death as its natural fulfillment, and continues beyond it into a state of wholeness, so mankind progresses towards a state of salvation and utopia. And just as in the life of the individual there is access to the fulfillment of death in the world of dreams, so we can grasp the ultimate utopia lying in the far future, the millennium, already here on earth, in the shape of a quasi-socialist utopia.

Having been "een machtig dromer, zolang ik mij kan herinneren", (p. 95) Muralto has, by virtue of this ability, become one of the world's "suggestie-brekers en padvinders". On the basis of his privileged information, he has a task to fulfill: that of being a prophet, a guide to the future: "Ik kan niet beproeven die Heros, die Sooter der mensheid te zijn... Maar ik wist en weet ook dat hij geboren zal worden... En zo ik hem zelf dan al niet zijn kan, zo kan ik toch zijn Johannes de Doper zijn, hem profeterend..." (p. 142) Though Muralto's efforts to establish a kind of philosopher-king on the American throne, and to found a colony, fail, the essential utopian message remains. There is no abandonment of the superior stance taken in the rest of the book. To be sure, Muralto's retreat means acknowledgment of defeat. But the very act of his writing also means a projection beyond this temporary defeat, towards a future more worthy of his ideas.

Fully aware of the problematic nature of Muralto's claims and consequently also his own, Van Eeden tackles the task of self-stylization, of vindication and justification in a variety of ways. It is in fact the wealth of narrative strategies, I would argue, which constitute the main interest of the novel.

The central element of self-stylization in *De nachtbruid* is that of contrast and difference. Muralto is unlike the majority of his contemporaries: when he finishes writing his memoirs in virtual exile in Holland, he has only reached the natural state for which his life seems to have prepared him. Muralto is different from other men: he is a loner and confesses to having had few friends, while his relations with women were problematic. More important than these biographical or psychological factors is Van Eeden's conscious removal of Muralto from the dominant Zeitgeist. Muralto is conceived as in opposition of the spirit of the "the herd", and for two main reasons. In order to define Muralto as an exceptional being, Van Eeden must let him overcome not only the conventions of his social class (the aristocracy) and his religion (Catholicism), but of his times in general. The second reason is that Muralto must become an anticipating thinker, whose destruction of the old lays the foundation for the new. This does not mean that Muralto ignores the past completely: on the contrary, to strengthen his own arguments he constantly draws upon past thinkers. But such authorities as he quotes tend to be, as we saw, intuitive thinkers: Plato, Goethe and Spinoza, whereas Ibsen, Shaw and other "witty" contemporaries come in for criticism. These references are typical for Van Eeden, whose bookish knowledge certainly contributed to his failures in the workaday world. But they are also typical for the kind of leaders whom Van Eeden considers important: they are poets, even when they are philosophers.

Muralto himself is clearly conceived as such a figure, and *De nachtbruid* postulates an intimate connection between poets on the one hand and revolutionary thinkers on the other. In Muralto there emerges the ideal fusion of poetic and revolutionary characteristics. Muralto himself expresses this in an important passage:

> Men heeft mij in mijn jeugd wel eens een dichter genoemd, en hoewel vaag en op goed geluk, toch niet geheel onjuist. Want ik ben een suggestie - vernieler, een groep - breker, een weg- zwerver van de kudde, een afgoodenhater, - maar ook een vreugde-, schoonheid- en zaligheidzoeker, een werkelijkheids-

minnaar. En dat alles zijn dichter-kenmerken... Maar verzenmaken was mijn werk niet... (p. 56)

Muralto's efforts to define himself go in two directions: on the one hand he makes of himself a slightly larger than life figure, on the other hand, he observes certain limitations to his character. This aspect we could call complexity. Muralto points, for example, to his youthful pride (p. 9), and to his sensuality which makes him the easy victim of women. Though he calls himself a fighter in his struggle against sexual temptation, he blames his cowardice for having equivocated so long before leaving Lucia. The examination of traditional religion throws him into intellectual confusion, but he is proud to have formulated some of the most fundamental philosophical questions. And whereas he glorifies the revolutionary character of his thinking, many a passage is devoted to his inability to fuse the ideal with the real. The limitations on the talents of Muralto are also significant. Lyric poetry and drama seem a closed book to Muralto, and what remains as a forum for the exposition of his theories is either the philosophical treatise, the novel, or, as *De nachtbruid* exemplifies, a combination of both. Van Eeden's care to create a figure in the round results in a rather ambiguous portrait, but one which is more realistic and therefore more convincing than the roman thèse formulation would suggest, and which justifies Van Eeden's pride in the creation of Muralto.

The claim of exceptionality is generally maintained, however, and Muralto's refusal to accept the dictates of the herd is cited repeatedly. An important device, in this context, is the recourse to Nietzsche. Nietzsche's own disdainful attitude towards the herd undoubtedly provides the model for Muralto's unconventionality. The fact that Nietzsche combines the talents of the poet and the philosopher could certainly not have escaped Van Eeden's attention.[14] But more important than as a genius and rebel, Nietzsche has a role to play as prophet. This can be seen in Van Eeden's occasional emulation of Nietzsche's "Zarathustrian" language, but particularly in his imitation of the relationship Nietzsche maintains with his reader. One need only compare the preface of *Der Antichrist* with the opening pages of *De nachtbruid* to notice this. Nietzsche writes in *Der Antichrist*: "Dies Buch gehört den Wenigsten. Vielleicht lebt selbst noch keiner von ihnen. Es mörgen Die sein, welche meinen Zarathustra verstehn... Erst das Übermorgen gehört mir. Einige werden posthum geboren..." He then continues by outlining the requirements to be met by an ideal reader:

> Eine Vorliebe der Stärke für Fragen, zu denen niemand heute den Mut hat;der Mut zum Verbotenen... Neue Augen fur das Fernste. Ein neues Gewissen fur bisher stumm gebliebene Wahrheiten... die Ehrfurcht vor sich; die Liebe zu sich; die unbedingte Freiheit gegen sich... Das allein sind meine Leser, meine rechten Leser, meine vorbestimmten Leser: was liegt am Rest? --Der Rest ist bloss die Menschheit. --Man muss der Menschheit überlegen sein durch Kraft, durch Höhe der Seele - durch Verachtung...

There can be no doubt that Van Eeden borrowed from Nietzsche, for the opening of *De nachtbruid* states: "...[it weet] dat mijn gedachten te groot zijn om door mijn levende medemensen zonder onderworpenheid, uit vrije erkenning, te worden aangenomen."(p. 6)...Toch heb ik de vrede, want dit zal gelezen worden... Het zal de toppen raken...(p. 7)

Van Eeden, too is relying on the ideal reader:

Neemt gij zelf niets aan op hoger gezag, maar alles op uw eigen zelfstandig oordeel? Dat moet ik juist hebben... Gij zijt verstandig genoeg niet te willen oordelen zonder trouwe aandacht gegeven te hebben...(p. 7) ...Ik schrijf dit voor u, de onwillige en opstandige, die genoeg heeft van alle slavernij. Ik schrijf dit voor u, die zich mondig voelt en niet langer als kind wil behandeld worden. (p. 8)

Like Nietzsche, Van Eeden sets up a certain complicity between author and reader. The reader can be called upon to have faith in the author because he already shares the latter's exceptional insight, he is like him and therefore receptive to the extraordinary claims advanced. This type of flattery works with the idea of an "us" against "them", it creates a sense of intimacy between author and reader, while at the same time creating distance between conventional ideas and the ideas advanced in the work under discussion. This is of course of the utmost importance, since the religious ideas of Nietzsche and Muralto's theory of dreams deviate so much from the norm.

Obvious though the connection with Nietzsche seems, one key idea is not taken over by Van Eeden: Nietzsche's "Verachtung". Muralto does not break completely with the herd; though it is the individual who causes the herd to progress to higher levels, an individual cannot exist alone. At one point Muralto confesses therefore: "Mijn geluk zou verrotten en verdrogen in mijn hoogmoed, als ik de lavende en verfrissende deemoed niet kende, de deemoed die mij door geduldige liefde-daden met de kudde verbindt". (p. 76) This is the thrust of the final chapters of the book, since Muralto's ideas are gradually used to underpin Van Eeden's own social theories. Particularly the chapters which precede Muralto's trip to America, and those in which he discusses his ideas about the ideal form of government with Judge Elkinson, provide the reader with a justification of Van Eeden's own continued concern with social and economic problems, and show that he could not abandon his belief that he had a special task in life. But for his activity to be successful, he once again needs the cooperation of the understanding listener, and the complicity of the sympathetic reader.

The play between the first person narrator and the reader, as a device to force the reader's acquiescence and complicity, is ultimately replaced by a more explicit rhetorical device in the second half of the novel, in that Muralto now acts as an instructor of his beloved Elsje. Whereas Elsje, as foundling and relatively uneducated person can be seen as a kind of Pygmalion figure, ready to be molded by the worldly and sophisticated Muralto, she also has precisely those innate qualities which Muralto seeks in his ideal reader: independence, intellectual openness, willingness to ask questions and to examine without prejudice. Unfortunately, the pedantic tone of many of the conversations between Muralto and Elsje become unbearable for the modern reader, whose own freedom to respond is dramatically reduced by the introduction of this implied reader. Muralto's arrogance is a natural product of his aristocratic background, perhaps, but there is also a fair amount of male chauvinism involved of which Van Eeden was most likely not aware. It is clear, in any case that Van Eeden wanted in the figure of Elsje to provide a kind of pupil to his Zarathustra-like Muralto. Even when (especially in the last chapters) Muralto admits to his inability to influence people as a true leader and his failure to fuse the philosopher and the king in his own character, he nevertheless solicits from Elsje, and through her from the reader, the acknowledgment that he is at least an important and original theorist.

Ultimately, of course, the effectiveness of all devices and strategies depends on the willingness of the reader to accept the intuitions of the author. That Van Eeden was aware of this, too, can be seen for example from the fact that he shows a basic unwillingness to share specific ideas and revelations which result from his dreams, for "dat behoort alles tot de wetenschap van het bovenzinnelijke, die op algemener navorsing wacht".(173) Van Eeden separates sharply between scientific evidence and the kind of information which can safely be dealt with in a work of fiction, and in this respect he does not transgress his chosen genre. If he plays a game here, it is a legitimate one. Yet even the few statements provided in the text caused enough alienation in contemporary critics and readers to make Van Eeden an increasingly lonely figure in his later years. "De latere Van Eeden maakt licht de indruk het contact met de realiteit verloren te hebben", writes Ilse Bulhof, "dat wil zeggen met de ontluisterde werkelijkheid die de moderne wetenschap ons heeft leren kennen".[15] In *De nachtbruid* we have a kind of "counter proposal" to such a view of the world. The way in which Van Eeden attempts by rhetorical devices and narrative strategies to overcome the readers' resistance to his counterproposal, rather than the somewhat outdated theories themselves, constitutes a large part of the fascination of this novel for the neerlandicus and the general reader alike.

NOTES

[1]Frederik Van Eeden, *Dagboek 1978-1923*. [Voor het Frederik Van Eeden Genootschap uitgegevan en toegelicht door Dr. H.W. Van Tricht]. Deel II (1901-1910), Culemborg, 1971.

[2]"den schemerenden voorhof van't generzijds." Quoted in H.W. Van Tricht, *Frederik Van Eeden. Denker en Strijder*, Utrecht 1978 (original edition Amsterdam 1934), p. 96.

[3]"Eigen schuld was daarbij, dat hij de wereld en de mensen onvoldoende kende, en de praktische waarde van de eigen bedoelingen overschatte." Van Tricht, p. 100.

[4]"Maar de Nederlander is praktisch, en Nederland voor profeten te klein." Van Tricht, p. 103.

[5] Van Tricht, p. 108.

[6] Van Eeden, *Dagboek*, 14 December, 1906.

[7] Van Eeden, *Dagboek*, 3 September, 1907.

[8] Van Eeden, *De nachtbruid. De gedenkschriften van Vico Muralto*. [Met een nawoord van Ilse N. Bulhof]. Amsterdam, 1984 (original edition 1909). [=Salamander 571]. All references in the text are to this edition.

[9] The most vociferous phase of Van Eeden's anti-religious thinking falls in the period of 1997, in connection with conversations with Henriet Ortt. See: Roger Henrard, *Wijsheidgestalten in Dichterwoord. Onderzoek naar de invloed van Spinoza op de Nederlandse Literatuur*. Amsterdam, 1977, p. 111.

[10] "[De] ervaring leerde hem, dat de mens niet geroepen is om het gevoelsleven de kop in te drukken en de nuchtere rede de vrije teugel te laten... Dit is trouwens de ethische les die al kan worden getrokken uit het eerste deel van *De kleine Johannes*." Henrard, p. 115.

[11] "Van Eeden's eerste mijmeringen over de dood vloeien voort uit zijn hypochondrische gesteldheid... Geleidelijk worden die mijmeringen met een existentiële betekenis geladen." Henrard, p. 104.

[12] "Dat Van Eeden aanhoudend door de dood wordt gekweld en er zich dan ook ernstig op wil voorbereiden bewijst meteen dat hij hem niet als een eindpunt beschouwd, maar er een raadselachtig ander leven achter speurt." Henrard, p. 105.

[13] See: Gerard Knuvelder, *Handboek tot de geschiedenis der Neder landse letterkunde*,'s Hertogenbosch,(2) 1961, vol. 4, p. 83.

[14] The diary entry of August 4, 1907 is full of praise for Nietzsche's *Zarathustra*, and Van Eeden draws parallels with himself, and between Nietzche's concept of the *Übermensch* with his own "soort-God," (The Christus-concept).

[15] Bulhof, in *De nachtbruid*, p. 234.

CONFLICTING CULTURES:
Edgar du Perron - an unusual temper towards the end of the Dutch Colonial Era

Kees Snoek
University of Indonesia, Jakarta

In the issue of December 5, 1936 of "Actueel Wereldnieuws en Sport in Beeld", a magazine of the Dutch East Indies which was printed on expensive paper and richly illustrated, and which had published a lengthy coverage of the encounter between Mussolini and Hitler, we find at the bottom of one page, with photographs next to each other, the pictures of Dr. Ernest Francois Eugene Douwes Dekker (1880-1950) and of Charles Edgar du Perron (1899-1940). The commentary states that Douwes Dekker had appeared before the Court of Justice on the charge of having publicly expressed his feelings of hostility, hatred or contempt towards the European Community of the Dutch Indies - and Du Perron is introduced as the well-known Dutch author whose works have drawn a lot of attention over the past years and who is staying in the Indies again after an absence of 15 years. Of this photograph Du Perron has remarked that he appears on it "als een kat in een vreemd pakhuis": like a cat in a strange warehouse - like a fish out of the water.

Let me introduce Douwes Dekker to you - D.D. for his friends and renamed Setiabuddhi after Indonesia gained its independence; he was a grandson of Jan Douwes Dekker: the brother of the most well-known member of the family, the author of the novel "Max Havelaar" (1860), Multatuli. Ernest Douwes Dekker had fought in South Africa on the side of the Boers, he was one of the first proponents of Indonesia's independence. In 1912 he founded the "lndische Partij", together with Soewardi Soerianingrat and Tjipto Mangoenkoesomo. He was banished to The Netherlands, returned in 1918 and established a complex of private schools. He was banished again, to Suriname, in 1940, but he returned in 1946 and became a member in one of the cabinets of the Indonesian Republic. He wrote a novel, *The Book of Siman the Javanese*[1] which was called "a romanticized report" by Du Perron who wrote an introduction to it in 1938.[2] This novel which relates the sad story of gross exploitation of Siman and his people, contains a lot of mathematics, deemed necessary as convincing proof to the colonial rulers. But D.D. was not at all appreciated by colonial government and community alike. He was scorned in the powerful colonial press, his publications were struck by boycotts, he found rejection everywhere, and even more so after he turned his sympathy towards the Japanese.

Edgar du Perron was a much more respected public figure. Born in Meester Cornelis - nowadays a neighbourhood of Jakarta - in a family of French ancestry, he got a much different start in life than D.D. Both were of mixed blood, but Du Perron was the son of a landlord who owned a huge mansion in Meester Cornelis. Du Perron, being a premature child, began his career early in life. At the age of 19 he translated a novel by Alexandre Dumas which appeared as a serial in a local newspaper. He liked this particular novel (*Gabriel Lambert*) because of the depiction of a certain duel in it. One of his first articles[3] is about the main figure of the three musketeers, D'Artagnan. Du Perron's fascination with D'Artagnan doesn't stand by itself: the sense of adventure and personal courage which surrounds D'Artagnan held a special appeal in a pioneering colonial society, and mingled with the indigenous concept of the "jago": the rooster, i.e. the brave and cocky individual. After he left the Indies in 1921 for France and Belgium, Du Perron collected fame as the relative outsider in Dutch letters, who was able to look at its products from a fresh and independent point of view. He was a feared adversary who did away with mediocrity, epigonism and literary rhetorics. He was uncompromising, aggressive and to the point in his criticism which dominated a whole generation of Dutch literary history. In the critics Menno ter Braak and Jan Greshoff he recognized his comrades; together they formed the three musketeers, sharpening their common weapons against everything they considered "half-baked", and united by strong bonds of friendship and the sense of a joint adventure. One may see this as an adolescent imagination, but it was able to sweep through Dutch literature and to sweep away a lot of humbug. Du Perron's foremost criterion was: personality. An author should not draw his value from form or from any kind of establishment - be it literary, religious or political; he should defend his own human value, with a sensitive eye for what is happening around him.

After having immersed himself in European literary life for 12 years, Du Perron felt compelled to render an account of his youth in the Indies which he interlaced with the literary and political discussions he had had in Paris with friends like Andre Malraux and Pascal Pia. This novel, *Het Land van Herkomst* (The Country of Origin)[4] established his fame once and for all. Yet this testimony alone wouldn't do for him: he wanted to see the Indies again with his own eyes, and by living there he wanted to test himself, looking for another perspective than could be gained in belligerent Europe. Du Perron's sojourn in the Indies, from July 1936 up to August 1939, was not a pleasant confrontation with his country of origin. As said before, he felt like a cat in a strange warehouse. The comrades of his youth had moved to other places and he missed the sense of joint adventure he shared with his literary friends in Europe. To one of his oldest friends in the Indies he wrote: "In olden times I had a self-evident center in life: a home, and friends, the way we used to be although we were not together , with such a "three musketeers feeling" as bondage (....) We have become older."[5] Du Perron's parents were dead, the fortune had gone lost to debtors, and here he found himself in a colonial society which only regarded position and titles, which didn't possess much of an intellectual life and which had become ever fiercer in its measures against the nationalists who threatened the very existence of that self-contented society. The leader of the Dutch National Socialists, Anton Mussert, had been received with full honors, and it was not until much later that the danger of fascism was recognized and - in reaction - a glorification of the House of Orange began in the media.

If we look upon Du Perron as a kind of D'Artagnan, who then were the enemies he had to fight? All those who had accumulated power, first of all the people who dominated the almighty media: those were the so-called "revolver journalists" who turned their weapons against people like Douwes Dekker. In 1919 Du Perron had worked as a journalist himself under the direction of one of them, Karel Wybrands, who had become known for his statement that the natives should be raised to the height of the gallows, and who insisted on using the term "inlands" (native) instead of the more dignified term "inheems" (aboriginal). According to him the latter term spoke of love for the natives. After his return to the Indies, Du Perron consistently used the term "Indonesian", which was a taboo word in official circles. He got upset when in one interview in a Dutch newspaper "Indonesian" was replaced by the word "inland": "My Indonesian friends will be painfully struck by it."

What divided Du Perron from the people around him, was certainly a matter of style, and since style is man himself, a case of different attitudes. Du Perron got a chance at last to cross swords with the revolver journalist Zentgraaff, in the magazine *Kritiek en Opbouw* (Criticism and Construction) which was brave enough to allow him space to battle one of the most feared figures in public life, founder (in 1929) of the rightist "Vaderlandsche Club" (Patriotic Club). In his attack Du Perron compared the Indies to a beaker full of scared fish, and Zentgraaf as a shark amidst them. This verbal duel was won by Du Perron, and he delighted clearly in his victory. But another group of people proved untouchable; namely the ones in power, the officials. Du Perron sought contact with the few intellectuals he could find among the colonial administrators, one of them being Hugo Samkalden, who had declared the government of the Dutch Indies to be "the great whore".[6] On the style of one of those officials Du Perron commented: "It is a style which - while giving the appearance of saying it all in a dignified, quiet, measured and nuanced manner - seems accurately calculated for concealing as much as possible the essential intention or truth: in one word, the style of an official." This person according to Du Perron, needs "10 or 20 sentences to rather wrap around one idea than to bring it out; a kind of cautious learnedness proffered to the reader with a specific solemnity of language."[7] It may be understood that we are not dealing with the style of a D'Artagnan! And for that reason, such people were difficult to fight. Especially after Du Perron began living in Batavia (nowadays Jakarta) he felt like a displaced person. Even more so than in smaller towns, money was the all-distinguishing factor here. In the club which was famous for its gatherings, "De Harmonie", was one table reserved for people who made one thousand guilders a month. Du Perron wrote to his friend who lived in the country-side[8]: "The country has a heck of a lot which is endearing to me, but the European community is below all. Either second rate or false, cowardish and caddish: everything purely geared boards position and money (...) You have to grow through hatred and jealousy to attain something over here. I pass." Menno ter Braak received an account of a garden party with Batavian authorities[9] "Gogol was innexhaustively a genius when he invented the formula of "dead souls". The more practical fellows I meet, that sort of people who are not "**weltfremd**", who stand "with both legs on the ground", etc., the more inexhaustible I find that formula. (...)God, oh my God, everything you tell those people - even when you approach them with the best of feelings - you feel become a lie before it has escaped your mouth, and whatever truth may have remained, has become pure shit when it has reached them." In another letter, after having complained about the rhythm of officialdom, he remarks about the light of Batavia[10]: "That evening I have also seen for the first time how barren and lifeless the Batavian light is; if you compare it with houses in the country, in a cool climate, where the light is humid and shiny, then every Batavian house is a house of skulls. No wonder that nothing but dead souls inhabit this place!"

A lot of the Dutch people in general were considered dead souls by Du Perron. He found the Dutch to be stiff and rigid in their ways and lacking in temper. But precisely the Dutch Indies attracted a lot of Dutch people who were more spirited than that: the real adventurers and eccentrics. Multatuli had been one of them, another one of those figures was Courier dit Dubekart, with the words of Du Perron: "An unsocietal fool, a little bit more headstrong than others."[11] Yet another one was Willem van Hogendorp: "This peculiar character, governor and adventurer, philanthropist and hunter after fortune, educated man from the 18th century and man of superficial socializing, yet the author of what with a grain of salt can be considered the **Uncle Tom's Cabin** of the Indies."[12] This equivalent of "Uncle Tom's Cabin" was called "*Kraspoekol* of De Droevige Gevolgen van een te verre gaande strengheid jegens de slaaven" (Mr. Hitting Hard or the Sad Consequences of a too far stretching severity towards the slaves). The people who had Du Perron's sympathy in the present were among others Douwes Dekker: "I have real admiration for this pluck: after the life he led (37 prisons!) 58 years old and with everyone (of "authority") against him (all "well-thinking" people even 10 times as much)".[13] At one point he also mentions another eccentric, the language specialist Gobee: "one of the most perfect people (Europeans) who ever lived in the Indies, into his old age considered a "Don Quichote" by the veritable officials."[14]

Under colonial circumstances the difference between D'Artagnan and Don Quichote was not great. The attribution of power often made the D'Artagnans seem Don Quichotes. Du Perron's very first short story, which was published in 1920, in a newspaper, was called "Don Quichote te Soerabaja".[15] It shows us the author sitting in the train while reading "Don Quichote". In the muggy atmosphere of two in the afternoon, all of a sudden the author is faced with the real Don Quichote in person, who tells him that he is not understood by the people, and therefore he hates Cervantes: "He was my father and he loved me, but he had one big fault: he thought humanity was clever enough. He thought they would understand him". Don Quichote, on a sudden spur, demands information from the author: "How much do you make?" The author is dumbfounded, and answers: "N-n-n-nothing...nothing yet. But I think..." "Nothing!" it resounded besides me. And when I looked up in amazement... he laughed, Don Quichote!...and he grasped my hand and shook it and patted me on my shoulder with his iron glove, with a thunderous noise,,,and his sallow parchment-face seemed to shine... "Thanks God! he shouted out. Nothing!!!...in Surabaya...one man...who...doesn't earn...a thing!" Later on, at the station, Don Quichote disappears out of sight. A railway official names him "Sir Echec": "He just potters about all over the place..." And the person who was recognized as Sancho Panza is referred to as "Mr. De Proll" Everyone knows him in Surabaya. He is a chief of various trading companies, superintendent of a score of sugar factories, big share-holder of...", but the author doesn't let the railway official finish his words; he boards the train to Solo, and looking out of the window he eyes Sancho who looks at him with his haughty gaze.

During his second stay in the Indies, Du Perron resumed the research of colonial literature which he had started as a young journalist. He finished two anthologies: *De Muze van Jan Compagnie*[16] and *Van Kraspoekol tot Saidjah*.[17] In his choice of pieces his anti-colonial point-of-view is obvious. It seems, that his historical sense was sharpened through his renewed confrontation with the Indies (and with the changes which had taken place in himself). He was planning a book on the hardened society he had found back, he published three books with new documents about Multatuli, he wrote some short stories and poems, and numerous book reviews, he wrote introductions to *Siman den Javaan* and to the only Dutch novel by an Indonesian author *Buiten het Gareel* (Outside of the Harness, written by Soewarsih Djojopoespito). Du Perron was considered a teacher, a guru, by young Indonesian intellectuals. Finally he was working on a series of documentary novelettes which was to get the title *De Onzekeren* (The Uncertain Ones). The first novelette, which carried the title *Scandal in Holland*[18], was about a Dutch nobleman who fell in disgrace, the second, unfinished, novelette was about Willem van Hogendorp - the writer of *Mr. Hitting Hard*. Du Perron lets his character say[19]: "To assert oneself. What is life else? I mean, how else could one exist? One has to assert oneself without taking a rest; against everyone; against the people who are inferior, equal or superior. All the time in a different way, but always just as hard. If one doesn't, then one has to resign to an existence as a nullity, as one asleep."

This self-convinced language is coming not from D'Artagnan, but from one of those Uncertain Ones. When explaining his project to a friend,[20] Du Perron wrote him that his persons would be uncertain ones and that he would write about dramas of uncertainty. "The whole series should just about prove that "free will" is a very relative something here on earth." Du Perron left the Indies in the philosophical acceptance that his place of belonging was with his friends in the Netherlands, where World War II was imminent. If he was to stay in the Indies (which he wasn't about to do with a wife and a child) he would feel compelled to join the Indonesian struggle for independence, because he could not assume half a role. Before his departure in 1936, Ter Braak had told him: "Even in the Indies you won't escape your fate as a European." To this fate Du Perron resigned at last. His words of farewell to Soewarsih Djojopoespito, the writer of *Outside of the Harness*, were "Life has nothing to do with career making." Your sense of self-esteem is the most valuable."[21] Du Perron died from a heart attack during a German air-strike in 1940, but his legacy of an unusual temper, honest, critical and uncompromising, remains, in the Netherlands well as Indonesia.

NOTES

[1] E.F.E. Douwes Dekker, *Het boek van Siman den Javaan, een roman van rijst, dividend en menschelijkheid* Amersfoort 1908.

[2] E.du Perron, "E.F.E. Douwes Dekker: Het boek van Siman den Javaan". In: *Verzameld werk* VI, Amsterdam 1959, p. 146-168.

[3] Idem, "Over den hoofdpersoon van "De Drie musketiers"". In: *De Revue* Vol. 1, nr. 4, 8 Jan. 1921, p. 158-160.

[4] Idem, *Het land van herkomst*. First edition: 1935. In : *Verzameld werk* III, Amsterdam 1954; also available in English translation.

[5] Letter of Sept. 9, 1937 to G.O. Tissing. In: E. du Perron, *Brieven* VII, Amsterdam 1981, p. 110.

[6] Information from Dr. F.R.J. Verhoeven.

[7] In *Verzameld werk* VII, Amsterdam 1959, p. 433. "Vierde brief uit Holland".

[8] Letter to G.O. Tissing, May 24, 1938. In: *Brieven* VII, p. 377.

[9] Letter to Menno ter Braak, April 30, 1937. In Menno ter Braak/E. du Perron *Briefwisseling 1930-1940*, vol. IV, p. 133-134.

[10] Letter to Adriaan Roland Holst, May 9, 1938. In: *Brieven* VII, p. 368.

[11] Letter to J. Greshoff, July 30, 1937. In: *Brieven* VII, p. 53.

[12] In: "Indisch Memorandum", *Verzameld werk* VII, p. 187.

[13] Letter to J.Greshoff, August 9, 1937. In: *Brieven* VII, p. 72.

[14] Letter to G. Stuiveling, October 26, 1939. In: *Brieven* VIII, Amsterdam 1984, p. 277.

[15] In: *Verzameld werk* V, Amsterdam 1956, p. 555-565.

[16] Eerste druk: A.C. Nix & Co. Bandoeng 1939. Tweede, herziene en vermeerderde druk: Bandoeng 1948.

[17] Unpublished.

[18] *Schandaal in Holland*. First edition: 1939. In: Verzameld werk III.

[19] In: *Verzameld werk* V, Amsterdam 1956, p. 524.

[20] Letter to Jan van Nijlen, October 31, 1939. In: *Brieven* VIII, p. 296.

[21] In: *De Engelbewaarder. Een Winterboek* 1979, p. 118, in the article G. Termorshuizen, "Een leven buiten het gareel".

DUTCH POETRY OF THE FIFTIES AND THE COBRA-MOVEMENT

Hugo Brems
Catholic University, Leuven

Dutch poetry before the second world-war was by-and-large a traditional one. Most of the revolutionary currents that had profoundly influenced European poetry, from futurism over dada, surrealism and other types of avant-garde, had never really taken root in Dutch literature. The center of the system was firmly dominated by a poetry that can be described as formally controlled and acceptable for the traditional culture. Of course there had been fluctuations, but they never really affected the overall picture.

That situation remained during the first years after the war. There was a search for renewal, but renewal was mainly searched for in matters of content and in what was called a new reflection on the traditional values. A few years later, Lucebert, the leading poet of the fifties, was to write about this poetry that it went on as if "Holland were a pink peach-garden" and that therefore poetry resembled "a cup of tea with rose petals".

However, from 1947, the first signs can be spotted of a seemingly entirely different kind of poetics. One that discards almost everything of the past and that claims to start from zero. Accordingly, the first publications are rejected by literary criticism, not as being bad poetry, but as not being poetry at all. That seems to be the case every time when a radical change in poetics occurs and not a mere shift in priorities. It is an index of the rise of a new poetic paradigm that will eventually lead to a complete reorganization of the poetic system.

Of course, as drastic a change as that, can only be explained by studying the entire web of intra- and inter-relations as it is being apart. But I will restrict myself to a few hints and focus on the role of the external relations with painting.

It is obvious that this new poetry, though it announced itself as unprecedented, as having no links whatsoever with the past, was deeply influenced by models from the European avant-garde, especially French post-surrealism (Artaud, Char, Michaux), by ideas from existentialism and phenomenology, by Marxism and so on. Only recently Dutch literary criticism is trying to untangle that intricate web of inter-relations.

However, a decisive role was played by the close relations to painting. Indeed, the first public appearances of this new, so-called 'experimental' poetry, in fact the whole period of its rise, before it became established and accepted, was (or were) characterized by common actions, publications and so on. I will not give you here a list of these cases of cooperation, but mention only a few. The very first manifestation of the new art and poetry was an initiative of some young painters. Opposing their concept of art to academism as well as to the dogmatism of surrealism and the still strong influence of Mondrian's geometrical abstract painting, they founded (in 1948) the "Dutch Experimental Group", with their own publication: *Reflex*. Among these painters were names such as Karel Appel, Corneille, Constant.

Almost immediately, they were joined by a few young poets such as Lucebert, Elburg, Kouwenaar. The result was that in the two existing numbers of *Reflex*, one could find drawings and reproductions as well as poetry. And a manifesto of the painters in nr. 1, was followed by one of the poets in nr. 2, almost echoing the main ideas of the former one.

Before discussing these ideas and how they are translated from one art to another, I shall briefly survey the further evolution. At the end of '48, on the occasion of an artistic conference in Paris, dominated by orthodox surrealism, the Dutch painters of the experimental group discovered kindred spirits in some of their colleagues from Denmark (Asger Jorn) and Belgium (Dotremont, Alechinsky). Together they founded the Cobra-movement (the name being formed by taking the first letters of the three capital cities: Copenhagen, Brussels, Amsterdam). One of their first big exhibitions is in Amsterdam, where again art as well as poetry are present. The following years, artists and poets work together on different levels: artists illustrate collections of poetry, poets write about the paintings, or let themselves be inspired by paintings in their poems, and on several occasions, common works of art are produced, so called 'peinture-mots' or 'tableaux-poèmes'.

Another remarkable phenomenon is that quite a few double-talents can be found among those young men. (Lucebert, Claus, Corneille, Dotremont...). I mention all these things because I am convinced, that a valid comparison of art and literature should be based on a close observation of facts. Of which this is only a summary. Their is no doubt that in this instance, we are dealing with a real case of interrelation between systems. On the other hand, the impact of this inter-relation is relative, because not all of the poets called Fiftiers were connected with Cobra and because many of their concepts are derived from the tradition of literary avant-garde.

But the importance of these relations should not be underestimated either, because we are dealing here with a kind of poetry, that is - at that time - emerging from the fringe of the system, but fighting its way toward the centre.

In the Amsterdam exhibition of 1949, one of the rooms, reserved for the poets had a wall, covered with only one slogan: "There is a poetry that we abolish". but, however challenging this may have sounded, at the same time, their renewal was, in the first years almost invisible. They wrote in obscure little magazines and had no access to the leading reviews and publishing houses. And as soon as they became visible, they were ridiculed as, e.g, in this quote from one of the leading traditional poets: "Having to read this only gives me a sensation as if the human brain, wilfully separated from the soil of the soul, has bestially been metamorphosed into a bull-frog, croaking loudly in the tropical night."

This position of both poets and painters largely accounts for their seeking support in each others work and company. But it is also an index of the importance of these relations for the entire poetic system, because it is situated right in the origin of a new poetic paradigm, striving to reach the dominating centre.

But, with this in mind, let us return to the origin of artistic and poetic conceptions. The starting point of Cobra painting is its desire to return to a kind of cultural zero, to strip off the entire cultural, artistic and ethical heritage of tradition. From that ideal, utopical starting-point, they want to express their emotions and experiences as directly and as spontaneously as possible. Moreover, this direct expression is conceived of as a continuous dialogue between the artist and his material. Such a dialog is only possible in as far as the artist excludes all a priori's concerning form as well as subject matter. They do not want to impose their will or their imagination on the material, but it is the material and the process of working with it, that suggests forms, images, meanings. Making and finding are to be completely blended.

A few quotations from the first manifestoes may illustrate this.

- "A painting is not a structure of colours and lines, but an animal, a night, a scream, a man, or all this at once."

- "The creative principle does not consist of ideas or forms, but is a result of the confrontation between the human spirit and the raw material, the latter suggesting its forms and ideas."

The 'experimental' features are stressed in these quotations:

- "The problematic period in the evolution of modern art has come to an end, and is now being followed by an experimental period. That means that, from the experience, gained in this state of complete freedom, the laws of future creativity will be derived."

- "An art that doesn't solve the problems posed by any a priori aesthetics, but recognizes as its only norm expressivity, and creates only and spontaneously what is inspired by intuition."

That could be completed by many other instances, all stressing the same key-concepts of direct spontaneity, materialism, a choice for the creative process over the achieved work, etc. I'll give you just one more to illustrate that last issue: "The creative act is of far more importance as it shows the traces of the process of which it is the result. A living art does not know the difference between beautiful and ugly, because it doesn't put aesthetic norms."

The fact is that all these key-concepts, designed to speak about painting, were almost literally adopted by the poets in their politics. For instance, Rodenko, the leading critic of the poets, wrote: "The experimental poet writes from a vacuum and creates, in the act of writing, his language, his form, his philosophy."

Such a process of concepts, wandering from one art to another, poses two closely related problems:

- What happens to the meaning of the concepts themselves?

- How are they put into practice in the different media?:

In order to answer these questions, I shall first turn to the paintings themselves, and try to explain what's really going on there. As the links between Dutch poets and Dutch artists were strongest, I will only discuss some of the Dutch Cobra-work.

1. Constant, *Twee dieren* (two animals), (1946).

    - The process of spontaneous painting can be traced here in the way these two creatures emerge from the play with colours. The overall shape of the bodies suggests completion and additions, as are the claws, teeth, eyes, tails. A painting like this one can be described as a form, a figure, emerging from the pure unpremeditated confrontation with the material.

    - Moreover, this painting, as some of the others will do, illustrates a point that is often stressed in the artistic manifestoes, i.e., the affinity with other so-called spontaneous or primitive forms of art, such as children's drawings, the art of primitive cultures and of the mentally disturbed. All of these forms of expression in which the distance between impulse and expression is minimal and in which the filters or screens of aesthetic a prioris, of reason, of realism and so on are lacking.

2. Appel, *Vogel, vis, vrouw* (bird, fish, woman)

    Visvrouw en haan (fishwoman and rooster) (1947).

    Similar ambiguities can be shown in this picture. Especially the figure on the left may be seen as one or as two representations: fish/bird or woman. In these different interpretations almost every item carries different meanings:

- fish -----> head

    - hair -----> fin / ears -----> fins

- bird -----> body

    - paws -----> legs / beak -----> breasts

    - eye ------> navel /

Thus creating what could be called pictural homonyms, i.e., different meaning in the same formal element. The effect of this is that a metaphorical relationship is being established between both possible interpretations.

3. Corneille, *Songes* (Dreams) is an even clearer example of what this art is all about. (1949)

Two main principles can be seen here:

- One is the use of these ambiguous forms as described in the former painting. Recurrence of the same motive-like elements in changing contexts, different meanings, creating a weblike interaction.

- The other one is the tension between figurative and non-figurative aspects, clearly showing the materialistic, improvisation-like creative process. Once could almost compare this kind of drawing to what you might do during a boring meeting or lecture, when you start almost unconsciously drawing some lines on a sheet of paper before you. But out of this mere play with lines emerge forms. Forms develop into patterns, and patterns into these ambiguous representations.

4. Corneille, *Het vrolijke ritme van de stad* (The merry rhythm of the city) (1949).

- Same principles, e.g., in the different functions of the cross-like motive (nose-mouth, human figure, fence, mast of a ship, etc.). A continuous interaction between line, shape, colour.

What I have been trying to prove is that all these key-concepts (spontaneity, materialism, improvisation, starting form zero, etc.) can easily be achieved in painting and the visual arts, since its material allows it. The main reason is that paint, or for that matter colour, line) have no distinct meaning themselves. Neither are they subject to laws concerning their possible combinations. There are no established rules of syntax or semantics in the visual arts.

I am aware of the fact that this may be objected to from different angles. There are, of course, semantic and syntactic restrictions in the visual arts of certain periods or styles, but these are the rules of that concept of art, not of visual art itself.

One could also argue that different colours have different meanings, that straight or curved lines, descending or ascending lines, etc., suggest different meanings. But even if that is so, the rigidity and complexity of this semantic code is so primitive that it can hardly be compared to language.

A poet, in using language as his material, is dealing with a pre-coded medium. As soon as he uses a word, he uses meaning, however unstable that meaning of the single word may be. At the same time the syntactic possibilities are restricted. If that is so, how can we imagine a poet writing spontaneously, in dialogue with his material and so on?

Of course, he could write pure sound-or-letter-poetry as it was practised, e.g., in dadaism and lettrism. A few attempts in this direction have been made by poets of the fifties. This however is a false solution because, whatever its results are, they are not poetry, as long as we think of poetry as made of language.

Moreover, this kind of automatic writing did not answer their aims. They were eager to find ways of direct, uncensored expression through language, to find a language capable of expressing the complexity, the ambiguities, even the chaos of life as it is experienced. They wanted to escape from the inevitable reduction the use of language operates on the experience. That is not a goal that could be achieved through mere sound or letter-plays.

So what is left is trying to use language as if it were as pure and as raw a material as paint, and at the same time being aware of its not being so. That's just what these experimental poets try to do: they are rope-walkers, searching for a balance between chaos and code, between the myth of God creating the world by giving names and the reality of a well established language, based on conventions, and at the same time between the destruction, or the undermining of that code and the finding of a new, original one.

They do so in the first place by focusing on these aspects of language that precede the meaning and at the same time omitting or opposing to the aspects that structure or limit the syntactic or semantic possibilities. The stylistic features they favour, therefore range from rather trivial and occasional items such as phonetic spelling, and neologisms (primarily to desautomatise the reading process and draw attention to the word as a thing, not just a conventional symbol) to omitting punctuation, frequent use of homonyms, disordering of syntax, paratactic structures, and especially metaphor. Moreover, the whole style is profoundly associative, paradigmatic. As it would be impossible to analyze here some entire Dutch poems, I will restrict myself to some fragments that could be translated without loosing too much of their complexity.

E.g., two lines of a poem by Lucebert, read as follows:

"ik ben een mens maar
ik ben soms iemand die liefheeft."

Here we have a combination of homonym and what is called apokoinou (a stylistic feature consisting of the blending of different syntactic structures). A translation would be:

"I am a man but
I am sometimes someone who loves."

However, the Dutch word 'maar', here translated by 'but' also means 'only'. The result of this homonymic use is that two statements are being fused into one ambiguous statement:

1. I am only a man. I am sometimes...
2. I am a man but I am...

The word 'maar' is then acting as a hinge between the two ways of reading the lines. It is clear that such an ambiguity, that can be compared to the ones I pointed out in paintings, is partly due to the absence of punctuation.

Another instance of the same kind is to be seen in the simple lines:

"waar ben ik
waar ga ik."

Here the most spontaneous interpretation would be:

where am I?
where do I go?

But here again, both the absence of question marks and the homonymic value of the word 'waar', account for another meaning. 'Waar' is not only the question-word 'where', but also the adjective/adverb 'true', 'in truth'. So the other interpretation could be translated as:

I am true
In truth I go,

the inversion here not being due to the interrogative sense, but a means of stressing the word 'true'.

The issue here, is not to decide or choose between the two possible interpretations, but to take them both into account. The lines then mean something like:

I may be true and I may go in truth,
but where does that leave me, and where does
it lead me?

This is merely a simple and isolated example of exploiting the ambiguities inherent to language. But in a poem, compiling these instances and constantly interrelating them, a thoroughly ambiguous and unsteady universe of meanings is created.

What is happening in these poems, is what Lucebert says in one of his best known poems:

"ik ben de schielijke oplichter der liefde
zie onder haar de haat"

This is a very complicated statement, especially because the word 'oplichter' is very unstable in its meaning. The normal, most used meaning would be 'swindler' or 'crook'. But it may also mean 'kidnapper', or 'one who lifts something up', and even 'illuminator' (especially since this is a constant motif in Lucebert's poetry, even echoed in his pseudonym "Lucebert", a combination of the Latin Luce, lux (light) and the old German 'bert' (light, bright). So the lines should be translated:

```
                    crook
"I am the swift lifter    of love
                    illuminator
see the hate underneath it"
```

This statement contains an entire poetic program, saying that he is opposing the 'lovely' poetry of tradition, unmasking it. At the same time, it shows that a concept as love has hate as its counterpart. He really lifts the word 'love' to see what is underneath: hate, as if he were lifting a stone and looking at the worms and bugs under it.

But most of all he is stressing the shortcomings of language, of such general, abstract words as 'love' that say everything and nothing about the unique and complex experience of it.

Lucebert states that the poet, by turning over, lifting up, swindling with the word 'love', he is at once the illuminator of it, showing its true meaning, or lack thereof.

Coming back to the comparison with Cobra-art, I would first like to quote a programmatic statement by Lucebert. (I use his work mainly because he is considered the model 'par excellence' of experimental poetry and because he is a Cobra-painter as well as a poet.)

"I paint anything that occurs to me, I draw and paint anything on every-thing. I value all ideas equally. I do not choose between motifs and I do not aim at syntheses. Contradictions are left as they are in my work, and while they are opposing, I do not interfere, I stay aside, experiencing the freedom that only they can hand to me, my paintings, my poems, these happy playgrounds, where no seesaws are pushing aside the swings, where in sand-boxes saharas and oceans coincide. (...) A good poem, a good painting, are never finished, they are open and careless. The poem doesn't shut up while it is suffering or laughing, it loves to be handed around, and changed by time, by strangers. Words hardly ever die a glorious death, and the same goes for paintings. But if ever one does so, its fate is worse than that of the most miserable mortal, because its dead body will go on smelling for ever."

This is of course a poetic and metaphorical statement, but it clearly illustrates an important issue. That is that painting and poetry are alike in their love for freedom, openness, contradictions.

And the basic conceptions of both art and poetry are closely linked to that conviction. Spontaneity, dialogue with the artistic material are starting points in poetry as well as in art, but as soon as they are put into practice, they reveal quite different implications.

The experimental poet, in adopting the same starting-point as the Cobra-painters, finds himself in a much more acute dilemma: the dilemma between his desire for unrestricted originality and expression of the unique, and on the other hand the demands of his coded, restricting material. The dilemma between a purely individual idiosyncratic use of language, that would become incommunicable, and the consciousness that language is related to a culture, a history, a society, which he is precisely opposing.

The closer one analyses this poetry, the more one sees how an associative style, disregarding the strict rules of the code, and playing around in the small area between complete anarchy and strict rules, can reveal potentials of language that are never used. Here as well as in painting, the making of sense and the finding of it in the associative process, are closely connected.

This kind of poetry is situated in the nameless area, where the self-confident presence and the transparency of structure and system blend into chaos, where they are being penetrated and dismantled by it. The marginal character of sense and meaning in this poetry is, however, not experienced as a shortcoming, a loss of sense, but, on the contrary as the very ground from which a whole new range of possibilities can emerge and can be explored.

What happens here can be compared to the continual shifts, knots and movements of a traffic situation. Here too, the aspects of meaning come together, bump up against each other, part and form new clusters in a continual process of conceptualization.

It is clear that this description of what is going on in a poem could very well be applied to Cobra-painting as well. The relation between non- or pre-figurative painting and referential elements, and the ambiguity of the latter, works in the very same way.

There remains, however, the decisive difference, that the poet is using language. That means that he has to make a detour, that implies a far greater contribution of consciousness and intellect.

In his work, as a result of the dilemma I mentioned earlier, there is not only a tension between the potential meaning of the material and what is realized, as it is in painting (the tension between pre-figurative and figurative elements, emerging from them). And not merely a tension between the established poetic (or artistic) code and his way of writing. But most essential is the triple tension between the established linguistic code, the potential meanings beyond or before the code, and the actually realized meanings. These are the essentially dynamic, tentative, ambiguous, shifting meanings, that I compared with the traffic situation.

The writing and the reading of an experimental poem, is in my opinion far more complex than the making or 'reading' of a Cobra painting, since it involves more different levels.

And, to finally make the point that I have all the time been trying to make, concepts such as: 'a cultural and artistic zero', 'spontaneity', 'dialogue' with the material, and so on, take very different meanings and have different implications when transferred from painting to poetry.

FIGURE 1

CONSTANT.
TWEE DIEREN.
1946
OLIEVERF OP DOEK
60 X 60 cm.
VERZ. DE JUNG,
ASCONA,
ZWITZERLAND

FIGURE 2

KAREL APPEL.
VISVROUW
MET HAAR.
1947.
OLIEVERF OP DOEK
110.5 x 80 cm
EIGENDOM
KUNSTENAAR

FIGURE 3

CORNEILLE.
SONGES>
1949.
INKT GEWASSEN
OP PAPIER
40.2 x 46.1 cm
EIGENDOM
KUNSTENAAR.

FIGURE 4

CORNEILLE.
LE RYTHME
JOYEUX
DE LA VILLE>
1949.
OLIEVERF
OP DOEK
58.5 x 49 cm.
VERZ STEDELIJK
MUSEUM
AMSTERDAM.

FIGURE 5

KAREL APPEL.
VRIJHEIDSSCHREEUW.
1948
OLIEVERF
OP DOEK
100 x 79 cm
VERZ> BIJKO
AMSTERDAM.

FIGURE 6

CORNEILLE.
VOGELS.
1948
GOUACHE
OP PAPIER
113 x 138 cm
EIGENDOM
VAN DE KUNSTENAAR
(BRUIKLEEN
STEDELIJK
MUSEUM
AMSTERDAM).

GERARD REVE'S WINDOW OF VULNERABILITY

Johan P. Snapper
University of California, Berkeley

The image of the window in Reve's early works, one of the best developed motifs since its employment in Couperus' *Boeken der kleine zielen* (1901-03) [Books of Little Souls] signifies a series of strained relationships not only between the house (of which it is a crucial component) and the world to which it leads, but also within the space on either side of it. Beginning with the second function, we see that the window basically signifies a detachment from the room in which the Revian hero happens to be, and/or from the people with whom he shares this space. Frequently this situation marks the setting preceding an urgent desire to get away. A typical example is Werther in *Werther Nieland*, (1949) who is repeatedly observed staring out of the window by an anxious Elmer. Their very first meeting shows Werther to be more interested in the window of his room than in Elmer. When a little later Elmer manages to invite himself once more to Werther's house, he again spots him standing in front of the window, quite oblivious to his visitor. This implied, and often misleading, detachment from one's peers is a typical thematic thread running throughout Reve's works and can be observed in many instances in which people - primarily young men or boys - are gazing aimlessly out of windows without apparent reason. Not uncommonly, such situations indicate the character's wish to be elsewhere, thereby turning the Revian window into a potential vehicle for escape for a trapped protagonist. And indeed in *Werther Nieland* Elmer has to flee from Maarten's room not the way he came in, but through the latter's window, lest he be detected by his mother. In *Erick verklaart de vogeltekenen* (1957) [Erick Explains the Signs of the Birds] the attic window has a similar function. Erick wants his friend Roy to install a fire ladder from his window, because the house poses a mortal danger:

> Begrijp je niet in wat voor dodelijk gevaar we verkeren? Roy knikte. Ten tweede. Hoe breng ik mijzelf in veiligheid? We zitten hier op dezelfde verdieping, en we lopen hetzelfde gevaar, waar of niet? (...) Luister! zei Erick dringend. Je legt dat ding aan, vanmiddag. En de korte tijd dat je hier nog woont, doe je je deur maar niet meer op slot als je weggaat.[1]

But usually this perception of the window proves illusory, so that the window tends to represent little more than a futile solution to an unresolvable crisis. Indeed, the window is not immune to the underlying deception which characterizes the relationship between the two opposing worlds in Reve's early works. In *Foreign Boy* (1956), for instance, when Darger's longing for his newly found friend Helmut continues long after the latter has been taken away, he walks to the window and looks out. Darger insists that Helmut will write to him; and when his brother Willem tells him that he is deluding himself, Darger is pictured as continuing to stare out of the window, as if someone or something might change his lonely predicament. But instead of bringing hope, the window responds with the dismal sound of the rain, accompanied, significantly, by the fateful striking of the clock:

> He got up and went to the window. He could not see anything outside except the street lights, which were changed by the wet pane into stars with needle-shaped rays. "Helmut's going to write a letter to me," he suddenly said. "Helmut won't write to you," Willem said. (...) Helmut didn't tell you he would write you a letter. That's only something you made up." (...) Darger kept staring out the window. His mother came back into the room bringing some cocoa. The clock struck a quarter to nine. There was a sound of rain. They waited.[2]

In *Gossamer* (1956) this application of the window metaphor is even more explicit. Mana, who has been abused by both her husband and her son, is desperately trying to bring some light into her dismal life by scrubbing the furniture on the balcony. But she is frustrated even in this last hope when it begins to rain. The story ends with her vainly turning once again to the window as a final resort, hoping for a miracle: "She stared aimlessly into the room, at the furniture, and then looked outside, into the yard, as though a solution might come from there."[3]

The gradual metamorphosis of the window as a motif signifying hope to that of gloom is particularly striking in the numerous scenes in which the people are portrayed as looking out of the window to consult the weather, which in Reve's works is generally turning menacing. Here again, the cyclical dilemma produced by house versus the outside comes into view, as the window conveys unwelcome messages from without to the bored or anxious inhabitant within. *Mana's* window of elemental depression can be recognized throughout Reve's early work. When Frits early in *De avonden* (1947) [The Evenings] wants to kill time, he sits down in front of the window and looks at a clear sky which is marred with a dirty yellow hue. His mother joins him and concludes that it is going to snow. Such scenes are familiar enough. The story *Winter* (1956), for instance begins with a description of Henry standing in front of the bay window, staring into the sweeping wet snow. The window, which looks out on a stretch of land, is described as being ideally suited for a storm; i.e, "where the storm could sweep along without any obstacle in it sway."[4] Darger in *Foreign Boy* also goes frequently to the window to look at the weather and inevitably sees it is raining or storming.

But the Revian window is more than a bad weather vane. It can also assume an active role. Like the clock,[5] it joins the other principals as a participant in life's peculiar drama. More often than not, the window functions as an early harbinger of ill tidings, or - more ominously - may itself become an agent of ruin, thereby hastening a demise that seems inevitable. Such is the case with *Winter*, where the window serves as an unwelcome and sly collaborator that permits the rain and the snow to seep through it and thereby expedite the ruinous process of the house inside. As a result even the furniture - an ever-present prop in Reve's works - is gradually decomposing, though this may not be evident to the outsider:

> The chair seats were so decayed that [Katie] ould press her fingers through almost any part f them, and the wood of the table and chairs and moldered away to such an extent that she could have easily torn off pieces with her hands All of this, however, was not visible to outsiders, so everything had been left as it was.[6]

Since the window makes the house inside vulnerable to the hostile elements outside, Henry's family looks for ways to deal with the treacherous link to these forces. Such a futile exercise is representative of Reve's middle class families. Henry's mother is listening to the storm in the living room, worrying whether the plants might be standing too near the window. And to minimize the potential damage provided by the window, she has placed rugs on the sill and against the lower part of the frame. But the reader is left with the impression that such measures do little to alleviate the destructive forces from without. The angry elements at the window tend to prevail and have the last word. This is particularly striking in the final scene in *Foreign Boy*, where the mother's plaintive sigh inside is answered with a cold and forceful response from outside representing an unspoken argument through the pivotal window between two hostile worlds: "She sighed. It was still raining. Sometimes the wind sent the rain against the window with great force."[7]

The threat by superior forces is intensified by a paranoia which almost invariably afflicts the principal characters in Reve's works. The latter tend to view life as a sinister conspiracy to destroy them. The enemy appearing at the window need not necessarily be limited to the elements, whether they are used metaphorically or not. No, he can also consist of one's friends and neighbors. As we have noted above, Mana's obsessive relationship to the window in *Gossamer* is not only frustrated by the rain which keeps her house and her furniture dark, but by another natural manifestation as well. When at one time she is relieved to see some patches of blue sky, she actually opens the window. But her momentary hope is quickly dashed. Out of the sky it is raining gossamer; thin, dust-like threads of cobwebs which, her brother John assures her, come from the trees and are made by spiders or caterpillars. But Mana does not see it that way. To her the gossamer is yet another enemy to her little house. She views the process as an aggressive act by the upstairs neighbors, dumping their dust through her window:

> "A dirty gang, all of them," she said bitterly, looking up and making a gesture with her hand toward the ceiling. "Look at all that dust coming down again! They don't even look to see if the windows or doors of other people are open." (...) "I can't put anything outside," she complained (...) "because they're likely to throw their dirt down on it. When you say something, they laugh in your face. It's no fun to live here, I can tell you."[8]

We have seen how the tense relationship between the Revian character and his immediate environment on both sides of the window is symptomatic of a peculiar and ubiquitous paranoia. But this does not mean that his anxiety is based on predicaments solely attributable to his own projections. For the character's penchant to see danger notwithstanding, Reve's world presents plenty of reasons to feel unsafe. In *Melancholia* (1951) Reve portrays two fearful young men, Andree and Ferdinand, standing in front of the upstairs windows of their respective apartments, anxiously watching a helmeted and uniformed enemy - presumably the invading German troops again - rounding up Dutch citizens. More frightening are the bizarre *Tien vrolijke verhalen* (1961) [Ten Merry Tales], where society seems to have little concern for the weakest among its people. We see this in the brutal maltreatment of little Allen at the hands of his stepfather and stepsister in the story *Bloed* [Blood], in the near murder of little Vernon by his greedy uncle in *Afgrond* [Abyss], and in the senseless and anonymous killings of innocent women in *Brieven* [Letters] as well as *in De kerstavond van Zuster Magnussen* [Nurse Magnussen's Christmas Eve]. These stories magnify the portrait of a world preying on itself. This realistic base for social and individual anxiety is also expressed in the domicile motif. Take the grandfather in *De laatste jaren van mijn grootvader* (1947) [The Last Years of my Grandfather] who is forced to move repeatedly and is unable to claim any place as his own. His desire to spend his time anywhere except at home is directly related to a domestic instability which is forced upon him by circumstances beyond his own control. In *De ondergang van de familie Boslowits* (1956) [The Decline of the Boslowits Family] the family's tragedy is pungently reflected by the spatial dimensions of the narrative. It, too, is repeatedly uprooted, dislodged, and dispersed. In this story about a persecuted Jewish family of Russian descent the youngest child, Otto, is retarded and lives in a home for mentally deficient children before he is moved again to yet another institution. When he is uprooted once more, the homeless child is not heard from again. Similarly, the father, whom the narrator calls "oom Hans," is an invalid who must also leave his home and live first in a hospital and then in the attic of acquaintances. When he has to move once again, this time to an old people's home, he commits suicide.

The story is set in World War II and the enemy consists of German soldiers as well as Dutch conspirators. In this atmosphere of despair, in which the two so-called healthy members of the Boslowits family, tante Jaanne and her son Hans, are not allowed to leave the city, it is but a matter of time before they, too, will be evicted from their own home. While they are waiting for the inevitable to happen, Jaanne and Hans continue to live in what the narrator's mother describes as a *spookhuis* (haunted house), an apt collective description of all the dwellings in which the individual members of the Boslowits family must reside. Reve portrays the house of the two lucky ones as a prison, in which mother and son have assumed the double and by now familiarly contradictory roles of inmates as well as guards. To magnify their passive plight, Reve reintroduces the image of the window, but now as viewed from the outside, drawing it has a frame (square noose) around their expressionless faces and emphasizing their vulnerability both inside and out. The narrator recalls visiting them regularly and comments on their frozen, sentry-like position at the left and right flanks of their bay window:

> Geregeld ging ik 's-avonds aan en steeds was alles hetzelfde. Het aanbellen, het van het slot draaien van de binnendeur en als ik in de gang trad, was tante Jaanne al weer binen. Kwam ik in de huiskamer, dan zat voor het linker raam van de erker tante Jaanne, voor het rechter Hansje. Was ik eenmaal binnen, dan verliet tante Jaanne voor een ogenblik haar post, schoot de gang in en sloot de binnendeur op het slot. Wanneer ik wegging, volgde ze me, sloot de deur achter me en als ik op straat stond, zag ik ze reeds weer, als beelden, voor het raam zitten. Ik maakte dan een wuivend gebaar, maar ze reageerden nooit.[9]

The early works of Reve deal largely with the interaction of social outsiders in a world which is perceived as dangerous or hostile. The resulting anxiety experienced by the Revian character is in turn greatly increased by his peculiar defensive stance vis-à-vis his environment, so that his paranoia, while reflecting reality, simultaneously alters it. Again the window represents a useful metaphor to illustrate the character's highly subjective interpretation of what he sees. An innocuous example of this is provided by the novella *Erick verklaart de vogeltekenen*, which begins with a description of Erick listening to the noises of the house and spending long periods of time staring out of the dusty window. Reve's description of him as an old man whose visual perception is colored by memories combines the temporal with the spatial factors, and shows how the window has turned into a reflector of Erick's own psyche:

> We moeten nog maar wat wachten, dacht hij, zich naar het venster begevend en door het enigszins bestofte ruit naar buiten starend. Ik heb al heel wat tijd nutteloos verbruikt. Als een oude man achter zijn raam. Hij had inderdaad een aanzienlijke hoeveelheid tijd besteed aan uit het raam turen, en het uitzicht was van het soort dat misschien oude mensen zou vermogen te boeien - die immers van de rauwste eentonigheid nog opwinding ondervinden, gekleurd als alles wordt door herinneringen.[10]

The story *The Acrobat* (1956) provides a more poignant example of mixed perceptions and images afforded by the window. Once again the familiar bored character, here called Philip, looks out of the window of Raimar's house, where he has been staying for a few days. Raimar has just been killed in a fall from the circus trapeze and Philip sets out to collect his belongings as well as some "souvenirs' before leaving town. Back at Raimar's house, he is about to steal some of the family's savings, when his attention is drawn to the window. He witnesses a scene in which a fully packed soldier must run around a courtyard in the scorching heat until even his disciplinarians become too tired. Fascinated with the drama below, he pushes the curtains aside, places his cheek on the pane, and then leans out of the window in order to join the persecutors in a verbal sadistic outburst: "Everyone should kick his fellow man whenever he gets the chance."[11] Through this image of the window the reader gains insight into the way many of the house-bound characters in Reve's earlier works view their world. But it is not a single view, for the universal formula of "kicking one's fellow man" implies that every kicker is in turn also kicked by another. This is vintage Reve. Indeed, the very same image of the window portrays Philip also as a victim in his own right, similar to the abused soldier below. The picture becomes more focused when it appears that the participants in this drama have grown in number, lending the particular experience a certain degree of universality. Philip is not the only one to observe the cruel maltreatment. The victim's fellow soldiers at the building next door are equally engrossed in the courtyard scene, as they watch through their windows. But as soon as Philip hears their boisterous laughter, the self-proclaimed misfit quickly withdraws from his look-out and closes his window, in an apparent gesture to distance himself from his fellow voyeurs who now apparently pose a threat to him.

The ambiguous revelations produced by the window reveal more about the dweller inside than about the outside world to which it ostensibly leads, for the Revian window frequently functions as a mirror which hurls its subject right back inside and often into himself, as we saw in the case of Erick. Initially, Philip actually uses the window to look at himself. While he examines himself in the glass, he takes special notice of his face and gazing eyes and observes that "his face was strained, and that his eyes were wide and staring."[12]

Reve intensifies the use of the window as a mirror of the character's physical appearance in a subsequent scene. After Philip leaves Raimar's house for good, the aimless dope addict walks to the center of town, sits down on the steps of a bombed-out house, and peruses the traffic and the passers-by. Again Reve returns to the house motif, fashioning it once more into a metaphor of insecurity and destruction. And once again he focuses on the window to underscore the point. But here he goes a big step further. He introduces the image of an imaginary window to portray the character's passive plight. Although Philip has left the house and is outside, waiting for the next train out of town, he is depicted as being helplessly confined to the bombed-out shell of a house, like a "convalescent sitting at a window," a description which poignantly recalls the images of the lifeless watchers in *De ondergang van de familie Boslowits*.

Reve's use of the window as a mirror of decrepency is of course quite deliberate and not an isolated instance. In a remarkable scene in *De avonden* Frits is portrayed studying an old painting with apparently disinterested objectivity, complimenting the artist on his sensitive creation. The picture with its broken picture glass represents a deformed old woman sitting at a window. Judging from her crooked mouth with its bulging tongue, Frits readily diagnoses her condition: she is paralyzed. But the art connoisseur does not have the last word. The scene is simply too overwhelming for Frits to maintain his critical distance. Clearly, the painting behind the broken glass is transformed into a self-portrait reflected by a shattered mirror. Frits, like most Revian characters, is looking at himself:

De afbeelding stelde een aan het raam zittende oude vrouw voor, uit een huiskamer gezien. "Verlamming," mompelde hij.

De mond van het portret hing scheef naar beneden en de onderlip puilde, met de tong, een eind naar voren. Hij bekeek het driehoekig gat in de ruit. "Hoe scherp, hoe zorgvuldig," dacht hij. "Het is verbijsterend."[13]

We have seen how the window motif in Reve's early works follows a circuitous route, similar to that of the larger house motif, which it complements. It is a contradictory image which ostensibly leads the house dweller outside of his restrictive room toward freedom or escape, only to counter him with an equally oppressive force from without. Similarly, the window changes from being a conduit of light into an antithetical circuit of darkness. No matter what particular function is ascribed to the Revian window it inevitably reflects the same fickle ambivalence of the room or house in which it is located. On the one hand the window confirms that the visual perception is deceptive, therefore unreliable and in constant need of interpretation. More reliable, on the other hand, is its message that the world outside is as dangerous as the one within, and vice versa, thus turning the window into a link between two hostile environments. To complicate things, the window also suggests that the world to which it leads (or which it brings inside) is translated into a subjective anxious reality which often becomes a self-fulfilling prophecy. But no matter where the Revian window reader is in relation to the window, he is nearly always on the wrong side.

NOTES

[1]Gerard-Kornelis van het Reve, "Erick verklaart de vogeltekenen," *Podium*, 12 (1957), 304.

[2]Gerard-Kornelis van het Reve, "Foreign Boy," in *The Acrobat and Other Stories* (Amsterdam/London: Van Oorschot, 1956), p. 160.

[3]Gerard-Kornelis van het Reve, "Gossamer," in *The Acrobat and Other Stories* (Amsterdam/London: Van Oorschot, 1956), p. 227.

[4]Gerard-Kornelis van het Reve, "Winter," in *The Acrobat and Other Stories* (Amsterdam/London: Van Oorschot, 1956), p. 7.

[5]For an analysis of the function of time in Reve's work, see my essay "From Cronus to Janus: The Problem of Time in Gerard (Kornelis van het) Reve's Work," *Dutch Studies* 3 (1977), pp. 36-69.

[6]Reve, "Winter," p. 35.

[7]Reve, "Foreign boy," p. 163.

[8]Reve, "Gossamer," p. 224-25.

[9]Gerard-Kornelis van het Reve, *De ondergang van de familie Boslowits* (1956; rpt. Amsterdam: Van Oorschot, 1964), p. 47.

[10]Reve, "Erick verklaart," p. 271.

[11]Gerard-Kornelis van het Reve, "The Acrobat," in *The Acrobat and Other Stories* (Amsterdam/London: Van Oorschot, 1956), p. 87.

[12]Reve, "Acrobat," p. 60.

[13]Gerard-Kornelis van het Reve, *De avonden; een winterverhaal* (Amsterdam: De Bezige Bij, 1947), pp. 19-20.

A. ALBERTS' THE ISLANDS AS AN EXEMPLIFICATION OF CONTEMPORARY NOVELISTIC TECHNIQUES.

A. van den Hoven
French Department
University of Windsor, Ontario

At present a battle is raging in Canadian semiotics circles about the scientificity of the definition of the "text" and about the relative merits of "contextualisation" and "decontextualisation".[1] It seems to me that these notions can play a useful role in the analysis of A. Alberts's *The Islands* because one's ideological preconceptions and one's methodology have a configurative influence on the ultimate conclusions at which one arrives about a text.

In the case of A. Alberts one must immediately decide if *The Islands*, which appeared under the title *De Eilanden* in 1952, should be read in conjunction with *Naming Names*, which appeared under the title *Namen noemen* in 1962 and which contains Alberts's reminiscences of the same period covered by *The Islands*. One must also decide, as do E.M. Beekman[2] and Hella Haasse, if it primarily forms part of the "East Indian belletrie", even though, according to Hella Haasse, it occupies in that subgenre "a totally unique place."[3]

It is not that I necessarily disagree with either Beekman or Haasse's very precise and detailed studies, but it is rather that one arrives at a different perspective on *The Islands* if first of all one does an immanent critique of it and, subsequently, one places it in a modernist Western context together with, for example, *L'Etranger* by Camus and Samuel Beckett's *Waiting for Godot*. This perspective will be significantly different from that which results if one reinserts the text immediately into a biographical or a socio-historical continuum. In the context of A.Alberts's life one requires *Naming Names*, or *Lifted in and out of Paradise* as it was retitled in 1975, as a necessary compendium to fill the gaps that characterize the writing of *The Islands*. Within the context of Dutch colonial literature *The Islands* then becomes an integral part of a passing historical phenomenon which is attempting to capture the nostalgia for a vanished exotic realm.

On the other hand, an immanent reading of *The Islands* compels one to focus on the relationship between technique and worldview and forces one to justify the sparse style and the often non-referential language in terms of the author's conception of man's role in the universe. In turn this makes possible comparisons of man's diminished role as expressed through the first person narration with similar treatments by writers of such diverse origins as Hemingway, Faulkner, Camus, Sartre or Beckett. This recontextualization places Alberts firmly within the modernist sphere, a realm with which he had become no doubt thoroughly familiar during his stay in Paris from 1936 to 1939. (*The Islands*, p. 18).

Let us now turn our attention to the stories that compose the text of *The Islands*, discuss their internal coherence and subsequently reinsert each into a broader Western literary context. This collection of stories introduce us into a universe without clearly definable biographical and geographical referents, because these texts are auto-referential as well as auto-generative. The first story, entitled "Green", assumes the form of a diary and one realizes quickly that the weeks, days, and hours which head the individual entries represent so many steps toward and away from Peartree's untimely end. Even Peartree's suicide emanates from language itself: his own name. As the narrator remarks:

> A la lanterne, Peartree. I am laughing my head off. If ha-ha, your name is Peartree, then you're going to hang yourself from a tree, ha-ha. Oh well.
>
> (*The Islands*, p. 44).

Just as the carved kobolds have provided the impetus for the narrator's "secret plan to make the Northwood a fairy-tale sanctuary" (*The Islands*, p. 38), so Peartree's name has generated in its bearer its own fateful conclusion. While reading "Green", one quickly realizes that something is seriously amiss with Peartree, he is obviously a desperate drunk, but ultimately the coherence of the text can be deduced intertextually from his name and from the expressionistic lullaby which the narrator inserts into the text after he comes upon Peartree's suspended body. These lines were most likely inspired by Paul van Ostaijen's poems "Huldegedicht aan Singer" and "Vlerken". A comparison of these three texts in Dutch highlights their common origin. This is the central core of Alberts's ironic lullaby:

> Wingerd bloem, slinger bloem
> Wingerd in de slinger in de wingerd in de slinger in de
>   wingerd in de slinger.
> Wingerd bloem.
> In de bloem.[4]

Here are the opening lines of van Ostaijen's "Huldegedicht aan Singer":

> Slinger
>
>   Singer
>
>   naaimasjien[5]

and now two lines from his poem "Vlerken":

> Nachtelijk vliegen vogels van
> de wilde wingerd weg.[6]

The combination of the traditional lullaby and the expressionistic form, the rhythm as well as the very words used reveal the evident filiation with van Ostaijen, certainly Flanders most outstanding proponent of modernism. We must not neglect to add that the phrase "A la lanterne, Peartree," evokes in French not just "poirier" and hence, through homophony, Pierrot but also, as a consequence, Francois Villon and "L'Epitaphe en forme de ballade que fit Villon pour lui et ses compagnons s'attendant à étre pendu avec eux" ("The Epitaph in the form of a ballad which Villon wrote for himself and his companions while waiting to be hanged with them"). Since it is a proper noun which creates the referent (and in turn provokes a lullaby, echoes of expressionistic poetry, a figure in popular literature, and a ballad by a fifteenth century French poet), we are obviously dealing with an auto-generative and auto-referential text so typical of the modernistic Western tradition. These intertextual relationships provide a simple surface to the text, which is composed of apparently discrete units because in the story all words and events are palimpsestically linked to pre-existent texts beyond which no other reality can be pinpointed. These remarks are also pertinent to an understanding of the second story entitled "The King is Dead." In addition to the title, the fact that its protagonist is named Mr. Solomon suffices to metamorphose and metaphorize the life of "a retired sergeant-major bandmaster" (*The Islands*, p. 46) into an existence that exudes regal splendor. It also provokes a reversal of hierarchical positions and results in the narrator, the official in the story, becoming the dying Solomon's "subject" (*The Islands*, p. 50).

In the third story: "The House of the Grandfather", the same principles are operative. Taronggi III, a trader in kapok, has built "a huge, low white house with pillars in front and at the back" (*The Islands*, p. 57). This house is modeled "on [a]n exceptionally bad painting" (*The Islands*, p. 55) which in turn is a copy of the building featured on "a postcard" (*The Islands*, p. 55) sent to Taronggi III and at the bottom of which was printed: "Casa de this or that and then Tarragona." The narrator comments further: "Taronggi III did not rest until he knew that casa means house, and from that point on the house was the one that belonged to his grandfather in Tarragona." (*The Islands*, p. 55). This story embodies a degraded version of Plato's myth of the cave. In modern terms its significance lies in the fact that regardless of the geographical location of Tarragona, a picture postcard has generated a painting which in turn has inspired the construction of a house. We also possess here in parodic form an illustration of Oscar Wilde's dictum that life imitates art. All those props were necessary in order that Taronggi III could acquire the appropriate antecedents and a concrete past which he can now insert into the mundane present and thereby obfuscate the fact that his grandfather, Taronggi I, in the manner of his literary forefather Robinson Crusoe, had been "shipwrecked and washed ashore on the big island seventy years ago." (*The Islands*, p. 53). Again the story's structure derives its configuration from other texts, and this is true as well of the exotic names and the character's fanciful preoccupations. Their ultimate significance is always mediated by the pictorial and verbal documents that function as their superficial excuses.

In the next story "The Meal", we are promptly introduced to the scriptural underpinnings of the character's psyche:

> Mr. Zeinal stood on a big sheet of paper in the front room of his house. The paper was at least ten feet long and six feet wide and it was completely covered with small letters. This is my family tree, Mr. Zeinal said.
>
> *(The Islands,* p. 58).

It is of course hardly a coincidence that the narrator also places his feet on the paper and that this family tree, lying as it does in a horizontal position rather than standing upright, is being trampled upon. We can see in this a modernistic commentary on the conclusion of Jean de la Fontaine's fable "Le chene et le roseau", ("The oak and the reed"). Only remnants remain of Zeinal's past and that of his distant relative the Prince. The latter possesses three houses one of which is called the birdhouse; its floors are covered with sixteen inches of bird dung, a product which the Prince sells. During a dinner at the birdhouse, at which only Zeinal and the narrator are present, Zeinal tells a fairytale of a princess who is a sorceress and who turns herself into "a senile old man" (*The Islands*, p. 63) whenever she wishes to stay out of the Prince's clutches. After Zeinal's telling of the story, a dialogue ensues which is initiated by the narrator:

> And her spirit returns here every so often, I said.
> I don't think so, Mr. Zeinal said.
> It may be a coincidence, I said; but just now, I thought I heard an old man giggling behind us.
> And at the moment I said this, I heard it again. It is probably your imagination, Mr. Zeinal said. I think so too, I said.
> It often happens, Mr. Zeinal said, that people imagine such things when they hear old stories.
>
> *(The Islands,* p. 63)

These casual remarks confirm what we have already stated about the inspirational underpinnings of A. Alberts's prose. The intricate relationship between narration and events is the result of the fact that in *The Islands* significance is provoked into existence by verbal and pictorial means.

This is even the case in stories where the intertext is not directly apparent at the surface, as in "The Swamp". Its protagonist Naman has built the house behind the swamp so that he may commune alone with Maria Winters, the woman of his dreams. Again we learn of their fateful liaison through a story which originally had been told by Maria herself and which is now recounted by the narrator:

> There had also been a girl. Rie Winters, Maria Winters, Naman had always called her. He worked pretty hard on her. One evening a month after Naman had been

transferred, a rather drunken evening, she told us about it, choking with laughter.

(*The Islands*, p. 67)

But in Alberts's stories information of this kind is not always transmitted directly; sometimes the narrator comes upon a scene which has its unstated prototype in previous texts, such as happens when Naman invites him to dinner:

> In the middle of the second room was a table covered with a white tablecloth on which candles were burning. There were red flowers on the white tablecloth, there were sparkling glasses and a bottle of wine. Naman was sitting at the table and I saw that it had been set for three people. I sat down at one of the empty places, and I heard Naman say softly: Don't pay too much attention to him, Maria. He is a bit drunk.

(*The Islands*, p. 72)

This scene reminds one of Dickens' *Great Expectations* and of the description Pip gives of Miss Havisham's room in which nothing has changed since her wedding day.[7] It may not altogether be a coincidence either that Naman has built his house in a swamp; after all Pip provides a similar location for his family: "Ours was the marsh country, down by the river within, as the river wound, twenty miles of the sea."[8]

While the narrator and Naman are partaking of supper, reality and phantasmagoria are suddenly blended and we are transported into a universe which is purely textual in its presentation:

> I yelled: Naman, it is dangerous! You shouldn't lean your elbow on the tablecloth like that. It is dangerous. Maria is doing the same. It rests on the swamp, only on the swamp, and you are sinking right through it.

(*The Islands*, p. 73)

The narrator maintains the tension between the imaginary and the real right up to the conclusion. When he awakes from his drunken stupor, the narrator describes the scene again:

> Before us ribbons of mist were moving across the open space in front of the house. Ribbons of mist? Did I see a white figure hurrying away in the direction of the swamp? Oh no.

(*The Islands*, p. 74)

It is not clear if Maria Winters has become metamorphosed into Miss Havisham's bridal gown as well as the cobwebs that decorate the wedding cake, but it is evident that in Alberts's self-contained universe it is language that engenders the worlds in which we are made to move.

The story entitled "The Thief" strikes one initially as a fairly straightforward account of an actual event until one is confronted with certain incongruities. Horan is not at all a typical thief, and also the demarcation lines between prosecution and defense quickly evaporate, so that the impression is created that the ostensible normality of the recounted events is purely an effect of narration. In the dialogue the thief's name seems to have been surreptitiously substituted for that of the owner of the beautiful bull calf, and consequently, one is actually surprised that the thief is to be punished:

> It is a beautiful animal, I said.
> It is a fat little fellow, Horan said.
> It is a beautiful little thing.
> And he slapped the animal on the flank.
>
> This is the bucket, the policeman said.
> What bucket, I said.
> The piece of evidence, said the policeman.
> I am sending it to the fair in the capital next year, the owner said.
>
> He is bound to win first prize, Horan said.
> Well, let's go back, I said.
>
> (*The Islands*, p. 77)

The thief receives a two months sentence but this does not prevent him, when on the way to prison, from greeting "the clerk of the court and [the narrator]" (*The Islands*, p. 78).

In the following story, "The Hunt", this blending of object and subject, of owner and thief, of the hunter and the hunted, becomes the principal leitmotiv. In this context one cannot help but think of Alain Robbe-Grillet's *Le Voyeur*, in which eventually one is unable to distinguish between the detective and the criminal.

This story, which deals with the pursuit and killing of Captain Florines, a Muslim rebel, contains a story within a story which retells the narrator's encounters with wild boars in the Netherlands. At one time he had allowed a wild boar to escape and on another occasion "One of the hunters had taken [him] for a hunted wild animal" (*The Islands*, p. 93) and previous to that, when trespassing and forced to hide, he had identified himself with the animal: "Or maybe it was the boar I had been myself, when I had lain panting and grunting in the Second Java Fort." (*The Islands*, p. 93).

It is the events of the framed story that provide the psychological impetus for the events of the framing story. We move from the Second Java Fort in the Netherlands to an unidentified island which is terrorized by fanatical Muslims led by Florines. The latter is finally tracked down to a "house standing in the middle of the flattened mountain top" (*The Islands*, p. 97). It is at that point that the narrator is confronted with the apparently insoluble dilemma which opposes (1) the authority figure to the rebel and (2) the hunter to the hunted. By identifying the rebel with the boar, the narrator finally accomplishes a reversal of roles and allies himself with the rebel:

> A man was standing by a round stone well. [...] It was Florines, but he was now also the wild boar and I was no longer the hunter. A boar at its watering hole and I had to warn it. I had to chase it into the safe underbrush before the others caught it. I had to save my friend the boar.

(*The Islands*, p. 97)

The narrator, in an automatic gesture which proceeds from his role as authority figure, blindly pulls the trigger and kills Florines; but when he has his body burned, he cannot help but comment: "I saw only the flames, my last salute to the boar, my friend." (*The Islands*, p. 98).

In the next story, "The Treasure", the decision to seek the treasure stems firstly from the opposition to the forester who has in "the drawer of (his) desk (...) a complete plan for the reforestation of the divide." (*The Islands*, p. 99). The protagonists prefer, instead of this paper promise, to listen to and be inspired by the "many old tales about treasures" (*The Islands*, p. 101). After the men arrive at the cottage of the prince a great amount of alcohol and food is consumed and they abandon the search. However, they promise to return "(t)omorrow(...) Tomorrow (...) Tomorrow" (*The Islands*, p. 104). In Beckett's *Waiting for Godot*, the latter never shows but the characters continue to wait for his arrival which is promised for tomorrow. In a like manner the narrator and the doctor decide to stay a little longer, all the while playing a ritual that is similar to that performed by Beckett's characters. The narrator remarks: "There was one small piece of meat left on one of the dishes." Subsequently, the following dialogue takes place:

> You take it, the doctor said.
> You take it, I said.
> No, you, said the doctor.
> I took it.

(*The Islands*, p. 104)

In this manner, so similar to that of Beckett's characters the narrator stresses the ultimate futility of their gestures.

The story "The Last Island" is about names, naming and seeking and not finding. This is the auto-referential text par excellence, as is made clear by the opening passage in which the narrator explains that he and Olon had, as a joke, suggested the name Threemaster because the "ship did not have any masts at all, it was to become a small tugboat and seconde, because of the complications (which would arise) when the threemaster would have to give her name at sea." (*The Islands*, p. 105). The natives baptize the ship Arimassa compounding the problematics of nomination already rendered famous by Faulkner's *The Sound and The Fury* in which the late uncle and his niece are both called Quentin. There is of course another parallel between Faulkner's novel and this story. Just as Candace, known as Caddy, is forever lost to her brothers even though the search for her continues, so Olan and the narrator will not give up the search for the island on which live the swimmers who can "swim after the (fishing) nets for them" (*The Islands*, p. 106). As was the case with Faulkner's Caddy, about whom we are left only with stories, the protagonists of "The Last Island" are also impelled only by "stories", though in this case these are "(s)tories about swimmers." (*The Islands*, p. 107).

The title of the penultimate story emphasizes two concerns which are central to modern literature: the question of narration and that of "estrangement". It is entitled "The Unknown Island. A stranger narrates." Its narrator is a member of an American plane crew who crash on an unknown island. By means of gestures the narrator succeeds in explaining to the natives that he wishes to reach a telephone. The fact that modern science has created a "lingua franca" in which "telephone" exists in the native's tongue (in the form tilpun) leads to his salvation. The right gestures and homophonic association lead to understanding. A summary of their state by a fellow crew member also provides an apt description of the metaphysical condition of man in modern literature: "we are abandoned by God and man alike, but we will give it a try." (*The Islands*, p. 115) As if to gainsay Donne's dictum that "no man is an island", A. Alberts's characters function as discrete entities who succeed in communication only when they speak in formulae. However hard they try, their language is no longer referential and characters, words, sentences and the stories themselves are severed from a clearly defined biological and geographical context.

The concluding story "Beyond the Horizon" strongly implies that for the author meaning is deferred (Derrida's term) or as the narrator puts it, "transferred" (*The Islands*, p. 127). Now that he is back in the country where "(t)here are bicycles and cars along the canal" (*The Islands*, p. 124), he is again a stranger, and together with many of the passengers he would have preferred "to stay behind on an empty ship and continue sailing on alone." (*The Islands*, p.124). Now that he is alone, he has also lost his collective identity and he has been turned into a solitary individual. As he states: "Then we are no longer we. (...) Then there is only me." (*The Islands*, pp. 124-125). As well, in his dreams the archipelago has become depopulated:

> I recognized the houses but there were no people. All
> the houses had big signs in their front yards, and on
> every sign was written in big letters: Transferred.

(*The Islands*, p. 127)

Two kinds of signs operate in this concluding passage. Firstly "the houses", which signify only negatively to the extent that qua sign they have been stripped of their inhabitants cum signifiers, and secondly, the "big letters" which proclaim their signifier blatantly while simultaneously suffusing the entire text retrospectively with the implication that all significance is constantly in the process of being transferred. The fact that Alberts decided to conclude his collection with the statement: "Transferred" provides a perfect illustration of the comments on narration which Sartre has Roquentin make in La Nausée:

> les événements se produisent dans un sens et nous les racontons en sens inverse. On a l'air de débuter par le commencement (...). Et en réalité c'est par la fin qu'on a commencé.[9]

> (things happen one way and we tell them backwards. You seem to start at the beginning(...). And in reality you have started at the end.)[10]

In circular fashion the end has brought us back to the beginning, compelling us to raise again the questions of text, context, decontextualisation and recontextualisation. Without wishing to invalidate the biographical, the literary-historical or the socio-cultural approach, it strikes me that my proposed re-ordering of the hierarchy of methodologies has the advantage of providing greater accessibility to a text such as *The Islands*. For that reason, I would propose an initial immanent reading of the text, in complete awareness that the imposition of this kind of "closure" directs the text's overall significance away from the themes and preoccupations that mark East Indian "belletrie" and re-directs one's focus to problems of narration, of language, of identity and of man's role in the universe. This new focus does permit a recontextualisation, but it places *The Islands* in an occidental modernist framework. This to us underlines the clear stylistic affinities with the works of Hemingway, Camus, and Beckett. It also singles out similar themes: those of modern man's isolation, his estrangement and his desperate search for meaning. Likewise Alberts's minimalist prose can then be shown to sustains a fictional universe severed from its referents and in which the only terra firma which is provided to the reader is that of the verbal indicators that allow his stories to stand as so many isolated islands reached by ships for occasional stop-overs. In Alberts's imagination the stories of *The Islands* clearly represent the touchstones of man's human condition. Therefore, whatever place they occupy in Dutch East Indian "belletrie", it is also evident that in international terms they beg comparison with luminaries of a different stature.

NOTES

[1]See for example, D. St. Jacques, "La clôture du texte," Sociétés savantes, atelier de l'APFUCC, Un. du Manitoba, Winnipeg, Man., le 2 juin 1986.

[2]"Introduction", A.Alberts, *The Islands*. Transl. by Hans Koning. Edited with an introduction and notes, by E.M. Beekman, Amherst, The University of Massachusetts Press, 1983, p.l. Further references to this edition will be included in the main text.

[3]H. Haasse, "tussen de regels. Over het 'Indische' proza van A. Alberts." *Bladspiegel. Een keuze uit de essays*. Amsterdam, E.M. Querido's Uitgeverij B.V., 1985, p. 175: "Hoewel zij maar een klein gedeelte van zijn oeuvre vormen, hebben zij Alberts gemaakt tot een van de merkwaardigste schrijvers behorend tot de zogenaamde 'Indische belletrie'. Juister is het te stellen, dat hij in die categorie een geheel aparte plaats inneemt."

[4]Alberts. *De eilanden*. Amsterdam: G.A. van Oorschot Uitgever, 1952, p. 34.

[5]Van Ostaijen, *Music-Hall*, Samengesteld en ingeleid door Gerrit Borgers, Den Haag: Daamen N.V., "Ooievaar 17", 1955, pp. 138-140.

[6]*Ibid.*, p. 153.

[7]C. Dickens, *Great Expectations*, ed. by R.D. McMaster, Toronto; MacMillan of Canada, 1965, p. 83.

[8]*Ibid.*, p. 1.

[9]J-P. Sartre, *Oeuvres romanesques*, Paris: Gallimard, NRF, "Bibliotheque de la Pléiade", 81, p. 49.

[10]J-P. Sartre, *Nausea*. Transl. by Lloyd Alexander. Intro. by Hayden Carruth. New York, New Directions Publ. Corp., 1964, pp. 40-41.

GENITIVES LEFT AND RIGHT IN VROMAN'S POETRY

W.G. Klooster
University of Amsterdam

Poems are intricate things. Because they are specimens of speech embedded in a much larger context than utterances ordinarily are, the context usually not being one of current interest, they are never readily understood, or hardly ever. A poem, taken by itself in isolation, is nothing but a syntactically and lexically ambiguous structure, sometimes containing deviant or ungrammatical strings of words. It will resist interpretation to the degree in which its universe of discourse comprises the diversity of the poet's personal experiences. Since these may include all sorts of facts and associations unknown to the reader, poems as a rule demand an extraordinary amount of interpretive power and linguistic ingenuity. Especially in modern poetry, there is, in addition, a tendency to convey as much as possible in as few words as possible (which is not to say, of course, that a good modern poem cannot be long). All kinds of unusual and subtle linguistic devices can be seen at work, heightening the information content of the poem, at the same time making it more complex and difficult to penetrate. This leaves us with a paradoxical state of affairs in modern poetry: although the negative entropy of information, so to speak, is very high, the degree of inaccessibility of that information is also very high. Modern poetry is like hidden tracks in the jungle: sparse but rich in information, hard to read because so much hangs on so little that is to be seen. The linguistic clues are there, but they are elusive most of the time. That is why poems are intricate things.

Leo Vroman's poetry answers to the above description in that it employs a great variety of devices that help convey a message in a very economical but subtle manner. These devices are largely of a linguistic nature in the sense that in most cases they do not so much serve to put across ideas or images through words directly - although of course that too is an element - as depend on alluding to fixed expressions and colloquialisms, using mock archaic words or turns of phrases, utilizing newly invented words, the comical clash of formal and informal language, etc., - in short, they are meant to appeal to the reader's linguistic knowledge and acuity in the broadest sense. One might call this particular kind of poetry "language conscious" poetry. Such poetry, of course, is attractive to the linguistically inclined. Since I am a grammarian rather than a student of literature, it should come as no surprise that Vroman's poetry is of the kind that interests me most. My treatment of the examples to be discussed, by the way, just possibly might be somewhat on the technical side at times. But I shall avoid esoteric terms and notions.

Through the years, Vroman's poetry has remained the same as regards "language consciousness". However, the focus of his linguistic awareness has shifted somewhat from the realm of highly convoluted grammatical constructions reminiscent of nineteenth century solemnity, to that of almost, but not quite facetious word-play and the possibilities of manipulating phrases of the present-day vernacular.

To give an example, taken from Vroman's earlier work, let me quote the beginning of one of the most difficult poems that I have ever tried to analyze (it will be repeated below as (30)):

>Schemering
>Hoe lelie welker blaren
>buiging Uw keelwit baren
>al sluit om kernrood merk:
>in 't wilde wimperstaren
>wil nog geen licht bedaren
>en fonkelt het stervend zwerk.

>['Dusk
>How lily whose leaves'
>curving already closes your throat-white birth-giving
>   around a kernel-red mark:
>in the wild eyelash-staring,
>no light will yet abate
>and the dying firmament glows.']

By giving a "literal" translation, I already partly disambiguated Vroman's text. As one can see, one of the things that make these lines so enigmatic and impenetrable is the forbiddingly complex construction that constitutes the beginning. I will return to this example at the end of my exposition and try to unravel its grammatical structure.

In the following, I will consider a number of examples of deliberately archaic turns of phrase in Vroman's poetry. They are not in all instances to be regarded as merely echoes of the archaic style. In some cases, in particular in the earlier work, they are meant to give the poem a certain air of loftiness, as we will see.

The main examples of Vroman's poetical language that I am going to discuss are all instances of a specific construction which might be called 'the prenominal genitive'. By a 'genitive' in this connection I mean forms like John's, as in John's book, of the house, as in the roof of the house, thereof, of which and their Dutch equivalents. More specifically, I am referring to the following forms in Dutch:

(1)   a   van de knaap   - 'of the boy'
                of the boy
    archaic:
        b   des   knapen -   -'of the boy'
           the-GEN-MASC-SING fellow-GEN)
        c   van de knapen   - 'of the boys'
           of the boys

<pre>
        formal/archaic:
            der   knapen   - 'of the boys'
            the-GEN-PLUR boys
     e   van de vergadering-'of the meeting'
            of the meeting
        formal:
     f   der   vergadering-'of the meeting'
            the-GEN-FEM-SING   meeting
     g   van de vergaderingen 'of the meetings'
            of the meetings
        formal:
     h   der   vergaderingen-'of the meetings'
            the-GEN-PLUR meetings

(2) a   waarvan   - 'of which'
            whereof
        formal/archaic:
     h   welker- 'of   which', 'who-
            which-GEN-FEM-SING, or   se'
            which-GEN-PLUR
</pre>

      The list given in (1) and (2) is far from complete, but these examples will do.

      For clarity, I will now illustrate what I mean by 'prenominal genitives', or 'genitives positioned to the left', as opposed to the normal case in Dutch for noun phrases with common nouns as heads, which we may dub 'genitives positioned to the right.'

      In Dutch, as in English, possessive personal pro-nouns are positioned to the left of their heads. They are instances of prenominal genitives:

(3)   <u>mijn</u> boek   my book

Normally, the genitive forms of proper names are also prenominal:

(4)   <u>Jonathans</u> boek   Jonathan's book

But genitives of proper names may also occur to the right of their heads, as in (5):

(5)   het boek <u>van Jonathan</u> - the book of Jonathan's

However, if the genitive is not that of a proper name, but that of a common noun, we would always expect the genitive to be positioned to the right, in its periphrastic form (i.e., with <u>van</u> ('of')):

(6)   de wandelstok <u>van de man</u> - the cane of the man

But this is only true of the modern, periphrastic forms. The archaic holophrastic form of the genitive of a common noun always appears in the position immediately to the left of its head, i.e. prenominally:

(7)   's   mans   wandelstok
      the-GEN-MASC-SING man-GEN cane
      'the man's cane'

(7), as I said, is archaic. It only occurs in everyday language if used facetiously. The form in (7) is much like the German example (8), in which the first part, the genitive, is literally the eguivalent of (1)b:

(8)   des   Knaben   Wunderhorn
      the-GEN-MASC-SING boy-GEN-SING miraculous horn
      'the boy's miraculous horn'

Note that in cases like (7) and (8) we have noun phrases that are definite, although an article marking them as such is absent (the inflected article marks only the first noun, not the whole phrase). In phrases such as (7) and (8), the genitive is in the position otherwise occupied by the article, or by a possessive pronoun or the genitive of a proper name (as in (3) and (4) respectively). In short, prenominal genitives occupy the so-called Determiner position, and somehow mark the noun phrase as a definite one.

As noted, the prenominal genitive is formal or archaic if it is the genitive form of a common noun. The same goes for such interrogative or relative pronouns as welker ('whose', 'of which'), that, in principle, always precede their heads and also mark as definite the noun phrase of which they are part. The reason that they are felt to be archaic most probably is that inflected forms such as these have given way to the periphrastic forms. They are no longer used in conversational Dutch except in fossilized expressions.

As we saw, however, there also are prenominal genitives that are not archaic, viz, possessives and proper names ending in the genitive marker -s. Hence we will distinguish between 'archaic' and 'non-archaic prenominal genitives'.

One expects the effect of archaic prenominal genitives to consist in lending the text an air of solemnity. In Vroman's earlier work such constructions appear to do just that, as I implied above. But in his later work, in which they also occur, the aim appears to be no longer that of imparting a solemn tone to the poem. Rather, it is to cause a subtle comical contrast with the much less formal character of the rest of the poem.

There are two other types of construction, both involving relatives, that I would like to mention here. I am referring to constructions like (9)-(10):

(9)   Deze doos, de binnenkant waarvan je rood moet
      This box, the inside whereof you red must

verven, (...)
paint, (...)

'This box, the inside of which you must paint red, (...)'

(10)   Dit is een envelop <u>op de achterkant waarvan</u>
       This is an envelope on the back whereof

       ik iets heb geschreven
       I something have written

       'This is an envelope on the back of which I wrote something'

Constructions like (10) are much more common in Dutch than are constructions like (9). Example (9), in fact, has a somewhat dubious status. It becomes even worse if we put the genitive construction in an environment similar to the one in (10): ?<u>Dit is een doos de binnenkant waarvan je rood moet verven</u>. Apparently, what is possible with prepositional phrases here, is not freely allowed with noun phrases. Instead of (9), it is much more natural to say (11),

(11)   Deze doos, <u>waarvan</u> je <u>de binnenkant</u> rood
       This box, whereof you the inside red

       moet verven, (...)
       must paint, (...)

On the other hand, if we change the word order in (10), so that we get (12), the result is rather doubtful:

(12)   ?Dit is een envelop <u>waarvan</u> ik <u>op de achterkant</u>
       This is an envelope whereof I on the back

       iets heb geschreven
       something have written

The point seems to be that the rule obligatorily putting the <u>wh</u>-phrase to the front of the subordinate clause has to involve the whole phrase, if it happens to be a prepositional phrase, whereas in the case of <u>wh</u>-phrases that are noun phrases, it should preferably move only the <u>wh</u>-word (in this case, <u>waarvan</u>), as illustrated in (13) (the hyphens mark the original position of the moved element, the moved element itself is underlined):

(13)   a   deze doos {je [de binnenkant **waarvan**] rood
            moet verven}
                              --> (not preferred:)

            deze doos {<u>de binnenkant **waarvan**</u> je [--] rood
            moet verven}
                              --> (preferred:)

        een doos {**waarvan** je [de binnenkant --] rood moet verven}

  b   een envelop {ik iets [op de achterkant **waarvan**] heb geschreven}
          --> (bad:)

        een envelop {**waarvan** ik iets [op de achterkant --] heb geschreven}
          --> (ok:)

        een envelop {op de achterkant **waarvan** ik iets [--] heb geschreven}

I will not go into the question why prepositional wh-phrases have to be moved in their entirety, whereas preferably only part of wh-phrases that are noun phrases are put to the front. Suffice it to note that relative clauses need not always have the relative pronoun at the beginning - they may start with a string of words of which the relative pronoun is not the first, or left-most one.

While sentences like (10) are perfectly correct, there still is something about them that makes them not quite natural in conversational Dutch. The tendency is not to have relative clauses start with elements other than either a relative or a preposition followed by a relative. The reason for this may be that perceptual strategies are such that relative clauses not starting with a relative are harder to recognize. However this may be, sentences in which the wh-phrase is part of a larger phrase, say a prepositional phrase as in (10), are avoided most of the time and replaced by paraphrases like (14):

  (14)   Dit is een envelop waarop ik iets
           This is an envelope whereon I something
           aan de achterkant heb geschreven
           at the back have written

Now on paper (14) may look terribly clumsy to a Dutch native speaker, but in a normal speech situation it will not be conspicuous at all, whereas (10) is somehow not natural and sounds slightly bookish.

    What if the relative is part of a phrase which is embedded in yet another phrase? Moving the entire complex wh-phrase (i.e., the maximal wh-phrase) to the front of the relative clause will simply result in a sentence sounding even more unnatural than (10). In fact, such a sentence does not seem to be well-formed. Compare, for instance, (15):

  (15)   *... een doos, de kleur van de binnenkant
           a   box, the color of   the inside

        waarvan rood is
        whereof red is

        '... a box, the color of the inside of which is red'

Sentences such as (15) remind one of Churchill's answer to the accusation that he too often stranded his prepositions at the end of sentences. His rebuke, it is said, was: "That is an accusation up with which I shall not put."

Only if we substitute the archaic-sounding inflected relative welker for the more modern waarvan in (15), will it be possible to leave part of the complex wh-phrase to the right of the relative, as in (16):

(16)   ... een doos, de kleur van welker binnenkant
a box, the color of whose inside

rood is
red is

'a box the color of whose inside is red'

However, (16) is hopelessly archaic, so that normally one would say something like (17),

(17)   ... een doos waarvan na de kleur aan de binnenkant
... a box whereof the color on the inside

rood is
red is

'... a box of which the color on the inside is red'

The situation is roughly the same with complex wh-phrases starting with a preposition, except that putting the entire complex prepositional wh-phrase at the front of the relative clause will not result in an ungrammatical structure, though it does lead to a rather forced sentence. Thus (18) is grammatical but awful. (19) is correct as well, but it suffers from stiltedness, because of the archaic relative welker:

(18)   ... een brief op de achterkant van de
... a letter on the back of the

envelop waarvan ik iets heb geschreven
envelope whereof I something have written
' ... a letter on the back of the envelope of which I wrote something'

(19)   ... een brief op de achterkant van welker
... a letter on the back of whose
envelop ik iets   heb geschreven
envelope I something have written

'... a letter on the back of whose envelope I wrote something'

In everyday speech, we would avoid (18) as well as (19) and say something like (20),

(20) ... een brief waarvan ik op de achterkant
 ... a letter whereof I on the back
van de envelop iets heb geschreven
of the envelope something have written

(20) will not stand up to grammatical scrutiny, but performance factors will cause it to be accepted.

We may conclude that in general, if the genitive is a relative, it may not occur too far to the right of the head of its maximal phrase. If, on the other hand, the genitive is something other than a possessive pronoun or the genitive of a proper name, it may not occur to the left of its head, unless we accept archaic constructions with inflected forms.

Let us now turn to examples actually taken from Vroman's poetry and see how they work.

The poem, titled *Kanji*, written in the Dutch East Indies in 1940 or 1941, consists of twelve two-line stanzas. It tells us about a philosopher who, standing on a rock, is listening to the peaceful sounds of nature as the sun is setting.

(21) ....
hij luistert, de stilte dreunt.

Hij herkent de juistheid van
der bomen takkengang
....
['he is listening, the silence rumbles.
He recognizes the correctness of

the courses taken by the trees' branches]

The word-for-word translation of de juistheid van der bomen takkengang is given in (22):

(22) de juistheid van der bomen
the correctness of the-GEN-PLUR trees'
takkengang
course-of-branches

Takkengang is a newly created compound. In forming it, Vroman admirably compresses in a single word the notion of paths traced by the branches of a tree as they grow. Shortness, too, is achieved by using the archaic prenominal genitive construction of the type illustrated above in (7) and (8). It is not just shortness, though, that is accomplished. The effect of the prenominal genitive here is the creation of an atmosphere of ancient oriental wisdom. Here, the archaic turn of phrase properly fits the sense of noble placidity pervading the text.

The above example may be compared with the following one, which is taken from the poem 'Eb en vloed' ('Ebb and flow'), in *Uit slaapwandelen* (*Out on a sleepwalk*), dating from rather a later period. In 70 lines, it evokes a dreamlike beach and seascape, populated with hollowed-out things, animals, roughly interconnected by the seaweeds of perhaps the poet's native country. The water is strange, wide, like the undulating interim time that separates him from Holland's surf. Heads of friends appear, as figments of the imagination. They take on some sort of reality, limbs drift along, voices seeming to come from far can be heard. The poet does not know who he is: maybe just a part of memories, maybe just a part of his friends. Am I floating (he asks), face down, above their world, which is so full and vague? Under the water surface and above it, it gets darker and later. It would be preferable to flee into dreamed forests, for lighting up the depths with softly sinking poems is going to take years of sleep and having slaves collect the poet's mutterings when he is not sleeping. There the caravan of slaves goes, heavily burdened, while the poet, writing, is stalking behind as the savages press closer. The caravan is walking down into the ocean,

(23) waar der waters kringelingen
labiale mompelingen
in het ruisen overgaan,
talmen in het nevelig zingen
waar de palmen...
waar de maan...

['where the waters'coilinqs
labial mumblings
blend into the rustle,
linger in the nebulous singing
where the palms...
where the moon...']

The lines quoted here form the end of the poem.

The phrase I would like to concentrate on is, of course, <u>der waters kringelingen</u>. In which-ever way we are to interpret (23), it is clear that we are dealing with an archaic prenominal genitive. The strange thing about it, however, is that the form <u>waters</u> is out of place here. <u>Waters</u>, of course, is the plural of <u>water</u> in Dutch, but it is the more archaic plural <u>wateren</u> which one would expect here. Possibly, <u>der wateren kringelingen</u> was rejected for reasons of euphony: in order to avoid repetition of the morpheme <u>-en</u>. Vroman may have substituted <u>waters</u> for <u>wateren</u>. There may also be an additional reason for choosing the unmarked form rather than the archaic one: using the archaic form could be regarded as overdoing it a little in this case.

One might want to consider the possibility that <u>waters</u> here should not be taken to be a plural at all, but a singular noun with the genitive ending.

But if <u>waters</u> would have to be regarded as a genitive, <u>der</u> <u>waters</u> would be incorrect. <u>Water</u> has neutral gender, therefore the genitive form of the singular noun phrase ought to be <u>des waters</u>.

Nevertheless, the possibility that <u>waters</u> is in fact a genitive cannot be wholly ruled out. But we would then have to accept that we are dealing with a violation of the case paradigm.

How does the construction we are looking at function in the text? It certainly does not conflict with the general tone of the poem. Other more or less archaic words and phrases occur in it, among them two more genitive forms: <u>des doods</u> ('of death') and <u>welker</u> ('of which'). Nor is there a hint of parody. For that, the archaisms are not conspicuous enough. Indeed, the effect of the archaic prenominal genitive has been softened by avoiding the archaic plural <u>wateren</u>, as noted. What, then, do they signify? It seems to me that the archaisms in 'Eb en vloed' have a function similar to that of the rather emphatic rhymes in it. They indicate that we are dealing with a text written in a clear tradition, that what we are reading is, emphatically, poetry, not a fragment of prose or poetical prose (which, incidentally, the book also contains). It is one of the devices to set a poem apart from other kinds of texts.

There is another aspect of the matter which we should not leave undiscussed, and that is that use of the prenominal genitive here is the only acceptable option. For let us consider what the possibilities are. First, one could replace the prenominal genitive by a postnominal one, leaving everything else as it is. This would give us (24).

(24)   ... de oceaan,
waar de kringelingen der waters
labiale mompelingen
in het ruisen overgaan,
(...)

Or we could replace, in (24), the holophrastic genitive by a periphrastic one, which would yield (25):

(25)   ... de oceaan,
waar de kringelingen van de waters
labiale mompelingen
in het ruisen overgaan,
(...)

Or we could substitute, in (23), (24) or (25), <u>wateren</u> for <u>waters</u>. Aside from the fact that all of these alternatives, to me, sound abominable, they all have the setback that the distance between <u>kringelingen</u> ('coilings') and <u>labiale mompelingen</u> ('labial mumblings') is hampering the linking of these two phrases. In (23), Vroman's version, there is no doubt as to whether it is <u>kringelingen</u> or <u>waters</u> that is to be associated with the adjunct <u>labiale mompelingen</u>. Therefore the prenominal genitive constitutes the superior alternative.

Let us now turn to an example actually containing a mistake, a mistake though, that hardly any Dutch native speaker would detect. It occurs in a poem called 'Lief, lief' ('Sweet, sweet'), also from *Uit slaapwandelen*. The poem is full of extraordinary combinations of words, violating all kinds of selection restrictions. Also, it contains a stanza consisting almost entirely of nonsense words, some of them violating word-formation rules on the phonological level. Archaisms, too, abound, and their effect is not exactly that of facetiousness, but something milder, very tender and playful. The poem at first seems to be some sort of ode to women, but it quickly turns out to be not in praise of women in general, but of the poet's wife, Tineke. It is not possible to quote it in full, since it consists of 84 lines, but I will try to give a general idea of its content.

The first seven stanzas are about women in general, how they speak, their voices, laughter and glances, the way they walk on stiletto heels, their charm. But then the poet makes it clear that he will not give himself up to women, or let them overwhelm him. The eleventh through seventeenth stanza then herald - but without giving anything away - what in the eighteenth stanza is to be revealed as the real subject of the poem, Tineke. Then the nonsense-word stanza follows, meaning, presumably, that existing words are simply insufficient to express how the poet feels about his loved one. The poem closes with a word to other women. Flee, jealous women, Vroman says; if you want a man, go away from here, or words (and an occasional non-word) to that effect.

I will now quote the three stanzas about the poet's not giving up himself to women. The second of these contains the phrase I want to discuss.

(26)   Moet ik nu heus vermoeden
om wat miljoenen jurken
zich grijnzend zitten te schurkenals zij zich doen bebroeden?

Neen, vrouwen zijn lange paarden, de binnenkant wier schoenen
ik nooit heb willen zoenen
en wier hoe schoon onthaarde

baddespons mij node
de mannemond mag laven;
neen, onder hen begraven
werd ik een platte dode.

['Must I really conjecture
as to what millions of dresses
are rubbing themselves for, grinning,
when they are having themselves sat and brooded upon?

No, women are long horses,
the insides of whose shoes I have

> never wanted to kiss
> and whose how beautifully depilated
>
> bath sponges are reluctantly allowed
> to quench my male mouth's thirst;
> no, buried under them,
>
> I would be a flattened corpse.']

The phrase in question is translated word-for-word in (27):

(27)   de binnenkant wier schoenen
        the inside who-GEN-PLUR shoes

(27) however, is not correct Dutch. It should be de binnenkant van wier schoenen ('the inside of whose shoes'). It is not surprising, however, that practically no-one would notice the error. First, since wier already is a genitive and as such may be said to incorporate van ('of'), the absence of van easily escapes notice. Secondly, the system of case inflection in Dutch is only feebly alive in the linguistic performance of native speakers; it is more than halfway on the way out. Hence errors will not easily be detected. A third factor possibly contributing to the acceptability of (27) is the fact that (28) is all right:

(28)   wier   schoenen binnenkant
        who-GEN-PLUR shoes   inside
        ('whose shoes' insides')

To the native speaker, the difference between (28) and (27) is minimal.

(28) is analogous to (7) ('s mans wandelstok, 'the man's cane'), (8) (des Knaben Wunderhorn) and to Vroman's der bomen takkengang in (21), that is, it is a prenominal genitive. But isn't a van, or some other genitive marker missing in (28)? The answer is yes, yet (28) is correct. Recall that the prenominal genitive occupies the Determiner position, thus, like the definite article, marking the whole noun phrase as a definite one. In (28), the prenominal genitive wier is occupying, as it were, the position of the definite article associated with schoenen. Since the definite article that would otherwise precede schoenen is now eliminated, its genitive case, too, is absent; harmlessly so, it appears.

Note, however, that the elimination of the genitive marker, together with that of the article, is not possible in constructions where the Dutch equivalent of the genitive 'of whose X' is not prenominal but postnominal, as is illustrated in (29).

(29)   prenominal:

        wier schoenen binnenkant [wier supplants der]

postnominal:

de binnenkant **van wier schoenen** [wier supplants de]

Let us now turn to the last example that we will discuss here, the opening lines of the poem that I quoted at the beginning and that I will repeat here as (30). It is the first stanza of the poem *Schemering*, dating from 1940 or 1941, written in the Dutch East Indies:

(30) Schemering Hoe lelie welker blaren
buiging Uw keelwit baren
al sluit om kernrood merk:
in 't wilde wimperstaren
wil nog geen licht bedaren
en fonkelt het stervend zwerk.

....

['Dusk How lily whose leaves'
curving already closes your throat-white birth-giving
around kernel-red mark:
in the wild eyelash-staring,
no light will yet abate
and the dying firmament glows.']

Schemering, I think, is about the finiteness of life. The person spoken to is, I believe, the poet's loved one. The lily of the first line depicts the sky, and at the same time probably also the loved one. The last stanza, not quoted here, roughly translates as follows: "Shadow is eating at your edges and your inward-turned hands, leaving you a vacant spectre. Come; inside these walls cold night extinguishes the burning, already bringing it to a chill worse than that of the horizon". The horizon may be interpreted as a symbol of death. Burning within the walls is the force of life. The night, not a symbol of death but its harbinger, coming at the end of dusk, reduces life to less than even death itself.

The noun lelie ('lily'), at the beginning of the poem, is used as if it were an adjective. Hoe lelie therefore should be taken to mean something like "How much (like) a lily". The first three lines can be regarded as an elliptical sentence. If I am right in thinking that the lily is the sky, the first lines can roughly be paraphrased as follows: 'How much like a lily, this evening sky. It is white as a throat and looking as if it is giving birth. The curve of its leaves is already closing its pallor over the red sun.' Het wilde wimperstaren (fourth line) then must be taken to mean the staring into the evening sky, causing one to blink. The light refuses yet to die down, the dying firmament still glows.

As already indicated in the rough translation in (30), the phrase welker blaren buiging is a prenominal genitive construction of the complex type shown in (29). The construction, because it is so complex and archaic, is very rare, even in Vroman's poetry. It occurs once more in the same poem, in a slightly less complex form. As the poet asks what woe causes soundless suffering in his loved one's eyes, he offers as a possible answer (31).

(31)   De verte waar <u>der wegen</u>
       <u>Willen</u> gaan saamgenegen,
       als onze na lange tijd?

       ['The distance where the wills
       of the roads goconverging
       like ours after a long time?']

Here, too, we have an archaic prenominal genitive.

Of course, the construction type that we have been considering although occurring more than once in this poem, is but part of what makes it such an abstruse and almost arcane piece of literature. Seldom, however, does a poem written in this tradition (set by such poets as Roland Holst, Achterberg and Bloem) contain such grammatically complex structures harking back to a period long past. In this respect, Vroman surpasses his contemporaries, as he does, in many cases, with respect to innovation.

As I said in the beginning, a poem is an intricate thing, linguistically speaking as well as in other respects. In looking at a specific class of constructions in Vroman's poetry I have of course not even begun to show just how intricate a poem can be. What I did show, however, is that grammatical analysis allows us a closer look at certain aspects of what is probably man's most highly structured form of art.

BIBLIOGRAPHY

Leo Vroman, *126 gedichten*, Amsterdam 1966 (Querido).

The
Dutch
in
America

THE HUISVROUW AND THE FARMER'S DAUGHTER
Images of Dutch-American Women in the Late Nineteenth and Early Twentieth Centuries

Suzanne Sinke
Department of History
University of Minnesota

A visitor to Orange City, Iowa watched the arrival of a number of Dutch-Americans at the local church. In particular he noted "a single amazon, a stout, young farmer's daughter who comes galloping over the fields, a delightful sight to see."[1] Images of the Dutch-American woman such as the one given in this account provide insights into the complex culture of an immigrant world. Moreover, they begin to illuminate a story, a history, which has received little attention, yet concerns half the population. Women have remained hidden in the shadow of their male relatives in much historical writing. Adding ethnicity into the picture, at least in the Dutch case, does not remedy the deficiency. What we need is a different lens, a different perception, of reality. To accomplish this the researcher must re-examine traditional materials, and then go beyond the conventional genres of historical inquiry.

I have begun a study of Dutch immigrant women and their daughters beginning in the mid-nineteenth century relying on such an approach, and focusing on gender roles. How do these women compare to their American counterparts? That is the question that drives this research. At an even deeper level is the related query: how does ethnicity relate to gender in the Dutch case? Among some Dutch-American women ethnicity and religion intertwined to create a kind of life that was far removed from the American standard.

My research has concentrated thus far on published sources by and about Dutch-American women. The life histories, reminiscences and letters that have found their way into print cannot be considered representative of the entire Dutch-American community for a number of reasons. First, they are predominantly from the Protestant groups, underrepresenting the story of Dutch-Catholics and ignoring that of Dutch Jews and other religious (or non-religious) groups. Hence my analysis deals only with Dutch Protestant women in this paper. Second, the writings come from a part of the population that is more educated than the average. Third, since many of the authors wrote long after the events, their interest frequently corresponded with family success and continuation in the Dutch-American community. Those who moved on or were dissatisfied were unlikely to write about their experiences. These factors, which make the families in published documents less representative, conversely make them excellent sources for determining community gender patterns. These individuals were likely to be leaders in norm definition, or at least on the forefront of adaptive changes.

My theoretical framework comes from the fields of Women's History, Folklore and American Studies. Researchers who have discussed gender roles have often focused on prescriptive literature, only to have their successors demonstrate that the rhetoric of the public forum did not match the reality of individual lives.[2] Hence I sought a middle ground. Private writings and family histories served this purpose, illuminating where the behavior of the individual met the belief system of the community. Similarly, accounts by outside observers of the community reflected how American ideas of proper behavior were upheld or challenged in an immigrant setting. Whether insider or outsider, individual accounts occupied a pivotal position, an excellent one to begin examining expectations for women.[3]

The image of a Dutch woman was normally the image of a huisvrouw, and with good reason. The familial nature of the Dutch immigration to America in the late nineteenth century meant that women constituted a significant proportion of the movement. But they came primarily as wives. Women's motivations for migrating were somewhat different than those for men. Industrialization and population growth put pressure on small farmers, farm laborers, and small craftsmen. With their livelihood threatened, these men sought better opportunities in the new world. Women emigrants, from the same background, also cited economics as their first priority in the Landverhuizers (emigration) lists, but social concerns were much stronger than among men. Many women left to rejoin husbands, while some emigrated as single adults hoping to find a mate in America. Still, unmarried women accounted for only 11% of Dutch migration between 1850 and 1880. The proportion of single men was also small in comparison to other west European migrant groups, but the ratio of Dutch single women per 1000 unmarried men was less than half the ratio for Swedes, indicating that the lure of jobs as domestics did not appeal to many Dutch girls.[4]

Once in America their rate of marriage was high, up to 100% in some communities.[5] Individual accounts verified this trend in impressionistic terms. A Dutch-American woman was expected to marry. For her, as well as for her native-born counterpart,[6] love was not a major consideration in nineteenth century marriages. One pressing reason for matrimony was economic: few women could survive on their own earnings. But men were not immune to economic motivations, as in the case of Jacob Quintus, for whom a youthful widow with a house proved tempting. He married the woman after a brief courtship.[7] For the majority of men, however, their economic need for a wife revolved around the services she could provide, services that allowed her husband to carry out his occupation without concern for domestic matters. As one newlywed put it, it was better to be married than to cook for yourself.[8] Whether domestic tasks were specified or not, the image of a Dutch-American wife in family histories and letters included the capability to handle such chores.

Not only did Dutch-American husbands value their spouses on this ground, they also valued their emotional support, as exemplified in an account of Geertje Bolks (nee Brouwer):

[Seine married] a modest and pious young woman. Everybody who has known mother Bolks will grant that she truly was a gift from God, being exactly the person to help and encourage her husband in his service of the Lord. .. She was deeply devoted to him.[9]

This was about as romantic as any of the mid-nineteenth century accounts. Cornelia van de Luijster surpassed it only slightly by explaining to her parents that you could tell her husband loved her because he bought her a straw hat.[10] In most cases the spouses would merely indicate that they were "happy" with one another if the marriage went well. Perhaps the most candid account concerned a young couple who faced economic hardship in their early years.

Jesus says, "These two," that is, man and wife, "shall be one flesh." But we human beings are still so imperfect that we need time and experience to become "one."[11]

At the turn of the century romantic aspirations became more important in the native-born community, resulting in increasing dissatisfaction with marriages where love was lost, and hence to an increase in the divorce rate.[12] Several factors mitigated against the transfer of this trend into the Dutch-American realm. Most importantly religious sanctions concerning divorce remained strong in Protestant Dutch communities. Group cohesiveness combined with the strength of the patriarchal family model to assure that (at least for church members) persons challenging their marital status would face church intervention and peer group disapproval if they carried their dissatisfaction to the extreme of separation.

Besides economics and emotional support, social considerations were important in the decision to marry since life in most Dutch-American communities was centered around family. To remain single was socially disapproved and often personally distasteful. Group norms dictated that a woman should marry within the religious and ethnic boundaries of her Dutch background, and in the Protestant case these two aspects were closely linked. One Dutch-American exemplified this norm:

"Gerrit isn't going with that girl anymore--the one he is in the picture with. She was an American girl and my folks didn't like that at all. But of course, he's got another girl again, and she is from Holland parents."[13]

The Tuininga family displayed some of the possible consequences of marrying outside the ethnic group. John's wife Elizabeth, an English woman, continually violated norms upheld by his Dutch relatives, such as failing to socialize with her in-laws, and not allowing her husband to smoke. Neither spouse appeared happy with the marriage.[14]

Reports by and about Dutch-American girls indicated they sought to prepare themselves for marriage by an informal apprenticeship in housekeeping, either in their own homes or as domestics in the homes of others. This process was illustrated by a woman who postponed her own wedding in order to learn American cooking and housekeeping through domestic service.[15] But she was an exception, more frequently a young woman in domestic service would gladly exchange her position for that of manager of her own home.[16]

For a wife, management did not mean total control. One example of this phenomenon concerned maternal socialization of children. Women had retained primary responsibility for child care over the century, but so long as the man remained at home, either farming or in some other home-based industry, he could exert a significant influence over child rearing. As men moved into the workplace they increasingly lost these opportunities. Simultaneously the growing recognition of early training as important to a child's development meant that women would take a greater role in this process. At least this was the way the shift functioned in the native-born community.

However, the change took a slightly different shape among Dutch-American Protestants. A prerequisite for this shift to maternal socialization was a stage of modernization that created the separation of male and female spheres. This condition was never fully in place on farms. Furthermore, since most of the Dutch immigrants came from groups escaping the economic consequences of modernization rather than the group that might have embraced the idea of spheres in the Netherlands, the immigrants lacked these gender divisions upon arrival.

The father's role in the home as prescribed by Dutch Calvinism, made it more difficult for him to abdicate the responsibility for a child's education to the mother, just as the family participation in Protestant religion meant a less spherically separated lifestyle. Still, by 1898 an article in *De Gereformeerde Amerikaan* illustrated that one aspect of the separation had entered the Dutch community. The author explained that for a man, the home was a refuge: "There one is refreshed and renewed and filled with a new courage to resume work every time."[17] Whether this recognition came as part of the acculturation process, or through late nineteenth century immigrants whose experience included a more industrialized setting in the Netherlands needs to be explored. In any case, the realization came late and with variations on the American pattern. Similarly, expectations for women's work in the Dutch community differed somewhat for later arrivals. One account from an immigrant of affluent background illustrated this thesis:

> "I never worked in Holland for it was considered disgraceful there for a lady to work, but in America I find it is thought to be disgraceful for a lady not to work."[18]

A woman's contribution to the family economy was substantial, as a few commentators recognized. Alieda Pieters gave an account of some "women's tasks":

Mothers of the large Dutch families were busy women for their daily duties included knitting, sewing, cooking, baking, keeping the house tidy, and tending the children.[19]

Women also produced other household manufactures, from candles and soap to cheese and foodstuffs, items that could sustain and enhance family life. Butter, eggs, and milk often provided a modest income if sold or bartered, and such marketing often fell within a woman's duties. Vrouw Arends, a woman of the Holland, Michigan colony, was a noteworthy example as she trudged from house to house, delivering milk "in pails, which hung from a yoke carried across her shoulders."[20]

Homemaking tasks changed significantly in the late nineteenth and early twentieth centuries as technology made certain tasks obsolete while others became less onerous. Improved transportation meant bringing butter and eggs to market was easier, while clothing manufacture became much simpler as machine produced fabric appeared on a widespread scale and as the sewing machine replaced hand-stitching.[21] These changes affected the Dutch-American community, though they rarely appeared in the writings I consulted.[22] The fact that men wrote many of the family histories could account for part of this lacuna.

Not only did the woman carry on household and marketing tasks, she often helped with jobs on the farm, from care of the vegetable garden and fowl to work in the fields. Childrearing entailed a greater work load during the years of infancy, but when the children grew both boys and girls assisted with housework and took over many of the outdoor chores that previously might have fallen to the wife. Thus Rosa Schreurs Jennings wrote: "What good food mother prepared! That and the endless patching of husking gloves were her contribution to the corn harvest."[23] Nonetheless, images of Dutch-American women in the fields were prominent in accounts of the settlement process, whether it was in the woods of western Michigan or on the prairies of the Dakotas.

The folklore surrounding women in the frontier setting focused on a number of stereotypes, the most prominent of which for the Dutch was that of the helpmate. The frontier woman needed to support her husband, and if she possessed extraordinary characteristics to do so that made her all the more worthy. As one storyteller recounted:

". . . the old Dutchman looked into the face of his deceased wife and said, "Doc, I believe it would have been easier for me to give up my best span of mules than that old woman."[24]

Another example demonstrated this principle, as well as the limits of what was expected from a woman. James de Pree reported that there was a family in Sioux Center which lived in a frame building without much sleeping space. Hence the six sons slept in the attic, despite the lack of a staircase.

The mother, a very tall, strong woman, weighing about two hundred and sixty pounds, was prepared for the emergency, . . .

every evening at bedtime she arose and bent forward, and allowed her boys one by one to climb on her back, and from it to raise themselves through the opening in the low ceiling to the attic....[25]

Strength was considered a useful quality for Dutch-American women. But courage, as manifested in other accounts, was considered exceptional. Women were not expected to take the initiative when faced with a difficult situation; to sit passively or to cry and call for help were the responses that writers often noted without comment, indicating they expected such behavior.

Attempting to be a good housewife under pioneer conditions was problematic. The image of cleanliness associated with Dutch households met the reality of sod houses and pine floors. One characteristic that differentiated Dutch-American cleanliness from that of the native-born was the use of wooden shoes in the early years. Numerous writers noted how the klompen could be shed easily upon entering a house. Other measures of cleanliness that paralleled standards in different ethnic groups still retained a Dutch flavor according to some writers. In the case of the Schreurs family the mother and daughter carried out the major house-cleaning on Saturday night in preparation for the Sabbath. The floor scrubbing was difficult because the mother refused to tolerate a quick mopping during the week "that would eventually make the boards grimy, which, Dutch born housewife that she was, she could not endure.[26]

Bedbugs, mosquitoes and snakes survived the best efforts at cleanliness in frontier dwellings. But still the efforts continued, upheld by group norms. At the turn of the century *De Gereformeerde Amerikaan* carried an article on domestic and family life among Dutch-Americans. The author professed that women needed to keep a balance between being ostentatious and being sloppy in housekeeping, but the criticism struck harder at the disorderly type:

> In the latter [sloppy housewife] case one also finds the greatest negligence about everything that belongs to her care and by which a woman can promote so much joy in domestic life. . . dirty and sloppy housewives are found only as great exceptions among Netherlanders.[27]

Besides cleanliness, the Dutch woman of popular image possessed a number of other virtues, or at least the community hoped she did. First, she was supposed to accept her lot without complaint. Christina Plemp's account of settlement in South Dakota upheld this view:

> ...our thoughts go back to those other women, isolated sometimes for weeks . . . uncomplainingly taking up their daily tasks. Strange it was there were so few complaints, so little murmuring of discontent.[28]

While silent suffering may have been the ideal, it was not always the reality. The things that women complained about, and the reactions of the commentators to these complaints were instructive as to proper roles. If her husband did not provide for the family adequately a woman had grounds for complaint. Similarly, if the housing was insufficient or if the bugs were bothersome, a woman might rail. Anna Brown portrayed her mother as a nagging wife, complaining about her husband's membership in the Masons, his selfishness, his ex-fiancee, and anything else that struck her.[29] The severity of her critique was striking since Brown demonstrated her mother had reason to be dissatisfied on several counts.

Another reason to complain came if the family moved without the wife's consent. In the case of migration she often faced a situation of divided loyalties. She could not retain the same intimate ties with her family and friends or care for her parents in their old age if she accompanied her husband to America. While most women may have supported the decision to move, numerous accounts noted the wife's reluctance to leave her homeland. Even when the decision was a joint one the record often indicated that she had to be convinced. In the Tamme van den Bosch family the daughter reported that they reached a point where everything was ready for departure "except mother."[30]

Subsequent moves within the United States could elicit similar responses, as exemplified by the Schreurs family. When Bette's husband quit his job and informed her that he was buying a farm on the prairie his wife was shocked and less than enthusiastic. Her dismay merely exacerbated her husband's anger.[31] He expected her to accept his decisions without complaint. Not all Dutch-Americans faced this kind of problem. Geographic stability for the group was high, and if Grand Rapids, Michigan was at all exemplary, the rate was much higher than for comparable groups in other cities.[32] Such permanence of communities would exacerbate the issue of moving for women who opposed their husbands.

Another situation of conflicting loyalties could occur in the case of religious disputes. Schisms were common in the Protestant community, and since Calvinist doctrine dictated that the husband was the religious head of the household, the woman supposedly followed him. But what about cases where the husband changed religions? The ramifications of a husband leaving the Hervormde Kerk in the Netherlands, or the Reformed Church in America could be tremendous. A wife might face persecution or at the least social ostracism from former friends. If she disagreed with him on theological grounds she faced a paradox of opposing his authority in order to maintain her position. Instead, the pattern could replicate that of Jacob Vander Meulen's mother, who began as a devout young woman, but lapsed from regular religious practice when her husband fell away from the church. Then, as her husband converted and joined the Seceders, she returned to her earlier role as a pious wife. Significantly, the commentator in this case did not indicate there was anything irregular in the fact that she changed her position.

Women retained a voice in evangelical pursuits, as seen in the case of James Moerdyke, who described his cousin's conversion:

> I cannot describe the change this produced in her character. She had been a vain, worldly woman, but was completely changed. She became sober minded, sedate, and ready to exhort everyone and lived earnestly for the Lord. Quite often she admonished me, spoke of God's service and exerted great influence on me.[33]

In other cases a woman could begin to train her children in Christian precepts in the home, or encourage them in their training at church. Further, a woman could console and encourage other women when they faced sorrow and bereavement, as with the death of a child, a common occurrence.

The image of a pious individual did not include tolerance of persons from other religious backgrounds. In such encounters gender was not particularly relevant. Adriaan Zwemer's account of meeting a Catholic woman upon arrival in the new world exemplified this prejudice.

> I asked her as well as I could if she knew and loved the Lord Jesus [she showed her crucifix] I said that . . . Christ must be in our heart, not only on the outside. The women now understood to what church I belonged, for her only answer was "Protestant".[34]

Such biases existed between the Protestant denominations as well, as revealed in a church trial where the accused woman was charged with desecrating the Sabbath by attending the Baptist church.[35]

The pious woman was one of the most common images of Dutch-Americans. But the piety of Protestant Dutch-American women differed from that of the native-born; there was little sense of the woman as moral superior, as arbiter of appropriate behavior in the family. In the writings of the early generations men held this role. There was a fine line between a woman's training in theology and going beyond the bounds of proper roles in the church. Unlike native-born women, the secondary sources indicate Dutch-American women were not the leaders of progressive reform campaigns in their churches, nor were they the primary purveyors of Christian education in the church. The feminization of religion that stuck the native-born community in the early nineteenth century did not become part of the religious adaptation that Dutch immigrants made to the United States.[36] By the turn of the century Protestant Dutch-American women had developed a number of organizations, particularly women's missionary societies. But in endeavors where native-born women predominated over their male counterparts in taking the initiative, Dutch men were less likely to have relinquished their leading role.

One area where women did hold sway was household management. Though they often did not have control of the overall budget, Dutch-American women, like native-born women, were in charge of making ends meet on the amount they were allotted. The image of frugality rests largely on the efforts of the wife. Letters and family histories supplied numerous examples of frugality in practice, from exhortations to exercise self-denial to delivering a baby without a doctor's aid, thus saving the family a bill.[37] Henry Lucas, inveterate commentator on Dutch-Americans, gave a more impressionistic evaluation:

> ...the mother managed [the household], frequently with an amazing resourcefulness, which overcame the greatest poverty.... Cooking was plain and, indeed, bordered on the monotonous. The excessive economy practiced by the Dutch restricted their diet, frequently to the point of endangering their health. In their desire to save money and to get ahead, the earlier immigrants subsisted on a diet of coffee, bread, and potatoes.[38]

But in contrast to this stereotype, the image of the Dutch-American woman as hostess incorporated an adequate if not abundant supply of food at her disposal, particularly little treats to accompany coffee. The Dutch-American woman was frequently pictured as a hostess for a koffie kletz, and whenever someone dropped in the coffee or tea water was soon hot. Or at least many writers reported this phenomenon. Edward Harrington demonstrated how this hospitality was carried out even under extreme conditions in his account of coming to visit a woman's home shortly after a losing battle with a skunk. Stench notwithstanding, the Dutch-American hostess offered her guests coffee and pancakes.[39]

The image of the hostess has not received much attention in writings in women's history, but I would speculate that the ethnic flavor of the coffee lunch meant it was more prominent among the Dutch than among some other groups. In accounts written by Dutch-Americans hospitality was a source of pride or condemnation. Rosa Schreurs Jennings complimented her mother on serving Indians, wandering tramps, and colored lecturers.[40] The prejudice against these individuals in the community came through as clearly as the fact that Mrs. Schreurs fed them. Withholding hospitality engendered disapproval from the Dutch-American community, as seen in the account of Anna Brown. Brown's mother, an English woman, held aloof from coffee lunches at her mother-in-law's on Sundays, "though in true politeness grandma's guests always came over and made a social call on Jan's wife."[41] During the week Jan would go to his parents' home to get his coffee lunch and to enjoy a chat in Dutch.[42] This ritual of sociability was a remnant of a pre-industrial world that had been lost to men in the wage work force. For paid laborers of many backgrounds the saloon fulfilled these functions, with a concomitant loss of status for women's gatherings in the old fashion.

A final image relating to Dutch immigrant women concerned their interest in beauty, both in terms of aesthetics and in terms of physical appearance. A history of Clymer, New York cited flower gardens filled with "old-fashioned" blooms as one manifestation of women's taste for beauty, while Henry Harmeling cited the pictures his aunt put on the walls to decorate the cabin. Alieda Pieters provided a somewhat different image of women seeking to share beauty, recounting how women in church might pass a colognedosje, a little box filled with cologne, up and down the women's pew for the olfactory enjoyment of the others.[43]

In some cases an enjoyment of beauty came in conflict with church norms, as with jewelry brought from the old country. Rings, beads, and the gold ornaments that highlighted head pieces became contributions in a fundraising campaign for an orphanage in Holland, Michigan. When a mother expressed her dismay at the loss of these heirlooms, the minister assured her that these were 'vanities,' not becoming Christians."[44]

But the most common reference to beauty relating to Dutch women occurred in the context of a man describing the process of finding a mate. Over and over men reported they were struck initially by the beauty of the woman whom they married shortly thereafter. Commentators associated beauty with a "successful" marriage, e.g. marriage to a financially well-off man.[45] But according to one writer after the turn of the century, a man had to be careful around American women:

> "There certainly is a good supply of lovely girls here, but you have to watch your step. If you attempt to make conversation with a young girl on the street, she may just call a policeman and he will toss you in jail . . . Yes, the stinkers do in fact have such a law here. . . But there are some lovely girls who will not report you . . . for example, who are happy to take a seat next to you in church."[46]

How Dutch-American men defined beauty differed, and included such adjectives as "stout," "buxom," and "healthy looking." The hefty frame that Americans associated with Dutch persons was the kind of build that attracted many of these men, at least until after the turn of the century when native-born norms emphasizing a thin physique began to intrude. Even then the change came more slowly to the Dutch-American community, perhaps owing to culinary habits.

Other commentators saw beauty in a woman's virtues, such as an anonymous poem titled "A Dutch Girl," which included the following stanza:

> Wherefore I wish, as is a maiden's way, to hold enchained one desire, that also for me a fair rose may bloom in wedlock's garden . Why, then, be misled by craft and appearance? False appearances I dislike; a woman's modesty is founded in her virtue.[47]

What do these images of Dutch-American women display for us? They demonstrate that the Dutch-American woman did not follow many of the patterns of native-born society during the late nineteenth century. The reasons for this difference included a variety of factors: the class background of these women, who rarely had lived in a world of separate spheres prior to emigration; the religious ideology among the Protestant group that maintained a strong patriarchal family authority long after it disappeared from the more popular culture of America; and the relatively stable settlement patterns that allowed the ethnic heritage to flourish. A second conclusion from this study is that we need to uncover the history of Dutch-American women, and to be sensitive to gender issues when looking at various aspects of Dutch immigrant life. My research has barely scratched the surface of this topic. As Nellie Van Kol wrote: "In all things there is a song; But the song lies in the soul of things, And deeply must thou enter in, Or thou wilt not, not find the song."[48]

NOTES

[1] Jacob Van der Zee, *The Hollanders of Iowa* (Iowa City: State Historical Society of Iowa, 1912), p. 299.

[2] See for example the discussion of Barbara Welter's "Cult of True Womanhood" in Nancy Cott's *The Bonds of Womanhood* (New Haven: Yale University Press, 1977), p. 197-198.

[3] What an impressionistic account of images cannot achieve on this generalized level is a sense of the diversity within the group. Rural/urban, regional, religious, and other divisions receive little attention.

[4] Robert P. Swierenga, "Dutch Immigrant Demography, 1820-1880," *Journal of Family History* 5 (Winter 1980): 398.

[5] See Suzanne Sinke, "Dutch Immigrant Women in the Late Nineteenth Century: A Comparative Analysis," Masters Thesis, Kent State University, 1983, Chapter 4.

[6] Native-born is used throughout this paper to indicate non-immigrant whites.

[7] Jacob Quintus, "A Backward Glance," in *Dutch Immigrant Memoirs and Related Writings*, vol. 2, Henry S. Lucas, arr. (Assen, Netherlands: Van Gorcum & Co., 1955), p. 87.

[8] Herbert J. Brinks, *Schrijf Spoedig Terug* (The Hague: Uitgeverij Boekencentrum, 1978), p. 103.

[9] James de Pree, "Reverend Seine Bolks," *Dutch Immigrant Memoirs*, vol. 2, pp. 379-380.

[10] John H. Yzenbaard, "'America' Letters from Holland," *Michigan History* 32 (March 1948): 49.

[11] Reijer van Zwaluwenburg, "Life Sketch," in *Dutch Immigrant Memoirs*, vol. 1, p. 426.

[12] Elaine Tyler May makes this argument in *Great Expectations* (Chicago: University of Chicago Press, 1980).

[13] Arthur Plaiser Correspondence, 19 December 1912, quoted in Herbert J. Brinks, "Immigrant Letters: the Religious Context of Dutch American Ethnicity," in *Dutch Immigration to North America*, Herman Ganzevoort and Mark Boekelman, eds. (Toronto: The Multicultural History Society of Ontario, 1983), p. 138.

[14] Anna Brown, "Life Story of John Tuininga," in *Dutch Immigrant Memoirs*, vol. 2, pp. 192ff.

[15] Rosa Schreurs Jennings, "A Scrap of Americana," *Annals of Iowa* 29 (April 1948): 291.

[16] Dingman Versteeg makes this comment in impressionistic terms concerning "comforting" lonely domestics in Kalamazoo, while Reijer van Zwaluwenburg provides one concrete example; D. Versteeg, *The Pilgrim Fathers of the West*, trns. Wm. K. Reinsma (Grand Rapids: C.M. Loomis and Co., 1886), p. 95; and "Reijer van Zwaluwenburg's Life Sketch," in *Dutch Immigant Memoirs*, vol.1 pp. 425-426.

[17] Walter Lagerwey, *Neen Nederland, 'k Vergeet U Niet* (Baarn: Bosch & Keuning, 1982), p. 82.

[18] Quoted in Van der Zee, *Hollanders of Iowa*, p. 325.

[19] Alieda J. Pieters, *A Dutch Settlement in Michigan* (Grand Rapids: The Reformed Press, 1923), p. 101.

[20] Anna C. Post, "Reminiscences," in *Dutch Immigrant Memoirs*, vol. 1, p. 403-404.

[21] See Joan Jensen, "Cloth, Butter, and Boarders: Women's Household Production for the Market," *Review of Radical Political Economics* 12 (Summer 1980): 14-24, on some of these changes.

[22] Rosa Schreurs Jennings, "A Scrap of Americana" is one exception, noting the purchase of a sewing machine, carpet, and hand washing machine, p. 296.

[23] Rosa Schreurs Jennings, "Second-Generation Americans," *Annals of Iowa* 29 (April 1949): 592.

[24] Quoted in Beverly J. Stoeltje, "'A Helpmate for Man Indeed' : The Image of the Frontier Woman," in *Women and Folklore*, ed. Claire Farrer (Austin: University of Texas Press, 1975), p. 37.

[25] James de Pree, "Reminiscences of Early Settlement at Sioux Center," in *Dutch Immigrant Memoirs*, vol. 2, p. 240.

[26] Jennings, "Second Generation," p. 593.

[27] Reproduced in Lagerwey, *Neen Nederland*, pg. 81 (my translation).

[28] Christina Plemp, "Memoirs," in *Dutch Immigrant Memoirs*, vol. 2, p. 333.

[29] Anna Brown, "Life Story of John Tuininga," in *Dutch Immigrant Memoirs*, vol. 2, see pp. 193-194.

[30] Mrs. J.H. Boone, "Journey and Arrival of Tamme van den Bosch," in *Dutch Immigrant Memoirs*, vol. 1, p. 259.

[31] Jennings, "Second Generation," p. 589.

[32] See David Vanderstel, "Dutch Immigrant Neighborhood Development in Grand Rapids, 1850-1900," in *The Dutch in Grand Rapids*, Robert P. Swierenga, ed. (New Brunswick, N.J.: Rutgers University Press, 1985), passim.

[33]James Moerdyke, "Autobiography," in *Dutch Immigrant Memoirs*, vol. 2, p. 911.

[34]Adriaan Zwemer, "Life and Emigration to America," in *Dutch Immigrant Memoirs*, vol. 2, p. 435.

[35]Suzanne Sinke, "Dutch Immigrant Women in the Late Nineteenth Century: A Comparative analysis," Masters Thesis, Kent State University, 1983, pp. 85-86.

[36]See Ann Douglas, *The Feminization of American Culture* (New York: Avon Books, 1977), Chapters 2, 3.

[37]See for example Yzenbaard, "'America' Letters," p. 53; and Jennings, "A Scrap of Americana," p. 295.

[38]Henry Lucas, *Netherlanders in America* (Ann Arbor: University of Michigan Press, 1955), p. 621.

[39]Edward J. Harrington, "Early Reminiscences," in *Dutch Immigrant Memoirs*, vol. 1, p. 386.

[40]Jennings, "A Scrap of Americana," p. 294.

[41]Anna Brown, "Life Story of John Tuininga," in *Dutch Immigrant Memoirs*, vol. 2, p. 193.

[42]Ibid., p. 193.

[43]Chautauqua County History, quoted in Sinke, "Dutch Immigrant Women," p. 74; Henry Harmeling, "History of Amsterdam and Cedar Grove," in *Dutch Immigrant Memoirs*, vol. 2, p. 111; and Pieters, *Dutch Settlement in Michigan*, p. 115.

[44]Engbertus van der Veen, "Life Reminiscences," in *Dutch Immigrant Memoirs*, vol. 1, p. 510.

[45]A clear example of this association appears in Edward Cahill, "Old Colony Days in Holland," in *Dutch Immigrant Memoirs*, vol. 1, p. 374.

[46]Arthur Plaiser Correspondence, 19 December 1912, quoted in Brinks, "Immigrant Letters," p. 138.

[47]Quoted and translated in Lucas, *Netherlanders in America*, p. 608.

[48]Quoted in Lagerwey, *Neen Nederland*, p. 266.

BIBLIOGRAPHY

Atteridg, Louise van Nederynen. "Dutch Lore in Holland and at Castleton, New York." *New York Folklore Quarterly* 10 (1954): 245-265.

Bannan, Helen M. "Warrior Women: Immigrant Mothers in the Works of Their Daughters." *Women's Studies* 6 (1979) : 165-177.

Bratt, James D. *Dutch Calvinism in Modern America*. Grand Rapids, William B. Eerdmans, 1984.

Brinks, Herbert J. "Immigrant Letters: the Religious Context of Dutch American Ethnicity." In *Dutch Immigration to North America*, pp.

131-146. Edited by Herman Ganzevoort and Mark Boekelman. Toronto: The Multicultural History Society of Ontario, 1983.

Schrijf Spoedig Terug: Brieven van Immigranten in Amerika 1847-1920. The Hague: Uitgeverij Boekencentrum, 1978.

Cott, Nancy F. *The Bonds of Womanhood: "Woman's Sphere" in New England, 1780-1835.* New Haven: Yale University Press, 1977.

Douglas, Ann. *The Feminization of American Culture.* New York: Avon Books, 1977.

Epstein, Barbara Leslie. *The Politics of Domesticity: Women, Evangelism, and Temperance in Nineteenth-Century America.* Middletown, Conn.: Wesleyan University Press, 1981.

Friedman, Jean E., and Shade, William G., eds. *Our American Sisters: Women in American Life and Thought.* Lexington, Mass.: D.C. Heath & Co., 1982.

Gordon, Michael. "The Ideal Husband as Depicted in the Nineteenth-Century Marriage Manual." In *The American Man*, pp. 145-157. Edited by Elizabeth H. Pleck and Joseph H. Pleck. Englewood Cliffs, N.J.: Prentice-Hall, 1980.

Herman, Sondra R. "Loving Courtship or the Marriage Market? The Ideal and Its Critics, 1871-1911." In *Our American Sisters*, pp. 329-347. Edited by Jean E. Friedman and William G. Shade. Lexington, Mass.: D.C. Heath & Co., 1982.

Honduis, Katherine N. "The American Folk Idea of the Dutch." *Western Folklore* 11 (1952): 29-31.

Jennings, Rosa Schreurs. "A Scrap of Americana." *Annals of Iowa* 29 (April 1948): 290-297.

Jennings, Rosa Schreurs. "Second-Generation Americans." *Annals of Iowa* 29 (April 1949): 589-598.

Jensen, Joan. "Cloth, Butter and Boarders: Women's Household Production for the Market." *Review of Radical Political Economics* 12 (Summer 1980) 14-24.

Kirshenblatt-Gimblett, Barbara. "Studying Immigrant and Ethnic Folklore." In *Handbook of American Folklore*, pp. 39-47. Edited by Richard Dorson. Bloomington: Indiana University Press, 1983.

Klymasz, Robert B. "From Immigrant to Ethnic Folklore: A Canadian View of Process and Transition." *Journal of the Folklore Institute* 10 (1973): 131-139.

Lagerwey, Walter. "Dutch Literary Culture in America, 1850-1950." In *The Dutch in America: Immigration, Settlement, and Cultural Change*, pp. 243-272. Edited by Robert P. Swierenga. New Brunswick, N.J.: Rutgers University Press, 1985.

_____. *Neen Nederland, k' Vergeet U Niet: Een Beeld van het Immigratenleven in Amerika Tussen 1846 en 1945 in Verhalen, Schetsen en Gedichten.* Baarn: Bosch & Keuning, 1982.

Lucas, Henry. *Netherlanders in America.* Ann Arbor: University of Michigan Press, 1955.

Lucas, Henry S., arr. *Dutch Immigrant Memoirs and Related Writings.* 2 vols. Assen, Netherlands: Van Gorcum & Co., 1955.

May, Elaine Tyler. *Great Expectations: Marriage & Divorce in Post Victorian America.* Chicago: University of Chicago Press, 1980.

Pieters, Alieda J. *A Dutch Settlement in Michigan.* Grand Rapids, Michigan: The Reformed Press, 1923.

Riley, Glenda. "'Not Gainfully Employed'": Women on the Iowa Frontier, 1833-1870." In *Our American Sisters*, pp. 267-290. Edited by Jean E. Friedman and William G. Shade. Lexington, Mass.: D.C. Heath & Co., 1982.

Ryan, Mary P. *Cradle of the Middle Class: The Family in Oneida County, New York, 1790-1865.* Cambridge: Cambridge University Press, 1981.

Sackett, Marjorie. "Folk Recipes as a Measure of Intercultural Penetration." *Journal of American Folklore* 85 (1972): 77-81.

Sinke, Suzanne. "Dutch Immigrant Women in the Late Nineteenth Century: A Comparative Analysis." Masters Thesis, Kent State University, 1983.

Smith-Rosenberg, Carroll. "The Female World of Love and Ritual: Relations Between Women in Nineteenth-Century America." In *A Heritage of Her Own*, pp. 311-342. Edited by Nancy F. Cott and Elizabeth H. Pleck. New York: Simon and Schuster, 1979.

Stern, Stephen. "Ethnic Folklore and the Folklore of Ethnicity." *Western Folklore* 36 (1977): 7-32.

Stoeltje, Beverly J. "'A Helpmate for Man Indeed': The Image of the Frontier Woman." In *Women and Folklore*, pp. 25-41. Edited by Claire R. Farrer. Austin: University of Texas Press, 1975.

Swierenga, Robert P. "Dutch Immigrant Demography, 1820-1880." *Journal of Family History* 5 (Winter 1980): 390-405.

Swierenga, Robert P., ed. *The Dutch in America: Immigration, Settlement, and Cultural Change.* New Brunswick, N.J.: Rutgers University Press, 1985.

Taylor, Archer. "Dutch in Proverbial and Conventional Use." *Western Folklore* 11 (1952): 219.

Vanderstel, David G. "Dutch Immigrant Neighborhood Development in Grand Rapids, 1850-1900." In *The Dutch in America*, pp. 125-155. Edited by Robert P. Swierenga. New Brunswick, N.J.: Rutgers University Press, 1985.

Vander Stoep, Arie. "Tulip Time in Orange City: a Brief History." *Annals of Iowa* 38 (Spring 1967): 598-609.

Vander Werf, Dorothy DeLano. "Evidences of Old Holland in the Speech of Grand Rapids." *American Speech* 33 (December 1958): 301-304.

Van der Zee, Jacob. *The Hollanders of Iowa*. Iowa City: The State Historical Society of Iowa, 1912.

Vanek, Joann. "Time Spent in Housework." In *A Heritage of Her Own*, pp. 499-506. Edited by Nancy F. Cott and Elizabeth H. Pleck. New York: Simon and Schuster, 1979.

Versteeg, D. *The Pilgrim Fathers of the West: A History of the Struggles of the Dutch Colonies in Michigan. Also a Sketch of the Establishment of a Colony in Pella, Iowa*. Translated by Wm. K. Reinsma. Grand Rapids: C.M. Loomis and Co., 1886.

Welter, Barbara. "The Cult of True Womanhood: 1820-1860." In *The American Family in Social-Historical Perspective*, pp. 313-333. Edited by Michael Gordon. New York: St. Martin's Press, 1978.

Yzenbaard, John H. "'America' Letters from Holland." *Michigan History* 32 (March 1948): 37-65.

VOICES FROM THE FREE CONGREGATION AT GRAND RAPIDS, MICHIGAN
An Introduction to the Holland Unitarian Church 1885-1918

Dr. Walter Langerwey
Calvin College

The broad outlines of Dutch immigration to America have been well chronicled and documented by eminent historians like Henry S. Lucas, J. Van Hinte, and Gerald F. De Jong. Increasingly historians are now engaged in analytical research into the broad economic and social factors of immigration after the manner of Robert Swierenga or providing a focus in depth as does James Bratt in his study of the intellectual history of Dutch Calvinism in America. Others were researching the many lacunae in the history of Dutch and Flemish, Protestant and Catholic immigration. Johan Snapper has high praise for *The Dutch in America: Immigration, Settlement, and Cultural Change*, ed. Robert P. Swierenga, but adds that... "this reader misses information about those immigrating Dutchmen who were neither Reformed nor Christian Reformed and may not have lived in Grand Rapids or Pella, but whose Dutch identity has not necessarily vanished. The book implies, at least through omission, that there is no Dutch-American history of immigration outside the church-dominated neighborhoods. And yet there is abundant empirical evidence to the contrary."[1] Whether that empirical evidence, in the absence of organized non-church communities, is sufficient to write a history is open to question. Indeed, even the story of church-dominated Dutch (and Flemish) immigration, particularly that of Roman Catholics and liberal Dutch Protestants is far from told. Thus there was between 1885 and 1918 in Grand Rapids, Michigan an organized non-Reformed community, one that preferred not to be identified as a church, *De Vrije Gemeente* (The Free Congregation), whose story is only hinted at in the standard histories. Most of these Dutch immigrants were *Vrijzinnigen* (Free Thinkers or Modernists) from the Hervormde Kerk (the national church) in the Netherlands who did not feel at home with the *Afscheiding* (Secessionist) Reformed Churches in America whether in Grand Rapids, Kalamazoo, Chicago, Orange City or Castalia (Dakota). These Dutch Modernists constituted a small minority within the much larger orthodox community which tended to shun and exclude them. For a period of some fifteen years they were held together under the dynamic leadership of the Rev. F.W.N. Hugenholtz. He served a congregation in Grand Rapids, Michigan from December 1885 until his sudden death from pneumonia in February 1900.

Historian Henry S. Lucas gives scant treatment to this unusual phenomenon: a liberal Protestant church in the midst of an overwhelmingly Calvinist community. Though he cites as his source no less than three volumes of Rev. Hugenholtz's *Stemmen uit de Vrije Gemeente te Grand Rapids* (Voices from the Free Congregation at Grand Rapids, Michigan),

125

Lucas devotes scarcely two pages to the Free Congregation(s) but does give a concise account of that history:[2]

> Among the Hollanders who settled in Grand Rapids were a few who represented the liberal movement in the Reformed Church in the Netherlands, and who therefore had scant sympathy for Reformed teaching. In 1875, these people made some effort to organize, but they failed. During 1883 and 1884 the group was revived, and in 1885 it effected a permanent organization. After correspondence with Professor Abraham Kuenen of the University of Leiden, Dominie W.F.N. Hugenholtz, the pastor of a Reformed church at Santpoort, near Haarlem, was called to lead the group. He was inducted on December 9, 1885. Hugenholtz was a capable person, and the editor of *De Hervorming* (The Reformation), a paper which advocated "advanced" ideas about religion. This movement, however, was not able to thrive among a population devoted to Reformed teachings. Similar efforts were aimed to found "free" congregations in Kalamazoo and Chicago. The Grand Rapids congregation speedily declined, and by the close of the First World War it had disbanded.

We must bear in mind that the *Stemmen* was the theological journal which for several years was the voice of liberal Dutch Protestantism in America. J. van Hinte gives a much more sympathetic treatment to the Dutch liberal community and gives it greater attention:[3]

> *De Stemmen* (The Voices) was edited by Rev. W.F.N. Hugenholtz, who was also the publisher from 1886 to 1890, while P.T. Hugenholtz took care of the administration. As the name indicates, the paper was the vehicle of the religious liberal Dutchmen who organized the Free Congregation in Grand Rapids. This group, which counted 316 members by the end of 1889, was supported by the Unitarians in the United States and was acknowledged as a foreign branch of the *Nederlandsche Protestantenbond* (The Dutch Protestant Confederation). The Free Congregation had like-minded friends in both Kalamazoo and in Chicago; in the latter city an independent group was established in 1889, numbering sixty members by the end of that year. Because of this *De Stemmen* appeared in 1890 as *Stemmen uit de Vrije Hollandsche Gemeenten in Amerika* (Voices from the Free Dutch Congregations in America), edited by the earlier-cited Reverend Hugenholtz, but now published by the congregation at Grand Rapids. Interesting information about the social importance of the Dutch labor element in the Furniture city appeared. It also took the intolerance of the orthodox Dutch severely to task.

This publication was followed by a bi-weekly, *Het Zondagsblad* (The Sunday Paper) which appeared for three years till July 1893, but no copies of it are known to exist.[4]

The Rev. F.W.N. Hugenholtz was a half-brother to two Dutch theologians, Dr. Philip Reinhard Hugenholtz and Dr. Petrus Hermannus Hugenholtz, who in 1877 seceded from the Hervormde Kerk (the national Reformed Church) and were instrumental in the founding of the *Vrije Gemeente* (Free Congregation) in Amsterdam. That history is the subject of a Master's Thesis by Ditsy Verdonk which demonstrates the relation of the Hugenholtz brothers to the origins of the *Vrije Gemeente*.[5] This congregation was the only one of its kind in the Netherlands, other seceding liberal preachers and their follower joining the *Remonstrantsche Broederschap* (The Remonstrant Brotherhood). The Amsterdam *Vrije Gemeente* was thus a sister-congregation to the congregation(s) in America.

The Rev. P.H. Hugenholtz was the leader of the Amsterdam congregation and editor of *Stemmen uit de Vrije Gemeente* (Voices from the Free Congregation) for nearly 32 years (1878-1909). The Amsterdam *Stemmen* (Voices) at times exchanged information with the Grand Rapids *Stemmen* (Voices). The Amsterdam *Stemmen* are especially valuable as a source of information on the Grand Rapids congregation after the Grand Rapids *Stemmen* ceased publication in 1880. Thus the Amsterdam *Stemmen* reports the death of the Rev. F.W.N. Hugenholtz and a eulogy spoken by his son F.W.N. Hugenholtz, Jr. at the dedication of a memorial tablet in the Amsterdam "church" on October 14, 1900.[6]

F.W.N. Hugenholtz, like his half-brothers, was a leader of the movement of religious modernism in the Netherlands during the last quarter of the 19th century. Since 1870 Modernist clergymen were associated in the *Nederlandsche Protestantenbond* (The Netherlands Protestant Federation). The weekly, *De Hervorming* (The Reformation), in 1875 became the official organ of the *Protestantenbond* and F.W.N. Hugenholtz was its editor from 1876 to 1885. The "advanced" theology of the Modernist clergy men embraced tenets like the following: 1) in matters of faith one is free from all authority; 2) miracles are impossible; 3) God works in the natural course of events; 4) the bodily resurrection of Jesus is denied by many; 5) Jesus is not the supernatural leader of the believers; 6) the Easter message is one of renewal after a wintry death; 7) to be a Christian is to live like Jesus and Modernism is but the continuation of the Reformation.[7] The Modernist view of the Bible is also radically different from that of orthodoxy. P.H. Hugenholtz articulates the radical Modernist view as follows: "The consistent Modernist does not have one bible, but numerous bibles, the bible of mankind; the voice of God sounds forth to him in all ages and so the testimonies of pious people and of wise people in all ages must be gathered."[8] Several volumes of such sayings were published by P.H. Hugenholtz under the title *Levenslicht* (Light of Life). These volumes of the sayings of the pious and the wise were regarded by the liberals as the bibles of mankind.

The Hugenholtz brothers, and that includes the half-brother in Grand Rapids, had distanced themselves greatly from orthodox Christianity. Verdonk summarizes the distance as follows:[9]

> They proclaimed...the immanence of God and departed from traditional Christology and soteriology. Their ecclesiology was very liberal, as was their view of the Bible. Their anthropology was un-Calvinistic: they did not view man as incapable of doing any good and of being inclined to all evil, but on the contrary as being very capable of doing good... the gulf between their faith and that of orthodoxy had become exceedingly great.

When he moved to Grand Rapids, F.W.N. Hugenholtz became the outspoken defender of this liberal theology as pulpiteer, as publisher, and as citizen. He engaged in a vigorous polemic with the editors of several leading religious publications, notably of *De Wachter* (The Watchman), *De Grondwet* (The Constitution), and *De Hope* (The Hope). It is this dialogue with orthodoxy as well as his active involvement in public affairs, and his perceptive commentary on the American scene that makes W.F.N. Hugenholtz's *Stemmen Uit de Vrije Gemeente* such an interesting and valuable document.

One of our principal sources of information on F.W.N. Hugenholtz is the eulogies spoken at the memorial service held at *De Vrije Gemeente* (The Free Congregation) in Amsterdam on October 14, 1900. It is especially the tribute spoken by his son, F.W.N. Hugenholtz, Jr., to which I am indebted for much of the information that follows. Hugenholtz Jr. highlights some of the traits which made his father, the religious idealist, such an outstanding leader.[10] Hugenholtz practiced what he preached: "...Everything that he proclaimed in public was deeply experiential and experienced truth; the ideal which he held up to others for attainment, he sought most scrupulously to realize in his own life."[11] Another characteristic reflected in his ministry is: ..."an unwavering faith in, an imperturbable love for all that was human."[12] Already in the Netherlands his love for mankind and his social involvement were evident:[13]

> That made him a democrat, the man of the people in the best sense of the word. He was so already in the Netherlands. Testimonials are still to be found in the nursery schools at Delden, Zierikzee, and Santpoort, and the so-called red village (*'t roode dorp*) in his second congregation, a series of workers dwellings well built and obtainable for ownership on easy terms; all these attest to his desire to bring about practical improvement in the lot of the working class. But America was the country where his democratic principles could flourish in fertile soil. After all, the class differences of the Old World had not yet penetrated here, society had not erected so many walls of separation here between one human being and another.

It is not surprising that this preacher should become an advocate of the working man in America. Hugenholtz Jr. calls attention, for example, to his father's Labor Day speech on the first American May Day in 1887:[14]

...the fear of a new revolution which many people had, he deemed to be justified, unless religion finally had a voice in matters and made its influence felt; religion which had been enjoined to silence by a political economy which preached that the development of society must be left to its own, that the common good was best served when everyone looked after his own interests. Only if everyone was thoroughly convinced of the wholesome true piety of Jesus, could the calamities which threatened our society be diverted.

The idealism of Hugenholtz is reflected in his belief that attempts to improve the lot of the worker will be futile unless they are preceded by character building, the inculcation of values. Hugenholtz was deeply impressed by the then famous work *Progress and Poverty* by Henry George who...

pointed to private property as the deepest cause of all social ills, and proposed as a remedy the 'single tax', a simple tax on land, equal to its rental value, by which land speculation might be ended once and for all and the rich treasury of nature would be available to all on equal conditions.[15]

The Dutch preacher joined the "Single-Tax Club" of Grand Rapids and even arranged for Henry George to speak in the city. Increasingly Hugenholtz became the spokesman for social reform in Grand Rapids, using his pulpit to proclaim his views. He argued that... "religion and life are one and inseparable. What is good outside the church is also good inside the church."[16] He insisted that "...religion must not be anxiously preserved in a neat container to be shown once a week, but it must be the yeast which leavens the whole loaf."[17] Since the ideal of national reform was a distant goal, Hugenholtz addressed himself to immediate ways of helping the poor. At a meeting of Unitarians in Chicago, he had been introduced to the idea of Associated Charities, "...a central information bureau which attempts to coordinate the work of many charitable organizations providing poor relief and often working at cross purposes, thus doing more harm than good."[18] The attempt had been successful in Chicago and Hugenholtz was determined to set up such an organization in Grand Rapids. He enjoyed the cooperation of Professor K. Hemkes of Calvin College and Seminary. In an article which appeared in *De Standaard* (The Standard) and in *De Vrijheids Banier* (The Banner of Freedom) Hemkes strongly urged all to participate. There was a good turn out for the planning meeting, though no clergymen, Hugenholtz notes, were present. But the plan failed, says Hugenholtz Jr., because of the "...dogmatic suspicion of orthodox diaconates which from the start had opposed the undertaking if only because it was initiated by the Modernists, and without this cooperation [of the orthodox community] nothing could come of the matter, because the greatest number of poor were to be found precisely among the Holland population."[19]

The Rev. Hugenholtz continued to study the ideas of the Socialists and finally became convinced that Henry George had not gone far enough: "...only Socialism, the common ownership of all that is essential to the conditions of life for every individual can bring a radical improvement in the existing conditions."[20] Since religion and life could not be separated they had to be integrated into what the Rev. Hugenholtz regarded as a higher understanding of the Christian religion. "Only socialism can provide the foundation on which Christendom would develop mightily. Christendom and socialism supplemented each other; in the most fundamental sense they were one and the same. Christendom had to be socialized and Socialism had to be christianized."[21] A strong impetus to the socialist conversion of Hugenholtz was given by the economic crisis of 1893. Hugenholtz Jr. reports that in Grand Rapids unemployment had risen to unprecedented heights. Many people were suffering from hunger, also among the members of the Free Congregation. In this impossible situation the Rev. Hugenholtz returned half of his salary to his congregation, and then organized a special exhibition at which products made at home by his unemployed parishioners might be sold to provide them relief.[22] This in turn led the pastor to organize a Labor Exchange in which he sought to put socialistic ideas into practice. An article which appeared in a Grand Rapids newspaper describes it better than does Hugenholtz Jr.:[23]

> Rev. Mr. Hugenholtz was an agitator of social reform and occupied a prominent position among those of his people who gave thought to the subject. At one time he established here what was known as a "Labor Exchange" with headquarters at the corner of Ottawa and Fairbanks streets. His principle was that labor not money was the unit of values, and he proposed that goods in all stores be purchased with tickets representing so many hours of work. Workmen were to be paid with "hours of work" and their "hours of work" brought them everything they desired. His scheme had worked in a Denver community and he saw no reason why it should not be successful here. The idea was not carried out, however, on account of the lack of interest manifested by the merchants and after a few months the "exchange" was abandoned. With it, it is said, a considerable portion of the minister's savings went too.

And thus the attempt failed to "...render the workers independent of the vagaries and stagnation of the market and the monopoly of the present means of exchange: gold and silver through a return to the simple exchange of the product of labor by means of "labor checks".[24] This radical socialist undertaking was quite incompatible with the prevailing ideas in our capitalist society.

The Rev. Hugenholtz also used his periodical *Stemmen uit de Vrije Gemeente* (Voices from the Free Congregation) to propagate his views on the need to reform the lot of the working man. There are numerous references, often case histories from within his congregation, that poignantly reveal the plight of the worker, and the prejudice in Grand Rapids against religiously liberal Dutch workers. The *Stemmen* (Voices) also contains translations from the English of stories (mainly from Unitarian sources) that tell the wretched tale of exploitation. Van Hinte observes that in Grand Rapids between 1890 and 1900 ...no group was more thoroughly exploited than the Hollanders."[25] The Dutch workers, if they were orthodox Calvinists, would not go on strike, but they did take over low paying jobs that Americans gave up. Again, it is the liberal minister, F.W.N. Hugenholtz who tried to do something about the hardships suffered by exploited laborers in Grand Rapids and environs: "As a step in improving their lot, he considered in 1890 the organization of an association of Dutch factory workers that would become a division of the Furniture Workers Protective Association. It was a good sign. However, it was mostly the more liberal element that joined the association, the Calvinists stayed away and continued to work for low wages."[26] When there were strikes in Michigan, notably in Muskegon, the orthodox workers refused to stop working and they also took over jobs from Americans who were on strike. though one newspaper praised the non-striking Dutch for "...their spirit of modesty, tolerance and peacefulness", it was again Hugenholtz who "...felt aggravated by these Dutch sneaks who caused our countrymen to be 'even more despised by the general public and to be even more the target of kicks and insults by the American workmen while losing their self-respect in the process.' The courageous man loudly exhorted orthodox fellow Dutchmen: "In the Kingdom of God one does not earn his bread by the death of his brother."[27]

The Rev. Hugenholtz now resumed his advocacy of socialism from the pulpit, by proclamation in his Sunday services, but in doing so he aroused considerable opposition among his congregation, especially, we are told, among the older generation. Nevertheless, the preacher did succeed in getting majority approval of the congregation to change the by-laws to state: "...that the goal of the congregation would also be the discussion and the promotion of social concerns."[28] However, only the Sunday evening services (which were less well attended) were to be devoted to social concerns and then only during the winter season. But this separation of so-called "purely religious subjects" at the morning service and of social concerns at the evening service was contrary to the principles of the minister. For Hugenholtz that was the main issue, "...why...the cleft between purely religious subjects and the application of religious principles to social life?"[29] A religious service in the morning with one audience and a socially oriented one in the evening with another was a violation of the very essence of religion, it fostered wrong ideas about religion especially among those only present at the morning service. Hugenholtz could not compromise on this issue. He now became "...unreligious for religion's sake, that is to say, just because religion was so precious and sacred to him, he could less and less accommodate himself to the official religion which in his judgment was so far removed from genuine religion."[30] At this critical juncture Hugenholtz became ill, developed pneumonia, and died unexpectedly on February 17, 1900, "as a Socialist", his son adds.[31]

The Dutch church of which the Rev. Hugenholtz had been the pastor was unique in Grand Rapids. At the welcoming service for the new Dutch pastor on December 6, 1885, words of welcome were spoken by the Rev. Charles Fluhrer of the Universalist Church and by Rabbi Rosenau.[32] During its first year the congregation met in the Universalist church. "Their fist year was eventful and prosperous," Albert Baxter reports in his history, "the membership increased to 253, and their commodious and pleasant edifice was built at a cost of $7,500, and dedicated December 22, 1886."[33] Financial assistance was received from friends in the Netherlands. The General Unitarian Conference at Saratoga, N.Y., to which Pastor Hugenholtz had appealed for aid, collected $1,000 for the new church. Baxter notes: "In 1887 Mr. Hugenholtz was formally acknowledged as a Unitarian minister and his church enrolled as "The First Unitarian Holland Church in the United States."[34]

In January 1887 the first society *Kennis en Kunst* (Knowledge and Art) was organized to realize one of the church goals: the promotion of general education and culture, notably the arts.[35] The Society organized debates, presented recitations and readings, gave concerts and even put on plays in the Dutch language at the local Opera House. The plays appear to have been quite a success, even in orthodox Grand Rapids. One can imagine what a stir this created in the Calvinist community which viewed the theater as a form of worldliness. Quite typically, pastor Hugenholtz welcomed the creation of the Knowledge and Art Society and defended its existence. That statement nicely illustrates Hugenholtz's liberal perspective on religion and life and his polemic with orthodoxy. It occurs in an article; "De lijn tusschen het heilige en onheilige", (The line between the sacred and the non-sacred)".[36]

> I do not wish to say ...that liberal piety is invisible - the leaven in the meal is also visible, at least in its effect. Still less do I wish to say ...that orthodox piety cannot permeate all of life and consecrate it as a leaven. I only affirm that orthodox religion is noticeable in the first place in its outward manifestation, while that of the liberals does not desire to be anything but an inner sanctifying principle of life.

> Therefore, the establishment of our young society "Knowledge and Art" is wholly compatible with our view of religion. Although it is not under the jurisdiction of our congregation, it necessarily exists on a good footing with it. Not only because its goal is innocent and ennobling enjoyment (genot), for that reason alone its establishment would be justified and give us joy, but because it seeks that enjoyment in the general development of the intellect, of the emotions, of taste, of clear insight into the many questions of the day, and of our own sense of responsibility toward them all; in a word, because it seeks the development of that genuine humanity, by which man alone becomes truly useful in God's vineyard. We fervently hope that it may succeed in the attainment of that goal, so that many join it and by means of cordial and cheerful cooperation are educated with and through each other to become people of solid character (degelijke menschen).

In a commentary on three plays put on by the Society the author distinguishes between good and bad theater, but strongly argues for the ennobling effect of good plays.[37]

The pastor, who was himself something of an artist and a good musician, assisted in the forming of two choirs, one for adults and one for children. He contributed twelve of 224 hymns to the hymnal of *De Nederlandsche Protestantenbond* (The Netherlands Protestant Federation).[38] Thus pastor and parishioners shared in the task of developing learning and the arts within the congregation and without.

A second society, prosaically named the Willing Workers, was organized in 1888. There were several sub-groups: for education, missions, practical and social matters. The Willing Workers ran a summer school for Dutch language instruction to children and gave lessons in English to newly arrived immigrants. They also gave lessons in sewing and drawing, for girls, and in gymnastics and fencing, for boys. The social circle promoted fellowship within the congregation and organized outdoor Sunday worship services (among others, at Lookout Park in Grand Rapids) and church picnics. It even organized a five-day kermis (carnival) December 20-24, 1889 and raised no less than $700 for the church in this, for Dutch protestants, highly unconventional manner.

The mission department assisted in the collecting of liberal protestant literature for the church library and was responsible for the distribution of pamphlet literature to the larger community of liberal Dutch protestants in America.[39]

When the pastor's brother visited Grand Rapids in 1888 the Church was flourishing, 150 children were enrolled in the Sunday School, and between 60 and 70 persons were enrolled in classes for religious instruction.[40]

The church had grown and prospered between 1885 and 1890, but then began to decline. The reasons given by the Rev. P.H. Hugenholtz (the pastor of the Amsterdam congregation) include: reduced contributions from parishioners due to serious unemployment problems and the growing dominance of the American element in the congregation which did not share the pastor's increasing sympathy for Socialism.[41] The great crisis came with the sudden death of the pastor in 1900.

The Evening Press of February 18, 1900 pays high tribute to the memory of the Rev. F.W.N. Hugenholtz:[42]

> Mr. Hugenholtz was probably one of the best known Holland citizens in the city. He was connected with nearly every organization with which his people were in any way identified and took a great interest in public affairs. Although he has been concerned in many Grand Rapids movements, and in several of them has been the leading spirit, still he will be remembered principally for his work with his church. A history of his life since the time of his coming to this country is an

account of the progress of the work of the Holland Unitarian denomination in Grand Rapids.

The tribute emphasizes the prominent role of pastor as an "agitator of social reform", his work on behalf of the working classes, and his work in the Social Science Club. He was much interested in the Boer War and had recently been elected president of a new Boer sympathizers association. The pastor's work on behalf of the poor is especially remembered:[43]

> As a member of the board of the city poor commissioners, Mr. Hugenholtz reached out his hand to do good to many. He was the vice president of the board and was invaluable as an advisor regarding conditions in certain sections of the city. Many times it was found that he could engineer matters through when no one else was able to do so... The city hall flag is at half mast today out of respect to Mr. Hugenholtz's memory.

After the death of the Rev. Hugenholtz, the Rev. B. van Sluyters became the pastor of the church. Dr. P.H. Hugenholtz was optimistic about the future of the church under its new leader: "It is fortunate that the continued existence of the congregation is assured, even though it is not as flourishing as in the past, and that a young and diligent man, a former student of my brother, recently assumed his labors in his stead.[44] We know nothing of the history of the church during the ministry of the Rev. B. van Sluyters. We also know very little about his successor, the Rev. Klaas Oosterhuis, who served for only two years, from 1916 to 1918, when he tendered his resignation.

In May 1917 the pastors of the two Unitarian churches in the city, Klaas Oosterhuis and Daniel Roy Freeman, were cited in the local newspaper for disseminating anti-conscription literature. The Grand Rapids Press of May 30, 1917 reports:[45]

> The Board of trustees of the Holland Unitarian Church has accepted the resignation of Rev. Klaas Oosterhuis, pastor of the church and secretary of the Grand Rapids Conference on Democracy and Terms of Peace. Mr. Oosterhuis's resignation came after the Board had informed him that because of pacifist activities he would not be retained at the end of his probationary period Aug. 1...

The Press also quotes the chairman of the board of trustees, Beke de Groot, who ..."said the great majority of the members of the church are opposed to their pastor's attitude...; he and others had remonstrated with him and warned him against voicing his personal views in a national crisis like this."[46] It is clear the pastor had agreed to this for on the fifth of June the Press reports that the Rev. Hugenholtz had been reinstated until August first, and that ..."He promised to confine his activities for the remainder of his stay here to church affairs."[47] However, on the first of August the Press reported: "Rev. Klaas Oosterhuis, Holland Unitarian Church pastor, under indictment for alleged draft law conspiracy, resigns."[48] Apparently the church did disband by the close of World War I, as Lucas suggests. But do the reasons given by H. van Hinte get at the heart of the matter? He conjectures: "Dutch Modernists are far more inclined to join an American Church than the Calvinists are. Their feeling of solidarity is much less."[49] Of course, the Dutch Unitarian churches in Grand Rapids and Chicago were free, noncreedal churches that lacked the confessional unity and authority structure and even the social cohesion of the orthodox churches. Their strength lay not in isolation, as was the case with the orthodox Calvinists, but in increasing involvement with other religious liberals, notably American Unitarians, and a very active involvement in the problems of American society. As democratic idealists they sought the good of the community and nation in the reform of economic, social, political, educational and religious institutions. This is surely a process of Americanization for the Holland Unitarian Church, but it should be noted that it flows as directly from religious principles as does the other-worldliness and isolation of the orthodox, Reformed churches. Ironically, the decline of the Holland Liberal Church in Grand Rapids coincides with the developing rift between the pastor and the congregation on the issue of socialism and radical socialist reform. The conservative liberals cannot follow their preacher in his identification of socialist reform with religion, the prophetic call from the pulpit to christian worldliness. It is equally significant that the final confrontation with the last pastor, the Rev. Klaas Oosterhuis, is on the issue of war and peace. When the dominie espouses the cause of pacifism (and resistance to conscription, or so it was alleged) the conservative congregation puts patriotism and the rule of the majority before that of pacifism and the freedom of the individual conscience. That is indeed the kind of Americanization that the Rev. F.W.N. Hugenholtz, the champion of religious freedom, would have regarded as a denial of their most cherished beliefs.

NOTES

[1] Johan P. Snapper, review of *The Dutch in America: Immigration, Settlement, and Cultural Change*, ed. by Robert P. Swierenga (New Brunswick: Rutgers University Press, 1985) in *Newsletter American Association for Netherlandic Studies*, April, 1986.

[2] Henry S. Lucas, *Netherlanders in America, Dutch Immigration to the United States and Canada, 1789-1950*, (Ann Arbor: The University of Michigan Press, 1955), p. 519. Lucas cites as his source: *Stemmen uit de Vrije Hollandsche Gemeente te Grand Rapids, Michigan*, 1886, 1887, and 1888. p. 709.

[3] J. van Hinte, *Netherlanders in America, A Study of Emigration and Settlement in the Nineteenth and Twentieth Centuries in the United States of America* (translation of *Nederlanders in Amerika: Een Studie over Landverhizers en Volkplanters in de 19e en 20ste Eeuw in de Vereenigde Staten van Amerika*, eerste en tweede deel, published by P. Noordhoff, 1928, Groningen, The Netherlands) Volumes 1 and 2, Robert P. Swierenga, General Editor, Adriaan de Wit, Chief Translator (Grand Rapids, Michigan: Baker Book House, 1985), Vol. I. p. 453. In footnote 24 on page 1060 Van Hinte reports that Volumes IV (1889)

Stemmen uit de Vrije Gemeente te Grand Rapids, Michigan and V(1890) *Stemmen uit de Vrije Gemeenten in Amerika* were present in the library of the *Vrije Gemeente* in Amsterdam.

When I checked several years ago that was no longer the case. I did locate the years 1887, 1888 and 1889 and zeroxed them. The four years 1886-1889 are now in the library of Calvin College. Only Volume V (1890) remains missing. It may be worth noting that Van Hinte quotes only from Volumes IV (1889) and V (1890).

[4]This is reported in the *Stemmen uit de Vrije Gemeente* published in Amsterdam by P.R. Hugenholtz, (a half-brother of F.W.N. Hugenholtz) XVI (1893), pp. 286-287. The last weekly issue of *Het Zondagsblad* appeared on July 30, 1893. Hugenholtz hoped to start a bi-weekly publication in October but unfortunately could not, apparently for lack of funds (the announcement speaks of people who are indifferent and of defaulters).

[5]Ditsy Verdonk, *De Gebroeders Hugenholtz en het onstaan van De Vrije Gemeente* (The Brothers Hugenholtz and the formation of the Free Congregation"), unpublished Master's Thesis, Municipal University of Amsterdam, 1981.

[6]The eulogy spoken by F.W.N. Hugenholtz Jr. is one of three which appear under the heading *Een Plechtige Inwijding* (A Solemn Dedication) in *Stemmen uit de Vrije Gemeente* (Amsterdam) XXIII(1900), pp. 319-350.

[7]Ditsy Verdonk, *op cit.* p. 23.

[8]*Ibid*, p. 30

[9]*Ibid*, p. 31

[10]F.W.N. Hugenholtz, Jr. *Stemmen uit de Vrije Gemeente* XXIII(1900), pp. 335-345.

[11]*Ibid*, p. 336.

[12]*Ibid*, p. 337.

[13]*Ibid*, p. 337.

[14]*Ibid*, p. 338.

[15]*Ibid*, p. 339.

[16]*Ibid*, p. 340.

[17]*Ibid*, p. 340.

[18]*Ibid*, p. 340

[19]*Ibid*, p. 340

[20]*Ibid*, p. 341.

[21]*Ibid*, p. 342.

[22]*Ibid*, pp. 342-343.

[23] *The Evening Press* (Grand Rapids, MI), Feb. 17, 1900.

[24] F.W.N. Hugenholtz, Jr. *op. cit.*, p. 343.

[25] Van Hinte, *Netherlanders in America* p. 822.

[26] *Ibid*, p. 823 (Van Hinte cites as his source *Stemmen uit de Vrije Gemeenten in Amerika*, V, No. 5, 1890).

[27] Van Hinte, *op.cit.*, p. 823 (Van Hinte cites *Stemmen* V, No. 6, (1890).

[28] F.W.N. Hugenholtz, Jr. *op.cit.*, pp. 344.

[29] *Ibid.*, p. 344.

[30] *Ibid.*, p. 345

[31] *Ibid.*, p. 345.

[32] P.H. Hugenholtz, the third speaker at the "Solemn Dedication", *Stemmen uit de Vrije Gemeente* XXXIII (1900), p. 347.

[33] Albert Baxter, *History of Grand Rapids, Michigan (With an Appendix - History of Lowell, Michigan)* New York and Grand Rapids: (Munsell and company, publishers, 1892, p. 348.

[34] *Ibid.*, p. 348

[35] P.H. Hugenholtz, *op.cit.*, pp. 348-349.

[36] F.W.N. Hugenholtz, *Stemmen uit de Vrije Gemeente*, II (1887), p. 36.

[37] The April issue of *Stemmen uit de Vrije Gemeente* in 1888 reports on three stage productions put on by the members of *Kennis en Kunst (Art and Knowledge)* during the winter season. The plays had been well received. "The quality of all plays performed was of such a nature that one could come away with wholesome impressions, assuredly the best, the only way to make the rejection of the theater by pious people yield to a more reasonable differentiation. Anyone who was ever edified in the true sense of the word by the presentation of a play, will therefore not defend the theater in general in its corrupted condition and praise it as wholly innocent, neither will he only damn the theater; but rather welcome every effort to raise it out of its corrupt state and so again become what it can be: an excellent means to develop [good] taste, also to tell "the truth with a smile", and to facilitate the moral development of the life of the people." p. 46.

[38] Rev. F.W.N. Hugenholtz had been the secretary of a commission which prepared and published a liberal hymnal in 1882: *Godsdienstige Liederen, Uitgegeven Door En Voor Rekening Van Den Nederlandschen Protestantenbond (Religious Hymns Published by and for the Netherlands Protestant Federation)*. Of the 224 hymns 12, including several translations, were by the Rev. F.W.N. Hugenholtz.

[39] Summary statements of the activities are given by both Albert Baxter and P.H. Hugenholtz (*op.cit*). Church and society activities are regularly reported in the *Stemmen*.

[40] P.H. Hugenholtz, *op cit.*, p. 347.

[41]*Ibid.*, p. 349.
[42]The tribute to Rev. F.W.N. Hugenholtz appears on the front page of *The Evening Press* of February 17, 1900.
[43]*Ibid.*, p. 1.
[44]P.H. Hugenholtz, *op.cit.*, p. 349.
[45]*The Grand Rapids Press*, May 30, 1917.
[46]*Ibid.*
[47]*The Grand Rapids Press*, June 5, 1917.
[48]*The Grand Rapids Press*, August 1, 1917.
[49]J. Van Hinte, *op.cit.*, p. 856.

RISKY RAILS
Dutch Investment in American Railroads

Augustus J. Veenendaal
Rijkscommissie Vad. Geschiedenis

The phenomenal growth of the Dutch economy in the late sixteenth and early seventeenth centuries had caused an accumulation of capital almost unparalleled in history. Fisheries (Amsterdam was built on herringbones), the Baltic trade (moeder-negotie) and the French and Iberian trades had all contributed to this spectacular growth. Part of this accumulated capital had been invested in the rapidly growing shipbuilding industry and its associated trades. Yet this burgeoning industry, although on a very large scale for those days and highly capital-intensive, was not enough to absorb the savings-surplus of the Dutch merchant. The Dutch way of life remained relatively simple despite this wealth, ostentatious living was considered outlandish and was not to be imitated. House building could and did absorb some of the accumulated savings of rich burghers and the arts benefited by this situation as well. Yet other ways had to be found to use this capital in an appropriate way. Land reclamation was popular for a time. It was a risky business, very capital- and labor-intensive, but if successful large gains could be realized in this field, where only large investors could operate. Technical and geographical limitations, however, soon ended further development here. The East India Company was another field for profitable investment, but again strictly limited, owing to the peculiar way of capitalization of the company. Dutch government loans soon became a much sought after means of employing surplus capital, for the big investor as well as for the savings of the small shopkeeper or artisan. Money was plentiful and these loans seldom yielded more than three percent, sometimes even less. But they were safe: interest was regularly paid and the loans were redeemed at the appointed time. Only once, after the end of the War of the Spanish Succession in 1713, the province of Holland had to close its paying offices for a short time, because there was no money in the till to service the outstanding debts.

In view of these limited domestic possibilities for investing surplus capital, it is not surprising that foreign governments soon found the way to the Amsterdam capital market.[1] Rates of interest were generally higher in the case of foreign loans than at home, caused, no doubt, by the higher risk incurred. Foreign governments could and sometimes did default on their payments of interest. In some cases the States General of the Dutch Republic guaranteed a loan for a foreign government, especially in case of war, when an ally like the perennially penniless Austrian emperor had to be given the means to continue the war on the side of the Dutch Republic. The Bank of England was founded with a large amount of capital from Amsterdam, and gradually every European nation became a debtor state, from Great Britain to Russia and from Sweden to Spain.

When the government of the newly independent United States approached the Amsterdam capital market for loans, the Dutch reacted cautiously at first, but soon confidence in the new state was established and other loans were advanced on more favorable terms than before.[2] When the French revolutionary armies overran the Dutch Republic in 1795, the total of Dutch loans to the United States government stood at approximately Dfl 30,000,000. Quite a sizable sum for those days. The period of French domination over the Netherlands did of course seriously hinder the free operations on the Amsterdam money market, but did not end them completely. A large part of the money needed for Jefferson's Louisiana Purchase of 1803 came from Amsterdam by way of the Dutch business relations of the London firm of Baring Brothers, who handled the loan.[3] After the re-establishment of Dutch independence in 1814 the Amsterdam capital market regained at least a part of its former importance, but it never again reached the position of prominence that it had had during the eighteenth century.

Despite the poverty, caused in part by the Napoleonic wars, and despite large scale unemployment, Dutch capitalists were again seeking an outlet for their money in the early years of the nineteenth century. Opportunities for investment in the Netherlands themselves continued to be scarce. Government loans were still much sought after, but their rate of interest remained low. The Indies offered a few opportunities, but not enough to absorb the savings-surplus. Dutch railways were slow in coming, and when they arrived on the scene their profitability was considered too low. Dividends of three or four percent instead of the promised seven and eight were not enough, so Dutch capitalists, after an initial enthusiastic reception of the new railway shares, soon sold their holdings to British and German investors.[4] Russian government loans were highly popular because of their high rate of interest and their relative safety. Russian railway loans too could count on a favorable reception on the Amsterdam stock market, because their bond issues were guaranteed by the Russian government and their rate of interest could climb as high as eight or even nine percent. These loans remained popular throughout the nineteenth century, only to be repudiated by the Soviet government after the Russian revolution of 1916.

Dutch interest in the young United States had remained strong during these years. Land companies, like the Holland Land Company or the Georgia Agriculture Company, both already founded in the eighteenth century, continued to be operated, although in some years with enormous losses to the participants. But they had kept interest in America alive. Federal and state loans had found a willing market in Amsterdam in the twenties and thirties; canal companies, like the Erie and Morris Canal Companies, had found a large part of their capital in Holland. The so-called "internal improvement" loans of some states were popular well into the forties, but then some states, like Michigan and Mississippi, ran into grave financial problems and simply repudiated their foreign debt.[5] Fortunately these were isolated examples, and they did not materially affect the credit of the United States in general.

In view of this Dutch interest in American transportation it is not surprising that early railroad companies tried to raise money in Amsterdam. Already in 1837 two railroads in New York State, the Tonnawanda and the Batavia-Buffalo Railroads, offered five percent bonds to the Dutch public, but the reaction was only lukewarm at that time, and nothing more was heard of these schemes.[6] Another, but more successful early road, the Baltimore and Susquehanna Railroad Company, supported by the state of Maryland, did raise some money on the Dutch market, but only in a roundabout way.[7] Maryland three percent state bonds were issued on behalf of the railroad in 1837 and the company managed to sell about half the total issue in Amsterdam.

Before we elaborate now on the main theme of this paper, it will be necessary to pay some attention to the technical side of foreign investment. The kind of investment we have discussed until now and that will be our main subject, is called portfolio investment, as opposed to direct investment, where business companies invest in subsidiary companies in other countries.[8] The latter type of investment is almost completely non-existent in the field of railroad business, so we will confine ourselves to the portfolio investment.[9] Early roads issued a large number of shares and these were sold to the public. Whoever held more than fifty percent of the shares was in control of the company, and so hot fights between rival groups of shareholders could take place. The fight over the Erie railroad is an infamous example of this kind of struggle for control. Later railroads only issued a limited number of shares and frequently the original promoters of the line retained at least a majority of these to remain in control. The money necessary for building and equipping a line was raised by bond issues. In the sixties and seventies we find railroad shares being offered for sale on the Amsterdam Stock Exchange, but gradually it became usual to raise money for railroads through the issuing of bonds. These construction bonds were often guaranteed by a mortgage on the railroad and its fixed plant and rolling stock, giving, at least in theory, some protection to foreign investors. An American banking house, acting as trustee for the railroad company, undertook to sell the bonds on the market. Although some early bonds were sold on the American domestic market, a more willing market was soon found in Europe, where London, Frankfurt and Amsterdam became the centers where this type of bonds was chiefly sold. From the seventies on we see a great preponderance of new bond issues instead of shares. Shares were considered too speculative at the time, especially shares in new and unknown companies, and it was considered highly improbable that any dividend would ever be paid. Shares were, however, distributed free sometimes as a bonus to boost the sale of a bond issue. Possession of bonds gave no actual control over a company, although a large number of bondholders could, and sometimes did influence the course of events, when railroads defaulted or were merged with other companies.

In 1857 the first American railroad company found the way to the Amsterdam stock market.[10] The Illinois Central Railroad, one of the more respectable companies, found itself caught by a sharp monetary crisis in the middle of a vast program of new construction. No funds were available in the United States, so the company had to look elsewhere, in London in the first place, but also in Holland. Shares and bonds were introduced tentatively at first, but they soon found a willing market in Amsterdam. The Illinois Central was a so-called "land grant" railroad which was considered an extra element of safety for the foreign investor.[11] Large blocks of shares were sold in Holland, and the original investors will not have regretted their step: dividends of ten percent were common during a number of years and even in the worst year of the depression of the seventies, they never fell below four percent. Despite this introduction of railroad bonds and shares on the Amsterdam market, it took some time before other American railroad companies took the step to float new loans on the Dutch market. The Civil War may have had a negative influence for a short time and only in 1864 some other American railroads managed to sell their bonds on the Amsterdam Stock Exchange. This trickle soon swelled to a torrent: twelve new loans in 1869, fourteen next year, eighteen in 1871 and twenty-one in 1872, roughly estimated at a total of $72,000,000.[12]

Why were these new loans so attractive to Dutch investors? We have seen the limited possibilities for Dutch capitalists in their own country and colonies. The cautious among them could choose the safe domestic and foreign government loans, giving a steady three of four percent return. The American railroad loans offered at least six percent and sometimes even more. Their price at introduction was usually between 70 and 80 percent, giving a nice ten percent return or more on their money. Many Dutch capitalists were apparently willing to take the risk. Buying bonds at the low introductory price, they could also hope to sell in a rising market before the possible crash came. Solid companies like the Illinois Central or the Chicago & North Western were safe enough and never crashed, but other new ventures introduced on the Stock Exchange were distinctly unsafe, overcapitalized and unnecessary from an economic point of view. Some even existed only in the minds of the promotors and in the glowing description in the prospectus, but were never to lay a single mile of rail or run a single train. Dutch investors apparently lacked the means to distinguish between the good and the bad or they did not even care while the mania lasted. They were soon to find out the hard way when the crisis of 1873 struck.[13]

How were these railroad loans introduced on the Dutch market? The first Illinois Central stock had been sold through British bankers, who were unable to sell all the shares offered on their own home market. The next loans, however, were introduced directly through Dutch stockbroking firms, mostly from Amsterdam, but a few brokers from Rotterdam or the Hague do appear now and then. Several large Amsterdam firms specialized in American railroad loans and gradually they acquired the necessary knowledge and experience to be able to protect the interests of the Dutch capitalists. Names like Kerkhoven, Boissevain, Wertheim or Tutein Nolthenius became well-known for their American business. These brokers formed the so-called "Administratie Kantoren", holding the shares of railroad companies in the name of the Dutch owners. They took care of the regular payment of dividends and passed them on to the owners. If they held large blocks of shares in this way, they could appoint a representative on the board of the company involved. This could be a Dutchman, but usually they choose an American or Englishman as their representative.

Dutch bondholders operated more individually. It was easy for the small capitalist to cut off the half-yearly coupons from his bonds and offer them for cashing to the broker. Only when a railroad ran into financial difficulties the bondholders needed help. If a company did not pay the interest due at appointed time and if a large part of the bonds was held by Dutchmen, the Stock Exchange Committee of Amsterdam could write out a meeting of interested parties. A special protection committee was formed and bondholders were invited to deposit their bonds with the committee in exchange for certificates. In this way the Dutch bondholders could act together and were in a better position to protect their holdings. More often than not a representative of the bondholders was sent out to the United States to try to save as much as possible from the wreck. Quite often the Dutch sought help from other interested parties, English or German, and acted together. The Amsterdam banker Boissevain, who helped to carry out the reorganization of the Union Pacific after the 1893 crash, was appointed by the Dutch and German bondholders jointly.[14] One particular company, the Denver Pacific, connecting the Kansas Pacific at Denver with the Union Pacific at Cheyenne, was turned over to the Dutch bondholders after it defaulted on the payment of interest. The Dutch committee toyed with the idea of operating the line on its own for a moment, but in view of the difficulties involved in running a railroad in a far away country they preferred to sell or lease the company to someone else. When Jay Gould, the famous railroad financier, at last made a bid, they were happy to sell. The deal was concluded in Amsterdam in 1879 when Gould happened to be in Europe. The Dutch bondholders did not come out badly in this case.[15]

The financial crisis of 1873 in the USA caused heavy losses to the Dutch capitalists. Railroad bonds, bought at 70 percent a few years before, fell to 4 or even 2 percent, and interest was hardly ever paid. In the reorganizations following the crash the bondholders did recoup at least part of their losses, and at last they became somewhat more cautious. The economic upswing in America soon caused a new wave of enthusiasm, but tempered with some measure of carefulness this time. The character of investment also changed: new issues of shares became rare, bond issues were the usual way now to raise money for the construction of new lines. The next economic and financial crisis, of 1893, again caused heavy losses to Dutch capitalists, but again some of the losses could be recovered in the next few years.[16] Investors should have been suspicious by now of new loans by unknown and untried American railroads with resounding names, but with little substance behind. Yet some new ventures did attract a sizable Dutch investment. This is all the more remarkable as other possibilities for investment did exist by that time. Large industrial companies, oil companies, both foreign and domestic, and public utilities needed large amounts of capital and generally promised a better return on the investment. The rate of interest on railroad loans had slowly fallen from the seven percent of the seventies to something like four percent at the end of the century. It is probable that the highly speculative element in the new railroad companies involved, like the Kansas City, Pittsburg & Gulf, must have had a strong appeal to the gamblers among the capitalists.[17] Most of these later ventures, but remarkably not all of them, ended in losses for the participants and they mark effectively the end of the strong Dutch interest in American railroads.

But this does not mean that Dutch investment in railroads ended then and there. The stock already acquired over the years was not suddenly sold and in 1914 the total Dutch investment in American railroads was still estimated at something like $300,000,000.[18] Shares and bonds of the more solid companies continued to be included in the price lists of the Amsterdam Stock Exchange and in the twenties even some new loans were floated. Illinois Central shares were still listed a century after they were first introduced and even now there is some trade in Illinois Central Industries, Burlington Industries and others.

One other way of investing in American railroads must yet be mentioned. Because the American railroad business proved to be a thorny field for the happy-go-lucky Dutch investors, some Amsterdam brokers formed investment funds.[19] The first one was the "Vereenigde Amerikaansche Fondsen", organized in 1869 by Kerkhoven and Boissevain, with a portfolio of some $2,000,000 in American railroad stock. Participants got a guaranteed five percent return on their money and these investment funds proved popular with the Dutch public. Several others followed in the next few years, all operating in the same general way. Most of them were only liquidated in the twentieth century. Despite their initial popularity they only represent a small part of the total Dutch investment in American railroads.

I want to conclude with a few selected examples of American railroad companies with an important Dutch participation. One solid, straightforward company, as representative of the many railroads of the same kind; one highly speculative, but in the long run successful line; and one late example of unfounded optimism, with a tinge of swindle in it.

The solid one is the Chicago & North Western Railway Company, connecting Chicago with Council Bluffs on the Missouri River and thus an important part of the transcontinental railroad. Other lines of this company criss-crossed the states of Iowa, Wisconsin and Minnesota. Preferred shares of this well-run company were first introduced on the Amsterdam Stock Exchange in 1868 and found a ready market, even to the extent that one of the Amsterdam brokers involved in this deal, Mr. J.L. Ten Have, was elected to the board of the company in 1872.[20] Dividends of between 2 1/2 and 10 percent were regularly paid and only in 1875, in the midst of the depression, the company had to pass the dividend. The major part of these preferred shares has been in Dutch hands for a number of years. And this did not represent all the Dutch involvement. Common shares were also sold in Amsterdam in large numbers and most, if not all of the several bond issues were listed on the Amsterdam Exchange. At least eight different bond issues, most of them giving a seven percent interest, were sold in Holland and found a willing market. Interest in the shares slowly declined and Ten Have gave up his seat on the board in 1878. But the several bond issues continued to be listed at the Amsterdam Exchange for many decades to come.

While this C&NW example may serve as general rule, the next company I want to discuss is more the exception. The Kansas City, Pittsburg & Gulf shows us a picture completely different from earlier Dutch ventures.

This 800 mile line was proposed to give the Midwest a direct outlet to the sea along the shortest possible route. The man behind the scheme was Arthur Stilwell, real estate tycoon from Kansas City.[21] When the company ran out of money, Stilwell went to Holland in 1894 to raise the necessary capital. So far everything is as usual, except for the singularly unsuitable moment chosen. KCPG bonds were sold in large numbers in Holland through the usual channels. But there was a difference: in this case not only bonds in the railroad were available, but the two construction companies that had been organized to build the line were taken over by Dutch capitalists. The formation of construction companies was a common practice in the American railroad business. Mostly they were really meant to do what their name implies, but quite often they offered golden opportunities for swindle. Promotors of a railroad organized a construction company under a different name, proceeded to build the line in the cheapest and most sketchy way possible, claimed large rewards for this "construction" to be paid from the proceeds of the sale of bonds of the railroad, and cleared out before the crash came. Then the road had to be reorganized and rebuilt, more often than not at the expense of the small bondholders. Dutch capitalists had been caught several times by this trick, but now they were resolved to do better. Both construction companies of the KCPG were taken over and they were well paid for their work for the railroad, mostly in valuable timberlands along the right of way. When the KCPG defaulted in 1899 and a receivership was necessary, the bondholders, many of them Dutch, had to swallow some losses, but the reorganized company, the Kansas City Southern, soon got into its stride and was able to give a reasonable return on the original investment. The participants in the construction companies did even better. In a long series of reorganizations, take-overs and mergers, they managed to sell their lands on favorable terms and they ended up with majority holdings in the Port Arthur Townsite Company and the Holland-Texas Mortgage Bank, both very profitable undertakings. One more difference with the usual practice of Dutch participation in American railroads is the extensive personal involvement. Many Dutchmen held high positions on the boards of the KCPG and its many affiliated companies. Stilwell's closest collaborator was Jan de Goeijen, a broker from Amsterdam; his name is honored in the town of De Queen, Arkansas, although few people will be aware that the names really are the same.

The last example I want to give is one of a short line, founded with too much optimism and not enough common sense. Around the turn of the century business in Oklahoma and Indian territories was booming. The country had recently been opened to white settlers, the unbroken prairie was converted into cotton and wheatfields and there was oil in the ground. New railway lines were needed and established companies like the Santa Fe, the Frisco and the Rock Island were busily building. Dutch capitalists were interested in these new lines, and when an independent company, the Oklahoma Central, was promoted to bring coal from the coalfields around Lehigh in the southeast of Indian Territory to the new industries south of Oklahoma City, its bonds found a willing market in Amsterdam.[22] Some doubts, however, must have existed in the mind of the Dutch broker who floated the loan. Salomon Frederik van Oss was considered to be the leading Dutch specialist in American railroad finance and his private bank introduced the OCR loan in Holland. He was careful enough to send two experienced Dutch railway engineers, father and son Middelberg, to Oklahoma to inspect the line. Despite their presence things went completely wrong. Traffic was never enough to pay for the interest of the bonded debt, and just when things promised to turn better, the company was caught in the panic of 1907. A receiver had to be appointed and the line was reorganized and later taken over by the Santa Fe. The construction company contracted to build the line proved to be one of the old-fashioned kind, meant to provide gain for the promotors at the expense of the Dutch bondholders. It is strange that an old hand like Van Oss was fooled by this old trick. Dutch losses were heavy this time. The Santa Fe soon abandoned most of its new acquisition, thereby clearly demonstrating that the line should never have been built. Only the small towns of Middleberg and Vanoss in central Oklahoma keep the memory of Dutch influence alive.

Looking back it may be concluded that Dutch money has played a considerable role in the development of the American railroad network during some fifty years since 1857. The motives of Dutch capitalists seem to be purely egoistic and financial: annual yields of the loans promised to be higher than elsewhere and large gains could be realized in a lucky quick sale. The possibility of large losses, on the other hand, seem to have been somewhat overlooked. A marked geographical preference can be distinguished: the railroads most popular with the Dutch public were those of the Mississippi basin and the West. Important eastern roads like the New York Central and the Pennsylvania were almost completely absent from the portfolios of the Hollanders, while roads like the Chicago & North Western, the Missouri, Kansas, Texas and the Kansas City, Pittsburg & Gulf were almost completely in the hands of the Dutch for a number of years. Without the influx of Dutch capital the territorial and economic expansion of the American nation would have been slower.

NOTES

[1] J.C. Riley. *International Government Finance and the Amsterdam Capital Market 1749-1815* (Cambridge, 1980).

[2] P.J. van Winter. *Het aandeel van den Amsterdamschen handel aan den opbouw van het Amerikaansche Gemeenebest* (2 vols. 's-Gravenhage, 1927-1933).

[3] The Amsterdam firm of Hope & Co. handled the Dutch participation in the loan. M.G. Buist, *At Spes non Fracta. Hope & Co. 1770-1815. Merchant Bankers and Diplomats at Work.* (s-Gravenhage, 1974).

[4] W. van den Broeke. *Financien en financiers van de Nederlandse spoorwegen 1937-1890* (Zwolle, 1985).

[5] Van Winter, *Het aandeel*, II, 410.

[6] Van Winter, *Het aandeel*, II, 412. The Tonawanda Valley Railroad did operate for a few years and became a part of the Buffalo & Rochester Railroad in 1850. W. Edson, *Railroad Names; A Directory of Common*

Carrier Railroads Operating in the United States. 1927-1982 (Potamataac, 1984), 127.

[7] This railroad was incorporated into the Northern Central in 1854, which in its turn was taken over by the Pennsylvania Railroad in 1974. Edson, *Railroad Names*, 15, 91.

[8] See for direct investment P.J. Buckley and B.R. Roberts, *European Direct Investment in the U.S.A. before World War I* (New York, 1982).

[9] F.A. Cleveland and F.W. Powell, *Railroad Promotion and Capitalization in the United States* (New York, 1909); S.F. van Oss, *Amerikaansche Spoorwegwaarden* (Groningen, 1903).

[10] K.D. Bosch, *Nederlandse beleggingen in de Verenigde Staten* (Amsterdam-Brussel, 1948), 154-156; J.D. Santilhano, Amerikaansche Spoorwegwaarden. *Overzicht van de in Nederland verhandeld wordende Amerikaansche spoorwegfondsen* (Rotterdam, 1884), 243-262.

[11] J. Moody, The Railroad Builders. *A Chronicle of the Welding of the States* (New Haven, 1920), 196-197.

[12] Bosch, *Beleggingen*, 162-163.

[13] Johan de Vries, (Amsterdam, 1976), 110; Bosch, Beleggingen, 163-165.

[14] Nelson Trottman, *History of the Union Pacific; A Financial and Economic Survey* (reprint, New York, 1966), 252.

[15] Archives of the Amsterdam Stock Exchange, file nr. 31, 17. I Want to thank Mr. H.W. Günst, archivist of the Exchange, for his kind help.

[16] Bosch, *Beleggingen*, 479.

[17] See for the KCP&G K.L. Bryant, Arthur E. Stilwell, *Promotor with a Hunch* (Hashville, 1971).

[18] Bosch, *Beleggingen*, 479.

[19] W.H. Berghuis, *Ontstaan en ontwikkeling van de Nederlandse beleggingsfondsen tot 1914* (Assen, 1967), 117-160.

[20] Santilhano, *Amerikaansche Spoorwegwaarden*, 141-165.

[21] Bryant, Arthur Stilwell, and Archives of the Amsterdam Stock Exchange, file nr. 454 and 578.

[22] Augustus J. Veenendaal, "Railroads, Oil and Dutchmen; Investing in the Oklahoma Frontier", in: The Chronicles of Oklahoma LXIII (1985), 4-27.

PROBLEMS OF CODE-SWITCHING
Dialect Loss of Immigrants of Dutch Descent

Jo Daan
Barchem, The Netherlands

1. Two Types of Dutch

In plain terms we can say that two kinds of Dutch have been spoken in the United States. They are separate and easily identifiable. The older type was spoken by descendants of Dutch immigrants in the 17th and 18th centuries; the other by immigrants who came over in the 19th and 20th centuries, especially between 1830 and 1850, and their descendants. In both types of Dutch dialect loss must have taken place, both communicative and structural.

2. Communicative Dialect Loss

We have information about this from the speakers themselves. They tell us, explicitly or implicitly, about the situations in which they maintained their mother tongue and those in which they switched to English (or what they supposed to be English). This information however is not always absolutely reliable; if you are fluent in more than one language it is sometimes difficult to realize which language you are using or in which language you are addressed at any given time.

2.1 Many accounts indicate prestige loss of the mother tongue. Prestige loss shows that the mother tongue is becoming restricted to less formal situations. Cleaf Bachman gives a very striking example in the first chapter of the introduction to a vocabulary of Jersey Dutch, Dutch spoken by descendants of 17th and 18th century immigrants. The introduction is complete in typescript, the vocabulary itself consists of a collection of material. One of his sources is an unpublished study of Mohawk Dutch by Walter Hill, who worked on it in the 1870's and 1880's. Mohawk Dutch is a variant of older Dutch as it was preserved in the Mohawk Valley until the end of the 19th century, "if a stranger be among them who will attempt to speak De tawl (that is the Dutch spoken in the Mohawk Valley) and he be not as fluent as his listeners they will change, almost at once, into English. Any deliberate attempt then, to learn the tawl will be thwarted at once." Bachman adds: "Hill's Low Dutch acquaintances never gave him a very satisfactory explanation for this reticence, simply professing great surprise that any Dutchman would ever want to learn their dialect. Hill was forced to infer that they were ashamed of what they considered a sign of boorishness and felt they would be called "Boor Duits" or "farmer" and so, looked down upon by their urban cousins".

For more than a century Dutch had been the lingua franca in the Hudson region. Hill indicated differences between Dutch dialects in New

Jersey and New York and he concluded that they must have resulted largely from the increasing restriction of the language to the household as the nineteenth century progressed and from the reluctance of the Mohawk Dutchmen to correct one another. "The reasons seems to be that none of them, even the most fluent, is ever quite certain that he had the right of it".

From this quotation we may conclude that there was no norm for this Dutch and that it was not used in formal situations, at least in the second half of the 19th century. In the 17th and 18th centuries, when Dutch was used by ministers preaching in the churches, a standard must have been observed - by the preachers actively and by the congregation passively. Recall to mind that the development and spread of a Dutch standard in the Netherlands was a very slow process until the beginning of the 20th century.

2.2 I have found nothing about a norm for the Dutch spoken by 19th century immigrants, but Dutch was spoken by ministers in church and was used for praying and Bible readings until about 1890.

2.2.1 I suppose the ministers and the teachers learned about a standard, but all the others who understood the Dutch of their ministers and mastered it passively, never spoke it. Perhaps every one knew the standard, but only the members of the upper classes, the intellectual ones were expected to observe it. The situations in which the standard was used were: in church, in school, at college, at meetings, and so on. Our informants who spoke a type of Dutch which approached the norm, belonged to the upper classes - ministers, teachers, bankers - or they were first generation immigrants who brought their speech habits with them. All the others retained the characteristics of their mother tongue.

2.2.2 Everyone except the educated used their regional dialect at home, out of doors a type of adapted Dutch, different for every speaker, in the interest of mutual comprehension. Material about this necessity will be found in a book about the languages of Dutch immigrants by Prof. Lagerwey and myself to be published next year.

2.3 We know a little more about the use of the dialects, the language varieties, spoken by these later immigrants from the accounts of the informants we contacted in 1966[1]. One of them told us that her mother immigrated and never learned English - she calls it "American" - because everyone spoke Dutch. She herself learned English at school, but she and her friends spoke it only at school. The following sentences are taken from her account: "Ja, maar zie je, vroeger leerden ze geen Amerikaans als ze uit Holland kwamme, want 't was hier alles Hollands. Maar da's met de wereldoorlog one is da veranderd, toe is't Amerikaans gekomme......O ja, we leerden wel Engels op skool, maar de minuut da we uit de skool kwamme, dan vloge we naar buite en dan was 't alles Hollands. Zo dajje in't schoolhuisje was, dan was't Amerikaans, maar as je na buite vloog, dan was 't Hollands. Nou, dan krege we wel es op ons dak en dan moste we......as de teacher zei: As ik je Hollands hoor prate, dan mojje inblijve, zie dan wel, dan prate we vanzellef Amerikaans, maar was je weer op de road na huis, dan was 't weer Hollands". The translation of this passage runs something like this: "In earlier days they did not learn English because everyone spoke

Dutch. This changed with World War I. We learned English at school, but as soon as we were out of the school we spoke Dutch. Sometimes we were scolded by the teacher and we had to stay in. We spoke English, for fear of punishment, but as soon as we went home we talked Dutch". Other informants learned English at night school, some only learned a few words in every day practice.

2.4 In this way immigrants and their children learned English primarily as a standard language. The language one learns at school is particularly a standard language. In some places parish schools were established in which the children were instructed in Dutch too, but presumably in Dutch as used in church, the Dutch of the Bible. This was already old-fashioned in the 19th century for the 17th century translation was still in use until the beginning of the 20th century.[2]

3. Dialect Development and Standard Language

The majority of the 19th century immigrants spoke a regional dialect and did not speak "standard" Dutch at the time they immigrated. In America they only learned some special styles of "standard" Dutch.

Are we entitled to say they did not speak "standard" Dutch? I am sure we are, for in the Netherlands where the immigrants came from, a part of the population only went to school for two or three years or in fact only in winter time. In 1825 35% and in 1835 28% of children of school age did not in fact go to school. The greater part of these truants were pretty certainly children of the rural population[3]. And a century and more ago the county children could only learn "standard" Dutch at school. Table 1 shows the varieties spoken by our informants; it gives Dutch only and Dutch with a regional dialect as two different groups. But I am almost sure the colloquial language of the informants of the latter group was a regional dialect only. They gave Dutch because they learned Dutch at school, they were able to read it and to speak it a little bit. Educated people are expected to speak the standard language and everyone likes it to be considered as an educated person. As shown in the table - less than 40% of the first generation, which immigrated from about 1885, when school attendance in the Netherlands was much higher than in the twenties and thirties, gave "standard" Dutch only as their colloquial speech. More than 60% of the second and third generation gave Dutch as every day speech. And yet I said just now they did not speak "standard" Dutch at the time they immigrated. What happened little by little, under the pressure of mutual comprehension and influenced by the Dutch of the Church, the regional colloquial languages spoken by the majority of the immigrants of all generations grew into one. Somewhat simplified you can say: (1) they spoke this variety of Dutch for mutual comprehension, but they did not consider it a standard; (2) they more or less understood the Dutch of the church and considered it a standard, but only for ministers and schoolteachers; and (3) they spoke English as best they could, they did consider it a standard, and felt ashamed when they did not conform to it.

Colloquial dialect

State	< Michigan		Wisconsin 2 (R.C.)			Iowa		Mass	
generation	1	1+	1	1+	1	1+	1	1+	1	1+
dialect										
Dutch/ Frisian	9	3	14	2	1	-	2	3	6	1
Frisian	1	-	1	1	-	-	1	-	15	6
reg. dialect	3	5	-	5	18	3	7	2	-	-
Dutch/	17	20	8	5	2	-	5	9	-	-
Dutch	13	15	5	2	4	-	5	28	-	-

I think a general understanding of the communicative aspect of the use of these languages presents few problems. Structural dialect loss is a very different matter, produced as it was by communicative dialect loss, by code switching and by the lack of systematic instruction; how are we to deal with this on the basis of our imperfect knowledge of the language varieties the immigrants spoke and the Dutch "standard" they heard, but did not observe?

4. Structural Dialect Loss

It is much more difficult to study this second type of dialect loss. We need to start from the original, the primary structure. And how can we know what it was like? Seventeenth century Dutch is only preserved in written form; the language of plays and farces is less formal than that used in other prose writings, but it is still not every day speech. In the 17th as the 19th century Dutch is only preserved in a restricted range of styles. The grammars tell us more about the ideal rules than about the actual realisations. We have vocabularies of dialects spoken in the Netherlands in the 19th century, but they are almost entirely restricted to words differing from the vocabulary of standard Dutch. The authors recorded the special words and features of the dialects but did not describe the dialect in detail, so that our knowledge of the spoken dialects in earlier days is not sufficient for us to assess dialect loss in grammatical structure and vocabulary. This is a very slippery ground, I will give a few examples. In 17th century correspondence the pronoun of address is "Uwe Edele" and variants, in some letters "gij", sometimes spelt with "gh", sometimes with "g" but almost never with "j". "UwEd" was used in formal letters at that time as we suppose, and the other pronoun in less formal writing and in colloquial speech. In Holland and Zeeland, the two western provinces, this "gij" was pronounced probably as "jij", while in

Brabant and Flanders it was pronounced "gij", as it is still today. I said "we suppose", but we do not actually know. Nowadays the formal form of address is "u", and we suppose the same for the 19th century. But one of our writers, Van Lennep, wrote in 1865: "Gij" is usually pronounced "jij". Fifty years ago respectable people used "uwee", as a form of address, but this is old-fashioned and the modern form is "u".[4] He supplies valuable information here about changes in the standard and about loss of formality. We have some information about other changes in standard Dutch too, but in most cases we do not know enough about variants and styles in colloquial speech. For instance, nowadays we say in standard Dutch "ik ben geweest", that is "I have been," literally "I am been". But Frisians say "ik ha west" and in the isle of Wieringen they said "ik heb weest", that is "I have been". In the Zaan region north of Amsterdam, we said in my young days "ik heb er weest, ik heb ebleve, ik heb gaan betale, ik heb er ekomme", and I hear my neighbours in the eastern Netherlands say "ik hef ewest, ik hef egoan". In the 17th century more verbs were conjugated in this way: "blijken" (to appear), "vallen" (to fall), "lopen" (to walk), "beginnen" (to begin). De Vooys notes in his grammar: Though Maerlant sometimes uses already "zijn", by the 17th century "hebben" is frequent in the colloquial language of the farces, as it is in most regional dialects today. About 1900 "hebben" was the norm in the Dutch of Belgium.[5] Fortunately in 1847 and 1848, the years of the first wave of the 19th century Dutch immigrants, there was a discussion in a Dutch journal about the use of "hebben" (to have) and "zijn" (to be) as auxiliaries. L.A. te Winkel, who's name is indissolubly connected with the spelling of Dutch in the 19th century, concluded that the verbs formed their past tenses with "hebben" except those expressing a change in situation or place; these were conjugated with "zijn", as were the verbs "zijn" and "blijven" (to stay).[6] So we may expect that the 19th century immigrants said "ik heb geweest, ik heb gebleven", contrary to the official standard. If we do not know this we will be apt to assume that "ik heb geweest" is a loan translation after English "I have been".

As a linguist and a student in Dutch language I was aware of this phenomenon. But I slipped up at an early stage in an other case. The greater part of our informants, speaking about their youth, said that they were "opgebracht", in English "brought up". When analysing their language in loan words, loan translations, regional dialect phenomena and so on, I classified "opgebracht" as a loan translation. But I had some vague doubts, and I looked the word up in the great Dutch dictionary and found that it was standard Dutch in the 19th century, and often occurs in the Bible.[2]

When I slipped you will not be surprised that Americans slip up too. Shetter published an article about "Brabants dialekt in Wisconsin".[7] In that article he analysed the Dutch dialect of Little Chute and surroundings. As he had an excellent command of standard Dutch he grouped words and expressions as loan words from English that are or were perfectly good Dutch. Some examples: 'smoken in the sense of English "to smoke", Dutch "roken", is old-fashioned and regional, for instance in the Wieringen dialect we have "smookteel" that is "smoked eel". An example of an expression is: "ik denk hij zal komme", "I think he will come". This construction can be used in colloquial speech, and it is not contrary to the rules of regional dialects, for instance Frisian. Here is an example from the Frisian Reference

Grammar: "Jo witte, Pyt it gjin buter", "You know Pete doesn't eat butter". It is normal in seventeenth century Dutch too "ick gis hy is niet veer", "I think he is not far away".

Shetter classified "Hij is hier veul better af" as a literal translation, but in colloquial Dutch you can say: "Hij is hier veel beter af" and the form "better" can be found for instance in Frisian and in dialects with vocal shortening, for instance in Noord-Brabant. Another American, Charles Gehring, now hard at work on the translation of the Stuyvesant archive, made similar mistakes. Together we studied the tape recordings to look for English influence. The following examples could be translations from English but they are and were Dutch, either colloquial speech or regional dialect. "Al zien leven -- all his life. Niet dat ik het weet - not that I know. Hij kennie veul werke - he couldn't work much. De wetenschap - the knowledge". I know Dutchman too who do not know the word in this sense and who use "kennis" instead.

Research on the phonetical/phonological level is even more slippery. I will give only one example, the pronunciation and articulation of "r". the majority of our informants articulated a lingual "r", some of them an uvular "r", and a minority, people of a higher social status, an American constricted "r", irrespective of whether they were speaking Dutch or English. Were the others not able to pronounce a constricted "r"? Were they perhaps not informed about the status of the constricted "r"? Was that status in the 19th century different from that it is today? Or did they just not care? I do not know. The literature about the "r" in America shows that the social status of "r"-constriction is changing in the course of time and depends on regional distribution.[8] The data about "r" pronunciation in Europe provide no certain information about pronunciation, articulation and the social factors affecting them.[9]

5. Conclusion

If we students of dialects loss wish to keep a firm foothold I recommend team work: collaboration between historical linguists, sociolinguists and native dialect speakers. Even the team will need to proceed with great caution. I have learned this lesson, I hope you will agree.

NOTES

[1]Jo Daan. Language Use and Language Policy among Americans of Dutch Origin - *Papers from the first interdisciplinary conference on Netherlandic studies*. Ed. by William Fletcher. New York/London. P. 207-217, 1982.

Jo Daan,"Communicatie-taalkunde". *Taalsociologie*. BMDC 32, 3-15, 1967.

Jo Daan. "Billingualism of Dutch immigrants in the U.S.A." *Actes du Xe congres international des linguistes* (Bucarest 1967). Bucarest. p. 759-763, 1969.

Jo Daan. "Trouw aan het Fries in de U.S.A." *Flecht op'e koai Stüdzjes oanbean oan Prof. Dr. W.J. Buma ta syn sechstichste jierdei* Groningen. p. 177-181, 1970.

Jo Daan. "Bilingualism of Dutch Immigrants in the U.S.A." *Dichtung, Sprache unde Gesellschaft. Akten des IV Internationalen Germanisten - Kongresses* (1970 Princeton). Frankfurt. p. 205-213, 1971.

Jo Daan. "Verschuiven van isoglossen" *Taal en Tongval.* XXIII. p 2-3, 1971.

Jo Daan. "Codewisseling en de oorzaken ervan - Miscellanea Frisica, red. N.r. Arhammer e.a. Assen. p. 229-236, 1984.

[2]The so-called Statenvertaling is translated between 1626 and 1637, and printed in 1637.

[3]L.W. de Bree. *Het platteland leert lezen en schrijven.* Amsterdam, 1946.

C. Hoppenbrouweres. "School, dialect en standaardtaal". *Werk-in-uitwoering.* red. J. Creten e.a. Leuven/Amersfoort. p. 159-171, 1986.

[4]J. van Lennep. *De vermakelijke spraakkunst.* Leiden, 1865.

C.G.N. de Vooys. "Jacob van Lennep over Hollandse aanspreekvormen in het midden van de negentiende eeuw". *Nieuwe Taalgids* 46. p. 31-32, 1953.

Jo Daan. "U en je". *Taal en Tongval XXX.* p 50-75, 1978.

[5]C.G.N. de Vooys. *Nederlandse spraakkunst.* 7e dr. Groningen. p. 140, 1967.

[6]L.A. te Winkel. "Nog iets over de hulpwoorden hebben en zijn". *Magazijn van Nederlandsche Taalkunde* 2. p. 31-34, 1848.

[7]W.Z. Shetter. "Brabants dialekt in Wisconsin". *Taal en Tongval.* IX. p. 183-189, 1957.

[8]W. Labov. "The social stratification of English in New York City". Washington,D.C. 1966.

Raven I. McDavid Jr. "Postvocalic -r in South Carolina: a social analysis". *Language in culture and society.* Ed. Dell Hymes,, New York/Evanston/London. p. 473-482, 1964.

[9]J.K. Chambers and Peter Trudgill. *Dialectology.* Cambridge, p. 190-191, 1980.

THE LANGUAGE OF DUTCH IMMIGRANTS
Dialect Museum or Laboratory for Dialect Loss

Henriette Schatz
P.J. Meertens Institute
Amsterdam Royal Netherlands Academy of Arts and Sciences

The Dutch have played an important role in the history of the United States. Since the foundation of the colony of Nieuw Nederland, in the early part of the Seventeenth Century, the Dutch were the most important segment of the population in the area around New York, despite the takeover by the British in 1664. Only slowly did this situation change, because in 1790 as much as eighty percent of the population in sixty-mile radius around New York still was of Dutch descent (Swierenga, 1985:1).

Nevertheless, the United States have generally not held a powerful attraction for Dutch immigrants. Even during the mostly economically motivated great immigration wave of the Nineteenth Century, the Netherlands contributed only modestly to the enormous stream of European immigrants entering the United States, particularly in comparison with other European countries. After France, Belgium, and Luxemburg, the Netherlands supplied the lowest percentage of immigrants in Europe, in the one hundred years between 1820 and 1920. Only 380,000 Dutch citizens moved to the United States during that period: an average rate of 72 per 100,000 Dutch citizens per year (Swierenga, 1985:27). In contrast, the total number of European immigrants entering the United States between 1821 and 1924, roughly the same one hundred year period, amounted to as many as 33 million (Ligterink: 1981:27).

After World War II, when the Dutch government formally encouraged emigration, fewer than 100,000 Dutch immigrants were admitted to the United States, as a result of the stringent and strictly enforced immigration quotas. Due to these limitations, many other prospective immigrants chose to move to Australia and Canada instead.

During the great immigration wave of the Nineteenth Century, the Dutch immigrants mainly settled in the Midwest. Here they founded a number of Dutch communities, which still exist in part, although they have lost much of their homogeneous Dutch character. These Dutch settlements offer interesting material for studying the processes of language choice and language use among immigrants in general, and the use of Dutch and its dialects in particular.

In 1966, Dr. Jo Daan and Henk Heikens of the Institute for Dialectology, Folklore and Onomastics -- now renamed the P.J. Meertens Institute -- of the Royal Netherlands Academy of Arts and Sciences, collected a large number of tape recordings of Dutch immigrants and their descendants. This corpus of data was collected with support of ZWO, the

Netherlands Organization for Pure Research, "in order to document the history of the Dutch language, its dialects, and the Frisian language in the United States" (Jaarboek KNAW, 1966:263). At the P.J. Meertens Institute, where these tapes are being kept, the material is now being investigated systematically to gain an insight in the processes governing language choice and language maintenance or loss among Dutch immigrants.

2. The Recordings from 1966

The material collected in 1966 covers approximately 75 hours of recordings of 285 different speakers. All these speakers either have immigrated before Word War I or are the children, and in some cases the grandchildren of immigrants from that period. In choosing the speakers the point of departure was that the speakers themselves, their parents, or their grandparents must have immigrated before the major social changes after World War I had taken place in the Netherlands. These changes had a profound effect on the use and the nature of dialects in the Netherlands. Expectations were that by using this method of data collection it would be possible to elicit data from earlier stages of the Dutch dialects, supposedly preserved in the American immigrant communities. These expectations were based on the notion that the immigrants would not have been subject to the same influences that conditioned dialect change in the Netherlands and would therefore have preserved older forms of the dialects.

The speakers who were eventually recorded are a diverse group. Among them are members of groups of Dutch immigrants, individual immigrants, their children, both Protestants and Catholics, speakers of Dutch dialects, and speakers of Frisian. The fact that so many different groups are included in the material should make is possible to compare immigrant Dutch or immigrant Frisian to their counterparts in the Netherlands.

The recordings all contain informal conversations about topics that are of interest to the speakers. Most often the conversations concern the situation of Dutch immigrants in the United States, their histories and their adventures. Sometimes a recording only contains one speaker, other times it contains several, including non-Dutch speakers. Besides recording informal speech, all informants were recorded counting to fifteen and naming the days of the week in Dutch. The immigrants were recorded in nine different places in the United States, mostly Nineteenth Century settlements in Massachusetts, Michigan, Iowa and Wisconsin.

3. The Recordings as a "Dialect Museum"

As has been explained earlier, one of the notions on which the collection of these remnants of Dutch, its dialects and Frisian was based was the idea that this material could provide interesting information about "older stages of spoken language which are no longer heard in the Netherlands under the influence of the standard" (Daan, 1984: 230). Having such older stages of the language on tape, as opposed to having them available only in written form, could provide us with a "dialect museum", as it were, located in the United States. Stagnating dialect change in the United States is assumed, for example, in the reconstruction by Daan (1971) of isoglosses in the North

Veluwe. These isoglosses are claimed to have moved further east in the hundred-year period between 1865 and 1966.

Still, this legitimate notion had already become subject to some doubts even on the part of those who recorded the material. Daan (1971: 77) herself suspects that the characteristics of the various dialects may not be so easy to track down any more "because of the contact of speakers from different dialect areas and the influence of [Standard (HFS)] Dutch, which was to a greater or lesser extent the language of the Church until as late as the post Word War I period."

Dutch dialects in the United States certainly have not undergone the same changes as their counterparts in the Netherlands, where the influence of the standard language, through the ever more important media and the increasing degree of education, has resulted in dialect change and dialect loss. However, apart from the influences mentioned by Daan, of the church and the contact between various dialect groups in the United States, there are quite a number of other influences that may indeed have changed the dialects of Dutch immigrants, though in different ways than the dialects in the mother country. Such factors conditioning changes in the immigrants' dialects will be discussed in more detail in a later section.

It is clear that the notion of a dialect museum has its problems. These problems are comparable to the methodological drawbacks of the apparent-time method used to study changes that have taken place in real time. The researcher can never be certain that the older group -- which supposedly represents the passage of time -- really shows the same phenomena that the younger group will exhibit in due course. It is equally difficult to ascertain in the language of immigrants whether the detected changes are in fact really due to dialect change.

Just one other possible cause of change may be illustrated by considering the age of the informants used by Daan to show the isogloss movement. De Bot (1985: 38) points out emphatically that in research on linguistic change not only internal and external mechanisms of change should be considered, but also the fact that, as a speaker gets older, physiological changes may influence linguistic phenomena within that individual. At any rate, this has been demonstrated to be true for the phonological level, because speakers of advanced age show changes in the production of both vowels and consonants (De Bot, 1975: 37). On the basis of this knowledge, a possible movement of isoglosses in North Veluwe dialect should be viewed with some reservations, since two of the four informants used by Daan were 84 and 86 years old, respectively, when they were recorded in 1966, while the other two were already in their sixties.

Apart from differences in possible processes of Dutch dialect change in the United States and the Netherlands, it is extremely difficult, under any circumstances, to compare material recorded on tape in the United States in 1966 with older Dutch dialect material.

In the first place, there is no reliable older material available for all Dutch dialects in the Netherlands. The existence of dialect monographs or other sources is generally a matter of chance and, more often than not, the dialect to be compared with its American counterpart does not even have a written source of material. In addition, such written material is always difficult to compare with oral material.

Secondly, it is difficult to analyze the oral language of immigrants, no matter what the circumstances are. For each individual immigrant a detailed knowledge is required of the dialect spoken by the person in question, in order to distinguish between real dialect change, interference from American English, and other phenomena which may have conditioned the differences between the immigrant's dialect and its counterpart used in the Netherlands.

Finally, comparison of Dutch written data about a dialect with audio recordings from a much later date and from a different country introduces a number of extra variables which can only be controlled by drastically limiting the choice of the material being investigated. Only then is it possible to gain a clear insight in the nature of language, language use, language choice and linguistic interference among Dutch immigrants in the United States.

4. The Investigation of the American Recordings

Despite these reservations, the corpus of tape recorded data from the United States is a treasure of valuable material for linguistic and other research. The recordings are not only of interest for the study of structural processes of language and dialect maintenance and loss, language choice, and linguistics interference. They also offer the possibility to investigate the relationship between these linguistic phenomena and a number of social and demographic factors. In addition, some of the material may be an interesting source for oral history research.

The plan to investigate the American material systematically comprises two components. In the first place, there is a linguistics component, which concerns the investigation of language and dialect maintenance and loss, language choice, and linguistic interference. Secondly, there is a socio-demographic component, comprising the collection of material about the social and demographic circumstances that contributed to the occurrence of certain linguistic phenomena.

5. A Selection of the Collected Linguistic Data

In setting up the investigation of the American corpus at the P.J. Meertens Institute, a selection of the material had to be made, chiefly for practical reasons. The total number of tapes is very substantial and investigation of all of them would require a long time. In addition, a judicious selection of the material makes it possible to control a number of disturbing extra variables, thus enhancing the possibilities for a systematic approach which will yield interesting results. The following decisions have been made regarding the selection of the material.

In the first place, it was decided to investigate only the speech of non-Frisian speaking informants. Exclusion of the Frisian speakers was a purely practical decision, since currently there is no investigator available with sufficient knowledge of Frisian to investigate the material. In a later stage this material may still be included in the project.

Secondly, all informants under investigation must be born in the Netherlands. The motivation for this limitation is the desire to exclude as many differences between the individual informants as possible. If those who were born in the United States are also included, there is no dimension on which all informants have the same characteristics, except for the fact that they all live in the United States. It seems reasonable for a study of the linguistic behavior of immigrants to investigate people who have actually immigrated themselves. In a later stage their behavior may then be compared to that of second or third generation immigrants. This decision still yielded a selection of almost 100 natives of the Netherlands who speak Dutch or one of its dialects.

The component of the study which specifically concerns dialect maintenance or loss will, for the time being, be restricted to two Dutch dialects: the dialects of Zeeland and Brabant. Within the Netherlands, these two dialects are currently still clearly distinguishable. In addition, there is a fair amount of literature available on these two varieties of Dutch and it is possible to find recorded data of modern-day dialect speakers from these two areas. The American corpus also contains a reasonable number of informants for each of the two dialects. There are about 10 speakers of Zeeland dialect and 20 speakers of Brabant dialect, who differ not only in terms of the dialect they speak, but who also have a very different social, demographic, and religious background. This should make a comparison of the two groups all the more interesting.

In order to investigate the specific processes of dialect maintenance or loss it is important to exclude as many other disturbing factors as possible. therefore, the choice was made to compare the American recordings with modern Dutch recordings of the same dialect and, if possible, from the same period. This method allows for the comparison of two similar bodies of data, so the results will not be muddled by apparent linguistics differences that are, in fact, differences resulting from a comparison of different types of data. Written material on the dialects under investigation will, of course, be used to support the conclusions that may be drawn from the comparisons of recorded data.

6. The Socio-Demographic Component

Apart from the linguistic data in the American corpus, there is also a body of socio-demographic data. Part of this information is already available, either because it has been supplied to the interviewers by the informants, or because it was collected by means of a questionnaire. Another part of this extralinguistic information must be gleaned from the tape recordings while they are being transcribed.

Facts that may be of interest to the investigation are, for example, the age of the informant at the time of recording, age of immigration, place of origin. Other information that should be included is, for instance, whether the immigrant was part of a group, and to what kind of group he or she belonged. All sorts of other general data about the behavior of immigrants may also be of importance, both concerning their situation before and after immigration. Other interesting facts may include the motive for immigration, the profession or trade of the informant in the Netherlands and in the United States, the immigrant's social status and wealth before and after immigration. Remarks about the use of language by the immigrants, the language of the spouse, the language used in the parental home or in the family, the language used in church and in school, and the immigrant's knowledge of English, both before and after immigration.

This summary of socio-demographic factors is by no means exhaustive and it stands to reason that during the course of the investigation other data may be included. When the socio-demographic information has been collected, it will be entered in a computer, in order to be able to use it, with as much flexibility as possible. By means of different selection procedures in a relational database the socio-demographic data will be related to the collected linguistic data.

7. The Status of the Investigation

The first order of business in the investigation is the transcription of the tape recordings, an extremely time-consuming task. So far, transcripts have been made of the speech of almost all 100 informants. Once all the material has been transcribed, excerpts of the transcripts will be entered in the computer. The excerpts of the American material will be analyzed on different linguistic levels in relation to the socio-demographic data.

At the same time, the socio-demographic information on the individual immigrants is currently being computerized. All the information gathered from the informants by the interviewers at the time of recording has already been entered in the database. It has been supplemented by data collected during transcription of the tapes, and information from other written sources.

On the basis of the transcripts available on paper, a first linguistic analysis has been started. In this analysis, all phenomena are noted which possibly contain linguistic information. These phenomena are then classified in a model for analysis based on the model devised by Weinreich (1953: 64) for describing language contact and interference. the Weinreich model will be modified, refined, and extended, as needed, to make it specifically suitable for analysis of the American corpus. Using this method will make it possible to quantify the linguistic data, so that the results of the investigation may be tested statistically.

When enough data has been analyzed in this way, a hierarchy will be set up, partly on the basis of the analysis and partly on an impressionistic basis. In this hierarchy, a number of informants will be rated on fluency by a panel of Dutch native speakers. Dialect differences will be controlled as much as possible, both on the part of the informants and on the part of the panel members. This method will serve to develop a fluency-measure which may then be related to the linguistic and socio-demographic data of the informants. Eventually, this method will serve to make statements, which may be tested statistically, about the relationship between the maintenance of loss of fluency in Dutch or a Dutch dialect and certain socio-demographic conditioning factors.

8. First Version of the Model for Analysis

For the analysis of interference phenomena it is necessary, first of all, to define the concept clearly. In this investigation it is defined according to Weinreich (1953:1), who considers interference "those instances of deviation from the norms of either language which occur in the speech of bilinguals as a result of their familiarity with more than one language." Weinreich himself remarks in the introduction of his descriptive model that there is no easy way to measure or characterize the total impact of one language on the other in the language use of bilingual speakers. His point of departure is that "the only possible procedure is to describe the various forms of interference and to tabulate their frequency" (1953:1). In effect, this is the method that will be used in investigating the corpus of American data.

In order to be able to quantify the various forms of interference, and, in particular, to be able to use the computer in doing so, the data will be categorized in a model for analyzing interference. The set of categories presented here represent only a first version of the model, which will be refined on the basis of the research results. So far, the following categories of interference phenomena have been distinguished.

    A.   Lexical interference

        I.   Domain-specific

        II.   Non Domain-specific

            a.   English to Dutch dialect
            b.   Dutch/dialect to English

                1.   loan
                2.   loan plus repair
                3.   habitual/frequent item
                4.   function word
                5.   loan transaction
                6.   other

    B.   Phonological interference

        a.   English to Dutch dialect
        b.   Dutch/dialect to English

    C.   Morphological interference

        a.   English to Dutch dialect
        b.   Dutch/dialect to English

D. Syntactic interference

    a. English to Dutch dialect
    b. Dutch/dialect to English

    1. word order

E. Code-switching

    a. English to Dutch dialect
    b. Dutch/dialect to English

    1. Triggered
    2. Untriggered

9. Examples of different types of interference

As an illustration of the different categories in the model, a number of examples of different types of interference will be given here.

Lexical interference can be divided into two types: domain-specific and non-domain-specific interference. The difference lies in the nature of the concepts for which the interference occurs. If the immigrant may be assumed to have learned the concepts he or she is discussing after immigration, the domain for the concept is most likely not known in Dutch. Such interference of English is of different order than seemingly random, non-domain-specific interference. Domain-specific interferences are, for example: "telephone operator", "telephone company", "medical school", "alleen voor de Young People Meeting". Non-domain-specific interferences are: "die namen een interest in mij", or "je direction vinden".

Examples of loans plus repair are: "onze next......onze naaste buren", or "onze second......tweede huwelijksreis". Interferences in frequent or habitual items are: "well", "and", "so", "see", "you know", "all right", "alrijt", "finally", "fijndelijk". Interference in function-words concern, for example: "but", or "because". Loan translations of various kinds are phenomena like "en zo aan" (= "and so on"), instead of "enzovoort"; "kom eens over" (= come over:), instead of :"kom eens langs"; "ik behoorde aan verschillende verenigingen" (= "I belonged to:), instead of "ik was lid van verschillende verenigingen", "hij leek het niet" (= "he didn't like it"), instead of "hij hield er niet van".

Phonetic interference may have the character of English sound patterns for the realization of Dutch sounds, like, for example, word-initial aspiration of plosives in words like "tante", "kopen", "pakje". English words or names may also be realized with Dutch pronunciations, as in "Grand Rapids", "Kalamazoo", "Young People Meeting", "lomberjard" (= "lumberyard"), "ze wouen m'n fonnie klozes zien" (= "funny clothes"), "in de ouwe kontrie" (= "the old country"), "alrijt" (= "all right"), "Fijndelijk" (= "finally").

When morphological interference takes place, sometimes Dutch morphology will be attached to English words, as in "schooltje", pronounced with English sound patterns, or "we hebben land gecleard" (= "we cleared land") or "reformde kerk"; "peggen" (= "to peg"), for "een houten pen indrijven"; "gepegd" (= "pegged"); "die roaden (= wegen) waren slecht". Other times, Dutch words are given English morphology, as in "offvijlen" (= "to file off"), instead of "afvijlen".

Syntactic interferences have not been very frequent in the material that has been analyzed so far. This is not surprising, since syntactic phenomena are generally less frequent than those on other linguistic levels. The syntactic interferences that have been found until now concern mostly word order, because many of the immigrants will use English word order in their Dutch. Examples of this type of interference are: "ze wisten we kwamen van Rotterdam", or "met al onze uitvindingen we kunnen de wereld haast kopen".

Code-switches, the final category of interference, may be divided into triggered and untriggered switches. When there is a clear linguistic or non-linguistic cause for the speaker to switch language, the code-switch is called triggered, while in other cases the code-switch seems to be unconditioned. An example of triggered code-switching is: "ik woonde op een farm tot mijn huwelijk...... (remark by interviewer) ......after I got married I moved to Grand Rapids". In this case the interviewer asks the speaker, first in Dutch and then, when he does not understand her, on account of his deafness, in English, where he lived after he got married. The question in English triggered the English answer and thus the code-switch. Untriggered code-switches are, for example "de eerste gereformeerde......reformde kerk in America, or say in Holland, see', or 'een paar woordjes, that's about it, because I was only a little kid, but ik kon 't wel lezen'.

The examples in this section are provided by way of illustration of the way in which the model for analysis will work. In the material that has been analyzed until now, not all types of interference have been found yet. In further investigation of the recordings an analysis will be made of the language of each individual informant, taking into account the dialect background of the speaker in question. By doing both a quantitative and a qualitative analysis of the speech of each individual and by relating the linguistic data to the socio-demographic information that is known about the speaker, it will be possible to draw documented conclusions about the nature of language, language use, and language choice of Dutch immigrants in the United States. The results of this research will not only shed light on the specific developments concerning the language of Dutch immigrants in the United States, they will also have implications for research on the language of immigrants in general, both in the United States and in other parts of the world.

BIBLIOGRAPHY

Bot, K. de. Onderzoek naar Taalverandering en het Gebruik van de "Apparent-Time" method. *Forum der letteren*, 26:1,33-40, 1985.

Daan, J. Codewisseling en de Oorzaken Ervan. In: N.R. Arhammar et al. *Miscellanea Frisica*. Assen: Van Gorcum, 1984.

Jaarboek. *Jaarboek der Koninklijke Nederlandse Akademie van Wetenschappen, 1966/1967*. Amsterdam: Noord Hollandsche Uitgevers Maatschappij, 1966.

Ligterink, G.H. *De landverhuizers*. Zutphen: de Walburg Pers, 1981.

Swierenga, Robert P. *The Dutch in America: Immigration, Settlement and Change*. New Brunswick, N.J.: Rutgers University Press, 1985.

Weinreich, U. *Languages in Contract*. New York: Publications of the Linguistic Circle of New York.

**History
and
Politics
of the
Low
Countries**

BLUE LITTLE BOOKS AND POLITICAL LIFE IN THE DUTCH REPUBLIC[1]

Craig E. Harline
University of Idaho

It is unusually pleasant to be in a setting where I am considered perfectly sane because I study the history of the Netherlands. During a recent visit to an unnamed school, I was told that I had been invited to interview for a particular job in the History department despite my interest in the Low Countries. I won't tell you the outcome of that visit, except to say that this was one case when I was more than willing to assume the attitude of the angry fox who walked away from the grapes.

Many people outside modern-day Belgium and the Netherlands continue to regard the Low Countries as merely cute curiosities, important for windmills, dikes, wooden shoes, and paintings; what significance could they possibly have in European history? Yet clearly this picture is beginning to change among inhabitants of the non-Netherlandish world. Within the past twenty years English-speaking historians have turned out an unprecedented number of books and articles which illustrate what Dutch and Belgian scholars have argued for over a century in their native tongue--the economic, cultural, and political significance of the Netherlands in medieval and early modern Europe.

I am particularly interested in cultural developments during the early modern period. In the general sense, my current project may be viewed as part of the effort to understand better some of the consequences of print for European society and thought. Specifically, I have studied the "little books," or pamphlets, in the years between 1565 and 1648. I should note at the outset that the word "pamphlet" was actually not used in Dutch until about 1700. I use it in the generic sense, as it encompasses a variety of contemporary terms such as pasquil, libel, little book, or tiding. All such writings had two things in common: (1) they provided information and commentary on current events, and were therefore usually of political consequence; and (2) they were printed, which to a modern-day observer might seem obvious but it should not be taken for granted.

Because they are numerous and often lively, pamphlets have long been recognized as valuable historical sources, indeed that is how I became familiar with them in the first place. But we know very little about their contemporary significance. Under the influence of studies by Eisenstein and Darnton on printing and the diffusion of ideas, I began to wonder, who wrote pamphlets and why? To whom were they directed? If, as commonly supposed, to the "common man," then why? Who read pamphlets? How and by whom were pamphlets brought to press and distributed, and what does this reveal? Who wrote them? What made pamphlets different from other media of the time? What were the major themes and approaches used by pamphleteers? In short, I approached pamphlets as a medium, not as repositories of historical facts but as a historical phenomenon in their right.

Obviously, I could not begin to answer all of these questions in any detail today, but I have reviewed them to give you an idea of the general context in which this study was conceived. I looked for pieces of these puzzles in governmental resolutions and proceedings, church resolutions and proceedings, private letters, publishing records and related materials about book dealers and pamphleteers, and in the pamphlets themselves. I read thousands of pamphlets for impressionistic pieces of evidence, and I analyzed them systematically as well. The statistical basis of the study became two samples from the important pamphlet collection in the Royal Library: a sample of 500 titles selected at random, and a "bestseller" sample of 87--for practical purposes, those titles printed four times or more. With the aid of quantitative techniques, I analyzed three basic kinds of variables: biographical information about the persons involved in production, bibliographical information about the pamphlet itself, and general pamphlet content.

The first thing that emerged from all this digging was a clear pattern in pamphlet growth. Assuming that the number of pamphlets which remains is representative of what was published at the time, pamphlet production would suddenly surge, level off for years or even decades, surge again to a new plateau, and so on. The major turning points occurred about 1565, 1607 and 1649. Before 1565 pamphlets appeared in quantities of about one to ten per year, and their production was well controlled. The range of production rose to between 30 and 75 during the four decades from 1565 to 1606, and pamphleteering continued to be dominated by governmental propaganda, particularly in the early stages of the Revolt. The next and most important turning point in Dutch pamphleteering was in 1607. After this date, not only did decennial production averages increase nearly four times over previous decades (between 130 and 240), but the character of pamphleteering changed as well--for the first time in history, outside of periods of civil war, we see major pamphlet campaigns launched from within a European country against official policies and personalities of that country. Most pamphlets were now coming from unofficial sources. After 1648, tracts appeared consistently at the rate of about 200 to 300 per year, and the government was in effect almost helpless to stop them. Partly out of convenience, and largely in light of this general pattern, I decided to focus on the first two periods of growth, between 1565 and 1648, what I considered the formative years of Dutch pamphleteering.

In order to understand how and why this growth occurred, we need to know something about the political nation of the Republic, those whose voices mattered. Most of you are familiar with the major institutions: the Princes of Orange, the States General, the Provincial States, the local political bodies. In theory, these formal institutions and the 2,000 or so regents who controlled them were all that mattered politically. There were no elections or other kinds of direct participation among the ruled, nor did most people consider such formal participation necessary. But in practice, at least in the urban areas of Holland, Zeeland, and Utrecht, there were many more people whose political opinions mattered--the large populations of merchants, over 1,000 strongly opinionated Calvinist preachers, even a good number of wealthy craftsmen and shopkeepers. And this is why people bothered to write pamphlets--they came to serve as a forum for, or as a means to reach, these unofficial political elements.

Since pamphlets were technically illegal, how did they not only survive but increase? This was also largely a consequence of the political structure. There was no strong central institution in the Republic; local and provincial "privileges," or virtual autonomy, were held up as political ideals. The result of this decentralized government was that the production of pamphlets was in practice impossible to control beyond the local, perhaps the provincial level. A banned pamphlet or author would soon be found in the next town or province.

With this fundamental understanding of the Republic (and let me emphasize that it is fundamental; I have presented to you in two minutes what observers of the Republic have tried to solve for centuries) and the conditions which promoted pamphleteering, we are now able to examine in more detail the actual place of pamphlets in political life. Were pamphlets indeed directed to the non-elite elements of Dutch society, and did these persons bother to read them? Without broad interest in pamphlets, their effect would have been inconsequential.

Again using 1606 as the dividing point, pamphleteers generally went from addressing an elite international audience to a socially broad domestic one. This is based partly upon direct statements, but especially upon indirect clues, such as the efforts of pamphleteers (who were usually not of common origins) to identify with the common man, the brief length of pamphlets, their relatively cheap price, the trend toward more pamphlets in the Dutch language, the shift in pamphlet content from international to domestic topics, or the increasingly common practice of using imaginative, entertaining approaches and appears in pamphlets. Dialogues, for instance, were set in everyday surroundings, in canal boats, taverns, wagons, or the street, with familiar Dutch characters.

That brings us to a major problem--who read the pamphlets? We do not know whether or how many small merchants and craftsmen and women and non-nobles and modest burghers read a particular pamphlet. But we again have indirect, general clues such as the ability of common people to read. Based on quantitative analysis of signees in the Amsterdam Marriage Register--about 60% for the men and 35% for the women--and on qualitative evidence taken from church records, a picture emerges of comparatively high literacy in the Republic.

This is a start, but it obviously does not solve the puzzle of pamphlet readership. Clearly not everyone could read, and those who could did not necessarily read pamphlets; there were all kinds of other media available to 17th century Dutch men and women: songs and poems on the market, town criers, parades, the Bible, devotional works, folk books, sensational accounts about smothered heretics, miracles in the Amsterdam work house, a woman who carted her sick husband all over Europe looking for a cure, or the scandalous tale of a quiltworker's wife who bought a baby and pretended it was her own. Could people find pamphlets in this forest? Given the high rate of literacy and the general availability of printed materials, this actually boils down to a matter of interest. Were people interested enough in current affairs to search out pamphlets?

They were indeed. Booksellers assumed their audience's knowledge of current affairs, dialogue scenes show boatmen, wagoneers, cloth-shearers, carpenters, sawyers, and masons discussing politics around the fire, in taverns, in boats, and on the street. Men and women are frequently portrayed reading, discussing, and lending pamphlets, and angry officials tried to track down offensive pamphlets but discovered they had come to late--the tracts had been sold out.

The best evidence of political interest lies in the book and pamphlet trade itself, with those persons who depended upon their knowledge of what people read for their livelihood. Besides the four-fold increase in pamphlet production and in the number of booksellers, besides scattered direct statements about the perception of political interest among booksellers, I have also examined the organization and methods of the book and pamphlet trade to see what these might reveal. Books and pamphlets were distributed throughout the Republic thanks to extensive communication networks. Sometimes tracts were spread by hand, or through the mail, or sent in bulk by boat or wagon. One 23 year old student, needing money for school, smuggled books for pay during a summer or two. But especially important were small-time itinerant merchants who sold tracts and other wares for a living.

For the printers and sellers of pamphlets, this economic element was paramount. Very few were forever loyal to a particular cause--Albrecht Hendricksz of Delft even stopped taking communion so he could print and sell as he pleased. Book dealers were concerned first and foremost with making a profit, and the profits from pamphlets came through sales, not stuffy dedications to some wealthy patron. Printers and "publishers" had an average overall output of only about 10, at most 20, issues per year; one had to be very careful about what one published, particularly when it was a work which depended on sales and not subsidies. A book dealer would not risk publishing a work that he (or she) did not think would sell; but book traders continued to publish pamphlets, and in increasing quantities, attesting to the public's interest in them.

This prospect of widespread interest is of great importance for the next and most difficult part of the puzzle--that is, just what influence did pamphlets exert upon political life? Direct evidence about the effect of a specific pamphlet or series of pamphlets is as scarce as a warm winter's day in Friesland. There are scattered statements about the grumbling and murmuring which a pamphlet could cause among the populace, but little else. This is not really surprising, since people probably did not read pamphlets and then run out and riot. Pamphlets could add to the store of information and contribute to forming currents of opinion, but these kinds of gradual changes are not usually recorded and do not lend themselves easily to measurement. In the end, what is clear, and ultimately most important, is that the politically interested believed people were eager to read pamphlets, and that pamphlets could influence how people thought. Their increasing actions to control the press show that in their view it was becoming more and more important to win the hearts and minds of the gemeente.

Religious and secular officials not surprisingly sought to restrict any kind of public discussion. Dutch regents were in perfect accord with their counterparts in monarchical states: "ask not what the people states: desire of your rule," said an old maxim. And this meant there was no need for unauthorized critics and pamphlets. Both the state and the church tried to control the press by restrictive laws and by promoting pamphlets of their own. Restrictive efforts were largely unsuccessful, primarily because of the political fragmentation I discussed earlier, but these efforts illustrate how seriously they regarded public discussion of what were once their own "secret" affairs. Let us not become too caught up in the extensive praise for the freedom in the Republic--it existed, but we must remember that it was in large part the result of certain conditions, and not of enlightened, "modern" attitudes. Had they been able, Dutch regents would have suppressed as many works as their counterparts in other European states.

Critics of the government took advantage of the relatively free Dutch press, and were especially instrumental in broadening the extent of political discussion in the Republic. Only when critical pamphlets began to appear in significant quantities did Dutch pamphleteering really blossom. This encouraged not only other critics, but an unprecedented number of apologists. Hesitant at first about openly opposing their rulers, many pamphleteers eventually overcame their scruples, concluding they had no other choice but to make their opinions known, and soothing their consciences with the balm of simplified Calvinist doctrines of resistance, or even the works of high political theorists such as Althusius. Appeal to one's rulers was not a new practice, but printed tracts offered a new twist to this venerable tradition: instead of being directed to the regents only, they were now presented to the public as well. Critical pamphleteers hoped that open discussion and the prospect of a potentially dissatisfied public would put the fear of riot into their rulers. What is striking is that the largest groups of critical pamphleteers--preachers, nobles, and even some political officials, had the legal right to remonstrate directly to ruling bodies. They obviously felt that their wishes were more likely to be granted if presented in a public forum as well.

One fragment of evidence illustrates nicely how Dutch rulers could have been affected by the perception of widespread interest in pamphlets and politics. A person opposed to public political discussion remarked offhandedly that he sat on a market boat to Harderwijk and observed a distinguished looking gentleman across from him. He couldn't tell who this man was, since he said little, but supposed "he was a regent, for while traveling they normally keep very still and don't reveal themselves, saying very little, in order to hear what the common man is saying, both on wagons and on boats." Regents did not necessarily hear or read what was being said and then act accordingly, but they did feel the need to keep an ear to the ground. This was much different than the situation of many decades before.

Let me tie these various ideas up here. The proliferation of pamphleteering clearly reflected extensive political interest among the Dutch. It cannot be quantified, but it was significant enough to cause the politically powerful and interested to take notice and to increase their efforts to win the loyalties of the gemeente. This in turn made the political importance of the gemeente even greater. Issues were no longer known only to "those who ought to have knowledge of such affairs," but were brought before the "common man, who possesses no discernment and judgment for such matters." Pamphlets did not replace the protest riot, but the prospect of information in the hands of the inexperienced was new and effective means to compel regents to listen, as the regent sitting quietly in the boat illustrates.

How do Dutch developments compare to those in other European countries? France, England, and Germany all had pamphlets in quantities comparable to Dutch totals. They appeared in large numbers in Germany during the Reformation, in France during the Wars of Religion, under Cardinal Richelieu, and the Fronde, in England during the Civil Wars, and even to some extent in Spain. But Dutch developments were different in two importance respects: (1) the practice of critical pamphleteering in the Republic grew consistently during periods of normal government as well as in times of crisis; and (2) on the other side of the press, in the case of Richelieu and the Spanish arbitristas, pamphlets were well controlled and produced for the most part by the government. This was not the case in the Republic after 1600, when unofficial pamphleteers far outnumbered those of official station. So we see in the Republic perhaps the first state in which political discussion became routine, and I use that word recognizing that it represents a development which was hardly automatic, inevitable, or even well-liked, but that's the best way I can describe it.

Finally, a last word about the role of the unique features of print. Contemporaries clearly recognized the major features of print culture: standardization, increased output and audience, and amplification of time-honored ideas. Limitations of time have kept me from saying much about these features today. But let me close with an incident from 1572 which reflects something about the importance of print. In that year, the States of Holland met to decide their plan of defense against Spain. Their primary objective was to restore the ancient privileges of the Land. No one knew exactly what these privileges were, but it was known that the valuable documents on which they were written were secured in a chest in a locked castle near Gouda. (Important documents--important partly because they were scarce--were often secured in this manner for fear of their being lost). The rebels appointed a delegation to go get these privileges and to see what they said. Three years later, the delegates finally left, taking with them a blacksmith to force the door and to break open the chests. They discovered that some of the chests were empty, some of the papers were very damp, and that some were completely decayed. They ended up finding nothing specific which could help them determine the exact privileges granted to Holland. In this situation, it didn't matter, since the myth of privileges was far more important than their content; people continued to fight for them. But this search in 1572 for political information was in striking contrast to the situation of the 1620's and 30's and 40's. Although the privileges continued to be locked up in chests, a great deal of other political information was not, either figuratively or literally. No longer was it restricted to the knowledge of a privileged few, but brought out into the open, and this made the gemeente of greater political importance. Pamphlets helped to provide not only information and to present ideas but were themselves an application of the principle that the subjects had to be considered in government, having at least--but also at most--an informal say in it. That's all those who were interested wanted, and I hope I have persuaded you that they largely succeeded in getting it.

NOTES

[1] For more extensive treatment of this subject, see my Pamphlets, Printing and Political Culture in the Early Dutch Republic (Dordrecht:Martinus Nijheff, 1987).

PROLEGOMENA FOR A BIOGRAPHY OF
JAN RUDOLPH THORBECKE, PART I

F.L. Van Holthoon
University of Groningen

Introduction

Usually when a biographer starts his work, his first task is to assemble his sources. Letters to and from his personage have to be solicited and documents and personal notes have to be sifted and dated. Not so in the case of Thorbecke. His personal archive is in perfect order and it is unlikely that a search for other material outside this collection will turn up new material of importance. Thorbecke started the collection himself, his wife pursued his work and his children and grandchildren rounded off the task. At present this collection is in the General State Archive in The Hague and - with minor restrictions - it is open to the public. The publication of his correspondence is well under way. This year a third volume will be published bringing it up to the date of 1840.

So Thorbecke prepared the road for his biographer very well, but it did not help him in getting a definitive biography, that is a biography based on this archival material. We, the Dutch, have no tradition for biography. Great men make us nervous, because they so obviously transcend the boundaries of average merit which as a nation we like to set for ourselves as a goal in life. The Dutch are not great admirers, they feel more comfortable criticising greatness.

In the case of Thorbecke there is also a special reason why his biography still has to be written. His contemporaries regarded him as an outsider. Political opponents made it the point of their acid criticism that Thorbecke did not understand his countrymen. This criticism touches on an important point. Indeed, though Thorbecke is justly regarded as the founding father of Dutch liberalism, his version of liberalism clashed with a political culture which had its roots in the history of the Dutch republic and which helped to mold the liberalism of a political establishment to which Thorbecke did not belong by birth. In fact one might say that he never became a partner to it. Thorbecke's liberalism resembled that of the French doctrinaires or the German constitutional liberals, and like them he regarded the State as the highest ethical goal which a civil society could reach for itself. For his opponents - which very often also called themselves liberals - or even many of his admirers and supporters the State was a means. Or to put it in different terms, Thorbecke adhered to the ideal of positive liberty, and the other Dutch to the ideal of negative liberty, or freedom from restraint. Politically this was a major source of controversy, less perhaps so when translated in terms of concrete issues, more so in terms of political attitudes. An older and experienced colleague once remarked to me that it is still too early to write the biography of Thorbecke. Too early more than a hundred years after his death! But there is a lot of truth in his remark, for it is still difficult to measure the meaning of his existence, of his public as well as his private life. He was different from the average Dutchman and his biographer has to deal with this fact before he can write the story of Thorbecke's life.

For me the fact that Thorbecke was an outsider is a major challenge to study his life and works. The next number of the *Bijdragen en Mededelingen betreffende de Geschiedenis der Nederlanden* will publish an article of mine entitled "De Genese van Thorbeckes Organische Staatsleer" (The Genesis of Thorbecke's Organical Doctrine of the State). Back in the Netherlands I hope to be able to devote a considerable part of my research time to the writing of a definitive biography of the Netherland's most distinguished nineteenth century statesman. There are two aspects to this study which makes it particularly worthwhile:

1. The fact that Thorbecke was an outsider makes it possible to use the study of his life as a kind of yardstick measuring the political culture of his age.

2. Thorbecke entered politics as an intellectual and became a statesman. This change of career opens an interesting vista on the role of the intellectual in nineteenth century Dutch (in fact European) politics.

Let me briefly discuss some of the formative influences on his life and career.

Thorbecke's Relationship to His Father

Thorbecke was the son of a tobacco merchant in Zwolle who lost his trade during the continental blockade in the reign of Napoleon. Father Thorbecke had to struggle all his life to make ends meet. Plaintively he petitioned the Dutch King William I time and again for a job, but he never succeeded in getting a government post. The education of his bright son was clearly seen as an investment for the family. Father borrowed right and left to get his son to the gymnasium in Zwolle, the Athenaeum in Amsterdam, and to the University of Leiden. The relationship between father and son was warm, always respectful and indeed very complicated. As a young student Thorbecke wrote his own protector, the Leiden professor Melchior Kemper, a very sharp rebuke in which he accused Kemper for not having been diligent enough in helping his father, demonstrating that astounding lack of tact which was so often taken for arrogance. Here we meet the loyal son, as in so many of his letters home. Yet when his father died, Thorbecke was probably absent at his funeral and we don't know the reason for his absence.

It would take many pages to unravel their complicated relationship, but one remark can be made in this short compass. Thorbecke by his upbringing - his provincial background and his poverty - was an outsider to the establishment and for him the way to become a member of it was through his intellectual achievements. His intellectual ambition was shaped by the circumstances of his upbringing, and his ambition egged him on to prove himself in the eyes of others. What - or if anything - happened between father or son we do not know, but it may well be that the father gradually changed from a revered figure into an object of pity as Thorbecke began to earn success and distinction in his own career. The father always complaining was a vivid reminder of the years of mortification which was born with a stoic countenance.

The psychological roots of Thorbecke's intellectual ambition were never fully understood by his contemporaries. And we cannot blame them. For Thorbecke had never any difficulty in mixing with the noblemen and patricians of the establishment. His intellectual achievements were always acknowledged. He won prizes as a student, he obtained a scholarship from the king which enabled him to spend two years of his life in Germany travelling and teaching. He was not appointed to a chair of philosophy in Leiden, but not long afterwards he got a chair as extraordinarius in Gent. And when a refugee in Leiden, after the Belgian secession, he was made a professor in the juridical faculty of Leiden, and he became one of its most distinguished and respected members. Why could this man act as if he had a chip on his shoulder? When slighted - or when he felt slighted - he could act with relentless arrogance. The trouble with an outsider is that he can only become an insider when he accepts the unwritten rules of the establishment, and Thorbecke could never do that. And that is why he was so extraordinarily sensitive of his honour.

His Relationship to His Wife, His Children and His Friends

Thorbecke married a girl 17 years younger than himself. She was the daughter of the German philosopher Solger and the marriage was very happy. When she died a few years before her husband his contemporaries noted that he was a broken man. Visitors to his house coming for the first time were always amazed that a man so aloof and forbidding in public life was such a gentle pater familias. His letters to his wife are effusive and sentimental. They portray the emotions of a Biedermeier.

This sharp division between the public and the private sphere which is one of the distinct elements of nineteenth century bourgeois family life demonstrates how much Thorbecke was a romantic at heart. He wanted to gather around him his family and his devoted friends whom he could trust completely and without afterthought. He needed the private sphere to give full vent to his feelings. The public, the hostile world was encountered with stoic restraint and a set of rigid principles of conduct.

Time and again Thorbecke broke with old friends. Often we don't know what the reason was, but the pattern is always the same. They were banished from the private sphere and then became aliens and often enemies. Thorbecke knew no gradations of friendship and love.

His two eldest sons who apparently had no aptitude for learning were sent off to sea against the wishes of at least one of them. Both of them died almost immediately after their arrival in the Dutch Indies. It almost looks as if they were banished. Did they disappoint their father? What made Thorbecke decide to send them off with such disastrous results? Was he feeling that they had to succeed on their own like he had done, and if not by intellectual achievement then by the traditional alternative of going out East to make a fortune? It is the task of the biographer to try to understand not criticise his personage and these questions require a long and delicately phrased answer. All I can say at this stage is that the example of the sending away of his sons fits in the pattern of his relationship to other people. They could not stay within the protected sphere of the family, they had to make their mark in the world. To be dependent on someone else was the worst fate which Thorbecke could imagine for a person. The dichotomy of the public and the private sphere was geared to that fact. A man (not a woman!) could only have a private sphere if he had earned his place in the world.

Thorbecke's Shift from Philosophy to Political History

Thorbecke travelled in Germany between 1820 and 1824. He deeply underwent the influence of the Biedermeierzeit. The characteristic of that age may be summed up as romanticism tamed within the mold of Restauration politics and government. Metternich, the Prussian king, and other German princes wanted to set their house in order after the onslaught of Napoleon on their states. Political opposition was eliminated and philosophy was relegated to metaphysics. Metternich's maxim was total quietness, but he did not succeed, not in the long run at least. Heine was making fun of Germany in Paris and even Hegel, that paragon of Prussian respectability, claimed for philosophy a measure of independence which was slightly disturbing (offset by the soothing thought that his philosophy was too difficult to understand anyway).

The Germany which Thorbecke was visiting was simmering beneath the surface, but there is no reference to politics in his letters or diaries of the time. He came to Germany as a philosophy student with the task to study German philosophy. Only gradually we notice a shift of attention. Thorbecke in 1822 had the prospect of becoming a professor of philosophy in Leiden, but he was disappointed in his hope. This may have been a boon and not a misfortune after all. Though he immersed himself deeply in German idealist philosophy he recoiled from its implications. He would not have been much of a philosopher. His point of view was a middle of the road pragmatism which betrayed his Dutch background as he acknowledged himself in the thirties.

Two early works: *Ueber das Wesen und den Organischen Charakter der Geschichte* (1824) and *Bedenkingen aangaande het Regt en den Staat* (1825) should be read as statements in which Thorbecke distanced himself from speculative philosophy and aimed at a concrete analysis of historical change. Reading the notes of his lectures in Gent (1825-1830) we can see how he distilled from the study of the French Revolution a point of view which he could apply to the study of constitutional law as well as to its implementation. The principle tenet of his political philosophy was that the French Revolution had heralded a new era in history and that liberals and conservatives alike had to learn to understand the fact that there was no return possible to the *Ancien Regime*.

The Development of his Constitutional Ideas

For many of his contemporaries, and even for some historians today, Thorbecke who defended the Dutch king against the Belgian revolutionaries, was a conservative legitimist who turned into a liberal during the political battles of the forties. I argue in the article which I mentioned before that Thorbecke remained consistent in his basic idea that the necessary political reforms should be accomplished in an organic way. As he explained to his friend Groen van Prinsterer in 1831: "If the doctrine of popular sovereignty is not again to lead to the result of the first revolution, it must be made into a system which is organic into all its details". His draft for the constitution of 1848 was his final answer to this problem.

Liberalism in the nineteenth century has two faces. First there is what may be defined as radical liberalism. It was prominent in England. It was ideological, had a large following in the population (the anti-cornlaw league, chartism), it was not very sophisticated, nor consistent in its aims. Popular sovereignty, a favourite notion of this type of liberals, was as its critics remarked, very vague. As a populist movement this type of liberalism easily changed its ideological cloak and became a form of reformist socialism. The transition in arguments was easily made, because liberty was associated with equality the socialist argument being that greater emphasis should be given to equality before true liberty could be gained for all people.

Then there was a second type of liberalism, let me call it constitutional liberalism.

This type of liberalism was prominent on the continent of Europe and it was represented by men like Guizot and Tocqueville in France, by Dahlmann and Gervinus in Germany, and by Thorbecke in the Netherlands. For these liberals the State was not a means but an end of human endeavour. In the wake of Hegel (and of course Aristotle long before him) they argued that the State is the product of the pursuit of the just and the rational and to the extent that human beings succeeded in this pursuit the State would determine what was just and rational in any existing civil order. The State in its actual configuration derives its authority from the degree to which a higher moral consensus is accomplished and only to the extent of this accomplishment it becomes the 'moral boundary' for the behaviour of its citizens. These constitutional liberals were very distrustful of the doctrine of popular sovereignty, because in their eyes the lawmaking process cannot be decided by majority vote. There must be a higher authority which ensures that liberty is guaranteed and justice is done. That is why they made sovereignty reside in the law-making and law-enforcing agencies of the State. They believed in what I have termed before positive liberty, that is the freedom - almost duty - to perform certain moral acts.

In actual history these two types should be rather called the two faces of liberalism, because in practice - regarding persons as well as doctrines - these two types intermingle. In one respect, however, they can be sharply distinguished as types. Radical liberalism remarkably enough attracted no intellectuals of major importance while constitutional liberalism had the backing of first class theoreticians. It was no accident that a major theoretical effort was spent in the service of constitutional liberalism. It was seen by its intellectual authors as a corrective for the popular ideology of radical liberalism, and as such constitutional liberalism was also seen as an instrument to shape the forces of social change which were the outcome of this ideology so that they would fit within an organic mold. Radical liberalism was the liberalism of the OTHERS, that is the vast masses of people, entrepreneurs and workers together, who by their scramble for wealth, security, happiness and distinction were building the industrial world. Constitutional liberalism was the effort of the WE, that is of liberal intellectuals, to contain the liberalism of the OTHERS by leaving an imprint of higher values on public life. Thorbecke belonged to the WE, and if only because of this it made him an outsider in a society which basked itself in a rather complacent and selfindulgent form of liberalism. There is some irony in the fact that he nevertheless became the architect of the constitution of 1848 which determines the structure of Dutch politics to this very day. But perhaps his prominent role in March 1848 was no accident, because the Dutch needed an outsider at that particular moment of crisis. And his role was beneficial. To quote myself: "Perhaps because Thorbecke was an outsider his constitution bore so much fruit, his extraordinary intellectual gifts have given an extra element of distinction to our political culture by which the Dutch state has become more than a handle for particular interests".

A Biography, Part I

These are some of the formative influences which made Thorbecke into the man and statesman he was. 1848 or perhaps 1849, when he relinquished his professorship in Leiden and became a professional politician, constitutes a watershed in his life. Since then Thorbecke had to deal with the stubborn facts of daily political issues which were less amenable to higher principles. Quite naturally I have divided my biography in two parts. In the second part the vista of Thorbecke's life will change. He entered politics as an intellectual, he became a politician, sometimes a statesman.

CRISIS, INSTABILITY, CONTINUITY IN THE DUTCH POLITICAL SYSTEM:
The Cruise Missiles and the 1986 Election

Samuel J. Eldersveld
The University of Michigan

Anyone who has followed Dutch politics in the Eighties is certainly aware of the crisis atmosphere within which political decisions had to be made. The election of May 21, 1986 in a sense is to be seen as reflecting the turmoil of the four years. This is again an expression by the Dutch public of their evaluation of political parties and their leadership. It is also a major event in the continuing process of the re-stabilization of the Dutch system. In this election although 27 parties presented slates of candidates, it appears that the "Big 3" (the Labor party, the Christian Democratic party, and the People's Party for Freedom and Democracy) won overwhelmingly. Labor secured 52 Parliamentary seats, less than expected but five more than in 1982 (for 34.7% in 1986), CDA secured 54 seats, a big jump over the 45 in 1982 (for 36% in 1986), and the VVD dropped considerably to 27 seats, compared to 36 in 1982 (for 18% in 1986). Hence the present coalition of CDA/VVD will return to power with exactly the same number of Parliamentary seats as before. And the small parties, especially the Communists, have been further squeezed out. Only D'66 did better than previously, securing 9 seats in 1986 compared to 6 in 1982. There are many significant implications of these election results, some of which we will comment on later. But clearly the trend back to the dominance of the "Big 3" which began in 1977, then dropped in 1981, and was revived in 1982, is in evidence.

Among the crises facing the Netherlands recently, the cruise missile crisis has been most visible, a crisis which extended at least from 1979 to November 1, 1985, when the government decided to deploy the missiles. The election of May 1, 1986 was conducted in an atmosphere of sharp confrontation over this decision, its consequences, and its possible renegotiation.

In addition there have been other problems confronting the Dutch society. The economic recession hit the Netherlands very hard, producing high unemployment (still over 15% according to recent reports) and leading to severe budget cuts in, among other things, social welfare payments and education. The unemployment in the youngest age cohort was reported even recently over 30%. The Pope's visit in May, 1985 produced a raucous, if not violent reaction. Only 18% of the Dutch public approved the Pope's tour, it was claimed. The controversy over the collapse of the RSV shipyards and the government's financial losses in and administrative handling of that affair led to a Parliamentary Commission of Inquiry in 1984 and a report critical of the company and the government, a debate which continued into 1985. The election of May, 1981 had led to a new Center-Left government, but this coalition lasted only a year, when the Socialists left the cabinet. New elections in September, 1982 led to a revival of the Center-Right coalition under Ruud Lubbers, the new Prime Minister. Throughout the past six years or more there have been mass protests, especially over unilateral disarmament and the deployment of nuclear weapons. There have also appeared new pressure groups organizing on a variety of issues, new political parties, and the defection of parliamentary leaders in the parties of the governing coalitions.

These developments have occurred during a period when it is alleged that the Dutch political system has continued to undergo major changes in the basic structure of its party system, in the roles of political elites in decision-making, in the role of the public in politics, and in the "rules of the political game" by which critical decisions are made. If this is so, certain key questions can be posed:

1. Has the Dutch political system changed in recent years and if so have these changes been basic structural changes?

2. How have these changes influenced the processes by which the key political decisions are made -- are these decisions being made today in the context of a new model of politics in Holland?

3. How has all this structural and process change affected democracy and political stability in the Netherlands?

I will attempt to comment in this paper briefly on all three of these questions, from the perspective of an American observer somewhat removed recently from the Dutch scene!

The Netherlands political system poses an interesting question for students of comparative politics: How does a democracy manage its crises and solve its problems when the structure of politics changes and the rules of the political decision-making process are altered. When political structure and process change ,the equilibrium of the system could be disrupted and could lead to instability. Has this been so in the Netherlands, and, if not, why not?

For a long time it was argued, at least for the period from 1917 to the 1960's and some claim before 1917, that the Dutch had a special type of system which guaranteed stability and order. This system was called "consociational democracy", and the scholars specified in great detail the features, practices, and rules of politics which accompanied this model. But in the past twenty years most scholars have agreed that the consociational model has been in decline, it not almost completely changed. The Dutch, it is now argued, have been moving toward a different model of democratic politics, attended by major changes in the way politics is conducted.

Arend Lijphart called the Dutch system which emerged from 1917 to 1967 a "consociational" democracy, one which had a "fragmented culture" and a "coalescent" pattern of elite behavior (as opposed to a "competitive" pattern).[1] He spelled out the key features of such a system, emphasizing the autonomy of the subcultures ("verzuiling"), the pragmatic bargaining which elites at the apex of the system had to engage in, elite commitment to the system, and a business-like approach to governance. Specific requisites for such a system to work were: grand cabinet coalitions (where the key decisions were made), proportionality in the allocation of awards to the major subcultures, mutual vetoes, a limited role for the public, a discussion role but not a final decisional role for parliament, the postponement of decisions on which there are irreconcilable differences, secrecy in top level elite decision-making, and elites at the apex who are not primarily accountable to their subcultural supporters. As Lijphart put it, "consociational democracy means government by elite cartel designed to turn a democracy with a fragmented political culture into a stable democracy".[2] Daalder referred to it ("consociational democracy") as "a deliberate counter-model to the Anglo-American type of democracy".[3]. these two Dutch scholars accepted this concept although they disagreed somewhat over its historical origins and whether the accommodationism of elites was a response to social cleavages or preceded them and facilitated the emergence of such cleavages. There are other scholars who disagree with the Lijphart thesis and his way of conceptualizing the Dutch system, but for the most part much of the argument and theory were accepted.

Whatever the validity of the historical argument, virtually every scholar for some time now has argued that consociationalism, "verzuiling" (or the pillarization of society and politics), and the special type of politics of accommodation which Lijphart operationalized, has been in a state of decline since the 1960's and no longer the model of democracy which obtains in the Netherlands. Andeweg writes that "Since 1963 fundamental changes have taken place in the Dutch party system"[4]. Lijphart titles the last chapter of his revision "The Breakdown of the Politics of Accommodation", claiming that "by the late 1960's, it had broken down completely".[5] Irwin and Dittrich have developed an impressive argument for the "dealignment" of the Dutch system.[6] The question is whether that is in fact completely true, and if so, or even partially so, what model has replaced it? Above all, how does the Dutch system today with the decline of consociationalism handle its problems, and make its key decisions -- successfully, effectively, and without a deterioration in the system?

Twenty Years of Changes in the Dutch System

Significant political changes have indeed taken place in the Netherlands from 1963 on. "Deconfessionalization" of party politics have occurred, by which is meant the decline in attachment to religious parties by those with a religious preference, and hence a decline in the relevance of religious affiliations for voting behavior. Studies have revealed the following changes over time (Table 1):

- the percent of those with a religious preference who voted for a confessional party was 55% in 1967 but only 41% in 1982.

- the percent of the electorate which was religiously active (attended church at least once a week) and voted for a confessional party was 44% in 1967 but only 20% in 1982.

- the percent of Catholics voting for the KVP declined from 84% in 1956 to 38% in 1972, rising to 51% for the CDA in 1977.

The religious parties suffered a steady decline in the vote they could mobilize -- it dropped from over 50% in the fifties to 34% in 1982 but, one should note, rose to 38% in 1986 (Table 1). There are few observers who dispute this development, although it was a phenomenon which was less true for Orthodox Calvinists than for the Catholics (Table 2).

A second change which occurred was the "pluralization" of the party system and the rise of small new parties on the "Left" and "Right". In the 1986 election there were 27 parties which presented slates of candidates to the people. This mushrooming of small parties is a development which was particularly noticed after 1963, although there had been small parties earlier. The proportion of the vote captured by small parties increased from 11% in 1963, to almost 19% in 1971 and 1972, and was still 22% in 1981 (Tables 3 and 4). Small parties declined in their total vote to below 17% in 1982 and 15% in 1986. Many of these parties survived, but they rarely were able to build any sizable following. The Communist party has declined from 6% in 1952 to under 2% in 1982, and lost its seats in Parliament in 1986. The D'66 has been quite successful, although its strength has fluctuated between four and eleven percent. Most small parties stay at the one to three percent level if they survive at all.

What this has produced is great "volatility," a third characteristic of the Dutch party system. This phenomenon can be conceptualized and measured in different ways. In one study, it is seen as the "floating vote", that is those who switch parties from one election to the next. The data reveal that the proportion of switches increased from 17% in 1948 to almost 35% in 1972, declining to 28% in 1982.[7] If one calculates volatility in terms of the average shift from election to election in party strength for the major parties one sees also an increase after 1967 (Table 3). But the Dutch figures in recent years of 10.3 and 9.1 percentage points are far below that of some other countries, such as France (23.6) and U.S. (19.3). The volatility of young votes in the Netherlands in recent elections has been particularly noticeable (Table 4). The youngest voters who have appeared at each election from 1971 on have a volatility of 18.5 percentage points, far above that of all voters (Table 5). Yet, one notices two interesting developments for the youngest cohort of voters: (1) they stabilize over time in their voting behavior patterns, becoming less volatile, and (2) they tend to return to support the major parties. The youngest cohort (born 1947-1953), for example, in 1971 only gave 40% of their votes to the major parties (The Big 5) in that year, but by 1977 it was over 60%.

A fourth concern about Dutch elections has been the variation in turnout, a concern about what some American scholars call "demobilization", or the tendency of voters to stay home from the polls and withdraw from politics (46% did in the recent U.S. Presidential election!). In the Netherlands over 90% in earlier years voted, but this declined in 1971 to 78.5% after compulsory attendance at the polls was eliminated. Turnout returned to high levels again and was 80% in 1982, and reportedly 86% in 1986. Turnout rates vary, however, by age groups, as the analysis of Andeweg has demonstrated (Table 6). About 25% of the youngest cohorts stayed home in 1982, and in earlier recent elections. The reasons given for such abstention are increasingly "political", that is, they don't vote because they are not interested in politics, reveal political cynicism, and hold negative views about the system. Despite all of this, however, one must note that comparatively voting turnout is high, very high if compared to the U.S.

These types of changes in party politics -- deconfessionalization, pluralization, volatility, and variations in turnout -- suggest to many scholars "fundamental changes" (Andeweg) and "convulsions" (Lijphart) in the Dutch system. To what extent is this indeed true? Is it not also possible to see the Dutch system revealing a "new stabilization" while at the same time undergoing changes in the patterns of mass support for the system? Certain key developments indicate that this may be the case. First, we have the revival of the vote monopoly of the "Big 3". By 1986 they are moving back to the 90% dominance which they held in 1956 and 1959. Small parties continue to appear and disappear and some do secure a minimal level of support. But it is almost as if the Dutch public, while appreciating the opportunity to vote for small, new parties, feels that the basic questions of politics can only, and will only, be resolved in and by the major parties (with D'66 as a possible adjunct for the "Left"). Thus the Dutch despite their 27 parties really have a sort of three party system or a "three-and-one-quarter party system". While pluralization may continue, fewer Dutch voters see such small parties as realistic alternatives. This is similar perhaps to the post-war change in the German party system (whose smaller parties received 28% of the vote in 1949 and only 2% in 1980 while the CDU/CSU and SPD controlled 87% in 1980 plus 10.6% for the FDP).

Along with this development is the strengthening of the Center, which Lijphart called "weak" in 1975. Actually, the CDA is stronger than ever with its 54 seats today, the largest party and one which probably will be involved in any coalition formation process. Further, the vote which the CDA gets from Catholics is considerable (67% of regular Church attenders in 1977), as well as from the Orthodox Reformed (75% of regular Church attenders), and only somewhat less so from the Dutch Reformed (51% of Church attenders) (Table 2). In fact over 90% of the CDA vote in 1977 was "religious" (Table 7). This indicates a "recombination" of two pillars -- the old Catholic and

Calvinist pillars -- into one new solid block of religious voters in the center of the Dutch system.

Further, in the same vein one must remark about the survival and increasing strength of the Labor party. It is truly a strong party of "the Left", a party of opposition, and it, too, with its 35% of the seats is at a very high point in its history, close to its 1977 record of 34%. Despite pluralization, the PVDA has grown into a strong adversary and with the D'66 now commands over 40% of the seats. While the VVD has declined in strength recently, prior to 1986 it showed a remarkable rise in popularity, increasing from 10% in 1971 to 23% in 1982. With new leadership perhaps it will again become stronger. For the meantime it is a secondary partner in the coalition. Is this a type of "partial pillarization", a modified version of the old system, despite the volatility in voting behavior revealed by the past few elections?

Other observations possibly reinforce this perception. One of the things to remember about the Dutch developments is that voting turnout is up, quite contrary to what has happened recently in the U.S. And the young voters, while participating less (yet their 75% turnout is far above that for American young voters), have been returning to the "Big 3" parties (Table 5). In 1982 75% of the youngest voters supported the "Big 3", compared to 55% in 1971. In 1982 the young shifted heavily to the VVD. We shall have to wait for the analysis of the 1986 Dutch studies to see what happened to young voters in 1986.

A final point must be made about the "expansionism" of the Dutch major parties, or what Kirchheimer, writing about European parties elsewhere, called the "catchall" tendencies of modern parties.[8] This development has been denied as to its applicability to the Netherlands. Yet, in one sense the major Dutch parties have been "expansionist", in that they have increasingly appealed to, and been attractive to, voters from different social classes and religious preferences. I have tried to picture this trend in Table 7. To illustrate in terms of the religious dimension: In 1956 only 5% of the VVD and PVDA supporters were Catholic, but by 1977 this had increased to 29% and 24%, respectively. In addition large proportions of the PVDA supporters were Dutch Reformed. This has declined somewhat recently (only 22% in 1977). Yet, PVDA and VVD today are coalitions of very diverse religious preferential groups of voters (only 33% of the VVD and 53% of the PVDA were nonreligious in 1977). On the other hand, in social class terms the parties always have been and continue to be diversified coalitions. The VVD is by no means exclusively upper and upper middle class, and the PVDA is by no means exclusively working class. What we see then is party structures which are diverse coalitions in terms of both dimensions, except that the CDA is apparently rather clearly homogeneous on the religious dimension. Although more analysis needs to be done, the Dutch party system consists of strong party structures which appear to be part of a re-stabilized system. These coalitional structure are apparently quite adaptive and responsive to the changing characteristics of Dutch society.

In concluding this section on developments in the Dutch party system one must admit that Dutch politics is different today than twenty years ago.

The system has been through several crises which may well continue. The evidence of switching in party affiliation is strong; there has been more volatility than before. There has emerged a confrontational atmosphere and a polarization in ideology which many deplore. If we add to this the increasing protest activity by the Dutch public, over nuclear energy, the Pope's visit, and cruise missiles we see a side of Dutch politics which in the immediate post-war period was not evident. Up to the Sixties the Dutch public was fairly passive. Yet, after 20 years the Dutch system may now be restored to a new type of equilibrium in its party politics -- a stable "three-plus" party system which is essentially not pillarized (but has a strong religious party), in which the major parties are adaptive to social problems and able to mobilize diverse groups of partisans, and where the potential for change is considerable. This appears to me to be more like the coalitional, expansionist, volatile, populist ideological adversarial politics of other Western democracies than the "consociational" politics of the past. But the "stabilization" elements of the Dutch system, the strength at "the Center", and other centripetal elements still set the Dutch system apart. In a very real sense the Dutch party system has not come apart, has not deteriorated. Rather it shows signs of coping rather effectively with the problems of the society and resisting threats to its existence. At least in 1986 the Dutch voters, 86% of whom voted, expressed opinions of considerable confidence in that system.

Implications of the Cruise Missile Crisis for Dutch Politics

Overriding all of the political tumult of this tortured decade was the crisis of the cruise missiles. Although opposition to the neutron bomb had been active earlier, the cruise missile crisis came into focus in December, 1979 when the Dutch Parliament voted 76-69 to reject "at this time" the 48 Tomahawk missiles as its part in the NATO weapons development program (which the U.S. had been pressing). Ten CDA deputies voted against the government. The Socialists pressed for a vote of no confidence, which Parliament rejected 81-66, with the ten dissident deputies returning to the fold. The VVD threatened to withdraw from the Cabinet if the CDA capitulated to Socialist pressure against deployment. A compromise was worked out (with NATO concurrence) which permitted the Netherlands a two year delay in the decision and made the decision contingent on the progress of the Geneva arms-reduction talks, while on the other hand plans for the deployment of the missiles would proceed. The crisis decision was postponed, and the parties had saved face for the time being.[9]

In May, 1981, the CDA/VVD government lost its majority and a new Cabinet consisting of CDA/PVDA/D'66 was formed. The cabinet could not, and did not, act on the cruise missile question. there were strong differences in positions of the parties: CDA pro-deployment, PVDA strongly against, and D'66 against "in present circumstances". As a result in December, 1981 the government postponed the decision until 1983 when the plans for missile sites would be prepared, pending of course a final decision to go ahead.

There was a Cabinet crisis in May of 1982 when the Socialists left the government, and new elections in September, 1982 which returned the

CDA/VVD government to power. But there was a split in the CDA on the deployment question (29 to 14 in the Parliamentary caucus). The new PM, Lubbers, decided to postpone the site preparation, and emphasis was placed on waiting for progress at the Geneva talks. October, 1983 saw over a half-million people demonstrate in the Hague, similar to the 400,000 who previously had protested in Amsterdam in May, 1981.

During 1984 the government was working towards some sort of compromise solution. One proposal was to reduce the number of missiles for the Netherlands, discussed by the Dutch foreign minister Van den Broek in Washington. And the U.S. defense secretary Caspar Weinberger in turn, visited the Netherlands. Many observers felt the Dutch could not go ahead on schedule, if at all. The New York Times reported the Dutch as "Unready to Fulfill Missile Plan" (May 13). There was a great deal of public protest against, as well as support for, the deployment. But the balance appeared to be in opposition. The IKV (Interchurch Peace Council), created in 1966, had been active for some time against nuclear weapons. Now, 300 notable Christian Democrats pressed Parliament to reject deployment. On June 1 the Cabinet proposed a 6-point plan which included a vote by Parliament to accept 48 missiles, while reserving the final deployment decision until November, 1985. The plan proposed a definite deadline of December, 1988 for delaying the actual deployment. The contingencies were: failure of the U.S. and the Soviet Union to reach an arms agreement by 1985, increase in the number of SS-20's deployed by the Soviet Union; and if a re-negotiation of the missile agreement between NATO and the U.S. took place (pursuant to a U.S. - Soviet arms agreement), the Netherlands would accept its share of the missiles. This 6 point plan was approved by Parliament 79-71, with the defection of 7 CDA-ers. The bottom line was that November 1, 1985 was to be the date of final decision!

All during 1985 the controversy continued although it was fairly clear that the decision to deploy was virtually assumed. Lubbers did say, however, that there were certain conditions under which deployment would not take place. At the elite level, there were visits to Washington by the Dutch foreign minister and by Lubbers, as well as to the Hague by Weinberger and Bush. The Soviets also made representations to the Dutch. Public opinion in January of 1985 was reported as 16% definitely favoring the missiles, 39% reluctantly accepting them, 40% definitely opposing, and 5% with no opinion. The opinion of the party supporters varied greatly: 83% of the VVD favored (27% strongly), 80% of the CDA favored (19% strongly), but only 36% of the PVDA favored (only 9% strongly). Thus the public was split and the parties were polarized. (NIPO poll, January 2, 3, 4, 1985 reported in Benelux Report, February 25, 1985).

The public was mobilized by a new group in a petition drive against the missiles. The group, KKN (Committee Cruise Missiles: NO!) recruited apparently over 50,000 volunteers. It was opposed by other groups -- ICTO (Interchurch Committee for Mutual Disarmament), HBV (Reformed Council on Peace Issues) and SVP (Peace Politics Foundation). In October, 3.7 million signatures had been secured and were delivered to the Government. Yet the polls now disagreed on the state of public opinion:

Vara/DeHondt, 55% favor a delay; NIPO, 59% favor deployment; Nijmegen Study -- 48% will protest decision to deploy.

Other aspects of the decision were raised from September, 1985 on. For example, the question was raised who would have final decisional power on ignition. Further, Den Uyl argued that there should be no decision until after the next summit between Reagan and Gorbachev. The question was also raised about the 6 nuclear tasks which the Netherlands already had under NATO, and whether these could be reduced if the Dutch agreed to deploy. This in fact became a very important part of the final compromise. Lubbers in October came out definitely in favor of deployment, arguing that otherwise the Soviets would see it as a victory and would not work towards an arms control agreement. The PVDA then raised a constitutionality question, asking whether a two-thirds vote of Parliament would be necessary. Despite all of these actions, protests, and confrontations on November 1, 1985 the Dutch government made the decision to go ahead, but still dependent on NATO's agreement to drop 4 nuclear tasks which the Dutch had been committed to. This NATO did in December. In the meantime on November 4 the U.S. and the Dutch government exchanged letters of agreement. And then the Dutch waited for the May 21, 1986 election. The results of that were a great victory for Lubbers and the CDA and a clear majority for the CDA/VVD government, with 81 seats out of 150.

It is difficult to completely understand and evaluate the meaning of this series of events and the agreement reached without having been in the Netherlands during this period. A foreigner can only suggest some possible interpretations. One of the first that seems clear is that the lower house of Parliament played a significant role during this controversy, much more so than in "consociational" days. The Cabinet deferred to Parliament throughout this period, delaying a decision until adequate support clearly existed. Defections from the CDA, and a split in its caucus in Parliament, contributed to these postponements, in May 1982 and earlier in December, 1979. One notices also greater deference by Parliament to the protest movements and to public opinion. As Peter Baehr observed after the 1981 demonstrations in Amsterdam: "Many -- if not most -- Dutch political leaders tried somehow to identify themselves with the cause of the demonstrators......(Prime Minister) van Agt said that he was sure that this event would influence the behavior of governments......"[10] The magnitude of the protests, of course, was phenomenal -- 400,000 in Amsterdam (May, 1981), 550,000 the Hague (October, 1982), and 3.7 million signatures on a petition submitted in late October, 1985. The public was certainly no longer passive and perhaps never again would be.

If "depoliticization" of the issues, and secrecy in governmental deliberations, were the marks of the earlier "consociational" system they were certainly now passé. In place of this one found open confrontations by political leaders and political groups and much ideological polarization, with leaders taking dogmatic and hard positions. Politics was also very personalized, with popularity polls conducted regularly.

Yet the basic compromise process on the part of the politicians at the apex of the system continued. There were two key points when this occurred -- December, 1979 and June, 1984. In the former it was agreed that no agreement was possible and there should be a two year delay. In the latter it was agreed that a decision had to be made and could be made, and a six-point compromise was presented and adopted. In between in May, 1981 the government was hopelessly split and the issue was "iceboxed", a favorite strategy of consociational politics. The basic point is that a compromise bargain was finally struck, the whole process delayed until that could be done and the support theoretically had been mobilized -- at the public level and at the parliamentary level. But it was not an "overarching" cooperative agreement as in the past. The vote in June, 1984 was, after all, close -- 79 to 71. Thus "profound disagreement" (Lijphart's term in 1975) by the top level elites existed, and yet a decision was made. Is this part of a new model of Dutch democracy? Or is it not so different from Daalder's characterization of the system in 1974: "consociational democracy therefore tends to show a curious mixture of ideological intrasigence on the one hand and pragmatic political bargaining on the other......"?[11]

What emerges from this analysis is then perhaps an awareness certainly that the system has been changing considerably. The rules of the political game are not the same, the roles of parliament and of the public are greater than before, the party system is more volatile. Further the political elites are more ideologically distinctive, more populist and more interested in citizen involvement in politics than ever before, more accepting of conflict, and less deferential to the Cabinet. These changes in elite orientations were demonstrated and anticipated in earlier research we did on Dutch MP's and top civil servants during the 1970-1973 period.[12] Nevertheless, despite these changes in the system one sees still the influences of the consociational period -- the stabilization of the party system, the commitment of elites to the system, the ability of elites to compromise, the discipline within parties in the Parliament, the competence of elites in the last analysis to govern. This is in a sense a blend today of old consociationalism and new populism, of old residual pillarization and new coalitionalism, of old elite discipline and new independence, of old pragmatic bargaining and new ideological confrontation. To meet the needs of a modern society this system is probably better than the old -- less elitist, more democratic; less anachronistic, and more a competitive and truly responsive democracy.

TABLE 1   Basic Trends in Dutch Parties and Elections

		'46	'48	'52	'56	'59	'63	'67	'71	'72	'77	'81	'82	'86
Voter Turnout		90.2	90.8	92.1	93.5	93.3	92.8	92.3	78.5	84.9	87.5	86.6	80.4	85.7
Party Vote 1..% cast for religious parties		54	57	54	52	51	52	47	41	36	35	35	34	38
2. cast for parties of the "Left"	- PVDA	28	26	29	33	30	28	23.5	25	27	34	28	30	33
	- other	11	8	6	5	4	6	11	14	15	10	17	10	9
TOTAL		39	34	35	38	34	34	34.5	39	42	44	45	40	42
3..% cast for the parties of the "Right"	- VVD	6	8	9	9	12	10	11	10	14	18	17	23	17
	- other	2	4	6	3	4	5	8	12	11	5	4	3	3
4.% cast for the "Big 5" "Big 3" (PVDA, VVD,	KVP-ARP-CHU, or CDA)	86	87	87	91.5	91.6	87.5	79	72	73	84	76	83	85

Sources:

Maurice de Hond, Hoe Wij Kiezen (Amsterdam, Sijthoff, 1986).
Galen Irwin and Karl Dittrich, "And the Walls Came Tumbling Down: Party Dealignmen in the the Netherlands", in Russell Dalton et al, eds., *Electoral Change in Advanced Industrial Democracies: Realignment or Dealignment?*, (Princeton University Press, 1984).
C. van der Eijk and B. Niemuller, eds., *In Het Spoor van de Kiezer*, "Stemmen op godsdienstige partijen sinds 1967", (Amsterdam, Boom Meppel, *Acta Politica*, 1983/2
Rudy B. Andeweg, *Dutch Voters Adrift*, 1982.
Statistiek der Verkiezingen, The Hague.

TABLE 2 Deconfessionalization in the Party System

	1967	1971	1972	1977	1981	1982
1. % of the electorate who were active religiously and voted for a confessional party						
- attended church at least once a week	44%	40%	32%	26%	24%	20%
- attended church sometimes	22	19	24	27	25	27
TOTAL	66	59	56	53	49	47
2. % of those with a religious preference who voted for a confessional party	55	45	42	47	50	41
3. % of those voting for a confessional party who were religiously active (attended church at least once a week)	79	64	69	77	80	75
4. Age and Religious Voting						
A. % of new voters in 1971 (born 1946-1950) who were active in the Church (attended at least once a week)		34	24	11	16	12
B. % of new voters in 1977 who were active in the Church				21	14	7
5. Denominational Voting	1956	1967	1971	1972	1977(CDA)	
A. % of Catholics voting KVP (or CDA)	84%	67%	51%	38%	51	
- (% of regular Church attenders voting KVP)	(90)	(77)	(70)	(53)	(67)	
B. % of Dutch Reformed voting CHU (or CDA)	26	24	22	18	28	
- (% of regular Church attenders voting CHU)	(43)	(54)	(50)	(44)	(51)	
C. % of Orthodox Reformed voting ARP (or CDA)	80	82	61	56	66	
- (% regular Church attenders voting ARP)	(87)	(88)	(67)	(61)	(75)	

Sources:

C. van der Eijk and B. Niemoller, eds., *In Het Spoor van de Kiezer*, (articles by the editors and by Rudy Andeweg), *Acta Politica*, 83/2.
For the 1977 data, *De Nederlandse Kiezer '77*, pp. 150-162.
Steven Wolinetz, "Electoral Change and Attempts to Build Catch-all Parties in the Netherlands", Canadian Political Science Association Meeting August 18-19, 1973, Montreal (using data from *De Nederlandse Kiezer '72*, and from Arend Lijphart NIP Survey, 1956).

TABLE 3   Dutch National Elections: Summary for Three Periods

	1946-1963 (average)	1967-1972 (average)	1977-1982 (average)	1986
A. "The Left"				
PVDA	29.0	25.2	30.8	33.3
D'66				
PPR	6.6	13.3	12.3	9.2
PSP				
CPN				
	35.6	38.5	43.1	42.5
B. Confessional Parties				
Catholics (KVP)	31.0	22.0	30.7	34.6
Protestants (ARP)	10.9	9.1		
Protestants (CHU)	8.5	6.4		
	50.4	37.5		
C. Liberals (VVD)	9.4	10.5	19.4	17.4
D. "The Right"				
SGP	2.3	2.2	2.0	
GPV	0.3	1.4	0.9	
KNP (RKNP)	0.7	0.3	0.1	
BP	0.5	2.6	0.4	
DS'70	—	3.1	0.6	
RPF	—	—	0.9	
	3.8	9.6	4.9	
E. Others				
EVP	—	—	0.3	
CENTRUM	—	—	0.3	
NMP	—	0.6	—	
F. Summary				
1. Total for "the Big 5" (the "Big 3")	88.8	73.2	80.9	85.3
2. Volatility of Party System (Average shift in party strength from election to election)				
1946-1982				
PVDA	2.9	2.8	4.7	3.35
CDA	1.9	6.0	1.1	2.79
VVD	1.5	1.5	3.3	2.03
	6.3	10.3	9.1	8.17

TABLE 4 Small Parties: Their Strength and Their Fate

	1952	1956	1959	1963	1967	1971	1972	1977	1981	1982	1986
A. Durable Parties											
PSP	—	1.8	3.0	2.9	1.4	1.5	0.9	2.1	2.3	1.2	—
GPV	0.7	0.6	0.7	0.8	0.9	1.6	1.8	1.0	0.8	0.8	1.0
D'66					4.5	6.8	4.2	5.4	11.1	4.3	6.1
PPR						1.8	4.8	1.7	2.0	1.6	1.3
CPN	6.2	4.8	2.4	2.8	3.6	3.9	4.5	1.7	3.2	1.80.6	
SGP	2.4	2.3	2.2	2.3	2.0	2.3	2.2	2.1	2.0	1.9	1.8
	—	—	—	—	—	—	—	—	—	—	—
	9.3	7.7	7.1	8.9	13.9	17.8	19.0	12.8	20.1	12.7	12.0
B. Parties Which Disappeared											
Farmers		0.7	2.1	4.7	1.1	1.9	0.8	0.2	0.3		
DS 70					5.3	4.1	0.7	0.6	0.4		
Middenstands Party					1.5	0.4					
Catholic National Party						0.9	0.4				
		—	—	—	—	—	—	—			
		0.7	2.1	4.7	7.9	7.3	1.9	0.8	0.7		
C. Recent Parties											
RPF								1.2	1.5	0.9	
EVP									0.8	0.2	
Center Party									0.8	0.4	
								—	—	—	
								1.2	3.1	1.5	

Source:

Thomas R. Rochon, "Mobilizers and Challengers: Towards a Theory of New Party Success", in Robert Harmel, ed., New Political Parties, International Political Science Review, Sage Publications, Volume 6, No. 4, pp. 419-439.

TABLE 5   The Volatility of the Young Voters

p		1971	1972	1977	1981	1982	Average Shift
1. Vote Preferences of the Youngest Cohort in Each Election:							
	PVDA	20	24	35	25	26	6.5
	CDA	27	18	23	21	19	4.5
	VVD	8	17	17	18	30	7.5
TOTAL "Big 3"		55	59	75	64	75	18.5
2. Analysis of Same Age Cohort over Time:							
A. Youngest Cohort in 1971 (born 1947-1953)							
	PVDA	17	21	36	26.5	23	8.0
	CDA	17	17	18.5	21	19	1.5
	VVD	6	12	14	15	19	3.3
TOTAL "Big 3"		40	50	68.5	62.5	61	12.8
B. Middle Aged Cohort in 1971 (Born 1937-1942)							
	PVDA	20	19	24	27	28	2.5
	CDA	27	25.5	30	31	27	3.0
	VVD	8	16	24	15	20	7.5
TOTAL "Big 3"		55	60.5	78	73	75	13.0

Source:

Rudy Andeweg, "Wie de juegd heeft, heeft de toekomst?" in C. van der Eijk and B. Niemoller, Eds., *In Het Spoor van de Kiezer, Acta Politica*, 1983/2.

Galen Irwin and Karl Ditrich, in Russell Dalton etal., eds., *Electoral Change in Advanced Industrial Democracies*, 1984, p. 294 (Based on Infomart Parliamentary Studies).

TABLE 6 Public Involvement in Politics

		1967	1971	1972	1977	1981	1982	1986
A.	Voter Turnout							
	- Total Population	92.3	78.5	84.9	86.5	86.6	80.4	85.7
	- Age Cohorts Born:							
	Before 1901	90	84	77	85	78	–	
	1902 - 1916	93	84	82	88	92	90	
	1917 - 1931	93	78	85	91	92	87	
	1932 - 1936	90	77	88	86	86	88	
	1937 - 1942	96	76	84	88	89	84	
	1943 - 1946	92	77	81	91	86	75	
	1947 - 1953	–	71	82	84	85	75	
	1954 - 1959	–	–	–	86	82	75	
	1960 - 1963	–	–	–	–	79	75	

		1967	1972	1977
B.	Political Activities			
	1. Held discussions with people in order to get them to vote for a particular party	9	16	14
	2. Hung up a window poster	5	5	10
	3. Went to an Election meeting or forum	5	5	5
	4. Contributed money to a party for the election campaign	4	4	5
	5. Distributed election posters or other propagand materials	1	2	2

		1971	1972	1977	1981	1982
C.	Reasons for non-voting					
	1. Practical Reasons	48	50	52	41	42
	2. Political Reasons (lack of interest, cynicism, lack of self confidence, anti-parliamentary views, etc.)	42	43	40	56	56
	3. Not ascertained, don't know	10	8	8	3	3

Source:

C. Van Der Eyk and B. Niemoller, In Het Spoor Van De Kiezer, Acta Politics, 1983-2, pp. 142, 161-2.
De Nederlandse Kiezer, 1977, p. 126.

TABLE 7 Social Group Homogenity and Diversity in Dutch Party Coalitions

A. Religious Composition of Party Support Groups

	1956 KVP	1956 CHU	1956 ARP	1956 VVD	1956 PVDA	1970 KVP	1970 CHU	1970 ARP	1970 VVD	1970 PVDA	1977 CDA	1977 VVD	1977 PVDA
Catholic	98	0	3	5	5	97	0	0	13	13	57	29	24
Dutch Reformed	0	94	25	61	41	1	82	11	43	30	17	28	22
Orthodox Ref	0	4	71	20	0	0	82	1	0.5	18	5	1	—
No Religion	1	0	0	29	44	2	0	4	37	52	7	33	53
Other	1	2	1	5	8	0	18	3	6	4.5	1	5	1
N =	333	111	144	85	367	240	71	96	89	210	421	162	415

NOTE: 1956 and 1970 are based on party preference; 1977 is based on the vote.

B. Social Class Composition of the Party Support Groups

Objective Social Class	1966 KVP	1966 CHU	1966 ARP	1966 VVD	1966 PVDA	1977 KVP	1977 CHU	1977 ARP	1977 VVD	1977 PVDA
Upper-old middle	4	4	4	10	2	3	6	6	9	1
Lower-old middle	17	23	18	18	5	15	22	15	17	3
Upper-new middle	16	25	21	42	16	14	11	25	36	13
Lower-new middle	24	33	24	20	26	22	31	26	24	28
Manual working	39	15	33	10	51	46	30	28	14	54
N =	1634	475	519	636	1505	207	54	110	214	407

Sources:

1956 Religious Vote: Steven Wolinetz, op. cit., 1973 (using NIPO Survey, 1956)
1970 Religious Vote: 1970 Dutch Election Study
1977 Religious Vote: De Nederlandse Kiezer, 1977, p. 151
1966 and 1977 Social Class data, Rudy Andeweg, op. cit., p. 93 (Objective social class based on employment status, specific occupation and size of firm; KVP, CHU and ARP percentages in 1977 are survey estimates of their strength if there had been no CDA.)

NOTES

[1]*The Politics of Accomodation: Pluralism and Democracy in the Netherlands*, (Berkeley: University of California Press, 1968,1975).

[2]"Consociational Democracy", *World Politics*, Vol. XXI, No. 2, January 1969, p. 216.

[3]Hans Daalder, "The Consociational Democracy Theme", *World Politics*, Vol. XXVI, No. 4, July, 1974, p. 620.

[4]RudyB. Andeweg, *Dutch Voters Adrift* (Ph.D. Thesis, Lerden, 1982).

[5]*op. cit.*, 1975 ed., p. 196.

[6]Galen Irwin and Karl Dittrich, "And the Walls Came Tumbling Down: Party Dealignment in the Netherlands," in Russell Dalton et al., eds., *Electoral Change in Advanced Industrial Democracies*, (Princeton University Press, 1984).

[7]Irwin and Dittrich, *op. cit.*, p. 288.

[8]Otto Kirchheimer, "The Transformation of Western European Party Systems" in Joseph La Palombara et al., eds., *Political Parties and Political Development* (Princeton University Press, 1966). pp. 177-200.

[9]A Good review of these events is found in Myron A. Levine, "Continuity and Change in Dutch Politics: the Dutch Approach to the Cruise Missile", Midwest Political Science Association Meeting, Chicago, April, 1985.

[10]Peter Baehr, "Democracy and Foreign Policy in the Netherlands", *Acta Politica*, 18, 1 (January) pp. 37-62 (quoted by Levine, *op. cit.*, p. 14).

[11]Hans Daalder, "The Consociational Democracy Theme", *World Politics*, 26, No. 4, (July, 1974), p. 607.

[12]S.J. Eldersveld et al. (University of Michigan Press, 1981).

History and Structure of the Dutch Language

MISTRESS OF MANY:
How Dutch was Grammatically Stripped

T. L. Markey
The University of Michigan

This paper attempts to show when, how, and why Dutch (Netherlandic) grammar became simplified in the course of the later Middle Ages and Early Modern Periods. The major sorts of simplification that occurred (e.g. case syncretism/elimination, gender stripping, feature coalescence, etc.) are shown to be characteristic of neighboring Germanic dialects, principally those that are traditionally catalogued as Ingvaeonic, e.g. English, Frisian, and Saxon (Low German). Major emphasis is placed on sociolinguistic aspects of the feature-stripping periods: the Netherlands as a commercial meeting place, a multi-cultural and multi-dialectal/lingual center. Then, too, it will be shown that Dutch was linguistically expansive during the periods of feature stripping, for Dutch provided the Scandinavian languages, for example, with numerous fixed, frozen phrases that became hallmarks of Nordic slang and colloquial speech --- even today. In an attempt to account for Netherlandic grammatical simplification, a thesis of Balkanization is proposed.

From the earliest available shreds of textual evidence (glosses, even the generally opaque Malbergian glosses to the *Salic Laws*, the Old Low Franconian corpus, etc.). as well as justifiable imputations from both comparative and internal reconstruction, one can only reasonably assume that "Netherlandic" entered the linguistic scene with much the same roster of morphological wealth that is evidenced by other Germanic dialects attested from earlier periods, e.g. 3rd century runic inscriptions, or the 5th century Gothic of a Dacian Wulfilas.[1] A contrary assumption would defy both empirical evidence and principled inquiry.

After a millennium, however, certainly so by the outset of the 14th century, Netherlandic had divested itself of the bulk of its inherited inflectional morphology and, consequently, been dramatically stripped of the major grammatical features that characterized a Proto- or Common Germanic.

The following is a selective inventory of the salient features that must have characterized the anterior stages of the Germanic of the Netherlands. At its earliest remove (c. 100 BC, let us say), this particular brand of West or Northwest Germanic must have had three nominal and pronominal (albeit only in the singular of the anaphor) genders, but no "verb" gender as in Hebrew or Slavic; four (nom., gen., dat., acc.) nominal and pronominal cases with traces of a vestigial instrumental only in the pronouns; three numbers (singular, dual, plural); tense/aspect inflection for a present and imperfect, as well as an optative/conditional, besides composite (Aux + MV) formations for modality/logical entailment, if not futurity and perfectivity; inflection of the cardinals "1" through "4" for both case and gender; a "strong" vs. "weak" inflectional contrast of adjectives constrained by divergent syntactic environments; strictly observed government and binding relations that obtained between nouns/pronouns on the one hand and adjectives and prepositions on the other hand; dominant SOV order and concomitant Adj + N sequencing; a predominance of "strong" (apophonic) vs. weak (non-apophonic, dental preterit) verb formants; apophony as a primary derivational strategy (cf. the moribund state of apophony in Early and Classical Latin) besides prefixing and suffixing; a low degree of definiteness (definites, but only exceptionally indefinites); a full set of unbound, uninflected (cf. Celtic) prepositions; absence of pronominal infixing (again cf. Celtic); a virtual complete lack of aspectual semantics at the lexical level (cf. Goth. hausjan vs. gahausjan procedures as a dialect-specific instance); absence of a fully developed Aux-assisted passive (diathesis); relativization marked by pronouns rather than verbs (i.e. absence of dependent vs. independent verb forms, cf. Celtic); absence of a consuetudinal/non-consuetudinal contrast in copularity (again, cf. Celtic); a single set of unbound personal pronouns (i.e. not keyed to tense/aspect/ mood distinctions as, for example, in Algonquian or Hausa); three and only three non-finite verb forms (an infinitive, a present participle, and a past participle, albeit with two divergent shapes from *-to- and *-e/or); and, in addition to primordial root nouns (so-called "consonant stems"), eleven (-a, -wa, -ja, -o, -jo, -i, -u, -n, -tᵉ/or,r, -e/or, -nd) distinctive nominal stem formants, presumably originally some sort of classifier secondarily reinterpreted asagender marker, some of which (i.e. -uu, -ᵉ/or, *-e/os) were quite probably moribund, but among which there was a major distinction between n-stems ("weak") and the others ("strong").

In addition to the ancillary, empirically motivated questions of when and how, the major question that arises here is the question of why it was that Netherlandic divested itself of much of this inflectional inventory? Why, indeed, did Netherlandic embark upon a course of deflection that would eventually give it the morphological appearance of a quasi-creole?

Certainly, at the dawn of Germanic-Roman contact and recorded history of the Germanic peoples in the Netherlands and the Rhineland in the first decades of our era, the Germanic of the area was rather more representative of a speech, than a language, community. There was no standardized language or dialect in the area. The onomastic evidence alone attests the presence of numerous entities, however distinct they may or may not have been linguistically. Note, for example: *Usipetes, Cannefatium, Tencteri, Texuandri* (modern-day Texel), *Tubantes, Bructeri*. However, it is doubtful whether these groups or tribes, if indeed they really were groups or tribes, were purely Germanic or a mixture of Celtic and Germanic peoples, possibly seasoned with even a smattering of Roman descendants, as well as a sprinkling of traders from the Near East, perhaps even North Africa, and their cohorts. One must also necessarily assume a Celtic substratum for the Netherlands, the original homeland of the legendary *Fir Bolg*, identifiable with the *Belgae*. Then, too, German-Celtic was laid down on a largely indeterminable Pre-/Non-Indo-European substratum, a predominantly matrifocal, non-stratified society with a sedentary agrarian aristocracy with refined plastic arts, highly developed maritime skills, and a penchant for monolithic constructions, all of which are traits that were notably absent among the intruding Indo-Europeans from the northeast.

It was this substratum in a Pre-Indo-European Netherlands that Hans Kuhn (e.g. 1959, 1960, 1961) used to support his "Northwest Block" hypothesis when he attempted to account for, inter alia, putatively unshifted initials (p-, t-). Whether one accepts or rejects Kuhn's hypothesis, the fact remains that an arrestingly high percentage (c. 28%) of the Germanic lexicon (e.g. such common items as folk) remains intransigent to etymological analysis and is presumably non-Indo-European.

We presume --- and this is the assumption that is justifiably made in all the handbooks, that the major differences between and among Germanic and quasi-Germanic groups in the prehistoric Netherlands were phonological, that is, of a micro- rather than a macro-dialectal nature. The morphology of the area was quite probably highly uniform. In its later stages of phonological development, Netherlandic certainly displays proto-typically West Germanic tendencies, e.g. a predisposition toward eliminating cardinal vowels (a, i, o, u, by umlaut and/or diphthongization. On the other hand, there are certain phonological strategies at work in the "Netherlandic Block" that cast it as a real entity and as part of a once larger Ingvaeonic (Saxon, Frisian, English, but not Frankish, neither West nor East Frankish) speech community.

Note, for example, the marked tendency toward assibilation (a graduated shift that commences with palatalization and ends with lenition: Old Saxon kebire 'beetle' + *kyever > *ktyever > *ktsyever > *tsever ' Low German sever, cf. High (Standard) German Kafer) throughout the area. English must have participated in this shift from its earliest periods, and the tendency toward assibilation must have been brought to Britain by the Anglo-Saxon emigrants, thereby dating the change to sometime prior to c. 450 AD. It is attested from Old Saxon from c. 850, but may well have been present there before it was indicated in the orthography. The tendency toward assibilation is most pronounced in Frisian, and it is recorded there from the earliest records onward, cf. OFr. tzise 'cheese', OE clese (and other variants) and Germ Kase < casius; OFr. szetel 'kettle', OE cietel and Germ. Kessel. Comparable assibilation, though not completed to lenition, is known elsewhere in Germanic only from Scandinavian, particularly from Northern Swedish dialects, but there the shift is medieval, having been initiated in the 14th century. Such assibilation, or even a tendency toward it, is unknown from Frankish, while it was probably weak in Saxon, but definitely strongest in Frisian, where palatalization was carried even further by the definitely later, secondary change known as "West Frisian Breaking", see Markey (1975, 1977).

In addition to such collectively enjoyed phonological tendencies or predispositions, there are also morphophonological innovations that are common to Ingvaeonic and the Netherlandic Block. One such morphophonological change is the diffusion of h-, beginning with the nom. sg. masc., throughout the anaphoric series (he, she, it); cf. OS, OFr., OE, OLF, MDu he (hi) 'he' and High German er; ME, MDu. hit 'it' and High

German es; OFr. hire, OE hiere, MDu. haer 'her' and OS iru/ira, High German ihr, see Markey (1972).

Now, such cataloguing of common results certainly supports an assumption of commonly shared tendencies and predispositions, but it fails to answer why grammars, here particularly Netherlandic, get stripped, pruned, simplified why, in effect, inflection gives way to deflection, or even give a prognosis of the probable extent of deflection in one language or, via contact, its genetically or allogenetically related neighbors.

With specific reference to stripping in Netherlandic, we note the following:

1. Loss of the dual and reduction of number marking to a singular : plural contrast (in nouns, pronouns, Verbs), and there was no supplementary creation of singulatives to counter this loss as was the case in Modern Irish for parals (e.g. 'eyes', 'hands', 'legs').

2. Loss of grammatical gender in nouns for which gender marking is provided only by the definite article in the singular with de (com.) vs. het (nt.). Thus, tripartite (masc., fem., nt.) gender gave way to bipartite common (de) vs. neuter (het) gender, in effect a con-trast between animate and inanimate, the same distinction that is found in Hittite. The plural is uniformly de and, hence, genderless. The bipartite gender-in-the-singular-only rule also holds for demonstratives and relativizers: dit, dat nt. sg. : deze, die com. sg. and pl. Neuters cannot be used after prepositions. Gender is also absent in adjectives and adverbs. The indefinite (een) is genderless, cf. German with its masc./nt. ein vs. fem. eine contrast. Tripartite gender is preserved only in the singular of the anaphor: hij 'he', zij 'she', het 'it'. This tri-gender anaphoric distinction is also maintained syntactically in coreferencing and here a comparison between Dutch and English is instructive:

DUTCH

1. hij = masc. persons and non-persons only and animals of common gender (e.g. Daar is de ketel. Zet hem even op het gas.

2. zij = female persons and the female of and the large animals (e.g. De koe en harr kalf.)

3. het = non-persons of neuter gender

ENGLISH

he = masc. persons

she = female persons and the female of large animals (e.g. The cow and her calf.)

it = non-persons (e.g. There is the kettle. Just put it on the gas.)

Interestingly enough, for this series,Continental (Danish, Dano-Norwegian, Swedish) Scandinavian makes a four-way distinction: han = masc. persons, hon (hun) = female persons, den = non-persons of common gender, and det = non-persons of neuter gender.

3. Distinctive noun classes (stems) are given up, and the earlier plethora of plural markers is reduced to three (i.e. -en, -s, and ex-ceptionally -eren), where -en dominates, cf. -s in French and English. Historically speaking, the n-stems were generalized at the expense of other formants/classes.

4. Case is lost except in personal and anaphoric pronouns, as well as a few personal nouns (e.g. vaders father's). For concrete case relationships, the primary function of which is semantic and the secondary function syntactic, prepositions are employed, cf. English. For grammatical case (= Subject/Object, nom./acc. resp., while the genitive is ambivalent, being both concrete and grammatical). the primary function of which is syntactic and the secondary semantic, word order and focusing have replaced marking devices, again cf. English, but note that whereas English has SVO exclusively with the verb consistently pivotal, Dutch has VO (verb-second) independently and OV dependently, except where the conjugated verb is one of "full meaning": Ik hoor, dat hij niet denkt te komen. 'I hear (that) he does not intend to come.', but not *Ik hoor, dat hij niet te komen denkt. Vestigially, in formal (archaic) registers, the genitive is preserved together with a masc. : fem. gender distinction: eens goeden zoons 'a good son's', eener goede dochter 'a good daughter's'. Fossilized genitives are preserved in standing expressions, proverbial sayings, adverbial adjuncts of time ('s Avonds 'in the evening') and place ('s-Gravenhage) as well as in some compound adverbs (e.g. destijds 'at that/same time (ago)', cf., similarly Continental Scandinavian, e.g. Swedish till bords 'at table', till fots 'on foot'. Only traces of the dative are found in frozen phrases, e.g. der'halve 'consequently'.

5. Adjectives make only a number (sg. : pl.) distinction, but only attributively and not predicatively, cf. Continental Scandinavian which still makes a gender/number distinction for adjectives both attributively and predicatively and English which fails to make any such distinctions.

6. Person markers are coalesced in verb plurals (-en), thereby permitting only a sg. : pl. distinction, e.g. in the

"weak" preterite with sg. -te vs. pl. -ten, that is, essentially, sg. -0 : pl. -n

7. Aux-support dominates tense construction ('have/had' + MV). Note that, in minor Frisian dialects such as Hindeloopen (Hylpers) where there is no standard or normalized "text" grammar for an appeal to authority, untutored informants are simply unable to generate anticipated or historically probable preterites and regularly employ 'have/had' + MV (PP). Thus, the natural, unmonitored tendency is clearly in the direction of lexicalized, analytic tense formation and away from grammaticalized, synthetic tense formation. Recall the situation in Bavarian, Yiddish, and, most significantly for our purposes here, Afrikaans, where synthetic preterites have been completely ousted by compound tense formations with 'have' Afrikaans: Ek het geskryf (gehad), have (had) written' perfective vs. Ek was (toe) aan die skryf 'I was (had been) writing' imperfective.

8. Corresponding to the tendency toward analytic/lexicalized, rather than synthetic/grammaticalized, tense, modality and logical entailment are exclusively realized by analytic procedures, that is, with Aux (mogen, kunnen, zullen, willen, moeten) + MV. An inflected optative/subjunctive (IE *-ye-/-i-, -oi-) is preserved only in frozen phrases, e.g. hij leve lang 'long may he live!', cf., identically, the situation in Continental Scandinavian, e.g. Swedish leve konungen 'long live the king!', cf. Engl. if .... were and Sw. vore, but note preservation of the subjunctive, signalled by umlaut, in German. Afrikaans mirrors the Dutch state of affairs, as does Yiddish and Bavarian.

9. A major innovation, characteristic of the later stages of all Western European languages, including Slavic, is the introduction of an analytic, Aux-supported passive, and note that an inflected passive, as opposed to the middle/medio-passive, isalate development in Indo-European. The inherited inflected medio-passive in -a-da (lst. & 3rd sg.), -a-nda pl. all persons, -a-za 2nd sg. < IE *-(n)t + o, analogical *-so resp. (see Watkins 1969:129-31) is attested only from Gothic with but feeble traces in Old Norse. It must have been lost in Northwest Germanic earlier than in East Germanic, where it is preserved only defectively. The historical medio-passive was very likely absent from Proto-Netherlandic/Ingveonic; note its absence in Anglo-Saxon. Northwest Germanic developed two analytic passives: (1) an inchoative passive with Aux = 'become'

(worden, werden, veroa, etc.) and (2) a stative passive with the copula (zijn, sein, vera, etc.). Historically, the stative (2) is the more stable of the two, while the inchoative Aux was frequently replaced, e.g. by 'become/get' in English and by bliva 'become' < Low German bliven 'remain' (marginally also 'become') in Continental Scandinavian. Cf. Dutch Het ei wordt gekookt. 'the egg is (being, begins to be, gets) boiled' and Het ei is gekookt. 'the egg is, has been boiled', that is, inchoative vs. stative resp.

10. A nuclear present that also served as a future, particularly when coupled with tense-sensitive adverbial adjuncts (e.g. 's morgens 'tomorrow'). was restricted to serve as a present, while futurity became marked analytically with Aux-support (i.e. zullen + infinitive). where the infinitive may represent a petrified and abbreviated present participial: lopen < lopend(e). Periphrastic futures (skal/will + infinitive) are rare in Gothic, but became increasingly frequent during the Old High German period (c. 600 - 1050 AD).

11. Of the non-finite forms, only the infinitive and the past participle flourish, while a gerund(ive) is entirely lacking and the present participle is largely restricted to use attributively, especially in fixed phrases, e.g. de gierende wind 'the whistling wind'. The replacement of dependent clauses by participial constructions, though grammatically correct, is regarded as formal and stiff and the natural tendency is to avoid them in colloquial speech: Wetende dat hij ziek was, Daar ik wist dat hij ziek was, ... 'knowing that he was sick'. Essentially, then, Netherlandic continues a general Germanic and Western Indo-European tendency, namely, displacement of participial forms and constructions. Note the state of affairs in German dialects, the vast majority of which have given up the present participle, which is best preserved in Upper German (particularly in Carinthia and the Alpine Sprachinseln). Note the English remaking of nd-forns as ing-forms, a procedure that contributed greatly to their survival. For a common Indo-European we may posit four basically distinctive participles: present active (*-nt-) and middle (*-mn-) vs. preterite/perfect active (*-wo-) and middle (*-to-). Moving from east to west across the Indo-European community of languages, there is a very appreciable impoverishment of participial morphology. Germanic continued only the present active (*-nt-) and preterite/perfect middle (*-to-), while Irish lacks participles altogether.

By way of summary so far, we have now pointed out that Germanic in the Netherlandic/Ingvaeonic Block was deposited on a Celtic substratum which, in turn, was deposited on a pre-/non-Indo-European substratum. Traces of that earliest substratum would appear to be primarily lexical, while traces of the intermediate Celtic layer, though also essentially lexical (onomastic), are also vanishingly slight. In line with the justifiable and well documented assumption offered in the handbooks, we reasonably assumed that the dialectal Germanic of the area was relatively uniform morphologically, surely also syntactically, but must have displayed minor phonological differences. We then cited critical phonological and morphophonological innovations that served to define the area as a speech, rather than a language, community. These shifts are termed probatively critical precisely because they are graduated shifts. This gradation shows that the aggregate of lects in the Netherlandic/Ingvaeonic Block could collectively and sequentially participate in changes: assibiliation is naturally a serial change that commences with palatalization and terminates with lenition and the spread of h- throughout the gendered anaphors graduated from the masculine via the neuter to the feminine forms, or so the historical (textual) evidence clearly shows us. We then sketched salient properties of a putative input grammar for early Netherlandic and proceeded to inventory typologically significant losses within that grammar which occurred in the course of the medieval and early modern periods. We have thus descriptively accounted for the when aspect of the major questions we have posed. It remains for us to answer how and why Netherlandic was stripped in the fashion and to the degree we have indicated.

The particularly and intrinsically linguistic aspects of feature stripping (pruning/simplification) are as yet poorly understood. Feature stripping is akin to language death, and that phenomenon too is as yet poorly understood. The results of feature stripping/simplification leave a highly reduced grammar that has the appearance of a quasi-creole, and we have just begun to comprehend the processes that underlie creolization. The point is that it is very difficult to document morphosyntactic, as opposed to purely phonological, change in progress. Indeed, few such changes have been observed with synchronic spans, and such spans necessarily afford the detailed scrutiny that is seemingly required to yield a penetrating and explanatorily adequate analysis.

Changes, particularly contact changes, fall into one of two fundamental categories: divergent/mutually non-supportive and convergent/mutually supportive. The latter assume and/or require an essential congruity, while the former do not. Quechua, with its highly marked palatal lateral, was hurled into contact with Spanish, which also had such a lateral: Quechua preserved, an instance of convergent mutual support, as was the preservation of case, albeit in streamlined form, in Rumanian, for Slavic, Latin, and the indigenous languages of the area all had case, cf. French.

Convergent/mutually supportive changes generally result in retentions, though with alterations of original materials. They are theoretically the less interesting of the two types, as they are highly predictable, usually easily explainable and comprehensible in terms of underlying congruities, and are thus somewhat trivial. Divergent/mutually non-supportive changes are more interesting theoretically, not only because they are far less predictable than convergent changes, but also because they raise interesting questions about naturalness and preference, certainly about preference as a manifestation of naturalness. When essentially prefixing languages come into contact with essentially suffixing inflecting languages, then prefixing usually gives way to suffixing. Witness the erosion of prefixing in Munda languages of the Savara or Sora group that have been in sustained contact with suffixing languages in India, see Ramamurti (1931). Nevertheless, the detailing of preference (and naturalness) in such cases may be difficult, difficult that is in strictly linguistic terms, for sociolinguistic factors may have played an important role: Munda languages suffer from low prestige, while the surrounding suffixing languages enjoy high prestige.[2]

The shift from any word order other than SVO to SVO is, however, a well known and unencumbered display of preference. In all synchronically and numerous diachronically observed cases of word order change, the result is consistently SVO. The shift from SOV to SVO within the last century for many languages of New Caledonia is a case in point, so Claire Moyse-Faurie and Francoise Ozanne-Rivierre (CNRS, Paris, 1981, p.c.). All true creoles are consistently SVO.

Feature stripping (simplification) seems preferable to feature adding (complication). Nevertheless, the initial stages of morphosyntactic change may be generally characterized as an additive processing that does not result in organic units. New material is usually merely added, though in an integrated fashion, to old material, whereupon reduction may set in. Note the following staging from Bavarian. For 'both', the basilect has alle zwa(o) lit. 'all two', to which the mesolect adds beide (bade) from the Standard, but in an integrated fashion: alle bade zwa(o). Finally, reduction spread from the acrolect and alle bade zwa(o) was "stripped" to bade (Willi Mayerthaler, p.c., 1983). The point is that bade (beide) did not immediately replace alle zwa(o).

Invocation of "drift" as an explanation of change, particularly changes of the Balkanization (*Sprachbund*) type, is a specious precision at best and superbly circular and ad hoc at worst (pereat Robin Lakoff 1972 and adherents of such views). An appeal to "drift" is tantamount to peddling description as explanation. A result is recast as a cause. Consider the following example. Replacement of an infinitive with a finite subordinate clause introduced by a conjunction in Modern Greek (with virtual total loss of infinitives), Bulgarian-Macedonian, Albanian (Tosk, but not Geg). and Serbian (preferentially, but not exclusively) might be construed as "drift" (a state of affairs). But states and static descriptions do not explain developments, though the converse is true: developments explain states. Merger of the infinitive and the 3rd sg. present in Byzantine Greek as the result of phonological changes presumably led to pernicious homonymy that triggered replacement of the infinitive by the finite form. Bilingualism then spread the finite construction (I want to drink + I want that I drink)[3] centrifugally as a model from Greek to the other languages of the Balkans.[4]

211

The Balkan languages did not, either individually or collectively, simply "drift" aimlessly toward adoption of the finite construction.

The initial causes of change are primarily linguistic, while determination of their paths of diffusion in time and space is largely social. Sometimes language affects people (in its strongest form = the Whorf-Sapir Hypothesis) and sometimes people affect language (the initial assumption of all current sociolinguistic inquiry), while at still other times language leads, or seems to lead, a life of its own apart from people, but a life that is also regulated by its own implicational hierarchies, preferences, and typological parameters.

This assessment conveniently leads us to what may be termed "the contact syndrome". It is a well known fact that language isolates, that is, languages with minimal contact and external interference, routinely evidence highly complicated grammars. Such languages are regularly typified by a wealth of inflectional morphology, word orders other than SVO, difficult phonological patterns, and a preponderance of what Hansjakob Seiler (e.g. 1986) has called predicativity. Conversely, languages with maximal contact and external interference routinely evidence deflection, SVO word order (so in all true creoles), highly streamlined phonologies (e.g. CVC syllabics, few morphophonemic complications, actually none in basilectal creoles), and a preponderance of what Seiler (*ibid.*) has called indicativity. Isolates are, or tend to be, far less immediately iconic in their grammaticality than maximal contact languages, where creoles represent an ultimate in contact. Bailey (1982:10-11) has fittingly and quite correctly portrayed the contrast between isolates (-contact) and non-isolates (+contact) as follows:

I. isolate: with synthesis, which groups, or tends to group, syntagmatically arranged items into paradigmatic bundles (+ inflection).

II. non-isolate: with analysis, which tends to break down paradigmatic bundles into syntagmatic arrangements (deflection).

The greater the number of inputs and the more intensive the contact, then the more extensive the break-down of paradigmatic bundles, the fewer the grammatical complications, the higher the degree of streamlining and feature stripping. What is grammaticalized in isolates tends to become lexicalized in non-isolates.

With reference to these observations, the historical development of Dutch, specifically its history of feature stripping as we have outlined it thus far, is a clear indication that Dutch was afflicted by "the contact syndrome."

With reference to the instances of Dutch stripping listed above, it is abundantly clear that the over-all movement of Dutch grammatical reanalysis was toward lexicalization and away from grammaticalization. Gender (2,3) was lexicalized by marking it on definites or anaphors, but only in the singular, while the plural became genderless, obviously an analytic strategy.

Case (4) was also lexicalized by marking it pronominally or, localistically/ concretely, by prepositions, again a lexical strategy. Verb person (6) signalling was largely extrapolated from the verb, which became marked primarily for number and tense: verb person became lexicalized by marking it with (now obligatory) personal and anaphoric pronouns. Contrast this turn of events with the situation in Italian, which has carefully maintained personal endings and where the personal pronoun is non-obligatory and generally lacking. Tense, aspect, mood, and diathesis (7,8,9,10) were all generally lexicalized by means of introducing Aux-support. Participial (present) phrases (11) were restructured as lexical strings, and a gerund(ive), if indeed it had been inherited, was lost.

We have thus shown how Netherlandic was stripped. Moreover, given our prognosis of the effects of contact, Netherlandic stripping points unequivocally to intensive contact and external influence/interference, reflected by a distinct move toward lexicalization, greater analycity, and, hence, greater indicativity and iconicity. This observation, the realization of contact as a rationale for how stripping was conducted, also provides a partial answer to the question of why Netherlandic was stripped: it was stripped, in part, as the result of intensive contact and external influence/interference.

During the later Middle Ages and early modern periods the Netherlandic Block was both culturally and linguistically pluralistic. The Hanseatic League transformed the Netherlands and Baltic/North Sea Europe into a Germanic Sprachbund of the Balkan type. The same sort of diffusion mechanisms that were at work in the Balkans were also unleashed in Northern, Germanic Europe. The level of mutual intelligibility was presumably appreciably high among Scandinavians, Anglo-Saxons, members of the Netherlandic Block, and Low Germans. Trivially, note that the absence of the High German Consonant Shift alone would have maintained a higher level of mutual intelligibility in the North Sea Germanic speech community than between that community and its Germanic neighbors to the south. More significantly, this was not only the Golden Age of Dutch literature, arts, science, and philosophy, but also the height of Netherlandic commercial and linguistic influence in the North. Dutch, as well as Low German, both gave and took linguistically: there was an egregious reciprocity of lingual exchange between Norse and Ingvaeonic as never before. Thousands of lexical items were shifted back and forth across the North Sea, and recall the dialectologist's maxim that seas unite while mountains divide. An arsenal of frozen phrases and set expressions entered the Scandinavian languages, and it is difficult, if not impossible, in many cases to determine the source, Netherlandic or Low German. Nw. hulter til bulter (Sw. huller om buller) 'hurly-burly, pell-mell' (Fr. pele-mele) can just as well derive from LG hulter de bulter as from Du. holder de bolder. Etymological dictionaries and monographs and articles in the literature abound with examples, see Foerste and Heeroma (1955). But far more pervasive than a seasoning conferred by individual lexical items or freezes was the implementation of critical elements of a Hansesprache, as Willy Sanders (1982:126-74) has called it, in the grammatical restructuring of Scandinavian, e.g. replacement of native varda 'become' by a borrowed (MLG, MDu.) bliven (bleiben) as a primary Aux-support in forming the passive.

Previously, we asserted that, while determination of the paths of change in time and space is largely determined by the socio-operative dimensions of language as a communicative device, the initial causes of change are primarily linguistic, that is, rooted in a private life of language apart from people (= autonomous grammar), a life that is regulated by a language's own implicational hierarchies, preferences, and typological parameters. While it is empirically obvious that greater contact interference and a higher number of inputs results in greater lexicalization and analyticity and, hence, in greater indicativity and iconicity, it merely begs the question and is ultimately circular to persist in citing contact interference/input diversity as a primary cause. This fails to penetrate the real issue of why it is that stripping or simplification occurs, and simplification (as a minumum oper- ationnel) may well, as Hagege (1985:35-41) has pointed out, be a mirage. Nevertheless, the empirical fact remains that prolonged contact interference/ increased input diversity pushes grammars in the direction of a reduced creole or quasi-creole, see n. 2. Even $L_1 + L_2$ input situations may result in reduction and a "fusion creolization", e.g. as in the case of English from a Norse-modified Anglo-Saxon + Norman French, or Bavarian from Alemannian + Proto-Ladin, see Mayerthaler (1984). Note, too, the stripped, deflected, quasi-creole status of languages such as Chinese that would hardly be considered "creoles". Do languages "naturally" prefer stripping and its apparent goal of enhanced iconicity? Seemingly, then, if we were to succeed in understanding, in some highly principled fashion, sufficiently satisfactory epistemic reasons for why it is that Netherlandic was stripped and stripped in the manner it was, then we would have simultaneously uncovered a basis for all such stripping, even the stripping in true creoles.

Obviously, by reasoning in this manner we are appealing to the explanatorily powerful, essentially biological notion of functional analogy. Dispersed, but convergent similarities (the similarly reduced, albeit to different degrees, grammars of Netherlandic, Afrikaans, English, true creoles) that emerge from different forms can only be adequately understood if they are attributed to chance encounters of various internal conditions (originally inflectional grammaticality) with the same external conditions (contact interference/input diversity and multiplicity). As Rupert Riedl (1979:132-4) has pointed out, in a similarity only its interpretation can be false, and our interest in an interpretation declines with an increase and grows with a decrease in similarity. Let us now return to the results of Netherlandic stripping with greater analytic precision.

With respect to a fundamental (station vs. motion, viz. Noun vs. Verb) dichotomization between basic grammatical categories that have been stripped, there are essential surficial differences, as well as underlying similarities.

First, consider the general, surficial result of verb stripping (7,8,9,10). Signs for propositional qualifiers (PQs). that is, essentially tense/aspect/ mood/diathesis, that were originally inflectionally grafted to radicals and variously integrated with personal endings as stem formants (e.g. IE *-o-i- = thematic optative, *-(n)t + i = plus hic et nunc particle i in the present vs.

lack of this particle in the injunctive, *-(n)t + o(i) = medio-passive) were deleted from the radical and lexicalized in the form of Aux-support constructions. As vectors of PQ-properties, Aux-elements then effectually preceded a nuclear (= infinitive) form of the verb as PQs. Formally, Aux-preposing is equivalent to preposing TMAs (tense/mood/aspect particles) to a bare, uninflected nuclear verb lexeme in all true creoles. Now, note that a major typological difference between creoles on the one hand and pidgins on the other hand consists in the fact that, whereas TMAs are preposed sentence internally to verbs in creoles, PQs are generated sentence externally in pidgins, see Markey (1982:f. 11) for details. Note the complete absence of inflectional tense/aspect in Afrikaans and Yiddish, both of which employ Aux-support for these values, vs. partial retention of inflectional tense/aspect in Dutch. The transition from inflectional PQs to lexical PQs is presumably gradual. Serial constructions, found in many West African languages, also present a lexicalization of PQ-properties: serials confer a sort of deictic-aspectual modality on motility or eventual or reportative conception. Translational equivalents of verbs that may be construed as essentially deictic (take, give, come, go). in Western European languages are typically the non-reportative operators in languages with serialization, see Markey (1986:516-7). The formal result of the shift from synthetic PQ-incorporation to lexicalized, analytic PQexpropriation is equivalent to composition (as opposed to paradigmatic constellations):

COMPOSITION	Tense #V	(particle # root)
(Non-Inflection)	Aux # V	(particle # root)
PARADIGMATIC	V-Tense	
(Infection)	V-Tense-Mood	

Analytic composition is the principal formal morphosyntactic procedure employed by all true creoles. Composition in creoles corresponds to inflection in non-creoles, but composition in creoles also characterizes grammatical domains in creoles that are not characterized by composition in non-creoles. Irrespective of the typology of known or putative inputs, all creoles structure kinship terms compositionally. Cf. Engl. boy : girl, Black Engl. man-chail : woman-chail and Papiamentu yia homber : yie muhe. The point is that kinship terms are normally suppletive in inflecting languages and agglutinating languages, and it is a well known rule of thumb that inflecting languages are far more prone to suppletion than agglutinating languages. Cf. Engl. son : daughter (suppletion) and Lat. fili-us : fili-a (inflection). Then, too, composition is far more frequent than suppletion in isolating than in either inflecting or agglutinating languages.

The composition vs. suppletion contrast and comparison of that contrast with the degree of suppletion in, for better or worse, the Sapirian typologies (agglutinating, inflecting, isolating, polysynthetic) is, I think, highly indicative of what it is that is really going on in creolization and contact simplification generally.

There are but four categories of what may be termed "basic suppletion sectors" in the world's languages: (1) kinship terms (mama : dada), (2) first person pronouns (I : me : we : us). (3) comparison of basic, no matter how you slice semantic pies, adjectives (good : better - best), and (4) initial ordinals/cardinals (first : one, second : two), see Markey (1985).

Based on a survey of suppletion in these sectors in 131 languages from all over the globe (Markey forthcoming, 1987), the following pertinent observations can be made. Prevalence of suppletion within categories is subject to implicational hierarchies: in kinship terms, suppletion in terms that are more distant from ego implies suppletion in terms that are ego-proximate; suppletion in the plural or dual of first person pronouns implies suppletion in the singular of first person pronouns; suppletion in ordinals implies suppletion in cardinals; and suppletion in less basic adjectives implies suppletion in more basic adjectives. Suppletion in these categories, among the first acquired by children, is indicative of a pregrammatical stage of acquisition. Note, incidentally, the skewing of suppleted forms by English-speaking children: I one, me first, that is, an association of the subject with the cardinal and the object with the ordinal, an instance of pregrammatical predication. We never really lose this pre-grammatical suppletion strategy, for otherwise we could not process onomastic information.Toponyms, for example, are not paradigmatically related, but highly suppletive when related, e.g. New York : Brooklyn not *New York : New York-ila.

The degree of suppletion in these basic categories in terms of the Sapirian typologies is as follows: it is virtually absent in agglutinating languages, more prevalent in strongly than in weakly inflecting languages, and most prevalent in isolating languages. But then, as we observed, composition is more prevalent than suppletion in isolating languages. Suppletion is virtually absent in all true creoles, where composition is rampant. There is an immediate correlation between the degree of suppletion and the degree of morphophonological "bonding": where that bonding is strongest (i.e. agglutinating languages), there is the least suppletion and conversely, where that bonding is weakest, there is the most suppletion. Suppletion, then, apparently takes up the slack of morphophonological bonding deficits, and morphophonemic complexity (e.g. vowel harmony, balance, apophony, umlaut) is a manifestation of such bonding. Creoles, particularly basilectal varieties, are notoriously impoverished morphophonemically, but begin to acquire elementary morphophonemic rules as they move down the road of creolization or decreolization, e.g. the well-known instances of elementary morphophonemic alternations in Papiamentu, a creole that is far down the road of the creolization process. Obviously, suppletion severely complicates a grammar, and a totally suppletive language would be unlearnable. Isolating languages, those typology most deficient in morphophonological bonding, fall off the suppletion scale and "naturally" capitulate to composition. Roughly speaking, then, we have the following continuum:

TURNING POINT

most bonding			least bonding
least bonding	less suppletion	more suppletion	
	more suppletion	marked increment	
			in composition

Clearly, both suppletion and composition may be viewed as purely lexical, rather than inflectional or otherwise "bonded," morphologization strategies. Note, for example, that the role of lexical semantics is more prominent and suppletion far more prevalent in languages that favor aspect over tense or accord aspect a prominent role, e.g. Polish with chodz- 'go, walk, attend, frequent' present (imperfective) stem vs. szedt- id. past (perfective) stem. Recall the high degree of verb suppletion in Celtic, particularly in Old Irish. (Engl. go : went is an historical accident.) Both suppletion and composition are highly indexical indicators of semantactic distinctions. However, there are dramatic differences between the two, and these differences are highly significant for the topic at hand.

Both processes are highly indexical, but suppletion, with its X vs. Y patterning, is icon-blind, while composition, particularly where present in interrelated sets (e.g. man-child : woman-child, formally X-Y : Z-Y), is highly iconic in its constant + variable constellations, its chains of Hegelian Aufhebungen, its difference that has far more "hooks" than suppletive patterns. Composition is formally comparable to juxtaposition strategies (e.g. John house for 'John's house') that are prevalent in many African languages (e.g. Kpelle, Mende), as well as creoles.

Aux-support, do-support, serialization (rather than bound TMAs), classifiers or prepositions (rather than case markers), gender by anaphora (rather than by bound markers), lexicalized (rather than grammaticalized) reflexives, and all such similar syntagmatic arrangements are all compositional in nature and isolating in character. With the review of feature stripping in mind that was presented at the outset, we now see that composition is a principal result of feature stripping.

Suppletive sets (X : Y) are generally characterized by etymological opacity, but this does not hold for compositional sets (X-Y : X-Z, etc.), which are generally etymologically transparent. The members of suppletive sets (such as Gmc. *bat-, whose source is unknown, in Engl. better/ best) tend to be opaque.

The ranges of suppletive items are strictly constrained by semantactic boundaries, e.g. postive (X) | comparative - superlative (Y) (so Engl. good | better - best), cardinal | ordinal, and so on. Such constraints are absent in composition.

Suppletive sets are extended by composition, e.g. mama : dada + mama-horse : dada-horse, but the converse does not hold.

The strict additivity of composition vs. the non-additivity of suppletion alone implicates a higher level of abstraction for suppletion than for composition. Indeed, the replacement of excessive suppletion by composition, mapped on the continuum above, is properly seen as a corrective measure to check excessive abstraction.

Suppletion, where not traceable to historical accident, appears to be arbitrarily introduced, while composition seems to be orchestrated by a sort of Boolean algebra, and, if pressed to assign a visual analogue, composition could be appropriately imaged as a Venn diagram, while suppletion certainly could not be.

As a highly iconic strategy, composition may be identified with what Haiman (1980) has isolated as the major functions of iconic motivation: intensity, plurality, and repetition/sequencing.

Feature stripping is apparently triggered by intensive contact and/or a plurality of inputs, particularly in the case of outright creolization. In many instances feature stripping results in composition, and composition is the principal grammatical strategy of all true creoles. As we have seen, composition is highly iconic, and we necessarily conclude that intensive contact and creolization are signalled by transitions from lesser to greater surficial iconicity.

Iconicity is a correlative of what Seiler (1986) has termed "indicativity," the complementary functional converse of which is "predicativity." Indicativity is also characterized as more grammaticalized and less marked, while predicativity is characterized by a reversal of these polarities:

PREDICATIVITY	INDICATIVITY
less grammaticalized	more grammaticalized
more marked/less stripped	less marked/more stripped
less contact/fewer inputs	more contact/more inputs
less iconic	more iconic
(- composition)	(+ composition)

Both during and well after the Hanseatic period (ca. 1150-1650), intensive contact between and among Netherlandic speakers and the speakers of the other, closely related Ingwaeonic dialects on the Continent and in Britain, as well as speakers of Scandinavian Germanic, must have fostered a sort of Germanic Balkanization. Indeed, the Dutch - Low German Hansa dominated the commercial scene of Scandinavia. Hanseatic control in Visby, Stockholm, Bergen, etc. is well known and well documented. This period of far-reaching trade and communicative contact triggered the feature stripping that made the languages of the North Sea Basin and the Baltic take on the appearance of a speech community with numerous shared traits.

Feature stripping conferred a semi-creole appearance on English and Netherlandic, and here we emphasize the fact that "creole" is a gradient notion. Modern Netherlandic is more creole-like than its medieval ancestor, and Afrikaans is more creole-like than Dutch, while the Negerhollands of the colonial Virgin Islands and the Berbice Dutch of Suriname were cast as true creoles.

That the flow of influence was from south to north, rather than the other way around, is indicated by the numerous fixed, frozen phrases of Netherlandic or Low German origin that became hallmarks of Nordic slang and colloquial speech: comparable Scandinavian elements in Dutch or Low German are lacking. These are valuable trace elements for reconstructing a sociolinguistic pattern. When a language borrows, rather than generates, its idioms and set phrases, then this is diagnostic of stigmaticization, even eventual death. Witness the wholesale introduction of English idioms, calqued or not, into Modern Scottish Gaelic vs.the general absence of Gaelic loans, slang or not, in English. Recall, too, the paucity of Irish loans in English, and these few (e.g. galore < Ir. go leor) are rarely perceived as loans.

We conclude that intrusive contact on a massive scale and/or multiple inputs triggers feature stripping. The goal of such stripping is increased indicativity which is evidenced by grammatical simplification and an increased iconicity. Increased iconicity is reflected, at least in part, by expanded composition. True creolization is an extreme case of stripping, as extreme as the social conditions and numbers of inputs that surround creolization, but the notion "creole" is necessarily gradient, keyed as it must be to degrees of contact interference and numbers of inputs. Netherlandic stands at some threshold level of creolization, while Afrikaans is a sort of "fusion creole" with many of the same characteristics of Yiddish, another "fusion language," and Negerhollands is a true creole. Feature stripping can be ranged along a continuum in much the same manner that creolization with its basilectal, mesolectal, and acrolectal spectra can be ranged along a continuum.

If indicativity is a result of stripping, then what is the cognitive basis that underlies it? How does stripping progress? A probative answer to the second question provides an answer to the first.

It seems obvious by now that indicativity is correlated with greater animacy than predicativity, that is, grammatical items and processes that are higher on the animacy scale are, or tend to be, more grammaticalized, less marked, more stripped and, generally, more iconic than those subsumed by predicativity, see Beechert (1982) for a thorough discussion of animacy scaling, cf. the pertinent sections in Comrie (1981).

Typically, case syncretism and elimination of nominal number markers is conducted in accordance with animacy scaling: syncretism is more frequent in the plural than the singular, more in neuters than in masculines and feminines, but the most frequent instances of loss of case marking are in the nominative and accusative singular.

It is a general rule-of-thumb that the higher the animacy, the higher the degree of specificity, definiteness, and participation, where participation is a cover term for pragmatic considerations, see Seiler (1986). Then, too, more animate entities will tend to act on less animate entities rather than vice versa, and reduction or elimination is usually in the direction of higher animacy: items and processes lower on the animacy scale are eliminated first, while those highest on the animacy scale persist longest. For example, a singular count noun is more animate than a singular (collective) mass noun, which in turn is more animate than a plural (distributive) mass noun. The higher animacy (+count) plural may attract (act on) a lower animacy (-count) collective, which may then, as presumably was the case in the anterior stages of Breton, emerge as a derived (-count) plural to which a singulative may be fabricated to supply "the singular" of (-count). This is a highly credible scenario for the historical development of the Breton number system.

Table 1 plots animacy scales. Only two polar values, most vs. least, are given. This is a simplification for the sake of diagrammatic clarity, but a more elaborate picture would show that animacy, too, is a gradient notion.

An item at the highest conceivable level on the animacy scale would be specified positively as single, masculine, adult, here/now, agentive, standing, and living, see Beechert (1982).

The course of stripping traces an overall pattern of movement from lower to higher animacy: morphosyntactic constructs with the lowest appreciation of animacy are stripped first, those with the highest animacy virtually never. Concomitantly, synthesis gives way to analysis, paradigmatic bundles to syntagmatic sets, and there is a marked increase in composition, where the last bastion of resistance to composition is core (sectors 1-4 above) suppletion, which, as in all true creoles, finally yields to composition, even in ego-proximate kinship terms (e.g. man-child : woman-child). In intensive contact situations, in highly diglossic encounters, whose pragmatic strings are marionetted by concessional rules, as well as in multiple input situations, speakers blot out fuzzy indeterminant predicativities and concentrate on or search for well-focused indicativities.

This assessment of stripping is firmly supported by the history of Netherlandic stripping: gender is lost in less animate nouns, but retained in more animate proforms; the arsenal of non-finite forms is reduced (generation of non-finite forms is an historical rarity); the less animate plural forms of verbs are coatesced and the overall inventory of plural markers is reduced, lative marking (case) is transferred to definites (cf. the discussion in n. 3) or prepositions (a compositional strategy). definites acquire expanded semantactic roles, certain forms that never functioned as discourse co-ordinators (e.g. NEGs) now assume these roles, and so on.

In comparison with what goes on in true creolization, the Netherlandic stripping movement from lesser to greater animacy and indicativity is liminal, while that same movement in Afrikaans and fusion creoles generally terminates at some intermediate range, and fusion creoles are postured as intermediate typologies.

Recently, Mufwene (1986a, 1986b) has gratifyingly devoted attention to creole diachrony and sought typological definitions. He is entirely correct in his critique of my earlier (1982) attempt to characterize creoles in terms of a roster of selected features, of particularistic saliencies, viz. in the matrix displayed in n. 2 above. While justifiably critical --- though such matrices are entirely suitable for phonological categorization, say, they are hardly commensurate with typological gradience and make no allowances for cognitive factors, Mufwene offers no new or credible solution as a replacement. Then, too, like most creolists, he is either uninterested in or ignorant of the benefits of etymological insight or procedure. The stripping scenario outlined here, whose final act is creolization, offers a probative, predictably adequate, model for simplification that relates observable surface reductions to cognitive motivations. The transition from inherent predicativity to inchoate indicativity outlined by the history of Netherlandic stripping defines a hypothesis for communicative survival in multilingual and pluricultural contexts. This was the same hypothesis for survival ---call it a bioprogram if you wish, that the children of multilingual and cultural plantation slaves resorted to in their primitive day-care centers. It is also the same hypothesis any native speaker of L:, but marginal speaker of Lz. resorts to when conversing with a partner whose competencies are inversely related to his own.

TABLE 1. Animacy Scale

MOST ANIMATE		LEAST ANIMATE
animate		inanimate
determinant		indeterminant
concrete		diffuse
definite		indefinite
participatory (most)		participatory (least)
here/now		there/then
topic		comment
VERB		**VERB**
active	middle	passive
personal		impersonal
non-stative		stative
finite		non-finite
agentive		non-agentive
volational		non-volitional
transitive		intransitive
NOUN		**NOUN**
count		mass
singular		plural
gender		gender
masculine	feminine	neuter
pronominal gender	nominal gender	verbal gender
grammatical case (nom./acc.)		concrete case (latives)
((classifier))		((classifier))
sortal		mensural
solid		liquid
standing		lying
(+human)		(-human)
(+edible)		(-edible)
(+color)		(-color)
(mature/adult)		(immature/young)

NOTES

[1] For a convenient, thorough, and reliable edition of the Old Low Franconian corpus and a lexical index to it, see Kyes (1969, 1983).

[2] The notion of "creole" as a typological label is most reasonably articulated as a gradient Value. Some languages are more creole-like than other languages. A gradient evaluation permits scalar ranking and thus a mapping of creoles and creole-like languages on a continuum. English is more creole-like than Dutch, as is Afrikaans, but Afrikaans is, in turn, far less creole-like than Virgin Islands Creole Dutch (Negerhollands) or the Berbice Dutch of Guyana, both true creoles, see Markey (1982) for a discussion and details of the feature matrix given below. A minimal requirement to be classified as a creole is positive specification for all of the following features diagrammed as a definitional matrix:

Feature Matrix for Creole Determination

(1) Lack nominal gender	(+)	(+)	(+)	(+)
(2) Nominal number by anaphora	(-)	(-)	(-)	(+)
(3) SVO-Order	( )	( )	(+)	(+)
(4) Anaphoric unity	(-)	(-)	(-)	(+)
(5) Three Tense-Aspect Markers	(-)	( )	(-)	(+)
(6) Lack nominal case	( )	(+)	(+)	(+)
(7) Lack non-finite Verb	(-)	(-)	(-)	(+)
(8) Lack inflected passive	(-)	(-)	(-)	(+)
(9) Certain semantic repartitions with respect to existence, location, ownership, and possession	(-)	(-)	(-)	(+)
(10) NEG-spread	(-)	(-)	(-)	(+)
	Dutch	Afrikaans	English	Negerhollands

[3] Statistically, there are fewer inflecting languages that are exclusively prefixing than there are infecting languages that are exclusively suffixing. Circumfixing, such as in some Caucasian languages, is a distinct rarity. This fact alone speaks for suffixing as preferential. Then too, prefixing languages tend to be isolates, as is certainly the case with the Munda languages, or geographically restricted in some way, or readily replaced by dominant suffixing languages, as was the case with Hattic, a prefixing language possibly related to Abkhasian-Circassian and Kartvelian that was ousted by Hittite, see Kammenhuber (1959). Diakonoff (1957). Recently, Ivanov (Engl. transl. 1986: 4-10) has correlated Proto-Kartvelian verb prefixes ("personal beginnings") with Indo-European verb suffixes ("personal

endings"). Other contact preferential results merit detailed attention: noun class languages seemingly give way to gender languages; case languages to classifier languages; ergative languages to non-ergative languages, abut note the trickle-down effect of ergativity in India from Dravidian to Indo-Iranian, e.g. Marathi.

[4]This example of Balkanization is well known and frequently cited. For further details and a discussion, see Comrie (1981:199-200). Other well-known instances are the merger of the genitive and the dative (i.e. genitive within NPs and the indirect object of verbs) in all languages of the area except Serbo-Croation; postposed definites (in Albanian burr 'man':burr'i 'the main'/burr-at 1the men'; Bulgarian-Macedonian maz 1man':maz-et 'the man'; and Rumanian om 'man': om-ul 'the man' with -ul < Lat. il-); formation of an admirative mood (cf. Alb. pjek-kam 'behold, I bake' and Rum. pacatuit-am 'behold, I have sinned').

Postposed definites would seem to be rare, but are, of course, a hallmark feature of Scandinavian (in direct contrast ato West Germanic), as is the double definite (both pre- and postposed) in Faroese, New Norwegian, and Swedish, but not in Danish or Icelandic, and here the double definite does not occur with genetives or posessives. Historically, the Scandinavian double definite is a new formation, a new strategy for conveying agreement/congruency that was introduced after weakening and eventual loss of case-gender agreement in the medieval period. While West Germanic and Continental Scandinavian have both definites and indefinites, both Insular Scandinavian (Icelandic, Faroese) and Celtic (Irish, Gaelic, Welsh) lack indefinites. Continental Scandinavian use of the indefinite expanded dramatically after intensive contact with both Dutch and Low German during the Hanseatic period. Emergence of a regularly employed indefinite is demonstrably late in Western Indo-European. For details of the Norse development, see now Lundeby (1965).

The rise of postposing and the evolution and diffusion of the double definite in Norse is an instance of Balkanization that is immediately comparable to the acquisition of definites by South Slavic and the diffusion of postposing in the Balkans.

There is an immediate tendential correlation between case and definiteness such that case flurescence implies definite decay, while, conversely, definite florescence implies case decay, schematically: (+case, -definite) vs. (-case, +definite). With their wealth of case morphology, Finnish and Estonian lack both definites and indefinites. Case is, as a semantactic prime, an expression of definiteness and definiteness plus case is an uneconomical redundancy. Here, Turkish is particularly revealing.

Indefinite objects are specified by an unmarked absolute case, while definite objects are signalled by a marked (-i) definite object case:

adam-lar gordum   INDEFINITE
men-PL saw I
"I saw men"

adam-lar-i   gordum   DEFINITE
men-PL-DEF saw I
'I saw the men'

As topicalizers, definites and indefinites are never marked on verbs, and definiteness is usually keyed to animacy hierarchies, see below.

[5]The substance of these statements is crucial for the argumentation that follows. Without further illustration, foregrounding, or definition they might well be cryptic.

A functional analogy is defined as a correspondence(s) in function between organs or items of different structure or origin. While they definitely have different structures and origins, the various anterior (= roughly, past tense) markers of all true creoles have the same function, namely, indication of an anterior action. Similarly, while all French-based creoles of the Caribbean Basin utilize what are etymologically body-part terms as reflexive pronouns, all English-based creoles of the area employ derivations of Engl. self.

Linguistically, then, functional analogies define allogenetic relationships, while homologies define genetic relationships. The monogenesis theory of creole origins necessarily subscribes to homology, while serious polygenetic hypotheses about creole origins are necessarily supported by appeals to functional analogy.

True creoles, as well as intensive contact languages generally, share convergent functional and strategic similarities, e.g. analytic, rather than synthetic, processing of certain grammatical saliencies such as tense/aspect signals, enumerative marking, and so on. These convergent similarities, which may well have had different language-internal origins, are presumed to have been triggered by encounters with the same (or very, very similar) external conditions, namely, contact interference that featured a high level of input diversity and/or multiplicity. The classic condition for creolization is more than a one-on-one confrontation of languages.

The contention that only the interpretation of a similarity can be false is illustrated by the following scenario. If, while walking with John, Bill sees what he thinks is Jane and says, "I think that's Jane," then John, who does not know Jane at all, must accept this interpretation until Bill says either, "no, that's not Jane, but that girl certainly looked like Jane," or, "hey, it really is Jane."

Room for counter-factual construal of similarities as correspondences and vice versa is a serious weakness inherent to any view of linguistic typology that persists in seeking only formal and functional analogues that are just short of identities. Unless such analogues are provided with a cognitive basis, they can only lead to a strictly taxonomic and ultimately trivial typologizing of surface structures < la Joseph Greenberg. Mere word order typologizing (VO vs. OV), no matter how extensive the subsidiary correlations with such macrocategorial position constraints may be (e.g. N + Adj. sequencing correlated with SVO order), will remain interpretively inadequate unless it can be given cognitive grounding. Even what at first appear to be sophisticated observations about such analogues, while fleetingly intriguing, will ultimately end by passing off description as interpretation. For example, the historical observation that "shorter" forms e.g. Engl. un-) are usually grammaticalizations of their lexical analogues (i.e. Engl. not) is not an adequate interpretation of a typological event.

The correlations ((increased similarity = decreased interest) vs. (decreased similarity = increased interest)) also require some clarification. In the case of the former, we assume that common cause is obvious. Here, we might be considering the resemblance of, say, different kinds of eggs, or pears, or tomatoes. In the case of the latter, illustrated by, say, a bat wing vs. a dolphin fin, common cause appears well hidden and we question reduction to some underlying prototype. The less similar things appear, the more hidden seems their common cause, if any, and the less soluble the problem appears.

In essence, the trick that Claude Levi-Strauss repeatedly performed was to claim common cause for things that normally appeared quite dissimilar, even outrageously different, and, hence, insoluble. Recall his frequent equation of smoking with eating in the structural context of cooked vs. raw.

It was the many similarities between creole structures and those of their acrolects that led to the earlier dismissal of creoles as objects worthy of real scientific inquiry. Just so, the many similarities between and among languages in a Sprachbund, such as that posed by Norse, or Ingwaeonic, or the languages of the Balkans, made them seem uninteresting. On the other hand, specification of the relationship between Celtic and an Indo-European parent, given the sharply decreased similarities between the two, was of real interest. The question of surface similarity was a distractor from the real issues posed by contact spill-over, grammatical streamling,and feature stripping that regularly result from prachbund-situations and creolization. Even the search for substratum effects in residual forms or residual syntactic scaffolding to account for similarities between Input X and Output Y, which were then frequently construed as evidence of correspondences, was a distractor. The surface similarities in contact spill-over effects, grammatical streamlining, and residual substratal retentions (e.g. the "surpass"-comparison formation found in many West African languages and Caribbean creoles) could neither be denied nor falsified: only the interpretation of these similarities could be falsified. Until Bickerton (1981) presented his bioprogram hypothesis, creolistics was going nowhere: data collection and exchanges of anecdotes do not constitute scientific inquiry. Until that point, conventional interpretations of similarities fell into just two theoretical categories: (1) a monogenetic hypothesis that argued homologies (or else it couldn't claim to be a monogenetic hypothesis), even when the empirical, extra-linguistic evidence was shaky, and (2) polygenetic views that apodictically contended that the similarities were due to samenesses in external conditions, to samenesses in specific sociolinguistic conditions (e.g. plantation economies equipped with multilingual slaves), or merely the natural, least common denominator (reductionist) result of any multi-input situation. Whatever his detractors' assessment of the bioprogram hypothesis per se may be, Bickerton (1981) succeeded in displacing similarity interpretation from mere surface observation to a cognitive base (preprogrammed nativism), however wrong-headed that base may be in his presentation.

BIBLIOGRAPHY

Bailey, Charles-James N. 1982. *On the Yin and Yang Nature of Language.* Ann Arbor: Karoma Publishers, Inc.

Beechert, Johannes. 1982. Grammatical Gender in Europe: An Areal Study of a Linguistic Category. *Papiere zur Linguistik* 26.23-34.

Bickerton, Derek. 1981. *Roots of Language.* Ann Arbor: Karoma Publishers, Inc. Comrie, Bernard. 1981. *Language Universals and Linguistic Typology. Syntax and Morphology.* Oxford: Basil Blackwell.

Diakonoff, Igor Miajlovic. 1957. Xattskij jazyk. *Vestnik drevnej istorii* 3.88-99.

Foerste, William and Klaas Heeroma. 1955. *Westfaalse en Nederlandse expansie.* (Bijdragen en mededelingen der Dialecten-commissie van de Kon. Ned. Akademie van Wetenschappen, 15.) Amsterdam: North Holland.

Hagege, Claude. 1985. *L'homme de paroles. Contribution linguistique aux sciences humaines.* Paris: Fayard.

Haiman, John. 1980. Iconicity of Grammar. *Language* 56.3.515-41.

Ivanov, V. V. 1986. Proto-Languages as Objects of Scientific Description. *Typology, Relationship and Time.* Ed. and transl. by V. V. Shevoroshkin and T. L. Markey, 1-26. Ann Arbor: Karoma Publishers, Inc.

Kammenhuber, Annelisa. 1959. Protohattisch-Hethitisches. *Münchener Studien zur Sprachwissenschaft* 14.63-9.

Kuhn, Hans. 1959. Vor- und frühgermanische Ortsnamen in Norddeutschland und den Niederlanden. *Westfälische Forschungen* 12.5-44.

―――― 1960. Vorgermanische Personennamen bei den Friesen. *Fryske studzjes oan Prof. Dr. J. H. Brouwer.* Ed. by K. Dykstra, K. Heeroma, W. Wok, and H. T. J. Miedema, 379-88. (Fryske Academy, 180. Studia Germanica, 2.) Assen: van Gorcum.

———————. 1961. Anlautend pi im Germanischen. *Zeitschrift für Mundartforschung* 28.1-31.

Kyes, Robert L. 1969. *The Old Low Franconian Psalms and Glosses*. Ann Arbor: The University of Michigan Press.

———————. 1983. *Dictionary of the Old Low and Central Franconian Psalms and Glosses*. Tübingen: Niemeyer.

Lakoff, Robin. 1972. Another Look at Drift. *Linguistic Change and Generative Theory*. Ed. by R. P. Stockwell and R. K. S. Macaulay, 172-98. Bloomington: Indiana University Press.

Lundeby, Einar. 1965. *Overbestemt substantiv i norsk og de andre nordiske sprak*. Oslo: Universitetsforlag.

Markey, T. L. 1972. West Germanic he/er --- hiu/siu and English "she". *Journal of English and Germanic Philology* 71.3.390-405.

———————. 1975. West Frisian -wV-/-jV- Breaking: A Generative Approach. *Folia Linguistica* 6.1/2.181-208.

———————. 1977. Societal, Phonotactic, and Paradigmatic Factors in Isoglossic Relations: Nordic Medial Affrication. *Dialectology and Sociolinguistics*. Ed. by C.-Chr. Elert, S. Eliasson, S. Fries, and S. Ureland, 92-108. (Acta Universitatis Umensis, 12.) Umeå: Centraltryckeriet.

———————. 1982. Afrikaans: Creole or Non-Creole? *Zeitschrift für Dialektologie und Linguistik* 49.2.169-207.

———————. 1985. On Suppletion. *Diachronica* 2.1.51-66.

———————. 1986. Some Verbal Remarks. *Linguistics across Historical and Geographical Boundaries. 1. Linguistic Theory and Historical Linguistics*. Ed. by D. Kastowsky and A. Szwedek, 513-24. Berlin: Mouton de Gruyter.

———————. forthcoming. Pidgin Provincialism: An Impolite Essay. *Lingua Posnaniensis* (1987).

Mayrthaler, Willi. 1984. Woher stammt der Name ‚Baiern'? *Das Romanische in den Ostalpen*. Ed, by Dieter Messner, 7-72. (Osterreichische Akademie der Wissenschaften, Phil.-hist. Klasse, 442. Bd.) Vienna: Verlag der bsterreichischen Akademie der Wissenschaften.

Mufwene, Salikoko S. 1986a. Number Delimitation in Gullah. *American Speech* 61.1.33-60.

———————. 1986b. Les langues creoles peuvent-elles être definies sans allusion a leur histoire? Paper presented at: Vé Colloque international des Etudes Creoles. Réunion, April 7-14, 1986.

Ramamurti, G. V. 1931. *A Manual of the Sora (or Savara) Lanquage*. Madras: Madras University Press.

Riedl, Rupert. 1979. *Biologie der Erkenntnis. Die stammesgeschichtlichen Grundlagen der Vernunft*.Berlin-Hamburg: Verlag Paul Parey.

Sanders, Willy. 1982. *Sachsensprache, Hansesprache, Plattdeutsch. Sprachgeschichtliche Grundzüge des Niederdeutschen.* Göttingen: Vandenhoeck & Ruprecht.

Seiler, Hansjakob. 1986. *Language, Object and Order.* (Language Universals Series, 1/III.) Tubingen: Narr.

Watkins, Calvert. 1969. *Indogermanische Grammatik. Bd. III. Formenlehre.* Erster Teil. Geschichte der indogermanischen Verbalflexion. Heidelberg: Carl Winter Universitatsverlag.

THE ORIGIN OF THE MIDDLE DUTCH SUFFIX -STER

Garry W. Davis
The University of Wisconsin -- Milwaukee

Etymological dictionaries of Dutch frequently maintain that the Middle Dutch suffix -ster (Mdu. bacster 'female baker', leerster 'female teacher', scepster 'female tailor'), a productive suffix for marking feminine agent nouns, was borrowed into Old English and early Netherlandic from the Vulgar Latin agentive suffix -istria. One such etymological dictionary states flatly that -ster was 'waarschijnlijk ontleend van Latijn -istria', and gives a few pairs of similar sounding agent nouns such as Latin tympanistria and OE timpestre 'female timbrel player' to support this theory. Schröder (1922), Frings (1932), and van Loey (1959) have favored this view. Others such as von Lindheim (1958) have concentrated on describing -ster's function as a feminine agentive suffix and have not concerned themselves with the question of -ster's origin.

According to van Loey (1959:220), "Het waren de Romeinse garnizoenen in het gebied van de Nederrijn, die de woorden aan de Germanen...leverden." Van Loey maintains that the Greek suffix -istria was borrowed into Vulgar Latin causing forms in -istria to appear parallel to the Classical Latin suffix -trix (Vulgar Latin meletristria vs. Classical Latin meletrix 'prostitute'). The formation of the new substantives using the suffix -istria many have been influenced by Classical Latin forms in -istria such as scitharistria 'lute player', tympanistria 'tambourine player'. Such Vulgar Latin forms were then borrowed into some Germanic dialects, according to van Loey (cf. OE miltestre 'prostitute').

Frings (1932:24) was apparently referring to forms such as OE miltestre when he wrote that the meaning of OE -estre was originally derogatory. After an extensive investigation of the Old English situation, von Lindheim (503), however, contradicted Frings, "Dass die ältesten -estre-Bildungen einen üblen Beigeschmack gehabt hätten, findet in dem ae. Material keine Bestätigung." Furthermore, it must be remembered that forms in -estre were very common in Old English. As von Lindheim points out (494), "Angesichts der stärkeren Frequenz sowie des späteren Schicksals der mit -estre gebildeten Formen läst sich schliessen, dass es sich um das wichtigste weibliche Genussuffix des Ae. handelt." The theory that the precursor of OE -estre and Mdu. -ster was borrowed from Vulgar Latin is deficient in several other respects, however.

The most damaging of these is the existence of forms containing -ster and -estre where the suffix cannot be said to have an agentive meaning. These forms instead have various meanings such as OHG wagastria 'lance', but are most often animal and bird names such as OS agastria (cf. Mdu. aexter) 'magpie', OE hulfestre 'golden plover', OE loppestre 'lobster', OE eowestre 'ewe', OS hamustra 'rye pest', etc. (cf. Kluge 1886:26 and Krahe/Meid 1967:III:184-186, also Palander, 1899).

Kluge (24) derived MDu. -ster and OE -estre from Proto-Germanic *-astrjon-/*-istrjon- and believed that reflexes of this suffix must have been passed into all the Germanic dialects. He supplied only two examples of such reflexes, however, Go. blostreis 'sacrificer' and ON bakstr 'baking', and he offered no explanation of how they fit into the overall context of the development of -ster/-estre. He further speculated that *-astrjon-/*- istrjon- had developed from an earlier jo-stem form (nom. sg. -stri) which then shifted over to the n-declension.

Krahe/Meid (1967:III:184) provide a clearer picture of the Germanic situation. They reconstruct PGmc. *-istrijo-/*-astrijo-/*-ustrijo-(n)- to account for the feminine agentive nouns ending in MDu. -ster and OE -estre. Krahe/Meid concur with Kluge in that, "Dass es jedoch auch Bildungen mit maskulinem Suffix -ja-gegeben haben kann, davon zeugt got. blostreis 'Opferer' (*blostrija zu *blostra 'Opfer').

Krahe/Meid also mention (186) many of the various animal names which end in reflexes of this reconstructed Proto-Germanic suffix, but offer no explanation for their existence. The most interesting aspect of Krahe/Meid's work is that they make a direct connection between feminine agent nouns in *-istrijo-/*-astrijo-/*-ustrijo-(n)- and Proto-Germanic instrumental and action nouns in *-stra-.

*-stra- (Krahe/Meid 184) is a variant of the Indo-European instrumental suffix *-tra- (PGmc. *-þra-/*-þro-) brought about by the juncture of roots having a dental final consonant + *-tra-where the final dental consonant of the root is consequently assimilated to an -s- as in Go. gilstr 'tax' (--gild-an, fra-gild-an, us-gild-an 'pay, vergelten'). This variant PGmc. suffix was attached later to roots containing a final velar fricative, i.e. -h#; OS, OHG lastar < *lah-stra- 'blame', next to OE leahtor; ON bolstr, OE, OHG bolster 'custion' < *bulh-stra-, cf. OHG balg 'animal skin'; ON mostr 'great amount' < *muh-stra-, cf. ON mugr 'pike'; ON bakstra baka 'to bake'. Root final -1# gave rise to doublets such as OHG galtar vs. galstra 'magic song', etc.

The basic points mentioned above were first articulated by Brugmann (1906:II,1:346). Brugmann, however, regarded the origin of certain other forms as unsure. These are, for example, Go. hulistr 'cover', OE heolostar 'hiding place', Go. awistr 'sheepfold' and ga-nawistr-on 'to bury'. He had good reason to find that the origin of these forms had yet to be adequately explained. At the time of his writing, several different etymologies had been proposed for Go. awistr and hulistr. Osthoff (1877:316) (see also Feist 1939:70) had suggested that awistr developed from PGmc. *awi-wistra. The suffix *-wistra was supposed to be derived from Go. wisan 'to be, stay' and is supposedly related to OHG wist 'soujourn, Aufenthalt'. Noreen (1894:30) also favored the reconstruction of *awi-wistr.

Bezzenberger (1879:267) suggested that Go. awistr could be derived from IE *oui-sth(e)-ro. This would then bring awistr into connection with Skt. -staras 'straw, camp'. In a somewhat similar attempt, Schulze (1888:270) tried to derive Go. awistr from IE *oui-sth-tro-. This, in turn, would have connected awistr with Skt. gosthas 'cowherd', 'cow barn' from Skt gaus 'beef cow' + stha- 'to stand'.

Pokorny (1959:784) analyzed the suffix attached to awistr as IE *-sto-, *-st[ə]tro- which belongs to the IE root *-sta -to stand', but he found that Go. hulistr (553), Go. huljan 'to cover; verhüllen' had made use of the Germanic suffix *-stra-. MHG hulse, OHG hulsa, hulis are supposed to rest on an old IE *-es- stem (cf. Latin color with later interchange of -r- for -s-). It is unclear whether Pokorny wishes to derive OE helustr, heolstar 'cover, Schlupfwinkel' from the Germanic suffix *-stra-, or whether he thinks that the suffix is related to the old -es-stem mentioned above. In any case, he mentions 'germ suffix-ablaut' as one possible source of the suffix in OE helustr, and suggests that it may be related to the IEstem *kelu-.

Krahe/Meid (184) analyze both Go. awistr and hulistr as root + PGmc. *-stra- though they still give at least lip service (170) to the possible validity of the theory (see my references to Bezzenberger, Schulze and Pokorny above) that *-stra- is related to the IE root *-sta- 'to stand'. They readily admit the problematic nature of this view, however, given the much more likely origin of these forms discussed above. Forms derived from PGmc. *-stra- are, however, according to Krahe/Meid mostly place designations, 'Ortsbezeichnungen'.

There is little basis indeed for Oshoff's and Noreen's proposed suffix, PGmc. *-wistra 'soujourn, Aufenthalt'. Such an explanation is clearly ad hoc, and does nothing to explain parallel forms such as Go. hulistr and agentive nouns in MDu. -ster and OE -estre. Theories linking PGmc. *-stra- to IE *-sta- 'to stand' are also deficient. The supposedly related forms in other IE languages are doubtful, and the question of agentive nouns, instrumental nouns, and animal names ending in -str-, -ster, -estre is left unexplained. Various other discrepancies are also evident. Whereas Go. awistr could perhaps be accounted for by comparison to forms in Sanskrit, Go. hulistr and *nawistr, though structurally similar, are left isolated.

The task, then, is how to explain how PGmc. *-istrijo-, *-astrijo-, *-ustrijo- were derived from PGmc. instrumental nouns in *-stra- and to account for those isolated forms in MDu. -ster and OE -estre which do not strictly speaking function as agentive nouns.

When PGmc. *-stra- began to combine with roots ending in a final guttural consonant, it set the stage for its further extension to all types of roots in Proto-Germanic. *-stra- would have had no theme vowel to bind it to specific forms, but instead came to be attached initially to consonant final roots, as in the example of Go. gilstr 'tax' (< *gild- + *-tra). Thereafter, it probably came to be attached to the thematic vowel of the form with which it was combined. Thus Go. awi- (cf. Latin ovi-s 'sheep', a feminine i-stem) + -stra would yield awistr 'sheepfold', Go. hulj-an (with -j- as the extension) + -

stra would yield hulistr 'cover, shelter'. Gothic naus (a masculine i-stem, gen. sg. nawis) + -stra would yield nawistr 'grave'. OE geolu 'yellow' (a u-stem adjective) + -stra yields OE geolostar 'ulcer', i.e. literally 'yellow spot'. The meaning of all these compounds is basically still just instrumental. awistr is a thing that holds sheep, hulistr is a thing that provides shelter, *nawistr is a thing that holds a corpse. Since such 'instruments' are also permanently located in one spot, the suffix may have secondarily come to have designated places, 'Ortsbezeichunungen', while retaining its basic instrumental meaning. Thus we get such extensions as OE geolostar 'ulcer'.

After instrumental nouns in *-stra had become productive, they must have been further modified to become masculine ja-stems, and thus became agentive nouns, i.e. PGmc. *blostra 'sacrifice', (< *blot- + *-tra) *blostrija 'sacrificer', thus Go. blostreis 'sacrificer', OHG bluostar 'sacrifice' (cf. Krahe/Meid 1967:III:185). Feminine agentive nouns would likely have been derived from the original instrumentals in a similar fashion. It is possible that these feminine forms were originally -jo-stems, as Kluge (1986:24) seemed to think since many feminines in -o- went over to the n-decension in Germanic. In any case, such feminine agentive nouns did emerge as n-stems in the attested dialects. Thus OE wyrt-gaelstere 'witch' i.e. literally 'singer of a magical song' is derived from *goelster 'song' (OHG galster 'song'), OE boecestre, MDu, bacster 'baker woman' are derived from an instrumental form, compare ON bakstr 'baking; pastry'.

Once such feminine agentive nouns in *-strijo-n- were firmly established, they were productive in forming feminine agentive nouns from verbs and occasionally from nouns (Wright 1925:316). In Old English -istrae > -estre was the most productive suffix in the language for forming feminine agentive nouns from verbs.

In summary, IE *-tra, an instrumental suffix, normally developed into PGmc. *-þra. It remained *-tra however, when suffixed to a root ending in a final dental consonant (*blot-tra > *blostra 'sacrifice'). This suffix subsequently came to be falsely segmented as *-stra and thereafter became productive in forming instrumental nouns, such as Go. awistr 'sheepfold', hulistr 'cover', and *nawistr 'corpse'. In these combinations, *-stra was suffixed directly to consonant final roots or added directly to the thematic vowel. *-stra was thus suffixed to Go. awi- (originally a feminine i-stem, cf. Latin ovis 'sheep') and became a neuter a-stem. In analogy with this instrumental use of *-stra, masculine and feminine agentive nouns emerged using (masculine) *-strija (*blostrija → Go. blostreis 'sacrificer'), (feminine) *-strijo-n. While the masculine forms fell out of use, the feminine forms became quite productive. This is evident from the high incidence of feminine agentive nouns in -estre and -ster in Old English and Middle Dutch. Certain animal terms may also be derived from agentive nouns in *-istrijo-n, but these developments are in need of further elucidation. Later, Vulgar Latin loan words ending in -istria were incorporated into this productive class of feminine agentive nouns because of their phonological similarity. They were comparatively few in number, however, and were basically limited to contact terminology, such as camp terms and items foreign to native Germanic culture.

BIBLIOGRAPHY

Bezzenberger, Adalbert. Awistr and *nawistr. *KZ* 22. 276-278. 1874.

Brugmann, Karl. *Grundriss einer vergleichenden Grammatik der indogermanischen Sprachen.* Vol. II, 1. Strassburg: Trübner. 1906.

Feist, Sigmund. *Vergleichendes Wörterbuch der gotischen Sprache.* Leiden: Brill. 1939.

Frings, Theodor. Persönliche Feminina im Westgermanischen. *PBB* 56. 23-40. 1932.

Kluge, Freidrich. *Nominale Stammbildungslehre der altgermanischen Dialekte.* (Sammlung Kurzer Grammatiken altgermanischer Dialekte. rgänzungsreihe, 1.) Halle: Niemeyer. 1886.

Krahe, Hans and Wolfgang Meid. *Germanische Sprachwissenschaft.* 3. Wortbildungslehre. (Sammlung Göschen 1218/1218a/1218b.) Berlin: de Gruyter.

Noreen, Adolf. *Abriss der urgermanischen Lautlehre.* Strassburg: Trübner. 1894.

Osthoff, H. Über das eingedrungene s in der nominalen suffixform -stra- und vor dental anlautenden personalendungen des deutschen, griechischen und altbaktrischen verbums. *KZ* 23. 311-333. 1877.

Palander, Hugo. *Die althochdeutschen Tiernamen.* 1. Die Namen der Saugetiere. Darmstadt: G. Otto's Hof Buchhandlung. 1899.

Pokorny, Julius. *Indogermanisches etymologisches Wörterbuch.* Vol. 1. Bern-Munich: Francke. 1959

Schabram, Hans. Bemerkungen zu den Ae. Nomina agentis auf -estre und -icge. *Anglia* 88. 94-98. 1970.

Schröder, Edward. Die Nomina agentis auf -ster. Niederdeutsches Jahrbuch. 48. 1-8. 1922.

Schulze, Wilhelm. Miscellen. *KZ* 22. 276-278. 1888.

Sommer, Ferdinand. Die Komparationssuffixe im Lateinischen. *IF* 11. 1-98. 1900.

van Loey, A. *Schönfeld's historische Grammatica van het Nederlands.* Zutphen: Thieme and Cie.

von Lindheim, Bogislav. Die weiblichen Genussuffixe im Altenglischen. *Anglia* 76. 479-504. 1958.

----------. Die weiblichen Genussuffixe im Altenglischen Korrekturen und Nachträge. *Anglia* 87. 64-65. 1969.

Wright, Joseph and Elizabeth Wright. *Old English Grammar.* 3rd ed. Oxford University Press. 1925.

RELATIONAL GRAMMAR, PASSIVES, AND DUMMIES IN DUTCH[1]

Thomas F. Shannon
University of California, Berkeley

1. Introduction: Relational Grammar

In recent research, linguists working within the theory of Relational Grammar (RG) have made a number of proposals concerning passives and purported syntactic "dummies." Although these proposals are by and large universal in scope, they are also directly related to Dutch syntax; in fact, in several instances (Perlmutter, 1978; Perlmutter and Postal, 1984a, b; Perlmutter and Zaenen, 1984), data from Dutch have been used to justify some of these claims. In this paper I would like to review these claims and attempt to refute them, arguing that more insightful analyses of the Dutch data are in fact available and that the universal claims are incorrect.

To see what is at issue here, consider first the examples sentences under (1-5).[2]

(1) Er spelen **twee kinderen** in de tuin.
'There are two children playing in the yard'

(2) Er werden **vele huizen** (door de storm) verwoest.
'There were many houses destroyed (by the storm)'

(3) Ik was verwonderd omdat er via Parijs **zo weinig mensen** naar New York vliegen.
'I was astonished because there are so few people flying to Paris via New York'

(4) Ik was verwonderd omdat via Parijs **zo weinig mensen** naar New York vliegen.

(5) Er wordt **(door de jonge lui)** veel gedanst.
'It is much danced (by the young people)'

Traditionally, the subjects of sentences like (1-4) have usually been considered to be *twee kinderen*, *vele huizen*, and *zo weinig mensen*, respectively, whereas sentences like (5) have often been analyzed as subjectless. Lately, however, these assumptions have been challenged by Relational Grammarians, who argue that in (1-5) the "dummy" *er* replaces another nominal (here in bold) as subject; even though there is no dummy present in (4) on the surface, it is claimed that there really is one and that it is subject, not *zo weinig mensen*. While the former claims may well find some supporters, I am sure that the latter will raise a few eyebrows among linguists

237

and non-linguists alike. To understand why these claims have been made, it is necessary to briefly review RG and some of the main theoretical principles to which these claims are related.

1.1 Relational Grammar: Some Concepts and Principles

Relational Grammar (RG) is a syntactic theory which emerged out of Transformational Grammar (TG), largely through the work of Paul Postal and David Perlmutter in the seventies (cf. Perlmutter and Postal 1974, 1977; Johnson 1977). RG challenged the assumption of TG that clause structure can be fully represented in terms of linear order and hierarachical configurations among the elements of a clause. As Perlmutter (1980: 196) says "[t]he basic claim of Relational Grammar (RG) is that grammatical relations such as 'subject of', 'direct object of', 'indirect object of', and others are needed to achieve three goals of linguistic theory:

a. to formulate linguistic universals

b. to characterize the classof grammatical constructions found in natural languages

c. to construct adequate and insightful grammars of individual languages.

Moreover, it is claimed that these grammatical relations must be taken as primitives of linguistic theory and cannot be defined in terms of other concepts such as word order, case marking, or phrase marker configurations. In addition, RG maintains that it is necessary to posit more than one syntactic (i.e. not semantic) level of representation, as opposed to other, 'surfacist' theories which claim that only one level of syntactic representation should be allowed, namely the surface level.

One of the important claims of RG is that as opposed to TG it could provide valid and insightful universal characterizations of constructions such as passive based on grammatical relations ("GRs"), while theories like TG, which did not accept GRs as primitives of linguistic theory, could not characterize such constructions universally in terms of transformations which altered linear order. Let us therefore take passive as an example to illustrate the theory and some of its central concepts and principles. We will only deal with those which are of direct relevance to our discussion. Take a sentence such as (6a) and its passive counterpart (6b).

(6) a. De terroristen verwoestten vele huizen.
'The terrorists destroyed many houses'

b. Vele huizen werden door de terroristen verwoest.
'Many houses were destroyed by the terrorists'

The relevant grammatical relations of (6a & b) can be represented in the form of the so-called "stratal diagrams" given in (6c & d), respectively.

(6) c. P   1   2
        verwoesten   de   vele
                     terrististen   huisen

    d. P   1   2
        P   Cho   1
        verwoesten   de   vele
                     terroristen   huizen

Here the numbers '1,2,3' refer to 'subject', 'direct object', and 'indirect object', respectively, which are referred to collectively as 'terms', whereas 'Cho' refers to the special chômeur relation, a kind of displaced term, if you will.

This analysis relates to several principles proposed by RG. First of all, it conforms to a very basic claim, embodied in the Final 1 Law:

FINAL 1 LAW: Every basic clause contains a final subject (1).

Note that this claim is different from the obvious falsehood that every basic clause contains a surface subject. Secondly, it agrees with the Motivated Chomage Law, which basically says that if a given nominal becomes a chômeur, e.g. a subject 'loses' its subjecthood (1-hood), it is because some other nominal takes place that GR. RG then offers a universal characterization passive (cf. Perlmutter and Postal 1977) as an advancement of a direct object (2) to subject (1) from a transitive statum (one containing a 1 and a 2) and the consequent demotion of the former 1 to chômeur. The latter demotion of the former 1 to chômeur is in term motivated by the Stratal Uniqueness Law, which claims that there can be no more than one element bearing a given GR in a given startum.

Now it has been observed (e.g. by Comrie 1977) that impersonal passives present potential problems for this analysis of passive and the laws given. Take the example (7a).

(7) a. Door deze mensen wordt er altijd gevochten
        'By these people it is always fought'

    b. P   1
        P   Cho
        vecheten   deze mensen

At first blush, it would appear that the stratal diagram given in (7b) properly characterizes this sentence, viz., the initial subject *de kinderen* becomes a chômeur spontaneously, with no other nominal replacing it as subject. This not only goes counter to the universal characterization of passive given above, but would also violate both the Motivated Chômage Law (the demotion of subject to chômeur is not motivated by another nominal assuming subject status) and the Final 1 Law (the sentence apparently has no final subject). We see the problem here: if this "spontaneous demotion" analysis of impersonal passives is accepted, then all these RG claims must be abandoned.

1.2 The Advancement Analysis of Impersonal Passives

Of course, Relational Grammarians have been rather reluctant to accept this conclusion and hence have tried to show that impersonal passives do not involve spontaneous demotion. Instead, they claim (cf. Perlmutter and Postal 1984a) that impersonal passives universally involve the insertion of a dummy element as direct object (2), which then advances to subject (1). thus the revised stratal diagram for (7a) would be (7c). This so-called "advancement analysis" of impersonal passives removes all the problems that spontaneous demotion had conjured up: passive still involves an advancement from 2 to 1, the Motivated Chômage Law is not violated since the chômeur is replaced by the dummy as subject, and the sentence has a final subject--the dummy *er*--in agreement with the Final 1 Law. Thus, it is claimed that impersonal passive always involves structures of the following form (8):

(7) c. P   1
        P   1   2
        P   Cho   1
        vechten   deze mensen er

(8)   P   1
        P   1   2
        P   Cho   1
        b   c   dummy

For Relational Grammar, Dutch provides a nice example of impersonal passive because the purported dummy subject *er* can always appear on the surface, although it does not have to. In some languages, such as Turkish, however, the dummy subject can never appear, while in others, like German (*er*), its appearance is limited to certain environments. However, it is claimed that even when no dummy can be seen on the surface, it is actually there and that therefore the advancement analysis of impersonal passives is correct. Perlmutter and Postal (1983: 126) state in this regard:

> "In our terms, regardless of whether an impersonal passive clause has a dummy nominal visible in its surface form, such as clause has a dummy 2 which co-occurs with a 1 in some stratum and advances to 1 in the next startum and thus is a passive clause in the sense of Perlmutter and Postal (1977), in the same way as passive clauses in which non-dummy 2s advance to 1."

Of course, positioning a dummy subject even when none is actually present seems to be nothing more than an ad hoc trick of the analyst to salvage an analysis which is clearly falsified by counter examples, and I will in fact later argue that this is the case here. Therefore, it would seem incumbent upon the RG theorists who defend this position to provide very strong, unequivocal evidence for their claim that the dummy is inserted as a 2 and winds up as a subject in all instances of impersonal passive. Unfortunately, precious little evidence of this kind has actually been forthcoming. The main argument for this conclusion is indirect and concerns the impossibility of certain (impersonal) passives, which can be 'explained' in RG by the interaction of the advancement analysis of impersonal passives with some other recent proposals made within this theory. Let us briefly review these proposals and the evidence they supposedly provide for this analysis.

2. The 1-Advancement Exclusiveness Law and Impossible Passives

In recent work, Perlmutter and Postal (1984a,b) have proposed a formal universal restriction called the '1-Advancement Exclusiveness Law' (1AEX).[3] This law states:

> 1AEX: The set of advancements to 1 in a single clause contains at most one member.

Thus, according to this law there cannot be more than one advancement to subject in a clause. Furthermore, they propose the "Unaccusative Hypothesis". According to this hypothesis, superficial intransitive clauses divide into two contrasting subclasses with different initial strata: so-called unergative verbs versus unaccusative verbs. Unergative predicts like *schaatsen* have an initial subject, as in (9).

(9) a. De kinderen schaatsen op het ijs.
'The children skate in the ice'

b. P   1   Loc
   schaatsen   de   het
               kinderen   ijs

Here there is not difference between initial and final GRs: *de kinderen* starts out and ends up as subject. However, unaccusative verbs such as *groeien* 'to grow'are claimed not to have an initial subject; rather, what appears as the surface subject, it is argued, is actually an initial direct object and only becomes subject through "unaccusative advancement", as seen in (10a-b).

(10) a. In dit weeshuis groeien de kinderen erg snel.
'In this orphanage the children grow very fast'

b. P   2   Loc
   P   1   Loc
   groeien   de   did
             kinderen   weeshuis

Now, as Perlmutter and Postal (1984a: 197) observe, "[t]he Unaccusative Hypothesis predicts that languages will have phenomena with

241

respect to which nominals in some intransitive clauses will behave like subjects, while those in others will behave like direct objects." Specifically, together with the IAEX, it makes one very important prediction with regard to passives (107):

(11) Noimpersonal passiveclause in any language can be based on an unaccusative predicate.

The reason for this is that unaccusative predicates already have an advancement to subject (unaccusative advancement) to get their active subjects; hence, if passive were to apply to an unaccusative predictate, under the advancement analysis of impersonal passives there would have to be a second advancement to subject, which is of course excluded by the 1AEX. This prediction is apparently borne out by a number of examples given in Perlmutter (1978) and Perlmutter and Postal (1984a). Impersonal passives of some intrasitive active clauses are possible, but not of others; it is claimed that the intransitive predicates which do allow impersonal passives are unergative, which do not violate the 1AEX, while the intransitive predicates which do not allow impersonal passives are unaccusative and hence would violate the 1AEX is passivized.

To take one example, sentence (9a) with the unergative intransitive predictate schaatsen has a corresponding impersonal passive given in (12).

(12) a. Er wordt door de kinderen op het ijs geschaatst
'It is skated on the ice by the children'

b.
P	1		Loc
P	1	2	Loc
P	Cho	1	Loc
schaatsen	de	er	het
	kinderen		ijs

Here there is only one advancement to subject and hence passive is not precluded. Compare, however, (13a), which contains an unaccusative predicate and this is ungrammatical in the impersonal passive.

(13) a. *In dit weeshuis wordt (er) door de kinderen erg snel gegroeid.
'*In this orphanage it is gtown by the children very fast.'

b.
P	2		Loc
P	1		Loc
P	1	2	Loc
P	Cho	1	Loc
Groeien	de	er	dit
	kinderen		weeshuis

As we see in (13b), here we have two advancements to subject, first *de kinderen* through unaccusative advancement and then *er* through passive.

Since the 1AEX rules out more than one advancement to 1 in a clause, impersonal passives of initially unaccusative strat are claimed to be universally impossible, as we see here confirmed for Dutch. Moreover, since this account crucially depends on the dummy *er* advancing to 1 from 2, these data are also taken as confirming the claim that impersonal passives always involve the insertion of a dummy as 2, which then advances to 1.

In addition to excluding impersonal passives from initially unaccusative clauses, this analysis also rules out impersonal passives derived from personal passives (cf. Perlmutter and Postal 1984b: 132):

"Impersonal Passives of personal Passive clauses cannot be well-formed in any language. Since impersonal passives of intransitive clauses are possible, and since personal passive clauses are superficially intransitive, the ungrammaticality of impersonal passives from passive clauses is a fact in need of an explanation. The 1AEX and the advancement analysis of impersonal passives provide one."

Though they use an example from German for some reason at this point, we can illustrate this with a corresponding one from Dutch.

(14) a. Niemand werd door de oude vrouw gekust.
'No one is kissed by the old women'

b. *Er werd door de oude vrouw door niemand gekust (geworden).

c.
P	1	2	
P	Cho	1	
P	Cho	1	2
P	Cho	Cho	1
kussen	niemand	de oude vrouw	er

Given the advancement analysis of impersonal passives, the stratal diagram for (14b-c) would be as in (14d). As we see, in order for there to be an impersonal passive of a personal passive there would have to be two advancements to 1: first *niemand* and then the dummy *er*, in violation of the 1AEX. Hence, under the advancement analysis of impersonal passives, the 1AEX once again predicts the ungrammatically of sentences like (14b), indeed of impersonal passives from personal passives in all languages.

Finally, the advancement analysis of impersonal passives together with the 1AEX predicts that impersonal passives of so-called inversion classes, which also involve unaccusative advancement, will be universally ill-formed. Inversion clauses involve an initial transitive statum containing a 1 and a 2, but in a later stratum the initial 1 retreats to a 3 ('1-3 retreat' or 'inversion'), thereby producing an unaccusative stratum with a 3 and a 2, but no 1; then finally the initial 2 is advanced to 1 by unaccusative advancement. Since there is already one advancement to 1 in such clauses, the 1AEX predicts that no other advancement to subject will be possible in the clause, and this prediction is corroborated by Dutch data. Take the following example with the verb *ontsnappen* 'to escape, elude'.

(15) a. Dat detail ontsnapt iedere keer aan onze voorzitter.

b. Dat detail ontsnapt onze voorzitter iedere keer.
'That detail escapes our chairman every time'

Perlmutter and Postal (1984a: 114f.) propose that *ontsnappen* is an inversion verb, and furthermore that the inversion nominal may also advance from 3 to 2, as in (15b). Therefore, (15a & b) would be associated with the stratal diagrams (16a & b), respectively.

(16) a.
P	1	2
P	3	2
onsnappen	onze voorzitter	dat detail

b.
P	1	2
P	3	2
P	3	1
P	2	1
ontsnappen	onze voorzitter	dat detail

Since these structures involve unaccusative advancement, the 1AEX predicts that they cannot undergo any further advancements to 1; hence there can be no impersonal passive corresponding to (15a), the example (17) demonstrates.

(17) *Er wordt aan onze voorzitter door dat detail iedere keer ontsnapt.

However, besides ruling out impersonal passives with *ontsnappen*, the 1AEX also rules out a personal passive. Although (15b) is finally transitive and should therefore be passivizable, the 1AEX precludes another advancement to 1 in a structure like (16b). This prediction is apparently correct: no personal passive corresponding to (15b) is in fact possible as we see in example (18).

(18) *Onze voorzitter wordt door dat detail iedere keer ontsnapt.

In addition, Perlmutter and Postal (1984a: 100ff.) also mention that their analysis correctly predicts the impossibility of English 'pseudo-passives' from unaccusative verbs, as well as the lack of passives from raising to subject verbs. Of course, such stratal diagrams a (16b), with nominals first retreating from 1 to 3 and then subsequently advancing to 2 will appear to many observers highly suspect and ad hoc. What are the constraints on such moves? The theory seems weak on this point.

Thus the main arguments for the advancement analysis of impersonal passives--i.e. the claim that impersonal passives always involve the insertion of a dummy as a 2 which then becomes 1, even if it is not visible at the surface--is that this allows the 1AEX together with the Unaccusative Hypothesis to rule out certain universally impossible passives. RG theorists take this to be a strong indication of the correctness of their approach in general as well as their specific proposals and analyses. however, this claim only holds as long as no other means is found to disallow these impossible passives; if another, more perspiciuous and explanatory solution to the problem were forthcoming, then this set of arguments in favor of the advancement analysis would lose its persuasiveness. We will discuss this point in a moment, but first let us consider and refute two other sets of arguments which have been offered to bolster the claim that er is a final 1, even when it is not visible at the surface.

3. The Evidence from the Indefinite Extraposition Construction

Other than these arguments from the 1AEX, only one other set of arguments has been given to provide that the "dummy" er is a final subject; as far as I know, no other arguments have been put forth to justify the claim that in the impersonal passive the dummy is inserted as a 2. Perlmutter and Zaenen (1984) discuss what they call the "indefinite extraposition construction" ("presentative" or "existential" sentences; cf. Kirsner (1979) on this) in Dutch with respect to a possible alternative to the 1AEX, namely the 1-Chomeur Initiality Law (1CIL), which says (172) informally that "if a 1 is demoted to chômeur, it must be the initial 1 of the clause." If the 1CIL could be maintained, then the arguments for the advancement analysis of impersonal passives just given would not hold. Even under the spontaneous demotion analysis of impersonal passives, the passifiziability of these clause types would be precluded by the 1CIL, since in each case the 1 which passive would demote would not be the initial 1, and the 1CIL would rule this out.

Perlmutter and Zaenen attempt to show that the 1CIL cannot be maintained but the 1AEX can, thereby saving the advancement analysis of impersonal passives. They claim that the indefinite extraposition construction in Dutch and German would violate the 1CIL but not the 1AEX, because the dummy 1 from indefinite extraposition puts not only initial 2s en chomage, but also no-initial 2s. e.g. advances from 2 to 1 through passive and unaccusative advancement. It is claimed that only subsequent advancements to 1 are precluded, and that while passive and unaccusative advancement involve advancements, indefinite extraposition does not, and therefore it can apply in classes where advancement to 1 has already taken place.

Important for our present discussion is the fact that Perlmutter and Zaenen (1984) claim that in the indefinite extraposition construction the dummy er, not the other nominal (here **bold**), which they refer to as the "pivot", is the final subject. Cf. the examples in (19-21).

(19) a. Twee en dertig staten hebben het ERA
geraticifeerd.

'Two children were playing in the yard'

    b.   Er hebben **twee en dertig staten** het ERA geratificeerd.

(20)   a.   Twee kinderen speelden in de tuin.
'Two children were playin in the yard'

    b.   Er speelden twee kinderen in de tuin.

(21)
P	1		Loc
P	Cho	1	Loc
spelen	twee	er	de
	kinderen		tuin

They offer two types of arguments for the final 1-hood of the dummy and the final non-1-hood of the pivot. It is claimed that the dummy acts like a final 1 with respect to word order and relative clause extraposition, while the pivot does not.

3.1 Arguments from Word Order

Consider first the arguments from word order. They claim that the final 1 can appear in two positions in main clauses: postaverbal in questions and sentences where some element is fronted, otherwise preverbal, as the following examples show.

(22)   a.   Spelen *de kinderen* in de tuin?
'Are the children playing in the yard'

    b.   In welke tuin spelen *de kinderen*?
'In which yard are the children playing?'

    c.   Vandaag hebben *de kinderen* in de tuin gespeeld.
'Today the children (have) played in the yard.'

    d.   De kinderen speelden in de tuin vandaag.
'The children played in the yard today.'

Since *er* and not the pivot *de kinderen* has the distribution of final 1s in examples like the following, it is concluded that *er* is in fact the final 1.

(23)   a.   Spelen *er* twee kinderen in de tuin?

    b.   In welke tuin spelen *er* twee kinderen?

    c.   Vandaag hebben *er* twee kinderen in de tuin gespeeld.

    d.   *Er* speelden twee kinderen in de tuin vandaag.

Moreover, they claim that the pivot *twee kinderen* in (23) does not have the distribution of a final 1, for the pivot can appear in places where a final 1 cannot as in (24-25).

(24) a. *Kwam door de achterdeur *Piet* binnen?
'*Did Piet come in by the back door?'

b. Kwam *er* door de achterdeur **iemand** binnen?
'Did someone come in by the back door?'

(25) a. *Gisteren kwam door de achterdeur *Piet* binnen.
'*Yesterday Piet came in by the back door.'

b Gisteren kwamen *er* door de achterdeur **verscheidene werklui** binnen.
'Yesterday several workmen came in by the back door.'

Finally, Perlmutter and Zaenen claim (177) that "in subordinate clauses, the unmarked position for the final 1 is immediately after the complementizer. For pronominal final 1s, this is the *only* position." Here two the dummy apparently behaves like a pronominal final 1 with respect to word order, as we see in these examples.

(26) a. Het verwondert me dat *er* gisteren niemand gekomen is.
'It astonishes me that no one came yesterday.'

b. *Het verwondert me dat gisteren *er* niemand gekomen is.
'*It astonishes me that yesterday no one came.'

This argues, they claim, that the dummy *er* is a pronominal final 1. Moreover, the fact that non-pronominal final 1s generally appear immediately after the complementizer and not after (certain) adverbial material as in (27a,b), but that the pivot can appear here, as in (27c), further supports their claim that the pivot is not a final 1.

(27) a. Ik was verwonderd omdat *Jan* via Parijs naar New York gevlogen is.
'I was astonished because Jan flew to New York via Paris.'

b. *Ik was verwonderd omdat via Parijs *Jan* naar New York gevlogen is.

c. Ik was verwonderd omdat er via Parijs **zo weinig mensen** naar New York vliegen.
'I was astonished because so few people fly to New York via Paris.'

Since the position of the pivot nominal in subordinate clauses is different from that of final 1s, they claim that their analysis, in which the pivot is not a final 1, is supported by this evidence.

However, several objections can be raised here which create serious doubts as to the correctness of these conclusions.[4] The main point is that Perlmutter and Zaenen simply assume that word order in Dutch is directly linked to GRs, at least for final subjects; but there is in fact little reason to believe that this is so. In fact, it is somewhat ironic that RG, which chastised TG for dealing with GRs in terms of constituent structure, would itself claim that for a language like Dutch, which is certainly much less "configurational" than, say, English, position is so closely tied to GRs. But it is simply not true that the final subject is limited to either pre- or postverbal position in main clauses; in fact, subjects in Dutch may appear in a variety of places, depending on a number of factors. To be sure, because of their normally high topicality/salience, subjects are frequently found toward the beginning of the sentence, but they are by no means limited to pre- or postverbal position. Other highly topical elements such as "situation setting" adverbials, for example, often may recede the subject. This entails that some elements such as *daar/ginds* may have a distribution similar to or even identical with that of "normal" subjects, but this certainly does not mean that they are subjects in sentences such as the following (cf. Schermer-Vermeer 1985: 68).

(28) a. Daar/Ginds staat nog een ouderwetse lantaarnpaal.
'There still stands an old-fashioned lamppost.'

b. Staat daar/ginds nog een ouderwetsel antaarnpaal?
'Does there stand there still an old-fashioned lamppost?'

c. Daar/Ginds schijnt nog een ouderwetse lantaarnpaal te staan.
'There seems to still stand there an old-fashioned lamppost.'

d. Er wordt gezegd dat daar/ginds nog een ouderwetse lantaarnpaal staat.
'It is said that there still stands an old-fashioned lamppost?'

Other examples can be found which lead to adsurb conclusions as to what is subject if the purported intimate connection between word order and grammatical relations is pushed further. In Geerts (1984: 981) it is noted that the nominal subject can be separated from the finite verb by other elements, for instance an ethical dative, as in (29), where the position of *me* after the finite verbs is "the only possibility".

(29) Nu heeft me die vuilik z'n handen weer niet gewassen.

'Now that dirty fellow hasn't washed his hands on me again.'

Is *me* now the subject in this sentence simply because it appears in "subject position"? Clearly this is not an acceptable conclusion. Furthermore, Nieuborg (1973: 283) had noted that when the subject is clearly a non-agent the reflexive pronoun normally precedes it postverbally, as in (30).

(30) In verschillende parochies vormden zich zogenaamde experimentele groepjes..
'In various parishes so-called experimental groups formed...'

Once again, however, it is hardly likely that anyone would want to claim that *zich* is the "final subject" here because of its position; case alone speaks strongly against such a conclusion, since the pronoun is objective in form, not nominative, as one would expect with subjects.

Finally, consider the position of the finite verb and the subordinating conjunction. It has been noted that in Dutch (Geerts 1984: 911ff.) and the German (Drosdowski 1984: 715ff.) the finite verb occupies a fixed position in main clauses, forming the "first prong" ('1e pool', 'erster Klammerteil') of the verbal frame ('tang', 'Satzklammer'), which in turn defines the middle field ('middenstuk', 'Mittelfeld'), whereas in subordinate clauses it is the conjunction which forms the first prong. Now on the basis of the distributional similarity, perhaps even identity, one might with some justification claim that the finite verb in main clauses and the conjunction in subordinate clauses in some sense occupy the same sentence position--thus in some Government and Binding analyses they are both located in COMP. But certainly this does not imply that they fulfill the same grammatical function, say "(head of) predicate". One would only be led to this absurd conclusion if one assumed a rigid mapping between structural positions in terms of word order and the grammatical functions of elements in the sentence.

More problems surface if we consider other GRs such as direct object and indirect object. Are they positionally definable in Dutch? If so, how? If now, why not? What is the "structural position" of direct object--right after the finite verb? What if some other element which normally follows the direct object, such as the "prepositional *er*", precedes it, as in the following examples--would we then claim that that element had advanced to 2?

(31) a. Ik heb het brood met het mes gesneden.

b. Ik heb het brood ermee gesneden.
'I cut the bread with it.'

Once again, I think it is evident that the claims about GRs based purely on word order in Dutch are not tenable. Therefore, in conclusion, it does seem that the prepared distribution similarity between *er* and other elements which are clearly subjects provides any support for the claim that er is a final 1.

3.2 An Argument from Initial Pivots.

Perlmutter and Zaenen also offer an argument for the final non-1-hood of the pivot, stemming from cases where the pivot appears in initial position from the indefinite extraposition construction. They note that when the final 1 is in initial position (32a), even when it is not an initial 1 (32b), the sentence can be neutral with no particular element sought out for special emphasis (presumably in terms of intonation and stress):

(32) a. twee mensen hebben de kindermishandelaar in dat gebouw gezien.
'Two people saw the child molester in that building.'

b. Twee mensen werden door de apoteker gedood.
'Two people were killed by the druggist.'

However, if a "prepositionless nominal" (presumably a 2 or 3, for instance) other than the final 1 appears in the initial position, they claim, it is emphasized (33).

(33) *De kindermishandelaar* hebben twee mensen in dat gebouw gezien.
'The child molester two people saw in that building.'

Now when the dummy is in initial position in the indefinite Extraposition construction the sentence is neutral:

(34) a. Er spelen twee kinderen in de tuin.
'There are two children playing in the yard.'

However, when the pivot appears in initial position, as it sometimes can, it receives emphasis:

(34) b. *Twee kinderen* spelen er in de tuin.

In this sense too the pivot supposedly acts like a final non-1, thereby providing a further argument that it is not the final 1 in this construction.[5]

But like the other arguments based on word order this one too does not hold up under scrutiny. In fact, Kirsner (1979) has already convincingly accounted for these facts, *without* having to postulate that *er* is the subject of such sentences. In addition, his account also gives a unwary account of both the meaning and the distribution of *er* and the "pivot". Essentially he says that *er* functions to signal the rhematic or backgrounded character of the subject, which is normally thematic or foregrounded. Now in accordance with the well-known tendency to place rhematic/unfamiliar elements later, this entails that the subject (Perlmutter and Zaenen's pivot) in this construction will normally occur later in the sentence; hence the function of *er* as "participant delayer". However, backgrounded or rhematic elements do not always have to appear late in the sentence; although this is the norm, rhematic or backgrounded elements can be fronted under certain circumstances, specifically under stress and/or contrast. This happens not just with backgrounded subjects in the indefinite extraposition construction. Direct objects are typically backgrounded (rhematic) in neutral sentences and hence tend to appear later in the sentence--in fact, for this reason they are not common in first position. However, normally rhematic direct objects may occur here under certain circumstances, namely when stressed or contrasted, as in the following example.

(35) a. Giseren heb ik het kind niet gezien.
'Yesterday I didn't see the child.'

b. **Het kind** heb ik gisteren niet gezien.

Note that in order to be fronted, the normally backgrounded direct object must be stressable; for subjects, however, the natural first position does not necessitate stress and so we can find unstressable subjects in this position. This is clearly the explanation for the remarkable distribution difference between *het/es* in Dutch and German in (36) and (37), depending on whether it is subject or direct object. If *het/es* is subject it can easily occur in initial position, as in

(36) a. het bevalt me niet.

b. Es gefällt mir nicht.
'It doesn't please me [i.e. I don't like it].'

However, if *het/es* is the direct object, then it cannot occur initially:

(37) a. *Het heb ik niet gezegd.

b. *Es habe ich nicht gesagt.
'*It I didn't say.'

This is clearly because in both languages, *het/es* is not stressable; as we have just seen, in order for normally rhematic elements like direct objects to appear initially, they must be stressed. This conflict provides a natural explanation for the ungrammaticality of (37a & b). If the neuter pronoun object is to be fronted, one must in. act use a stronger deictic than just the personal pronoun; thus the demonstrative, which *is* stressable, must occur here:

(38) a. Dat heb ik niet gezegd.

b. Das habe ich nicht gesagt.
'That I didn't say.'

Now if rhematic or backgrounded elements can occur in initial position, and the subject of "presentative" sentences is marked as rhemtic/backgrounded by the presence of *er*, then we would even expect this rhematized subject to be able to occur initially, under exactly the same conditions as other rhematic elements (such as objects), viz. under stress. Of course this is precisely what we find in examples like (34b). Therefore, such data do not provide an argument for analyzing the pivot as a final non-subject, but simply show that the subject, which is normally thematic/foregrounded, is rhematic/backgrounded, even though it occurs sentence-initially.

3.3 The Argument from Relative Clause Extraposition

Another set of putative arguments for the final non-1-hood of the pivot comes from the extraposition of relative clauses (RCE). Basing themselves on work by de Haan (1976, 1979), Perlmutter and Zaenen claim that RCE from final subjects is not possible, but that is is possible from final 2s and 1 chomeurs, as seen in (39-42).

(39) a. *Een buurman die van Brussel* is is aangekomen.
'A neighbor who is from Brussels has arrived.'

b. *Een buurman* is aangekomen *die van Brussel is*.

(40) a. Jan heeft *een jongen die pas in de buurt is komen wonen* geslagen.
'Jan hit a boy who just moved into the neighborhood.'

b. Jan heeft *een jongen* geslagen *die pas in de buurt is komen wonen*.

(41) a. Een *buurman met wie we nog geen kennis hadden gemaakt* werd gedood.
'A neighbor whom we had not yet met was killed.'

b. *Een buurman werd gedood met wie we nog geen kennis hadden gemaakt.

(42) Een buurman werd door *een apoteker* gedood *met wie we nog geen kennis hadden gemaakt*.
'A neighbor was killed by a druggist whom we had not yet met.'

Perlmutter and Zaenen dismiss certain possible counter examples to their claim such as (47).

(43) Zelfs *die mensen* zijn niet gekomen, *die we schriftelijk hadden uitgenodigd*.
'Even *those* people didn't come whom we had invited *in writing*.'

By pointing out that such cases of "focus Extraposition" require extra heavy stress on the determiner of the antecedent and on one element of the relative clause, whereas the first type, "non-focus extraposition," does not. Moreover, non-focus RCE (44) clauses occur before a dat-object, whereas focus RCE (45) clauses appear after it.

(44) a. Jan heeft tegen *enkele vrienden* gezegd *die een auto hadden*, dat hij naar huis wou gaan.
'Jan told several friends who had a car that he wanted to go home.'

b. *Jan heeft tegen *enkele vrienden* gezegd dat hij naar huis wou gaan, *die een auto hadden*.

(45) a. ??Jan heeft tegen *díe vrienden* gezegd, *die een aúto hadden*, dat hij naar huis wou gaan.
'??Jan told those friends who had a car that he wanted to go home.'

b. Jan heeft tegen *die vrienden* gezegd dat hij naar huis wou gaan, *die een auto hadden*.

All cases of RCE out of final subjects are, they claim, examples of focus Extraposition, as in (50).

(46) a. Zelfs *díe mensen* zeiden dat ze niet zouden komen, *die we schríftelijk uitgenodigd hadden*.
'Even those people whom we had invited in writing said that they would not come.'

b. *Zelfs *díe mensen* zeiden, *die we schrifttelijk uitgenodigd hadden*, dat ze niet zouden komen.

They then argue that the pivot in the indefinite extraposition construction is not a final 1: although non-focus RCE is not possible from the final 1 iemand in (47), it is possible with the pivot in (48).

(47) a. *Iemand die er geweest is* heeft verleden week beweerd, dat het leven in Mexico nog altijd goedkoop is.
'Someone who was there claimed last week that the cost of living in Mexico is still low.'

b. *Iemand* heeft verleden week beweerd, *die er geweest is*, dat het leven in Mexico nog altijd goedkoop is.

(48) Er heeft *iemand* verleden week beweerd, *die er geweest is*, dat het leven in Mexico nog altijd goedkoop is.

The fact that the extraposed relative clauses appear to the left of the *dat*-clauses proves that we are dealing with non-focus RCE here, and the possibility of RCE with the pivot argues that it is not a final 1, according to Perlmutter and Zaenen.

This argument stands and falls with the claim that it is final 1s which cannot undergo RCE. The first objection to this restriction is its arbitrariness-why should this be? Even assuming for the moment that this formulation is correct, it simply does not offer any explanation for the observed regularity. It is a completely arbitrary syntactic restriction with no apparent further motivation, so why should Dutch have it? More important, how could speakers learn it? It seems that in order for speakers to reach this formulation, they would have to attempt RCE with final non-1s and be corrected. However, as Baker (1979) has aptly pointed out in a rather different context, speakers (e.g. children) do not normally receive such negative feedback. Since this is not a plausible innate restriction, it is a puzzle how speakers could ever arrive at it.

An even more serious objection, however, is that consideration of further examples makes one very skeptical concerning the correctness of this purely syntactic restriction in the first place. Though Perlmutter and Zaenen claim to base their analysis on de Haan, I find nothing to indicate that he feels non-focus RCE cannot apply to final 1s.[5] Perlmutter and Zaenen reject a restriction against RCE for sentence-initial elements, but they do not show that it is possible from final non-1s in initial position. Without stress, there seem to be problems here too:

(49) a. ??*Door de kinderen* werd (er) op het ijs geschaatst *die pas in de buurt zijn komen wonen*.
'??By the children it is skated who just moved into the neighborhood.'

b. *In *de tuin* kan niet gezeten worden *waar net gesproeid is*.
'*In the yard it cannot be sat where it has just been sprayed (watered.).'

With stress of course, both these sentences are much better, but they would be "focus RCE".

In addition, it is not clear that final 1s are not susceptible to RCE: all their examples with RCE in the indefinite extraposition construction could in fact simply be taken to show that this formulation is false. It also leads to their highly improbable claim that in dialects where the dummy does not have to appear with indefinite extraposition, it is really there but simply "silent". Thus, in sentences like (50) the pivot *iemand* is supposedly not the subject for a 1 chômeur, and the final subject is the silent *er*, which for some rason does not happen to appear. It is claimed that since the pivot is not a final 1, RCE is possible.

(50) a. Heeft *iemand* gezegd, *die pas in de buurt is komen wonen*, dat mijnheer van Vliet van Brussel is?
'Did someone who just moved to the neighborhood say that Mr. van Vliet is from Brussels?'

b. Gisteren heeft *iemand* gezegd, *die pas in de buurt is komen wonen*, dat mijnheer van Vliet van Brussel is.
'Yesterday someone who just moved to the nieghborhood said that Mr. van Vliet is from Brussels.'

Of course this ad hoc ploy removes numerous counterexamples to their claim about RCE. Especially here a much more plausible interpretation is certainly possible, namely that the restriction as formulated is simply wrong; final subjects *can* have RCE, but only under certain discourse conditions, and there are no "silent dummies".[7]

Finally, contrary to Perlmutter and Zenen's claims, there appear to be examples of RCE from final 1s without indefinite extraposition, as the following examples culled from just two Dutch novels reveals.[8]

(51) a. *Jij* bent het *die mij zit te vertellen dat*...['tHart: 118']
'It's you who is sitting there telling me that...'

b. Omdat *ik* het ben *die door de Duitsers word gezocht*! [Hermans: 120]
'Because it's me who is being sought by the Germans!'

c. ...en *wie* zou dat ooit kunnen geloven *die dat niet zelf had ervaren*? ['tHart: 19]
'...and who would ever be able to believe that who hadn't experienced it himself?'

d. Dat kan toch niet *de man* zijn *die mij verdenkt van een moord*...['tHart: 47]
'But that can't be the man who suspects me of a murder...'

e. Hij stopte de foto in het borstzakje van zijn colbert en voelde dat daar ook *de foto* nog zat *die Elly hem had gegeven*. [Hermans:75]
'He slipped the photo into the breast pocket of his jacket and felt that the photo was still there that Elly had given him.'

f. Er moet rekening gehouden worden met de omstandigheid dat hij wist hoe *de jeugdleidster* heten zou *die zijn kind zou halen.* [Hermans: 157]
'One had to reckon with the circumstance that he knew what the name of the youth leader was who was supposed to fetch his child.'

g. Daarom wierp hij het gezonde been naar voren met een opvallend luide plof en verder dan *mensen* doen *die allebei hun benen normaal kunnen gebruiken.* [Hermans: 304]
'For that reason he tossed his healthy leg forward with a conspicuously loud thump and farther than people do who can use both legs normally.'

h. En weet je ook hoe *die personen* heetten *die je neergeschoten hebt*? [Hermans: 370]
'And do you know the names of the people who you shot down?'

Such examples seems to show that RCE is final 1s is possible, at least under certain circumstances. Of course, Perlmutter and Zaenen might wish to dispute this in terms of their description of the facts. For instance, (51a-b) might well be considered focus RCE with *jij* and *ik* stressed; with (51c) this interpretation is more forced, however. Moreover, they might wish to argue that in (51d) the initial *dat* is also some kind of dummy final 1 and *de man* a pivot, although this seems a bit far-fetched. However, examples like (51e-h) do not appear amenable to such reinterpretation and therefore are clearly countereexamples to their claim that final 1s cannot launch RCE. It is perhaps significant that several of the examples (51c, f, h) involve direct or indirect questions.

I believe that these conditions are sufficient to make us skeptical about Perlmutter and Zaenen's account. What we would like to find instead is a proper characterization of RCE and when it is possible. In fact, a true explanation of the distribution seems dependent on ascertaining the communicative function of RCE, for once that has been established, we can hope to show that the restrictions to be observed follow naturally from the fact that the given environments do not correspond to the communicative function of the construction. In this short paper, I cannot hope to accomplish this task; indeed at present I cannot claim to have a final, definitive account. But I do have a preliminary proposal which I think has some promise.

Briefly, I believe that the function of RCE is to delay a backgrounded or rhematic relative clause, a relative clause whose antecedent is relatively rhematic and perhaps in some sense in focus. If this is true, we would expect that (unstressed) elements in initial position would be hostile to RCE, since such elements are typically foregrounded/thematic. Since subjects are typically foregrounded, when a subject is in initial position, it should not be frequently associated with RCE. This is especially the case if the element in question is definite as opposed to indefinite, because indefinite elements are usually familiar (according to Kirsner (1979) the meaning of the definite article in Dutch is "differentiation [=identification, TFS] required and made"). If the element in question is foregrounded and assumed to be familiar, it not only is "nonrhematic" and should therefore not be extraposed, but to delay the relative clause, which contains information necessary for making the required identification, would be to lead the hearer down a garden path and unnecessarily burden his processing load. Indefinite (or stressed) elements, on the other hand, should be more susceptible to RCE, since they contain specific cues which alert the hearer to the necessity of identifying the referent which will thus be in focus.[9] Finally, since RCE violates Behagel's (1932) First Law ("das geistig eng Zusammengehôrige [wird] auch eng zusammengestellt"), once would expect that not too much material should intervene between the antecedent and the delayed relative clause. Note that this would potentially cuase processing problems by involving antecedence over an intervening NP. This may be part of the reason why elements in first (forefield) position are less subject to RCE. In fact, my preliminary review of examples from these two novels indicates that RCE by and large only occurs when the antecedent is the rightmost (rhematic) element in the middle field with next to nothing but the dependent verbal elements in between. Note that all but one of the examples given involve RCE from a final 1 which is not in the forefield, but rather in the middlefield of a subordinate clause.

Obviously these remarks only represent a first step toward a full explanatory account of RCE, both focus and non-focus. They are still in need of fleshing out and must be confronted with a larger range of data. However, I feel they are very promising and if they, or a similar account, can be maintained, then the claim that RCE is limited to final non-1s would have to be rejected. With that of course would disappear one more piece of purported evidence for the claim that in the indefinite extraposition construction *er* is the final subject and the pivot is a 1 chômeur.

4. Some Further Objections

In reviewing so far the arguments on whether the dummy *er* and not the pivot is the final subject in the indefinite extraposition construction we have disregarded what is probably the most obvious and convincing argument: the verbs agrees with the pivot and not the dummy, even though otherwise the final subject controls verb agreement in Dutch. In discussing this, however, Perlmutter and Zaenen do not even consider the possibility that this could easily be viewed as evidence that the pivot is actually the final 1, since they apparently consider their previous arguments to the contrary totally convincing. Instead, they simply discuss how to account for the verb agreement. Rather than being forced to complicate the agreement rule, they rely on another relation of RG, the so-called "brother-in-law relation" (1984) posited in Perlmutter and Postal (1974):

(52) **The Brother-in-Law Relation**

The brother-in-law relation holds between a dummy and a nominal if the dummy puts that nominal en chomage in the *lowest clause* and *earliest stratum* in which the dummy heads an arc.

They note that "not every nominal put en chômeur by a dummy is its brother-in-law." Thus the pivot in the indefinite extraposition construction is a brother-in-law, because the dummy is inserted as a 1 which simultaneously puts the pivot en chômage in its first stratum; however, in impersonal passives, the dummy is inserted first as a 2 and only subsequently puts the 1 en chômage--crucially not in the dummy's first stratum.

Given this new concept, verb agreement in the indefinite extraposition construction can be seen as an instance of "brother-in-law agreement" (1984):

(53) **Brother-in-Law Agreement:**

Where the nominal referenced by an agreement rule is a dully, agreement is determined by the dummy's brother-in-law instead.

Similarly, the pivot is assigned nominative case (seen more clearly in German than in Dutch) through the brother-in-law relation (187):

(54) The brother-in-law of the dummy in the indefinite extraposition construction agrees with the dummy in case.

But clearly these new "principles" of RG are nothing more than ad hoc tricks to make the analysis work and avoid having to admit what we have suspected all along--that the "pivot" and not the summit is the final subject. The brother-in-law relation is totally arbitrary and unmotivated and its sole purpose is to sweep embarrassing counter evidence under the table. Far from being "a new device for capturing... regularity" (186), this relation is a very dangerous instrument of obfuscation, for it now removes two more possible arguments for final subjecthood. Indeed these two arguments have traditionally been held to be among the strongest and most reliable ones available for languages in which they applied: (1) the final subject of a clause is the nominal with which the finite verb of the clause agrees; (2) the final subject is nominative. Kirsner, who argues (1979: 181) pointedly against the notion "dummy subject", underscores this point: "it is not at all clear that there is any validity to the term 'subject' in Dutch except as a synonym for "that noun or pronoun which is taken as specifying the participant-in-focus [= subject, TFS] referred to by the finite verb-ending'". Moreover, why should it be that the verb agrees with its brother-in-law? Why does the verb not agree with the dummy instead of the pivot in the indefinite extraposition construction? After all, the verb in the impersonal passive purportedly agrees with the dummy subject there, even if there is none present in the clause. So why doesn't the verb agree with the dummy subject in the indefinite extraposition construction when it is there?

Obviously, it is much more reasonable and plausible to admit that the so-called "pivot" is the final 1 in the indefinite extraposition construction, especially since only considerations of word order even remotely suggest that *er* is the subject. In fact, *er* otherwise has no properties characteristic of subjects. Not only does it in at least one instance not control verb agreement, it is difficult to see how it could, since subjects are nominal but *er* is *adverbial*. Therefore, how could it in principle control verb agreement--as it is supposed to do with impersonal passives--or pass on nominative case to its in-law? Furthermore, since it is a weak adverbial deictic referring to the spatio-temporal situation and not an entity (like *het*), it cannot control Equi, as subjects of verbs like beloven typically can, not can it be questioned or relativized. Finally, it does not share another trait of subjects: whereas subjects are typically obligatory elements in the sentence,[10]--obviously, since they are the focal point of the event--*er* is not. the pivot, on the other hand, still has all these subject properties: it (1) is a nominal; (2) refers to an entity; (3) has case; (4) controls verb agreement; (5) is not optional; and (6) can control Equi and be questioned or relativized. Clearly, this must be the subject.

In addition, Perlmutter and Zaenen are faced with the problem of explaining why the 1 chômeurs in impersonal passive and indefinite extraposition do not behave the same. If they both beaer the same GR ('1 chômeur'), why is it that the one is preceded by *door*, non-nominative, and does not condition verb agreement, whereas the other is prepositionless, nominative, and does control verb agreement? Giving them the same GR label implies that they should act alike, but as we see, they do not. The conclusion seems to be that they do not bear the same GR: while the former may be a 1 chômeur, the latter is clearly a final 1. On the whole, RG is terrible vague on any numbero "mechanical details" which would insure the proper surface form of elements which are only given labels in the theory.

Moreover, Perlmutter and Zaenen's analysis seems to compound the problem of "homonymous *er*" (cf. Kirsner 1979). As opposed to many traditional analyses which, while positing several different *ers* ("locative, prepositional, quantitive"), only refer to a single "expletive" or "existential" *er*, Perlmutter and Zaenen implicitly position two different, homophonous expletive *ers*. They are apparently separate elements, for they appear in two different constructions and have differing characteristics; dummy er_1 in impersonal passives, which is introduced as a 2 and later as final 1 triggers verb agreement, and dummy er_2 in the indefinite extraposition construction, which is introduced as the final 1 but does not affect verb agreement.8 Taken together with the traditional *ers*, this would give us a total of five homonymous *ers*. There seems to be little motivation for this except to make the other analyses proposed, especially the advancement analysis of impersonal passives and the 1AEX, work. Also, this account has no explanation to offer for why these two dummy *ers* cannot occur with the traditionally distinguished locative and prepositional *ers*. Because it takes an atomistic approach to the question, this analysis cannot offer a unitary account of the form, function, and distribution of *er* in modern Dutch.

Such a unitary account is in fact presented very persuasively in Kirsner (1979), which leads up to the final, and possibly most telling objection. *Er* can only be a dummy subject if it is a meaningless element, which is optionally present in certain environments purely for formal, syntactic reasons. However, as Kirsner shows, *er* is not meaningless; in fact, its meaning is actually coherent with its use in the various environments where it occurs. But if *er* is not semantically empty, then it cannot be a "dummy subject". Once we accept Kirsner's analysis as clearly superior, things which up to now had seemed anomalous fit into place. There is only one *er*, not a bunch of disparate elements which all happen to be homophonous; this also accounts for the lack of occurrence between the existential *ers* and the other *ers*. It is not a dummy but rather a meaningful pronominal adverb, a deictic signaling "weak situational deixis". Being an adverbial not a nominal, it is never an "underlying" direct object nor a subject, not even a "dummy" one, nor does it bear case or trigger verb agreement. Thus, impersonal passives are actually subjectless; the verb does not agree with *er* but rather is simply in the unmarked or "least inappropriate" (Kirsner 1979) third singular form. In the "indefinite extraposition construction", we are dealing with the same *er*, here used to background and delay the subject, with which the verb of course agrees.

Having dispensed with most of the arguments for assuming that *er* is a subject, we are left with only one. As we saw earlier, the argument for the advancement analysis of impersonal passives crucially depends on *er* being introduced as a 2 and advancing to 1, for otherwise the 1AEX cannot be invoked to exclude the impossible passives previously noted. In the final section of this paper, we return to this issue.

5. Toward a Universal Characterization of Passive

5.1 Objections to the Advancement: An analysis of Passive.

Although the advancement analysis of impersonal passives may at first glance appear convincing to some, upon closer examination it does not stand up; in fact, several criticism can be leveled at it besides those already given concerning the claim that *er* is a surface subject. First of all, no independent evidence is offered for the claim that in impersonal passives as opposed to the indefinite extraposition construction *er* is inserted as a 2; and yet this claim is crucial to the analysis, as it alone allows for the advancement of the dummy to 1 which is necessary in order for the 1AEX to exclude further advancements to 1. The only argument in favor of inserting *er* as a 2 here is simply that it makes the analysis work, certainly a very weak and highly suspect motivation. Why should er_2 have a different initial GR than er_1, other than that RG would like to have things this way? This ploy is ingenious, but nonetheless totally ad hoc and unmotivated by other considerations. Furthermore, why is it that the dummy can never appear as a surface 2 in the language? That is, to my konwledge there are no sentences in Dutch containing a dummy 2 such as (55), even though this might be expected on the RG account.

(55) a. *Ik bestudeer er.
'*I am studying *er*.'

b. *Ik zie er.
'*I see *er*.'

If *er* can be a non-initial 2, why doesn't it ever appear on the surface as a 2? The answer of course, is that the 2-hood of *er* is completely fictional: it is only a figment of the RG imagination, invoked to make the strictly syntactic analysis work out correctly. Otherwise if there are no empirical, theory-noninternal (and therefore testable) grounds for claiming that *er* is an initial 2.

Another objection to the analysis is its obviously arbitrary and to a large extent non-empirical character. For instance, the account relies heavily on the 1AEX, which disallows multiple advancements to 1; the problem is that this restriction is totally without any external motivation--why should languages universally obey such an odd principle? Assuming for the moment that the 1AEX correctly *describes* the data, it does not *explain* them and thus in the final analysis does not increase our insight into the workings of language and the nature of the phenomena in question. Moreover, since the principle is arbitrary, how direct object speakers come to have it? Once again, it hardly seems learnable without correction, and according to Baker (1979) this is highly unlikely. The only other alternative would seem to be that it is innate, but this too does not appear very plausible. Furthermore, why should only 1s be singled out in this way, why not 2s also, or terms in general.

Similar objections can be leveled at the Final 1 Law, the Motivated Chômage Law, and the insertion of invisible dummies as 2s. Are these in some sense innate? Hardly. How then do people learn them? For example, in a language like Turkish with only silent dummies, how do people know that impersonal passives contain a dummy which is inserted as a 2 and advanced to 1 if they never are confronted with data which force this conclusion? Why don't speakers simply take the data at face value and interpret apparently subjectless to be just that--namely subjectless? As long as silent dummies are allowed, the Final 1 law, the Motivated Chômage Law, and the advancement analysis of impersonal passives are largely devoid of empirical content, for they could never be falsified through empirical evidence.

However, since we have argued that impersonal passives (and other constructions in Dutch as well as other languages) are truly subjectless, we also reject both the Final 1 Law and the Motivated Chômage Law. Not having a final subject, impersonal passives constitute clear violations of any putatively universal claim that all basic clauses must have a final 1. Therefore, this claim cannot stand. Moreover, rejecting as we do the advancement analysis of impersonal passives, we must also reject the

Motivated Chômage Law. Since no dummy is inserted as a 2 in impersonal passives, there is no advancement to 1 and thus no "motivation" for the chômage of the initial 1. This amounts to accepting "spontaneous demotion", as proposed by Comrie (1977). As we see here, the arguments given in this paper have serious consequences for a number of important recent proposals made in RG.

5.2 Proposal for a Semantically Based Universal Charcterization of Passive

Thus, the mechanism for excluding the impermissible passives proposed by RG appears questionable, as does the whole advancement analysis of impersonal passives. In view of the problems posed by a purely syntactic analysis of passive, a semantically based solution seems worth pursuing.[11] Note that Perlmutter and Postal (1984a) were forced to admit certain connections between unaccusative versus unnegative distinction and the meaning of the predicates involved: thus unergative verbs frequently express voluntary actions, whereas unaccusative verbs express event not under volitional control.[12] Moreover, they observe that certain verbs can be either unergative or unaccusative, depending on meaning (volitional versus non-volitional), and even normally unaccusative verbs can be passivized when given a voluntary reading as in the following.

(56) a. De edelen buigen voor de koning.
'It is bowed before the king by the noblemen.'

b. Er wordt door de edelen voor de koning gebogen.
'*It is bowed in the wind by the flowers.'

(57) Op deze tafel wordt (er) altijd door de kinderen gestaan wanneer zij uit het raam willen kijken.
'On this table it is always stood by the children when they want to look out the window.'

(58) a. In het tweede bedrijf werd er door de nieuwe acteur op het juiste ogenblik gevallen.
'In the second act it was fallen by the new actor at the right moment.'

b. *Er werd door twee mensen uit de venster van de tweede verdieping gevallen.
'It was fallen by two people from the window of the second floor.'

Such observations led Perlmutter (1978: 1973ff.) to consider a characterization of passive in semantic terms, which he unfortunately rejected. However, the proposal he rejects is really only a straw man, since it is clearly too simplistic and strong in limiting passive to clauses with an initial 1 which is an agent. Sentences such as the following are then taken to be clear counter examples to such a restriction:

(59) a. Dat wordt door bijna iedereen geloofd / verstaan / verondersteld / voor onder steld / betwijfeld / vermoed.
'This is believed / understood / supposed / assumed / doubted / suspected by everyone.'

b. Zij wordt door iedereen gehaat / veracht / bewonderd / geacht / ger espek teerd.
'She is hated / despised / admired / respected by everyone.'

c. Deze hypothese wordt door de feiten weerlegd / bevestigd / gesteund.
'This hypothesis is refuted / confirmed / supported by the facts.'

Note that in these examples the active subject/initial 1 is considered to be not a literal agent; no examples are given where passive is impossible with a clearly agentive subject, although nothing in the theory seems to absolutely preclude this possibility.

While these observations certainly knock down this simplistic semantic restriction, they do not argue against a more sophisticated version which limits passives to *agentlike* subjects. In fact, Kirsner (1975: 99) has offered just such a characterization of passive for Dutch:

(60) The hypothesis then is that in both its 'true' use and its 'pseudo' [=impersonal] use passive morphology in Dutch is one single linguistic sign signaling the meaning...HIGH PARTICIPANT NOT FOCUSED.

This amounts to claiming that the Dutch passive in this view backgrounds or demotes a relatively agentlike subject, for Kirsner goes on to explain:

By HIGH PARTICIPANT I mean one which ranks *relatively high on a scale of relative agentivity,* [my emphasis, TFS] relative agent-like character with respect to the event name by the verb. In other words, participants can be ranked according to their relative potency, their relative degree of contribution to bringing about the event named by the verb. In terms of arbitrary absolute labels..., a HIGH PARTICIPANT covers roughly--but only roughly--the range of "causer" - "agent" - "instrument" ...

Such a proposal seems to handle the Dutch data very well; it not only accounts for the observed restrictions but offers a principled reason for the gaps--if passive demotes or backgrounds an agentlike entity, and only secondarily foregrounds/advances a patient-like entity if one is present, we would not expect passive to apply when the active subject (initial 1) is less agentlike/more patient-like. This explains the normal lack of passive with unaccusative verbs, since their subject is usually not agentlike.[13] Also, cases where a volitional reading on the subject makes passivization possible are perfectly in line with this analysis, since the subject is then viewed as more agentlike, which should make the sentence more susceptible to passive.[14] It also accounts for the lack of impersonal passives of personal passives; since the personal passive already backgrounds the one agentlike entity (subject) and foregrounds the patientlike entity, there is no reason to expect passive to work again--this would in fact be totally contrary to its basic function. The lack of passive with inversion and raising verbs also mentioned earlier is also correctly predicted: both these verb types take nonagentlike subjects. In addition, this analysis also accounts for something which Perlmutter and Postal do not mention: the lack of relatively agentlike subjects in personal passives. Because we hypothesize that the advanced or foregrounded object of a personal passive is patientlike, we would predict that more agentlike objects would not occur as passive subject, and as far as I can tell this is correct.

Time limits prevent me from documenting all these claims here (cf. however Shannon 1987a), but I think the superiority of this account over the RG account is already obvious. In light of the evidence offered against the advancement analysis of passive the abandonment of that proposal seems called for. But not that rejecting the RG analysis of passive as an advancement from 2 to 1 from a transitive stratum does not mean that a universal characterization of passive is necessarily impossible. Although Kirsner proposes his analysis as a characterization of passive in Dutch, I maintain that it stands a good chance of holding up as a universal characterization of passive. Certainly it accounts for the Dutch data very nicely and it seems to generalize to other languages I am familiar with such as English, German, French, and Russian. Furthermore, it can uncover the connections between passive and other passive-like constructions such as reflexable passives and mediopassives. Of course, to support this claim to universality much more work will have to be done. However, because of the initial success of this semantically-based analysis, I feel it holds great promise as a characterization of passive not only in Dutch but also universally.

6. Conclusion

In this paper I have argued against a number of universal and language-specific proposals made recently within RG. It has been argued that despite apparent evidence to the contrary given by Relational Grammarians, *er* is not a dummy subject, neither in the so-called indefinite extraposition construction nor in impersonal passives. This has several consequences for RG and a number of its universal principles. Most importantly, we have claimed that RG's universal characterization of passive is incorrect; it is not universally an advancement from 2 to 1 from an transitive stratum. Along with Kirsner (1975, 1976, 1979), we view passive as a strategy to background, or "demote" in RG terms, an agentlike subject-- advancement of the patient-like direct object is secondary. Hence the Motivated Chômage Law and the Final 1 Law proposed by RG are both false: impersonal passives in Dutch (and presumably other languages) involve the spontaneous demotion of a subject, without any consequent advancement of a dummy (*er*) to subject. Finally, we contended that the Unaccusative Hypothesis is a misguided attempt to handle essentially semantic restrictions on passive in syntactic guise. Since passive only backgrounds **agentlike** subjects, it is obvious that constructions with non-agentlike subjects, for instance so-called unaccusative verbs, inversion verbs, and personal passives, will not be susceptible to passivization.

In the end, it is concluded that the Dutch data considered here are much better accommodated in the present account, which therefore strongly suggests some radical emendations of RG theorizing. On balance, RG seems to have started with a basically sensible idea -- that GRs are important and should be referred to by grammatical theory -- but has for some reason made it practically the nly basis for grammatical description and theory. This elevation of purely syntactic, undefined primitive GRs to the major if not sole element in grammar has been most unfortunate. By postulating only a single syntactic level with different "strata", Relational Grammarians seem to have become prisoners of their own methodology, who seek to account for all phenomena which they consider relevant in strictly syntactic terms -- i.e. in terms of GRs -- even when factors from other levels seem to be at work. In so doing they have abandoned all hope of truly understsanding and ultimately even in some real sense explaining the phenomena in question by separating out the various levels -- semantic, pragmatic, and syntqactic -- which are crucuially involved. I hope to have at least suggested that the latter strategy will eventually prove to be much more frutiful and rewarding than the regretfully "autonomous syntactic" approach of recent RG work.

NOTES

[1] Thanks go to my colleague Robert Kirsner for very helpful comments on this paper; the influence of his ideas on my own thinking should be evident throughout. However, the usual disclaimers hold true; *caveat lector et auctor.*

[2] Almost all examples in this paper are taken from printed sources, mainly Perlmutter and Postal (1984a, b), Kirsner (1979), and Perlmutter and Zenen (1984). I have avoided changing the original examples from the published literature, even though native speakers may find some of htem unusual. For instance, Kirsner (1979) notes that *er*- clauses favor subject NPs containing indefinite quantifiers rather than (definite) numerals, so that examples like (1) are probably not typical. Also, the use of *zegden* in (46) is perhaps not the norm for most speakers nowadays. In addition, the preferred order of the adveribials in (22d) would undoubtedly be first time, then place. English translations are rather literal and not claimed to be fully idiomatic. Finally, for purely typographical reasons, the stratal diagrams are given in boxlike form and not hte usual arc-shapoed form. I trust that no serious misinterpretaions are introduced by this.

[3] As Perlmutter and Postal (1984a; 82) point out, this law is in effect a more constrained version of their previous *Advancee Tenure Law*:

An advance cannot be placed en chômage by an advancement.

[4]In arguing against Hoekstar's (1984) analysis of Dutch (an adaptation of RG claims into the Government and Binding framework), Schermer-Vermeer presents similar objections to some of those voiced here. I am indebted to Bob Kirsner for pointing out this reference to me.

[5]Perlmutter and Zaenen also offer two other arguments, one for the final non-2-hood of the pivot--relying on the fact that it receives nominative and not accusative case (at least in German, where we see this most clearly)--and other for the final non-termhood of the pivot, based on the Stratal Uniqueness Law, which disallows more than one given term in a stratum. I disregard these arguments here because they are only relevant once one abandons the position that the pivot is in fact the final subject, precisely the point which we are trying to maintain here despite the arguments to the contrary given above.

[6]At least not in de Haan (1979); unfortunately, de Haan (1976) was not available to me.

[7]Perlmutter and Zaenen consider and reject a "Silent Dummy Ban", which would disallow the use of such fictitious elements. I believe they are mistaken in doing so, but space does not allow me to elaborate on this here.

[8]The novels in question are *De donkere kamer van Damokles* by Willem Frederik Hermans (Amsterdam: Oorschot, 1971) and *De kroonegetuige* by Maarten 'tHart (Amsterdam: De Arbeiderspers, 1983).

[9]In fact, in many ways RCE may be sensitive to the same properties as the indefinite extraposition construction; at least this is to be expected, because they both have similar functions, in particular the delaying of a bacgrounded/rhematic element.

[10]With certain well-known exceptions such as "pro=drop" languages like Italian.

[11]For further development of the proposals made here, cf. now also Shannon (1987a).

[12]Perlmutter and Postal (1984a: 97ff.) even tentatively adopt the "Strong Alignment Hypohtesis," which states

> There exist principles of universal grammar which predict the initial relation borne by each nominal in a given clause from the meaning of the clause.

Personally, I do not believe that such a strong position can be maintained across the board, although there should be a relatively transparent mappying relation in the majority of cases, particulary the "unmarked" or prototypical ones.

[13]Kirsner's (1975, 1976b) account also explains the restriction of impersonal passives to human agents in Dutch. Perlmutter and Postal deny the

currectness of this claim, but they appear to be wrong. The same restriction holds for German passives as well, incidentally.

[14]For more on volitional control, especially with respect to verbal complements in German, cf. Shannon (1987b) and further literature cited there.

BIBLIOGRAPHY

Baker, C.L. 1979. "Syntactic theory and the projection problem". *Linguistic Inquiry*. 10:533-51."

Behagel, Otto. 1932. *Deutsche Syntax*. Vol. 4 Heidelberg: Winter.

Cole, Peter and Jerrold M. Sadock. (eds). 1977. *Syntax and semantics 8: Grammatical relations*. New York: Academic Press.

Comrie, Bernard. 1977. In defense of spontaneous demotion: The impersonal pasive. In Cole and Sadock, 47-98.

De Haan, Ger J. 1976. "Regelordering en domeinformuleringen op transformaties." In Koefoed, G. and Arnold Evers (eds.), *Lijnen van taaltheoretisch onderzoek*. Groningen: Tjeenk Willink.

Drosdowski, Günter (ed.). 1984^4. *Duden. Grammatik der deutschen Gegenwartsprache*. Mannheim: Bibliographisches Institut.

Geerts, G. et al. (eds.). 1984. *Algemene Nederalndse spraakkunst*. Groningen/Leuven: Wolters-Noordhoff.

----------. 1979. Conditions on rules. Dordrecht: Foris.

Hoekstra, Teun. 1984. *Transitivity. Grammatical relations in government and binding theory*. Dordrecht: Foris.

Johnson, David Dutch. 1977. On relational constraints on grammars. In Cole and Sadock, 151-178.

Kirsner, Robert S. 1975. "On the mechanism of the restriction of the Dutch 'pseudo-passive' to human actions." *Columbia Working Papers in Linguistics*. 2:109-143.

----------. 1976a. De'onechte lijdende vorm'. *Spektator*. 6:1-18.

----------. 1976b. On subjectless 'pseudo-passives' in Standard Dutch and the semantics of background agents." In Li, Charles (ed.). *Subject and topic*. New York: Academic Press. 187-215.

----------. 1979. *The problem of presentative sentences in modern Dutch*. Amdsterdam: North Holland.

Nieuwborg, E. 1973. De plaatsing van het substantivisch onderwerp inreflexieve constructies. *Leuvense Bijdragen*. 62:273-283.

Perlmutter, David M. 1978. Impersonal passives and the unaccusative hypothesis. In *Proceedings from the Fourth Annual Meeting of the Berkeley Linguistics Society*. Berkeley: University of California, 157-189.

----------. 1980. Relational grammar. In Moravscik, Edith and Jessica Wirth (eds),*Syntax and semantics 13: Current appraochs to syntax.* New York: Academic Press, 195-229.

----------. 1981. Functional grammar and relational grammar: Points of convergence and divergence. In Hoekstra Teun, Harry van der Hulst and Michael Moorgat (eds), *Perspectives on functional grammer.* Dordrecht: Foris, 319-352.

----------. 1982. Syntactic representations, syntactic levels and the notion of subject. In Jacobson, Pauline and Geoffrey Pullum (eds), *he nature of syntactic represntation.* Dordrecht: Reidel. 283-352.. 283-352.

----------, (eds). 1983. *Studies in relational grammar 1.* Chicago: University of Chicago Press.

----------. 1984. The inadequacy of some monostratal theories of passive. In Perlmutter and Rosan. 3-37.

---------- and Paul M. Postal. 1974. *Lectures on relational grammar.* Unpublished lecture notes, LSA Summar Institute, University of Massachusetts, Amherst, Mass.

----------. 1977. Towards a universal characterization of passivization. In *Proceedings of the Third Annual meeting of the Berkeley Linguistics Society.* Berkley: University of California. 394-417.

---------- and Paul M. Postal. 1984a. The 1-advancement exclusiveness law. In Perlmutter and Rosen. 81-125.

---------- and Paul M. Postal. 1984b. Impersonal passives and some relational laws. In Perlmutter and Rosen. 126-170.

---------- and Carol G. Rosen (eds). 1984. *Studies in relational grammar 2.* Chicago: University of Chicago Press.

---------- and Annie Zaenen. 1984. The indefinite extraposition construction in Dutch and German. In Perlmutter and Rosen 1983. 1971- 216.

Schermer-Vermeer, E.C. 1985. "De onthullende status van *er* in de generatieve grammatica." *Spektator* 15:65-84.

Shannon, Thomas F. "On some recent claims of relational grammar." In Aske, Jon et al. (eds.). *Berkeley Linguistics Society. Proceedings of the thirteenth meeting.* Berkeley: Berkeley Linguistics Society, 247-262.

----------, 1987b. *Aspects of complementation and control in modern German.* (Göppinger Arbeiten zur Germanistik, 424). Göppingen:Kümmerle.

REMARKS ON THE ORIGIN OF THE IE PRETERITIS STIERF, WIERP, ZWIERF, BEDIERF IN DUTCH

Robert B. Howell
University of Wisconsin, Madison

Germanists have long been aware that a small group of original Germanic class 3 strong verbs in modern Dutch possess preterit forms whose vocalism can not be derived by applying regular sound changes to the original Germanic preterit vocalism. Neither the original preterit singular *a vocalism nor the *u vocalism of the preterit plural and past participle forms could yield a modern reflex of -ie- as is found in modern Dutch stierf, wierp, wierf, bedierf and zwierf. It is therefore clear that the modern forms represent analogical innovations based on the model of other strong verbs which have -ie- vocalism in their preterit forms. In Dutch there are two possible sources of -ie- vocalism in the preterit forms of strong verbs. The richest source of verbs with -ie- preterit vocalism in the Germanic class 7 strong verbs, often referred to as the reduplicating verbs. From the Middle Dutch period onward these verbs are in general characterized by -a- vocalism in the present tense and in the past particle and by -ie- in the preterit, the regular reflex of WGmc. long e². Although phonological changes in the history of Dutch have in a number of instances obscured original ablaut alternation by altering either the present or preterit vocalism, the expected class 7 ablaut alternation is still reflected in many modern Dutch verbs:

Figure 1

infinitive	prest.sq.	pret.pl.	pastpart.
vallen	viel	vielen	gevallen
blazen	blies	bliezen	geblazen*
laten	liet	lieten	gelaten

A second possible model for the stierf-type preterit could be the small group of original class 6 strong verbs with *-jan presents which have themselves adopted the preterit vocalism of the class 7 strong verbs by the Middle Dutch period rather than retaining the expected long -o- preterit vocalism of class 6 strong verbs. This group of verbs is quite small and is represented in modern Dutch only by the verbs heffen and scheppen:

269

Figure 2

infinitive	pret.sq.	pret.pl.	past part.
heffen	hief	hieven	geheven
scheppen	schiep	schiepen	geschapen*

Handbooks dealing with the history of the Dutch language traditionally assume that the stierf-type preterits find their origin in an analogical formation during the 14th and 15th centuries based on the model of the verbs heffen/hief and scheppen/schiep (Van Bree 1977:317; Van Loey 1970:10).[1] In this paper I will demonstrate that it is in fact far more likely that the -ie preterits in sterven, werpen and the like result from a direct reinterpretation of these verbs as members of the class seven strong verbs in the Flemish linguistic area in the course of the 14th and 15th centuries. I will also argue that verbs such as heffen and scheppen play at most a peripheral role in the extension of the -ie- preterits to the original class 3 strong verbs.

According to the traditional view, the innovative preterit forms stierf, wierp, zwierf, etc. were introduced as a reaction to the neutralization of the inherited present/preterit distinction resulting from the raising of the preterit singular root vocalism of -a- to -e- before r followed by a consonant in much of the Dutch linguistic area during the Middle Dutch period. As a result of this phonological change, the present and preterit forms of these verbs share the same root vocalism:

Figure 3

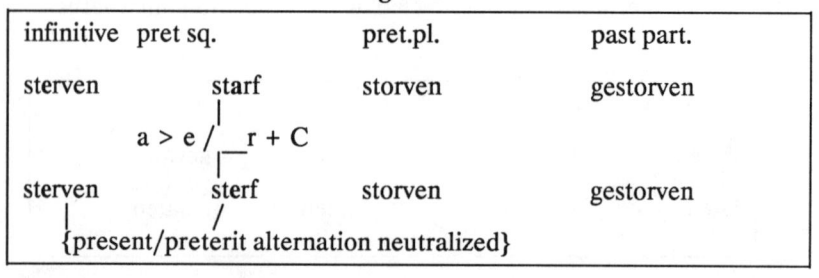

infinitive	pret sq.	pret.pl.	past part.
sterven	starf	storven	gestorven
	a > e / __r + C		
sterven	sterf	storven	gestorven
{present/preterit alternation neutralized}			

Van Bree (1977:317) characterizes the resulting forms as "niet erg functionele praeterita", a situation which then possibly favors the introduction of the more distinctive, and hence more functional, -ie- forms.

This traditional theory obviously depends critically on the assumption the original preterit singular vocalism -a- was raised before clusters of r plus consonant, since it is the identical -e- vocalism of the present tense forms of sterven and heffen which provides the formal basis for the analogical association of the two types of verb. One might also argue that the double consonantism in the present tense root in both sterven- and heffen-type verbs also provides at least minimal formal similarity with respect to the consonantal structure of the present tense root. Unfortunately, the double consonant in <u>heffen</u> is found only in the present tense forms, so this particular formal similarity is not a factor in the preterit alternants. These facts allow the following analogical equation:

Figure 4

<u>heffen</u> is to <u>hief</u> as
sterven is to X = = = > stief

While this explanation is certainly within the realm of the possible, the formal argument is weak enough to provoke questions. First of all it seems odd that the class 3 verbs introduce an entirely new preterit vocalism in both the singular and plural forms rather than employing what is in Germanic the more common strategy of simply borrowing the vocalism of one of the verb's other ablaut grades--in this instance -o-.

Figure 5

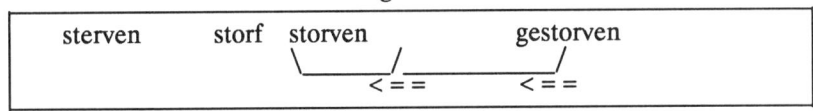

```
sterven     storf  storven          gestorven
            _____/_____/
              < = =         < = =
```

The second possible objection might be that the rather weak formal similarity between the two types of verb is simply not a very compelling argument for the analogical introduction of the preterit vocalism of one type into that of the other. Of course neither of these objections constitutes an insurmountable challenge to the traditional explanation of the origin of the stierf-type preterits. They do however provide enough room for doubt to motivate a reevaluation of the facts surrounding the introduction of these new preterit forms.

The most crucial fact pertaining to the origin of the stierf-type preterit is that they first make their appearance in Flemish texts of the 14th century:

Figure 6

wierde (pret.opt.) Brugge 1288; wierpen Brugge 1334; wierp Arnemuiden 1381; wiert Brugge ca. 1400 (Van Loey1976:77)

The characteristics of the Flemish dialects during the period must therefore be the focus of our inquiry. The appearance of these first -<u>ie</u>-forms in Flanders is of particular importance to our discussion because the raising of <u>a</u> to <u>e</u> before <u>r</u> followed by a consonant, the phonological development which is absolutely essential to the argument favoring analogy to the <u>heffen</u>-type verbs, tends not to occur in this dialect area. Even more interesting is the fact that at precisely this time in Flanders, original short <u>e</u> is lowered to <u>a</u> when followed by <u>r</u> plus consonant:

Figure 7

Before r + dental:	
darscen (<derscen) "to thresh"	(Van Loey:
warden (<werden) "to become"	1976a:8)
derde (<derde) "third"	"
dartien (<dertien) "thirteen"	"
dertich (<dertich) "thirty"	"
Carst (<Kerst) "Christ"	"
varde (<verde) "peace"	"
Varsch (<versch) "fresh"	"
Varsenare (<versenare) place name by Brugge	
varre (<verre) "far"	"
Before r + labiel	
aerve (<erve) "inheritance"	"
gearft (<geerft) "inherited"	"
karke (<kerke) "church"	"
karker (<kerker) "jail"	"
bescharmen (<beschermen)	"to protect"
arve (<erve) "inheritance"	(Willemyns:
arrvelijker (<ervelijker)	1974:84)
"inheritable""	

The result of this lowering is interesting for a number of reasons. First of all it yields infinitive and present tense forms of the sterven-type verbs with a vocalism: <u>starven, warden, warpen,</u> etc. this phonological change would render considerably less likely the equation of these verbs with verbs such as heffen and scheppen which retain e̱ vocalism in the present tense throughout the linguistic area. A second consequence of the lowering of e̱ to a̱ is the neutralization of the present/preterit opposition, just as in the raising areas:

Figure 8

orginally:	werpen warp worpen geworpen
Raising areas (a > e)	werpen werp worpen geworpen
Lowering areas (e > a)	warpen warp worpen geworpen

Thus in both the raising and lowering areas a similar loss of the present/preterit distinction occurs. As a result of the neutralization of this key morphological distinction throughout the Dutch linguistic area, any innovation which clearly reestablishes the tense alternation stands a chance of acceptance even outside of the area where its introduction is motivated by a strong analogical equation.

Finally, the new vocalism in <u>warpen, warden, starven</u> and the like results in verbs which formally resemble class 7 strong verbs both in their present tense vocalism and in their consonantal root structure, since a number of class 7 verbs are characterized by the root structure of liquid/nasal plus consonant. Examples of class 7 strong verbs with this root structure in Middle Dutch are vallen, wallen, vangen, hangen, bannen. Since the class 7 strong verbs represent numerically the richest source of -ie- preterits in Middle Dutch and because the lowering of the e to a corresponds exactly, both temporally and geographically, to the introduction of the stierf preterits, it seems highly likely that the old class 3 verbs have simply been reinterpreted as members of the class 7 vallen/viel kind of alteration as a result of the lowering of the present tense e vocalism to "a" before "rC":

Figure 9

vallen ==> vie
\<aLC>
warpen ==> ? ==> wierp

Because the class 7 strong verbs represent the most numerous source of inherited -ie- preterits (Van Loey lists 34 members of this class in Middle Dutch), this reinterpretation of the old class 3 verbs as members of class 7 would seem to represent a logical development. The sporadic appearance of past participles such has gewarden, gewarpen, gestarven (see Van Loey 1976:74 and Verwijs/Verdam 1985-1941 under individual word listings for examples) in place of inherited geworden, geworpen, gestorven suggests that at least in some dialect areas the identification of sterven-type verbs with the class 7 ablaut series was total:

Figure 10

	infinitive	pret. sing.	pret. plur.	pest. part.
originally:	werpen	warp	worpen	geworpen
innovation:	warpen	wierp	wierpen	gewarpen
class 7	vallen	viel	vielen	gevallen

The lowering of -e- to -a- before r followed by a consonant and the introduction of -ie- preterits in original class 3 strong verbs characterized by the consonantal root structure of r plus consonant both occur in the same time period (late 13th century to the 14th century) and in the same geographical area (Flanders). This fact provides strong circumstantial evidence that the explanation of the stierf-type preterits proposed above is a plausible one. The final convincing evidence linking lowering of -e- before r with the introduction of these new preterits can be found in the distribution these two features in the 17th and 18th centuries and in the dialects of modern Dutch.

In the centuries following the Middle Dutch period stierf-type preterits seem to enjoy little favor with northern writers. The frequency of the -ie- forms is so low that Weijnen (1968:38) makes no mention of them in his discussion of the 17th century Dutch although he gives a number of examples of alternate preterit vocalism in these verbs:

Figure 11

> u: versturf, verwurf, wurp
> a: starf, wart
> o: worp
> e: sterf, werp

It is interesting that in the few instances where an -ie- form does appear, it seems to be employed in order to emphasize the preterit meaning when a present tense form of the verb is in close proximity. An example of just this sort is found in P.C. Hooft's *Nederlandse Historien*:

Figure 12

> "Ook **werdt** [present] ieder gelast niet van zyn'hoefslagh te schieden oft hy **wierd** [preterit]'er afgehaalt by die van den Gerechte," from *Leiden ontzet* (Weijnen 1969:294)

Elsewhere in this same text Hooft employs <u>werd</u> as the preterit of <u>werden</u>:

Figure 13

> "...raakten vast aan den grond, en werden genomen."
> "...dat de beleegherden aangemaant werden."
> "...dat er slapper wacht...gehouden werd."
> "...daar werden zy ontvangen..."
> "...daar ze mee bewelkoomt werden van burghers.."
> "...Welke dankbaarheit....begenaadight werd..."
> (Weijnen 1968:292-296).

Clearly Hooft has employed <u>wierd</u> in the sentence in Figure 12 in order to avoid confusion with the present tense. The alternate form is clearly known in Holland, but is used in special situations, much as <u>zeuven</u> can be used in place of <u>zeven</u> in modern spoken Dutch to avoid confusion with the phonetically similar <u>negen</u>.

Other northern writers of the 17th century are equally reluctant to make extensive use of the -<u>ie</u>- preterits as well. Nauta (1893:66) cites in the works of Bredero only one instance of <u>stierf</u> and four examples of <u>wierp</u> beside the far more numerous -<u>u</u>- forms such as <u>besturf, wurp, verwurf</u>.

Perhaps nowhere is the southern origin of the <u>stierf</u>-type preterit so clear as in Lambert ten Kate's *Anleiding tot de kennisse van het verhevene deel der Nederduitsche sprake* of 1723. Although the lists the parallel preterits <u>stierf/storf, verwierf/verworf, wierd/word, wierp/worp</u>, and <u>wierf/worf</u>, Ten Kate also states flatly "bij den Vlaming is 't Imperf.: <u>Beedirf</u>" (Ten Kate

274

1973:565). Clearly even by the early 18th century the stierf-type preterits were perceived as Flemish in nature.

Modern evidence indicates that the stierf preterits never have been widely accepted in the dialects of the northern and eastern parts of the Dutch linguistic area. In an extensive discussion of the distribution of the stierf-type preterits in the modern dialects of Dutch, Van den Berg (1957) demonstrates that the introduction of the -ie- preterits in class 3 verbs has been quite limited geographically. In the northern and eastern parts of the linguistic area the -ie- forms do not appear at all. Instead, the vocalism of the preterit plural and the past particle has been extended to the preterit singular:

Figure 14

Groningen:	sturf, bedurf, zwork
Stadsfries:	swurf, bedurf, sturf
Ruinen:	storf, bedorf, zworf
Kampen:	storf, bedorf, zworf
N.W. Veluwe:	storef, zworef
Heerde:	bedorf, besorft, storf, worf, worp
Enschede:	bedorf, wor (= werd)
Elten-Bergh:	storef
Westerschelling:	wu: (= werd)
Oosterschelling:	wode
Wieringen:	swarref but stierref, wier
Urk:	storref, zworref
Drechterland:	bedurref, sturref, swurref
Zaans:	storf/sturf,bedorf, worp, worf, zworf
Katwijk:	sturref/stieref, zwurref/szieref, bedurref/bedieref
Roermond:	storf, bedorf
Heerlen:	bedorf, sjtorf, sjworf,worp
Maastricht:	bedorref, starref, zworref

(Van den Berg 1957:75-78)

The areas where the -ie- preterits do occur dialectally encompasses a region from Leuven westward including West Flanders, Southeast Flanders, Antwerp, Zeeland, Brabant, Grave, South Holland and North Holland as far north as Wieringen (Van den Berg 1957:80). The significant fact here is that this region in the south and west of the linguistic area essentially coincides with those regions where -e- was lowered to -a- before r plus consonant. This lowering had extended to Zeeland, South Holland and to parts of Brabant by the 15th century (Van Loey 1976a:8). Therefore the stierf preterits seem to occur precisely in the area where the formal relationship between the class 3 verbs with root r and class 7 verbs would have been strongest. Conversely the formal relationship between the class 3 verbs and heffen-type verbs would have been quite tenuous. The examples in Figure 14 show that in the non-lowering areas, where sterven- and heffen-type verbs reflect the greatest formal similarity, the stierf-type preterits simply do not occur. In these areas a different analogical strategy has been followed. The argument that the stierf preterits were formed on analogy to the heffen/hief alternation therefore does not appear to be tenable. On the other hand, the chronological and geographical coincidence of -e- lowering and of the introduction of -ie- preterits in sterven, werven, werpen etc. makes it seem exceedingly likely that the original class 3 verbs have been reinterpreted as verbs of the vallen/viel ablaut alternation.

It is interesting to note that even within the area where stierf preterits are numerous, the starf type of preterit shown in Figure 14 is quite common as well. These competing verb forms do not detract from the argument presented above. Throughout the entire linguistic area, including the -e- lowering regions in the south and west, the introduction of the -o- vocalism from the preterit plural and/or past participle of the class 3 strong verbs represents an analogical strategy which is equally effective in reestablishing the lost distinction between the present tense vocalism and that of the preterit singular. The important fact to recognize is that once outside of the lowering area the introduction of -o- vocalism seems to have been the only viable strategy. This restriction of the stierf preterits to the areas where vowel lowering before r was common would seem to indicate that the two phenomena were closely related. It also served to call into question any possible role that heffen and scheppen might have played in the origin of these preterit forms.

Of course this line of argumentation does not preclude the possibility that alternations such as heffen/hief might have promoted the eventual integration of stierf, wierf, wierp and the like into the standard language instead of forms such as starf, worp, worf. The presence of the alternations heffen/hief and scheppen/schiep could only have enhanced the status of -ie- as a suitable preterit marker. Nevertheless, hief and schiep would seem to have had little to do with the actual origin of stierf preterits in Flanders.

The explanation proposed here for the origin of the stierf preterits in Dutch might seem to represent but a minor adjustment to the standard interpretation that they reflect an analogical extension of the heffen/hief alternation. I am, in effect, simply replacing one analogy with another. It is however important from a methodological standpoint that we define as closely as possible the formal requirements for and constraints on analogical processes. Otherwise we run the risk of resorting to ill-fitting analogies before all of the relevant facts have been considered.

NOTES

[1]The idea that the -ie- preterits in the class 3 strong verbs represent analogical innovations to the class 7 preterits is not new. Franck (1893:102), for example, mentions the possibility without explaining the mechanism.

BIBLIOGRAPHY

Berg, Berend van den. De ie van bedierf, stierf, wierf, wierp en zwierf. *Taal en Tongval.* 9.75-84, 1957.

Bouman, A.C. *Middelnederlandse bloemlezing met grammatica.* Zutphen: W.J. Thieme. 1948.

Bree, C. va. *Leerboek voor de historische grammatica van het Nederlands.* Groningen: Wolters-Noordhoff.

Franck, Johannes. *Mittelniederländische Grammatik mit Lesestücken und Glossar.* Leipzig: T.O. Weigel. 1983.

Kate, Lambert ten, ed. *Anleiding tot de kennisse van het verhevene deel der Nederduitsche sprake.* Amsterdam: Wetstein. 1723.

Loey, Adolphe van. ed. *Schönfeld's historische grammatica van het Nederlands.* 8th ed. Zutphen: W.J. Thieme. 1970.

---------. *Middelnederlandse Spraakunst.* 1. Vormleer. 7th ed. Groningen: H.D. Tjeenk Willink. 1976.

---------. *Middelnederlandse Spraakunst.* 2. Klankleer 7th ed. Groningen: H.D. Tjeenk Willink. 1976a.

Nauta, G.A. *Taalkundige aantekeningen op de werken van G.A. Bredero.* University of Groningen doctoral dissertation.

Verwijs, Eelco and Jacob Verdam. *Middelnederlandse Woordenboek.* 1-11. The Hague: Martinus Nijhoff. 1885-1941.

Weijnen, A. *Zeventiende-eeuwse Taal.* 5th ed. Zutphen: W.J. Thieme.

Willemyns, R. *Het niet-literaire Middelnederlands.* Assen: Van Gorcum. 1979.

PREPOSITIONAL VERSUS 'BARE' INDIRECT OBJECTS IN THE WRITTEN DUTCH OF NOVELS AND NEWSPAPERS[1]

Robert S. Kirsner
University of California, Los Angeles

1. The Problem. This paper concerns the choice between two forms of the traditional 'indirect object' in Modern Dutch: the 'plain' form shown in 1a and the aan-form shown in 1b and 1c:

1) a. Hij heeft zijn vader het verhaal verteld.
      he has his father the story told

   b. Hij heeft het verhaal aan zijn vader verteld.
      he has the story 'to' his father told

   c. Hij heeft aan zijn vader het verhaal verteld.
      he has 'to' his father the story told

We shall here restrict ourselves to the opposition between the 'plain' form and the aan-form and will not discuss word-order shifts, such as in 1b and 1c. Generally, we want to know why the 'plain' form and the aan-form are used where they are, why there is apparent overlap of use in some cases, but no overlap in others. Specifically, we will report on an experiment in which we gave a questionnaire to 32 native speakers of Dutch living in The Netherlands and asked them to compare different versions of paragraphs taken from novels and newspapers. These consultants were thus confronted with the aan-form and the 'plain' form not in isolated sentences[2] but in a discourse context and they were asked to decide which alternative sounded better in that context.

The immediate purpose of this experiment was to determine, for the different passages, to what extent native speakers agree in their choice of the 'better' or 'best' form, first with each other, and, second, with the author of the original text. If our consultants did not agree either with each other or with the author, we want to know why. On the other hand, even when the choice of a form is nearly unanimous, we also want to know why. What about this example rather than that example makes the choice unanimous here, but random there?[3]

2. The Data. The passages our consultants were confronted with are displayed below, in Sets 1 through 3. The first example is taken from a short-story collection by Remco Campert:

Set #1

a. Het wordt later en duizelig van de warmte kom je naar beneden, waar je mij snurkend op de bank aantreft. Je schudt mij wakker en ik zie dat je geïrriteerd bent en ik weer vat op je begin te krijgen. Je ziet hoe het bier over mijn overhemd gutst en hoe ik dan opsta en op je afkom. Je wordt bij je arm gepakt en mijn mond gaat open en zegt je naam en dat je de enige bent en weer je naam. Je trekt je arm los en knikt ongeduldig en geeft me meer bier. Het is schemerig geworden en je duwt de luiken op en ik knijp in je schouder en val half tegen je aan... (Campert 1984: 76-77)

'It is later and sleepy from the heat you come downstairs, where you find me snoring on the sofa. You shake me awake and I see that you are irritated and I begin to get a hold over you again. You see the beer gush over my shirt and you see me get up and come towards you. You are grabbed by your arm and my mouth opens and says your name and that you are the only one and then your name again. You pull your arm away and nod impatiently and give me more beer. It has become twilight and you push up the shutters and I pinch your shoulder and half fall against you...'

b. Je trekt je arm los en knikt ongeduldig en <u>geeft aan me meer bier</u>.... (<u>aan</u>-form, preposed)
'...You pull your arm back and nod impatiently and give <u>to me more beer</u>....'

c. Je trekt je arm los en knikt ongeduldig en <u>geeft meer bier aan me</u>...(<u>aan</u>-form, postposed)
'..You pull your arm back and nod impatiently and give more beer to me...'

The actual order of presentation of these sentences was b, a and then c. The pattern of rankings we obtained from our consultants[4] is shown in Table 1.

As may be seen from the table, the 'plain' form was preferred by everyone and the preposed <u>aan</u>-form was considered worst by <u>almost</u> everyone. As shown from the Kendall's coefficient of concordance, the extent of agreement among the consultants is very high: 97% of the maximum that could be expected.

TABLE 1   Possible and Observed Rankings of Sentences

Ranking	Best >	Worse >	Worst consultants	Number of choosing
I	a	b	c	1
I (Kendall.s	a	c	b	28
III b coefficient		a	c	0
IV b concordance		c	a	0
V	c	a	b	0 W=.967
VI	c	b	a	0

X^2 (df=2)=56)

Sentence	Average	Rank
a.	1.00	me meer bier
b.	2.97	aan me meer bier
c.	2.03	meer bier aan me

A second group of paragraphs is given under Set 2, from a novella by Gerard Reve:

Set #2

a. Thuis vertelde ik van de uitnodiging. We gaan met een tante van Werther naar het kleine circus, zei ik. -- Wat voor een circus? vroeg mijn moeder - Het is een circus in het klein, zei ik, een soort variété met veel kleine dieren. Met apen en konijnen. Er zijn ook honden, die door een hoepel gaan. -- Je hebt toch niet aan die tante gevraagd of je mee mocht? vroeg ze bezorgd. -- Juist helemaal niet, zei ik. Die tante was niet eens bij hem. Ze hebben zelf gezegd dat ik mee moest gaan.

'At home I told about the invitation. We're going with an aunt of Werther's to the little circus, I said. What kind of circus? my mother asked. -- It is a circus in miniature, I said, a kind of variety show with lots of small animals. With monkeys and rabbits. There are also dogs, which jump through a hoop. -- You have after all not 'to' that aunt asked if you could go along = You didn't ask the aunt if you could go with them, did you? she asked worriedly. -- Not at all, I said. The aunt wasn't even there. They themselves said that I should come along.'

b.   ... Je hebt die tante toch niet gevraagd of je mee mocht?
     '...You have that aunt after all not asked if you could go along?'   (Reve 1970:131-2)

The original order of presentation of the sentences was b first, then a. There was no clear-cut preference for either form; the results are statistically indistinguishable from a 50-50 split:

Relative ranking

0 preferred = b preferred to a: 17 votes (53%)

aan preferred = a preferred to b: 15 votes (47%)

p > .85 by the binomial test, two-tailed   (Siegel 1956:41)

The third set of data are taken from a front-page article in the newspaper *NRC Handelsblad* about the scandal involving the concern Rijn-Schelde-Verolme and are presented in two parts. Part I is the headline and first paragraph of the story. Part II is the second paragraph:

Set #3, Part I:

LUBBERS: RSV KREEG GEEN EXPORTVERGUNNING WEGENS KANS OP CRISIS.
Door een onzer redacteuren.

a.   DEN HAAG, 2 mei - Het kabinet Den Uyl heeft in mei 1976 aan RSV geen vergunning gegeven voor de export van onderdelen voor een kerncentrale aan Zuid-Afrika omdat daarover anders een kabinetscrisis was ontstaan.

b.   DEN HAAG, 2 mei - Het kabinet Den Uyl heeft in mei 1976 RSV geen vergunning gegeven voor de export van onderdelen voor een kerncentrale aan Zuid-Afrika omdat daarover anders een kabinetscrisis was ontstaan.

'LUBBERS: RSV RECEIVED NO EXPORT LICENSE BECAUSE OF POSSIBILITY OF CRISIS.
By one of our editors.

THE HAGUE. 2 May. The Den Uyl cabinet did not give 'to' RSV a permit in May 1976 for the export of nuclear reactor components to South Africa because of the threat of a cabinet crisis.'

Set #3, Part II:

a. Overigens had de toenmalige minister van economische zaken, Lubbers, in maart 1976 met medeweten van premier Den Uyl aan het RSV concern een brief geschreven waarin hij schreef in beginsel positief te staan tegenover levering van reactorvaten aan Zuid-Afrika.

b. Overigens had de toenmalige minister van economische zaken, Lubbers, in maart 1976 met medeweten van premier Den Uyl het RSV concern een brief geschreven waarin hij schreef in beginsel positief te staan tegenover levering van reactorvaten aan Zuid-Afrika. (*NRC Handelsblad* 2 mei 1984, p.1)

'Moreover, in March 1976 the then Minister of Economic Affairs, Lubbers, had written, with Prime Minister Den Uyl's knowledge, a letter 'to' the RSV concern, in which he wrote that he in principle favored the sale of reactor drums to South Africa.'

Here it is interesting that the results for Part I and Part II were not the same. For Part I, 63% of the consultants preferred the 'plain' form. This was shown by a statistical test (the binomial test; cf. Siegel 1956:41) to not differ statistically from a 50 - 50 split. For Part II, on the other hand, 81% of the consultants preferred the 'plain' form, and this does differ statistically from randomness.

Part I:
a preferred to b: 12 (37%) (aan preferred)
b preferred to a: 20 (63%) (0 preferred)
(p >.25 by thebinomialtest(two-tailed).
[Not significantly different from a 50%-50% split]
(Actual order of presentation: b,a).

Part II:
a preferred to b: 6 (19%) (aan preferred)
b preferred to a: 25 (81%) (0 preferred)
(p <.002 by the binomial test (two-tailed).
[Significantly different from a 50-50 split]
(Actual order of presentation: a,b)

3. Questions Posed by the Data The responses of our consultants to these three passages contain several puzzles:

a) Why is there great unanimity in Set 1 among the consultants and in agreement with the author's choice of the 'plain form?'

283

b) Why do we find a <u>lack of unanimity</u> in Set 2 (apparently random results)?

c) Why do we get '<u>mixed</u>' results in Set 3?

d) Why, moreover, do we find <u>the particular pattern of 'mixture,'</u> with random results in Part I, but near unanimous disfavoring of <u>aan</u> in Part II, rather than precisely the other way around?

e) Why, in spite of this trend towards favoring the 'plain' form in Set 3, did the <u>author</u> use <u>aan</u> in both Part I and Part II?

4. Theoretical Interlude. An important clue towards an answer to some of these questions is provided by Table 2, below, which summarizes some important differences between the <u>aan</u> form and the 'plain' form:

Table 2.   Differences between the 'plain' and <u>aan</u>-forms.

'Plain' form	Aan-form
A. Information from which Other NPs phase containing the NPs	The preposition participant role is aan in the aan inferred for referent phrase of NP
B. Way in which Degree of Control in the event is taken as non-polar, i.e. MID rather than high or low.	Relative to other 'Absolute' participants.
C. Status of entity with respect to event named by main verb and, by implication, in the discourse. — Central	Peripheral
D. Demarcation of material referring to participant — None	Marked by aan.

Point A refers to the fact that the 'plain' form does not consistently mark which noun phrase refers to the 'indirect object' i.e. the entity MIDway in control between 'subject' and 'direct object.' When both post-verbal NPs are full noun phrases, as in sentences 2a and 2b below, the first is the 'indirect object.' But when both are pronouns, different orders are possible, as shown in 2c and 2d. Accordingly, with the 'plain form', the hearer must infer the role of the NP from both its specific identity (full NP or pronoun and, if the latter, what kind of pronoun) and its position:

2)   a.   Hij heeft <u>zijn vader</u> <u>het verhaal</u> verteld.(= la)
              "IO"   "DO"
   b.   * Hij heeft <u>het verhaal</u> <u>zijn vader</u> verteld. BUT:
               "DO"   "IO"
   c.   Hij heeft <u>het hem</u> verteld.
      he has it him told
              "DO"   "IO"
   d.   Hij heeft <u>hem dat</u> verteld.
      he has him that told
              "IO"   "DO"

The <u>aan</u>-form, in contrast, marks the MID role <u>mechanically and directly</u>, by means of the preposition. It will also be clear that the aan form clearly separates the 'indirect object' NP from other material in the sentence, while the 'plain' form does not. This point is summarized under D: 'Demarcation.' Point B in Table 2, on relative versus absolute characterization of the 'indirect object' role cannot be dealt with here.[5] Point C, however, is crucial. The <u>aan</u>-form, like other prepositional phrases, explicitly marks the 'indirect object' as a backgrounded or PERIPHERAL entity. The 'plain' form, on the other hand, being a 'bare' non-oblique noun phrase, can be taken as referring to a CENTRAL entity: one in the center of attention both with respect to (i) the event named by the verb in its particular clause, and (ii) the ongoing narration or discourse, to which the sentence in question contributes. Another way of describing this contrast is to say that the 'plain' form indicates that its referent is more <u>topical</u> than the <u>aan</u>-form does, either because it is something speakers find <u>inherently</u> interesting or because it has <u>come to be</u> important in the discourse at hand.

5. Supporting Evidence. Some quantitative evidence for this contrast between CENTRAL and PERIPHERAL entities, or in topicality, if you will, is provided by text counts in which we examine what kinds of noun phrases occur in the 'plain' form and in the <u>aan</u> form. First, however, consider the difference between referring to a person with different types of noun phrases. If the person is not familiar, we use an indefinite noun phrase, such as in <u>Ik heb iemand gezien</u> 'I saw <u>someone</u>,' or <u>Ik heb een man gezien</u> 'I saw <u>a man</u>.' Once the man becomes identified, we can use a definite full noun phrase: <u>Ik heb de man gezien</u>. 'I saw the man.' If he is even better known, we can shift from a common noun to a proper noun[6]: Ik heb Henk gezien 'I saw Henry.' Finally, when the referent is maximally known, maximally topical, we can use a pronoun: Ik heb hem gezien 'I saw him.' We thus have, as shown under 3, a

285

kind of ordinal scale running from minimally familiar or minimally topical entities, referred to with indefinite noun phrases, through definite NPs with common nouns, then definite NPs with proper nouns, and reaching maximally familiar or topical entities, referred to with definite pronouns:

3)

MAXIMALLY IDENTIFIED <------< MINIMALLY IDENTIFIED
    1   >   2   >   3   >   4
Ik heb hem / Henk / de man / een man gezien.
I have him   Henry the man a man seen

Now given the hypothesis that the aan-form portrays its referent as PERIPHERAL and the 'plain' form portrays its referent as CENTRAL, we would expect an interaction with this scale. What is CENTRAL in the event and the discourse should tend to get identified and become topical sooner than what is explicitly PERIPHERAL. Accordingly, if we examine which type of 'indirect object' co-occurs with which type of noun phrase, we should find that the percentage of aan-forms increases as one goes down the scale: topical entities should be treated as CENTRAL 'indirect objects' and occur in the 'plain' form; non-topical entities should be treated as PERIPHERAL and occur in the aan-form. Table 3, below, shows that this is exactly what we find. As we go from pronouns on the left to indefinite noun phrases on the right, the fraction of aan-forms rises:

Table 3.   Frequency of aan-form vs. type of noun phrase referring to the 'indirect object' in 3-participant sentences from four novels.[7]

	De facto scale: More Central <------------< More Peripheral.			
	1 Pronoun	2 Proper Noun	3 Def. Det + common N	4 Indefinite
No. with aan	15	13	19	8
No. 'plain'	195	21	14	2
Sample size N	210	34	33	10
% of aan	7	38	58	80

6. An Explanation for the Data. It will be clear that we now have an immediate explanation for the questionnaire results with Sets 1 and 2. To start with 2, the Gerard Reve example, first: die tante is a definite full noun phrase containing a common noun and falls under position 3 on the scale. In our text sample, the aan-form tended to occur 58% of the time, which is not too different from the questionnaire result of 47%.[8] Moving now to see with the first person pronoun me, we find that pronouns in the text counts, point 1 on the scale, overwhelmingly favor the 'plain' form: 93% of the 210 pronominal indirect objects occurred in this form. This agrees well with the 100% preference for the 'plain' form found in the questionnaire results for the Remco Campert example, especially when we recall that in the questionnaire we are dealing not with all definite pronouns but with a first person pronoun, referring to the speaker, who is by nature maximally topical.

But now what about the results to set 3, from *NRC Handelsblad*? There, the first paragraph came out random but the second showed a favoring of the 'plain' form. Why?

Here, I think, the answer lies in the fact that the more often an entity is mentioned in discourse, the more likely it is to be taken as important or 'central' rather than peripheral. Even when the referent keeps on being referred to with a full noun phrase containing a common noun, prior mention should favor the use of the 'plain' form over the aan-form.

Evidence that this is in fact true is given in Table 4, where we examined in their original contexts all the sentences used in constructing column 3 in our previous Table 3. As can be seen from the text-counts, when there was no prior mention of the referent, most of the 'indirect objects' -- 68%--occurred in the aan-form. However, when the referent was mentioned earlier in novel, most of the indirect objects -- 64% -- occurred in the 'plain' form.[9]

Table 4. NPs with definite determiner and common noun (= Column 3 in Table 3 above; N = 33). Relative favoring of the aan-form when the referent has not been mentioned previously.[10]

	Prior mentions of referent:		
	None	One or more	Total
Form: aan (58%)	15 (68%)	4 (36%)	19
plain (42%)	7 (32%)	7 (64%)	14
Total:	22 (100%)	11 (100%)	33

Now when we compare the questionnaire results for Set 3 with these text-count data, we observe the same sort of shift, but less pronounced:

Table 5. Set 3 data viewed as indicating increasing centrality of RSV with time.[11]

	Set #3; Part I (earlier)	Part II (later = prior mention)
Form: aan	12 (37%)	6 (19%)
plain	20 (63%)	25 (81%)
Total:	32 (100%)	31 (100%)

Furthermore, if we look for anything else conditioning the shift to the 'plain' form, we fail to find it. As Table 6 below shows, the choice of forms in Part II of set 3 is independent of the choice of forms in Part I. Of those who chose the 'plain' form in Part I, 83% chose the 'plain' form in Part II. And of those who chose the aan-form in Part I, 75% chose the 'plain' form in Part II: roughly the same proportion:

Table 6. Choice of plain vs. aan-form in Part I vs. choice of plain vs. aan-form in Part II. 'Plain' form favored in II independent of preference in I.[12]

Votes in Part I	1976 RSV	1976 aan RSV	Total
Votes in Part II			
Den Uyl het RSV concern	15 (83%)	(75%)	24
Den UYl aan het RSV concern	3 (17%)	3 (25%)	6
Total	18 (100%)	12 (100%)	30
	$p > .90$ (chi square test)		

The only other thing to go by would be the difference between the abbreviation RSV in Part I and the definite description het RSV concern in Part II. But this difference, too, seems to reflect a zeroing in on the referent as the discourse proceeds. In any case, if at this point we compare our as the discourse proceeds. In any case, if at this point we compare our consultants' responses on the questionnaire with the corresponding text-count data, we find a relatively strong correlation, as shown in Table 7:

Table 7. Comparison of % aan in Questionnaire Data and Novel Sample.

Set	NP Type	Prior Mention	Quest.	Text Counts	Difference	Text Data
1	pronoun		0%	7%	+7%	(Table 3, Column 1)[13]
3,II	common	yes	19%	36%	+17%	(Table 4, Prior mention)
3,I	common	no	37%	68%	+29%	(Table 4, No Prior mention)
2	common		47%	58%	+11%	(Table 3, Column 3)

Pearson correlation coefficient: r = 0.937 (N=4, p <.04)

Observe that the Pearson correlation coefficient between the percentage of aan-forms on the questionnaires and in the texts is high, r = .94, and is statistically significant (p < .05). This suggests that the same explanation, in terms of relative prominence or topicality of the referent, underlies both trends: (i) the percentage of choices of the aan-form by native speakers judging alternative versions of a single passage, and (ii) the percentage of aan-forms in a sample of comparable passages in distinct texts.

7. Remaining Puzzles: Grammar and Style. Still, in Set 3 we are left with a puzzle: if our consultants preferred the 'plain' form in Part I and, even more so, in Part II, why does the original newspaper article contain aan in both? Here, I think, we can appeal, first of all, to the explicitness of the aan-form, which uses a concrete chunk of morphology -- a preposition -- to mark the MID participant. All the necessary information is spelled out, which fits with the objective reporting style of a newspaper of record, such as *NRC Handelsblad*. Second, there is the clear demarcation brought about by the aan-form. This can certainly be seen in Part I. If the 'plain' form had been used here, the year 1976 would not be clearly separated from the abbreviation RSV and thereby at least a potential problem would be created for the reader. Consider 4:

289

4) DEN HAAG, 2 mei - Het kabinet Den Uyl heeft in mei 1976 RSV geen vergunning gegeven voor de export van onderdelen voor een kerncentrale aan Zuid-Afrika omdat daarover anders een kabinetscrisis was ontstaan.

Similarly, in Part II, without <u>aan</u> we would have three NPs in a row, which could be difficult to process. Consider 5:

5) Overigens had de toenmalige minister van economische zaken, Lubbers, in maart 1976 met medeweten van premier <u>Den Uyl het RSV concern een brief</u> geschreven
                                1   2   3
waarin hij schreef in beginsel positief te staan tegenover levering van reactorvaten aan Zuid-Afrika.

In this regard, it is at least suggestive that aan is also found in children's books, where native speakers regard it as, strictly speaking, not necessary. Consider the following quotation, from a book by Annie M. G. Schmidt:

6) 'Maar we hebben zo'n vreselijk lawaai gehoord...,' zei de vadermuis. 'Dat gebrom en gedreun...wat is dat dan?'

'Dat is de betonmolen,' zei Pluk. 'Maar ze doen er niets mee. Ze spelen alleen. En ze komen niet hier.'

'Kan ik nou <u>aan m'n vrouw</u> en <u>aan m'n kindertjes</u> gaan zeggen dat ze rustig mogen gaan slapen?' vroeg de muis. 'Ze hebben een hele week niet geslapen.' (Schmidt 1984:128)

'But we heard such a horrible noise...,' the father mouse said. 'That buzzing and rumbling, what is it?'

'That's the cement mixer,' Pluk said. 'But they aren't doing anything with it. They're playing. And they won't come here.'

'May I now tell <u>to my wife</u> and <u>to my little children</u> that they can calmly go ahead and go to sleep?,' asked the mouse. 'They haven't slept for a week.'

It might be suggested here that <u>aan</u> helps in spreading out, clearly demarcating, and individually role-marking <u>m'n vrouw</u> and <u>m'n kindertjes</u>, making the passage easier for children to read.[14] If so, then the use of the <u>aan</u>-form in *NRC Handelsblad* can be explained from a desire to achieve maximum clarity and explicitness in what are long and complex sequences, even though theoretically one could 'get away with less'.[15]

In this connection, however, it is instructive to consider a last example, a literary one, from Willem Frederik Hermans' best novel *De Donkere Kamer van Damokles*:

7) Hij ging terug naar zijn stoel, bedacht zich toen weer, draaide het nummer van de informatie en vroeg <u>aan</u> de telefoniste <u>naar</u> het nummer van de firma Bellincoff, Oudezijds Achterburgwal 28, Amsterdam. (Hermans 1981b:70; 23rd printing;4th revision).

'He went back to his chair, thought a bit, dialed the number of Information and asked to the operator for the number of the firm Bellincoff, Oudezijds Achterburgwal 28, Amsterdam...'

Here, native speakers who do not know which the original passage is indicate that what Hermans wrote is 'heavy' and 'overloaded with prepositional phrases'.[16] They prefer the alternatives under 8:

8) a. ...en vroeg   de telefoniste naar het nummer van...
   b. ...en vroeg <u>aan</u> de telefoniste het nummer van...
   c. ...en vroeg   de telefoniste   het nummer van...

On the other hand, since the quote is taken from the <u>fourth revised edition</u> of the book, one can hardly assume that as careful a stylist as Hermans has simply 'made a mistake'.[17] I suggest instead that Hermans is exploiting the relative precision of the prepositions to give a maximally careful and pseudo-objective description (cf. the above remarks on *NRC Handelsblad*) in order to thrust a kind of 'information overload' upon the reader. If there really are 'too many prepositional phrases' (as my consultants say), then the reader will be forced to go through the sentence haltingly rather than smoothly, and will feel <u>disoriented</u>. The <u>reader's</u> disorientation will then perhaps mirror *Osewoudt's* own disorientation at failing to reach the number he has been dialing.

8. Conclusions. We may perhaps summarize our discussion as follows:

[1] Concerning the puzzles mentioned earlier, in section 3, the degree of unanimity in the choice of the aan-form reflects the relative topicality of the entity in question, as may be inferred independently from either (i) the type of NP used to refer to it or (ii) whether or not the entity has already been mentioned in the discourse.

285

[2] The questionnaire data exhibit the same tendendies found in text counts, tendencies which evidence an interaction between (a) the <u>type of NP</u> used to refer to an entity, and (b) the <u>difference between the degree of involvement in the event</u> claimed for the entity by the

'plain' form vs. the aan-form. CENTRAL entities are more 'important' than PERIPHERAL ones, hence more likely to become identified first, and to be referred to with pronouns or at least definite NPs.

[3] Within the 'intermediate' category of definite full NPs (standing between pronouns and indefinite NPs), the more often a referent has been mentioned in the discourse, the more likely it is to be important rather than unimportant (hence CENTRAL), and the more likely it is in consequence to occur in the the 'plain' versus the aan-form.

[4] With this intermediate category, however, the advantages and disadvantages of the 'plain' form may be played off against the advantages and disadvantages of the aan-form. The aan-form, clearly delimiting and role-marking the noun phrase referring to the MID participant (non-polar; neither 'subject' nor 'direct object'), may be used when it is not strictly necessary, as in the examples from *NRC Handelsblad*, to communicate greater precision and thereby greater formality. This very same aura of objectivity and precision may, however, be exploited for 'stylistic' purposes, as in the example from Hermans.

[5] The present paper complements Kirsner (1986), which discusses consultants' reactions to isolated sentences where use of the aan-form forced an overly literal interpretation of the verb[18]. Here, the very same oppositions between (i) CENTRAL vs. PERIPHERAL involvement and (ii) relative vs. "absolute" claims of MID CONTROL lead to a favoring of different kinds of NPs in the two different forms and to the choice of the aan-form for its 'stylistic' effects.

NOTES

[1] The data discussed in this paper were collected while the author was a Visiting Scholar at the Netherlands Institute for Advanced Study in the Humanities and Social Sciences at Wassenaar. The additional support of a Fulbright Fellowship, a Visitor's Fellowship from the Dutch Organization for Pure Research (ZWO-Bezoekersbeurs B-130), and Grant 2964 from the UCLA Academic Senate is here gratefully acknowledged.

[2] See number [5] under Conclusions, below.

[3] The ultimate purpose of the experiment is to better understand the distribution of the aan-form and the 'plain' form with respect to messages, in order to explain why the two forms occur where they do and do not occur where they do not. Ultimately, this entails

determining whether or not either or both forms can be considered signals of meanings, what those meanings are, and whether and how the meanings might be organized into a larger grammatical system. For the concept of grammatical system assumed here, cf. Garci 1975, Kirsner 1979b.

[4] As may be inferred from the numbers, not all consultants were able to follow all the instructions for all the items on the questionnaire. Uninterpretable results were discarded. Note that in this particular example, we present (but cannot discuss here) data on the relative acceptability of pre-posed and post-posed aan-phrases. These ratings were the form in which the data were originally obtained See further footnote 13, below.

[5] For discussion, see Kirsner, Verhagen, Willemsen 1985.

[6] See Kirsner (1979a: 363) for additional implications of the contrast between proper and common noun.

[7] The novels were: Hermans 1981b, Mulisch 1975, Minco 1983, and Reve 1970. Only sentences in which all three participants were referred to with NPs were counted. (Object clauses, for example, were excluded from the count.) Various non-parametric statistics (e.g Kendall's rank-order correlation coefficient) show that the monotonic increase in the relative frequency of the aan-form with decreasing specificity of the referent of the noun phrase is significant at the .001 level.

[8] Strictly speaking, the comparison here can only be suggestive because the sentence from Reve contained an object clause rather than an overt direct object NP (as in *Je kunt het beter (aan) je dokter vragen* 'You can it better (to) your doctor ask = You'd better ask your doctor'). Nevertheless, we might expect a correlation between the behavior of 'indirect object NPs' in overt 3-participant sentences and in sentences with 2-participant NPs plus an object clause; cf. Garci (1975:90).

[9] Compare the studies of the influence of 'contextual motivation' on the form of the English 'indirect object' in Smyth, Prideaux, and Hogan 1979 and also Bock and Irwin 1980.

[10] The odds ratio = $(15/7)/(4/7) = 3.75$; the probability that the aan-form and the 'plain' form distribute the same with respect to prior mention is less than .05 (Mann Whitney U test, adjusted for ties). Because our theory predicted the direction of the difference between the two groups (namely that the plain forms would show a greater number of prior mentions than the aan forms), we computed the one-tailed p as .043. In addition, the Tau b statistic (Nie et. al. 1975:227-228) showed a significant association of the aan form with new mention ($p < .05$). Finally, computation of the asymmetric lambda statistic (Nie et. al. (1975:225-226) shows that knowledge of whether or not the referent has been mentioned previously increases one's ability to predict whether or not the aan-form will be used by 21%.

[11] The odds ratio (Reynolds 1977:20-25) is $(12/20)/(6/25) = 2.5$, indicating that aan is favored more than twice as much in initial mention of RSV as in later mention. Both the Mann Whitney test and the Tau b

statistic indicate that this skewing in the predicted direction (less aan with prior mention) just misses the .05 significance level (p = .057).

[12]These data are a subset of those presented previously. Only those subjects who responded unambiguously to both Part I and Part II were included in the table. It will be noted that two subjects who responded to I did not respond to II and that one subject who responded to II did not respond to I.

[13]Note that the task given consultants for set 1 was different than that for 2 and 3. However, since all 29 respondents ranked the 'plain' form as 1, we may interpret this result as equivalent to total rejection of the aan-form.

[14]I owe this hypothesis to Tineke Oosterhaven.

[15]It is at least suggestive that in an exploratory count of the 33 sentences in Table 3, column 3 and in Table 4 (where the NP referring to the 'indirect object' contained a definite determiner and a common noun), sentences with the aan-form were, on the average, two word-lengths longer than sentences containing the plain form. If the two forms of the traditional 'indirect object' were simply 'transforms' of one another, sentences with the aan-form should be only one word-length longer than sentences with the 'plain' form (because of the addition of aan).

[16]Thus far, I have interviewed eight native speakers, including one winner of the Nijhoff prize for translations into Dutch and one Professor of Dutch and Comparative Literature. All eight condemn what Hermans actually wrote and prefer at least one of the alternatives. Note also Van Weeren's claim (1977:83) that a sentence such as Hij vroeg aan mij naar de weq is ungrammatical.

[17]Compare Janssen 1980, especially p.77 on Hermans as an author 'seeking perfection,' and also Janssen (1976:56,61) on the stylistic precision associated with *De Donkere Kamer van Damokles*. See further Balk-Smit Duyzentkunst (1985: 33,35-36) on both the 'objective, 'neutral' and almost 'formal' character of Hermans' style and the identification that the reader makes between the narrator and the main character.

[18]Cf. Kirsner, Verhagen, and Willemsen 1985 for discussion of such pairs as Deze vondsten vertellen archeologen een interessant verhaal 'These relics tell archeologists an interesting story' versus Deze vondsten vertellen een interessant verhaal aan archeologen 'These relics tell an interesting story to archeologists,' in which vertellen is said to be taken more literally, e.g. as 'narrate.'

BIBLIOGRAPHY

Data sources:

Campert, Remco 1984. *Hoe ik Mijn Verjaardag Vierde*. Amsterdam: De Bezige Bij.

Hermans, Willem Frederik 1981a. *De Donkere Kamer van Damokles*. Amsterdam: G. A. van Oorschot

Hermans, Willem Frederik 1981b. *Uit Talloos Veel Miljoenen*. Amsterdam: De Bezige Bij.

Minco, Marga 1983. *De Val*. Amsterdam: Bert Bakker

Mulisch, Harry 1975. *Twee Vrouwen*. Amsterdam: De Bezige Bij.

Reve, Gerard 1970. *De Ondergang van de Familie Boslowitz. Werther Nieland*. Amsterdam: G. A. van Oorschot.

Schmidt, Annie M. G. 1984. *Pluk van de Petteflet*. Amsterdam: Em. Querido's Uitgeverij B.V.

References:

Balk-Smit Duyzentkunst, Frieda 1985. 'De Stijl van Willem Frederik Hermans.' *BZZLLETIN* 126: W. F. Hermans, 33-38.

Bock, J. K. and D. E. Irwin 1980. 'Syntactic Effects of Information Availability in Sentence Production.' *Journal of Verbal Learninq and Verbal Behavior* 19, 467-484.

Garci , E. C. 1975. *The Role of Theory in Linguistic Analysis: The Spanish Pronoun System*. Amsterdam: North-Holland.

Janssen, Frans A. 1976. *Over De Donkere Kamer van Damokles van Willem Frederik Hermans*. Amsterdam: Wetenschappelijke Uitgeverij b.v.Janssen, Frans A. 1980. "Varianten in Orde en Chaos: Over de Varianten in de Tiende Druk van *De Donkere Kamer van Damokles*', in F. Janssen *Bedriegers en Bedrogenen: Opstellen over het Werk van Willem Frederik Hermans*. Amsterdam: De Bezige Bij 1980, 55-78.

Kirsner, Robert S. 1979a. 'Deixis in Discourse: An Exploratory Quantitative Study of the Modern Dutch Demonstrative Adjectives,' in T. Givon, ed., *Syntax and Semantics*. Volume 12, *Discourse and Syntax*. New York: Academic Press, 355-375.

Kirsner, Robert S. 1979b. *The Problem of Presentative Sentences in Modern Dutch*. Amsterdam: North-Holland.

Kirsner, Robert S., Arie Verhagen and Mariette Willemsen. 1985. 'Over PP's, Transitiviteit en het zgn. Indirekt Objekt.' *Spektator* 14 ,341-47

Kirsner, Robert S. 1986. 'On Being Empirical with Indirect Objects: The Subleties of aan,' in J. Snapper and J. van Oosten, eds., *Papers from the Colloquium on Dutch Linquistics. Berkely, California, November 9, 1986*. Berkley: Dutch Studies Program.

Nie, Norman H. et. al. 1975. *SPSS: Statistical Package for the Social Sciences*. New York: McGraw Hill.

Reynolds, H. T. 1977. *Analysis of Nominal Data: Quantitative Applications in the Social Sciences 7*. Beverly Hills: Sage Publications.

Siegel, Sidney 1956. *Nonparametric Statistics for the Behavioral Sciences*. New York: McGraw-Hill.

Smyth, R.H., G. D. Prideaux, and J. T. Hogan 1979. 'The Effect of Context on Dative Position.' *Lingua* 47, 27-42.

Weeren, Jan van 1977. *Interferenz und Valenz. Zum Problem der "falschen Freunde" für niederländischen Germanistik studenten.* Leiden University dissertation.

WORD ORDER IN THE DUTCH INNER FIELD

Jeanne van Oosten
University of California, Berkeley

The current wisdom concerning the order of elements in the inner field of Dutch sentences (the part after the finite verb and before any infinitives and past participles), is that the most important rule determining the order is informational, that of news value: the newest, most important informational element occurs farther back in the sentence. For example, the Algemene Nederlandse Spraakkunst (ANS) says (1984:913):

In een groot aantal zinnen worden de informatief minder belangrijke elementen voor de elementen met een grotere informatieve waarde geplaatst.

Sentences in which this is the case are said to follow the "left-right principle": what is informationally less important comes before what is informationally more important.

The idea of information value and that the most important elements should come towards the end of a sentence were given prominence by the Prague School with their "Functional Sentence Perspective" (Firbas, 1964; Danes, 1974), by Halliday (1967) with his discussions of theme and rheme in a functional approach to language, and more recently by the Functional Grammarians headed by Simon Dik (1978, 1980, 1983; also Bolkestein, De Groot, and Mackenzie, 1985) in The Netherlands, among many others.

The idea of information value has thus proven its worth through its durability and its popularity. Nevertheless, I would take issue with the claim that it is information value alone, or even primarily, that determines the order of elements in the Dutch inner field. Certainly information value plays a role in the final ordering of elements in the inner field, but I will argue that there is a canonical, or standard, neutral or unmarked, ordering of elements in the Dutch inner field, and that in order to see what that canonical ordering is, one should distinguish between two separate ordering systems which in the resultant sentence mesh together: first, the nominal arguments, whose order is fixed in something which closely follows a stereotyped information gradient from informationally less important to informationally more important, and secondly, the non-nominal modifiers, mostly, but not exclusively, adverbials, which are bound to the contentive verb such that the most closely bound elements are at the end of the sentence.

In the latter point I largely follow Koster (1974), "Het werkwoord als spiegelcentrum," and Van den Hoek (1971), "Woordvolgorde en konstituentenstruktuur," but the former point, and the separating of these two type of elements into two ordering systems, is, I believe, new. It is only by separating these two systems that one can see the regularity of the ordering in the inner field clearly. Within these two systems the ordering is quite stable, especially of course in that of the nominals, but also in that of the non-nominals, except for variation made possible by special thematic and rhematic positions in the inner field itself. A third, minor, system, that of sentence adverbs, also interacts with these two major systems.

The inner field in a Dutch sentence is

- in a main clause, everything between the finite verb in second position and the non-finite verbs at the end of the clause;

- in a subordinate clause, everything between the conjunction and the verbs at the end of the clause;

- in an infinitive phrase, everything in the phrase before the infinitive and other non-finite verbs at the end of the phrase;

- in a participial phrase, everything in the phrase before the participle at the end of the phrase.

In these four contexts, the word order is the same (cf. Koster, 1974). In main clauses, the inner field is bound by verbs -- the poles, the finite verb on the left -- the first pole -- and infinitives and past participles, if any -- the second pole -- on the right, which in their turn are bounded respectively by a single element in first position -- the prefield -- and an optional number of elements in the end field, after any infinitives and past participles. In subordinate clauses and infinitive and participial phrase there is no prefield, but an end field is possible in all except participial phrases.

I am certainly not the first to suggest that the elements in the inner field have a canonical order. Van den Berg (1949), for example, speaks of a "neutral order," which can, however, be altered by "expressively" placing an element farther to the right than it goes in the neutral order. The "expressive order" is, of course, the one mediated by considerations of information value, but on a canonically-ordered foundation. An example:

1a. De kinderen gaan morgen (1) bij goed weer (2) met hun allen (3) op de fiets (4) naar Scheveningen (5).

b. De kinderen gaan morgen (1) bij goed weer (2) op de fiets (4) met hun allen (3) naar Scheveningen (5).

c. De kinderen gaan morgen (1) met hun allen (3) bij goed weer (2) op de fiets (4) naar Scheveningen (5).

Sentence 1a gives the neutral order, according to Van den Berg (adverbials of time, condition, accompaniment, manner, direction), with all adverbial elements stressed equally. In 1b, the adverbial of accompaniment *met hun allen* is moved farther to the right, with the result that it receives more emphasis. In 1c, the adverbial of accompaniment met hun allen finds itself farther to the left, with the result that *bij goed weer* receives expressive emphasis, according to Van den Berg. We will discuss such movement possibilities further below.

More recently, De Schutter & Van Hauwermeiren (1983) take another point of view. Although they state that the nominal constituents have a fixed order (Subject - Indirect Object - Direct Object - Prepositional Object or "voorzetselvoorwerp"), they hold that the adverbials are free in their ordering (1983:192), and offer the following as one of many examples (1983:194):

2a. Toch hebben in 1945 de Amerikanen in Hiroshima nog een atoombom afgegooid.

b. Toch hebben de Amerikanen in 1945 in Hiroshima nog een atoombom afgegooid.

c. Toch hebben in Hiroshima de Amerikanen in 1945 nog een atoombom afgegooid.

d. Toch hebben in 1945 in Hiroshima de Amerikanen nog een atoombom afgegooid.

These orders, too, are all explicable under the assumption of a canonical order for non-nominals as well as for nominals, as we will see below.

The mutual canonical ordering of the nominals in a sentence is fixed, as De Schutter and Van Hauwermeiren suggest. What alters the canonical order of the non-nominals in a sentence, among which I include the prepositional object, is the information value of the sentence, which is indicated by focal or contrastive stress. A heuristic for finding the canonical ordering of these elements, then, is to find sentences without stress on the inner field but rather on the element in one of the poles or the prefield or end field, and with a consistently falling intonation pattern on the inner field itself. By this test, all the sentences in 2 seem to have a fairly neutral order except 2c and there is nothing much to choose between them. By contrast, there are many other logically possible orderings of the elements in the inner field of 2, but most sound quite marked. Some possibilities:

3a. Toch hebben de Amerikanen in Hiroshima in 1945 nog een atoombom afgegooid.

b. Toch hebben in 1945 nog de Amerikanen in Hiroshima een atoombom afgegooid.

c. Toch hebben de Amerikanen in Hiroshima nog een atoombomb in 1945 afgegooid.

d. Toch hebben de Amerikanen in Hiroshima nog in 1945 een atoombom afgegooid.

What is the canonical ordering? For the nouns, it is, as mentioned, Subject - Indirect Object - Direct Object. I ignore here the pronouns, for which the canonical order seems to be subject - direct object - indirect object. For the non-nominals, the general order is:

circumstantial adverbials
Peripheral participants
sentence-level model and "small" adverbials
"inherent" completion of the verb

These terms will be explained as we go along.

Among the circumstantial adverbials, the order seems to be as follows:

time when
frequency
condition
duration
manner - instrument/means - accompaniment - concomitance - reason
place

Again, I ignore the proforms *hier, toen,* etc. As with the pronouns, the order seems to be the opposite from the order in the case of full forms. An attested example is found in 4, where place precedes time while both are proforms:

4. Ze hebben *daar toen* een oude man overvallen en vermoord.

Examples of the types of circumstantial adverbials on the list above are found in 5 to 13.

5. Time when: Hij moest *om tien uur* een pilletje slikken.

6. Frequency: Hij moest gisteren *om de twee uur* een pilletje slikken.

7. Condition: We zullen iedere morgen *bij goed weer* een paar uurtjes met de hond gaan wandelen.

8. Duration: Ze wil vanaf morgen om de twee uur *vijftien minuten* proberen te mediteren.

9. Manner: Ik moest gisteren *heel hard* lachen.

10. Instrument: Wil jij dat hek morgen zomaar *met je handen* afbreken?

11. Means: Ze hebben hem gisteren eindelijk *met dreigementen* weten te overtuigen om mee te doen.

12. Accompaniment and Concomitance: Zo liepen *samen onder veel gelach* de kamer uit.

13. Reason and Place: Hij is gisteren *wegens moord in de binnenstad* door de politie gearresteerd.

I am not sure of the mutual ordering, if any, of the adverbials in the middle of the list of circumstantials above. It may be that these do not have a mutual canonical ordering, also because it is very rare for several of these to occur in a single actually-attested sentence. The circumstantial adverbials are so-called because they give details about the event which cannot essentially change the nature of the event itself. These are elements on the periphery of the clause, in Foley and Van Valin's (1984) terms; Dik (1980:9) calls these satellites -- through the elements in the second category are satellites (and peripheral) also. Both terms point to the general consensus that this type of adverbial is less closely bound up with the verb than others, which we shall be considering below.

The second category, that of the peripheral participants, stands between the circumstantials and the inherent completions of the verb as far as the closeness of the bond between them and the verb is concerned. Peripheral participants are expressed inadverbials such as those listed below,

agent door-phrase
beneficiary (voor)
indirect object with aan
on-primary participant in a commercial event

and no doubt others. An example of an agent door-phase is given in 13; examples of the other three types of peripheral participants are given in 14 to 16:

14. Ik heb vorige week met Opa *voor Jantje* een vlieger gemaakt.

15. Ze wil voor haar zoon aan haar schoondochter een kookboek geven.

16a. We hebben het boek voor een gulden gekocht.

b. We zouden tien jaar geleden voor zo'n huis maar een ton hebben hoeven te betalen.

The mutual ordering of elements in the third category is still largely mysterious to me. It contains sentence-level modal adverbs and particles, sentence-level negation particles such as *niet* or *nooit*, the indefinite locatives *ergens, nergens, overal*, and "small" adverbs like *al, nog, gelijk*. Examples are nog in 2, *toch* and *niet* in 24 and snel in 26.

As for the last type of non-nominal in the inner field, the so-called inherent completions, the different types of inherent completions are as follows:

>   predicate adjective or noun
>   prepositional object (voozetselvoorwerp)
>   other necessary completion of verb, including separable
>   prefixes

Examples are given in 17 to 19:

17a. Hij is *dokter*.

  b. Hij is *zoveel ouder dan zij*.

18a. Ik legde het telefoonboek *naast de telefoon*.

  b. We wachten *op nieuws*.

  c. Ze hebben de hele dag niet *op de kinderen gelet*.

  d. We hadden niet *op ons horloge* gekeken.

19a. Ik heb nog het een en ander *nodig*.

  b. Hij heeft een flinke verkoudheid *te pakken* gekregen.

  c. Hij werd door andere schepen begroet, die er speciaal voor *uit de koers* gingen.

  d. Kun je dat hele stuk helemaal *uit je hoofd* spelen?

Adverbs of direction are generally prepositional objects rather than some kind of circumstantial. This explains why they are usually found towards the end of the sentence. Sentence 18a is an example. This point of view is also consonant with the fact that the auxiliary in the case of intransitive sentences is different: 20a sounds incomplete in a way that 20b does not.

20a. We zijn gelopen.

  b. We hebben gelopen.

Stranded prepositions are most frequently stranded out of a prepositional object, and come after an adjective or noun or before other completions of the verb, as shown in 19c and in 21 to 23:

21a. Ze kreeg 't er benauwd *van*.

b. Ze hebben het er erg druk *mee*.

22a. Dear heb je groot gelijk *in*.

b. Ik heb er honger *van* gekregen.

23a. Hij kwam er gisteren toch *mee* thuis?

b. Ik ben het er niet *mee* eens.

The nouns are sprinkled among these adverbials, in a fixed order of Subject followed by Indirect Object followed by Direct Object. This order reflects what is typically the news value of these elements, but no matter what the facts concerning news value are in a given sentence, this order has to be preserved. The placement especially of the direct object, however, is heavily mediated by considerations of news value: definite direct objects can occur anywhere from after the pronouns and before the locative proforms *er, hier, daar,* to the position of the sentence-level modal adverbials, the third major category of non-nominals given above. Examples are given in 24:

24a. Je had het boek hier laatst toch niet bij neergelegd?

b. Je had hier het boek laatst toch niet bij neergelegd?

c. Je had hier laatst het boek toch niet bij neergelegd?

d. ??Je had hier laatst toch het boek niet bij neergelegd?

e. ??Je had hier laatst toch niet het boek bij neergelegd?

Indefinite direct objects, on the other hand, occur almost exclusively immediately after the category of sentence-level modal adverbials, as in 25:

25a. Je had hier laatst toch geen boek bij neergelegd?

b. *?Je had een boek hier laatst toch niet bij neergelegd?

c. *?Je had hier een boek laatst toch niet bij neergelegd?

d. *?Je had hier laatst een boek toch niet bij neergelegd?

e. *?Je had hier laatst toch een boek niet bij neergelegd?

Specific indefinite direct objects can occur just before the category of sentence-level modal adverbials. The sentence in 26a is an attested example:

26a. Heb je 't geluk dat je *dingen snel* snapt of *snel goede gedachten* kunt formuleren, dan ben je vlugger klaar dan anderen.

b. Heb je 't geluk dat je snel dingen snapt... dan ben je vlugger klaar dan anderen.

c. Heb je 't geluk dat je de dingen snel snapt... dan ben je vlugger klaar dan anderen.

Snel in 26a is one of the "small" adverbs that is found in the category of modal sentence-level adverbials. In the first half of the disjunct, *dingen* is indefinite but specific; compare 26b and 26c. In the second half of the disjunct, however, *goede gedachten* is non-specific and so comes after snel. If it came before, it too would be interpreted as specific.

ANS (p. 993) suggests that circumstantials can be considered "de spilplaats" or the pivot of a sentence with the informationally less important elements before it and the informationally more important elements after it. I would rather suggest that it is this modal sentence-level category which operates as "spilplaats" in the sentence, especially because of its importance in direct object placement.

The prefield (before the first pole) and the end field are positions par excellence to put thematic and rhematic elements (thematic in the prefield and rhematic in the end field, except under emphatic stress, in which case the positions may be reversed -- see, for example, De Schutter 1985:152). However, the inner field itself has secondary thematic and rhematic positions. The thematic position, where an informationally less important element can be put for emphasis or contrast, is found at the very beginning of the inner field, after the proforms. The rhematic position, where the element that holds the informational peak can be placed, is found near the end of the inner field, in the position of an indefinite direct object or right before or after that position (I have not yet figured out when it is better to place the rhematic element before and when it is better to place the rhematic element after the indefinite direct object). Even the position of circumstantials like place and time can thus be altered, as was shown in 2c, where *in Hiroshima* is put in the thematic position at the front of the inner field, so that it (place) ends up before the time reference. Similarly, one could have a sentence like 27:

27. Toch hebben de Amerikanen in Hiroshima (ook) nog in 1945 een atoombom afgegooid.

We can now add sentence adverbs to the soup: they generally come at the beginning of the inner field (well into the thematic section), first or second after the pronouns. Attested examples are in 28:

28a. Ik ben waarachtig wel wat van hem gewend.

b. Hij voelde in feite weinig voor een discussie met de commissaris.

A made-up example is found in 29:

29a. Hij moet de hond *kennelijk* morgen bij goed weer voor een uurtje uitlaten.

b. Hij moet hem *kennelijk* morgen bij goed weer voor een uurtje uitlaten.

c. Hij moet hem morgen *kennelijk* bij goed weer voor een uurtje uitlaten.

d. Hij moet bij goed weer *kennelijk* morgen de hond voor een uurtje uitlaten.

e. ?Hij moet morgen de hond bij goed weer *kennelijk* voor een uurtje uitlaten.

f. *?Hij moet morgen de hond bij goed weer voor een uurtje *kennelijk* uitlaten.

The picture that results is somewhat complex: two major ordering systems, plus a minor one, that must mesh in a certain way, and a thematic and rhematic position in the inner field. In other words, a basically canonical ordering with modifications for the sake of considerations of news value. This while by far the majority of clauses have no more than three elements in the inner field. Isn't it preferable just to say that word order in the inner field is free and determined solely by information value, as so many have said, and have done with it? I obviously don't think so. In the first place, this would leave no way of explaining the order of elements in sentences with more than three elements in the inner field unless that were entirely free, which it isn't. Basically, using just the concept of news value, one can identify no more than three elements: an informationally least important constituent, a pivot or "spilplaats," and an informationally most important constituent. This leaves sentences with more than three constituents in the inner field, while uncommon, still in need of an explanation. De Schutter (1985:145f.) suggests that "sentences with quite a lot of information incorporated in them [i.e. with many adverbials] do not display a clear theme/rheme distinction, and so do not easily offer the conditions for splitting the constituents according to their pragmatic values." He makes this observation based on the fact that the more PP's there are in a sentence, the less is the tendency to put one or more of them into the end field. This type of sentence also needs to be described.

In the second place, there are several exceptions to the thesis that informationally most prominent elements come at the end of the inner field. In order to make this theory work, ANS makes clear that there are several notable exceptions. Two are of interest to us here. First of all, of course, the verbs in the poles are an exception. Their order is fixed no matter what their informational value is. Furthermore, inherent completions of the verb must be seen as exceptions, according to ANS (1984:914). This is an especially unfortunate exception inasmuch as the position of inherent completions of the verb is precisely the best position for the rhematic element. It is not the case, however, that inherent completions are the rhematic element an overwhelming proportion of the time, through certainly prepositional objects, in particular, are quite likely to be the information peak. That the prepositional object also often is not rhematic is seen by the fact that it is often pronominalized: old information, theme, par excellence. As I mentioned above, a stranded preposition is most often the residue of a prepositional object. With the basically canonical ordering in the Dutch inner field, modified for considerations of news value, the way the Dutch language has developed to get around the problem of how to harmonize the conflicting tendencies of thematicity and canonicity, is ingenious: when the prepositional object, or in fact any other object of a preposition, is pronominalized, the position of the pronoun is far to the front of the inner field (or even in the prefield) as a concession to its thematic status, while the preposition remains at the end of the inner field as a concession to its canonical position.

As supporting evidence for the argument that non-nominals are ordered canonically, we may note that the canonical ordering of modifiers in the Dutch inner field is generally, though not totally, the opposite of the ordering of modifiers in English. Thus an acceptable sentence in English is 30.

30. That piece was played from memory (1) by everybody except my sister (2) at her recital (3) yesterday (4).

while the corresponding Dutch sentence is 31:

31. Dat stuk is gisteren (4) op het recital (3) door iedereen behalve mijn zus (2) uit het hoofd (1) gespeeld.

It would be absurb to suppose that this difference is attributable to differences in thematicity in English and Dutch: rather, it must be differences in canonicity that account for it. The difference between English order and Dutch order is not random: rather, the one is basically the mirror image of the other, at least as far as the adverbials and inherent completions of the verbs are concerned. The fact that the adverbials bound most closely to the verb are found at the end of the inner field, has led many linguists, notably Koster (1974, 1975), to conclude that Dutch is basically on OV language, while English is basically a VO language. Certainly this is evidence in favor of this view. However, nouns are generally also considered to bind to their predicates, and in this respect Dutch and English are identical. It would seem then that, discretion being the better part of valor, it would be more judicious to conclude that Dutch has both OV and VO characteristics, perhaps leaning more heavily towards the OV end of the spectrum, though in an earlier paper (Van Oosten, 1975) I have shown that if one bases oneself on Greenberg's (1966) substantive word order universals, Dutch leans more heavily towards the VO side.

BIBLIOGRAPHY

ANS: Algemene Nederlandse Spraakkunst, ed. by G. Geerts, W. Haeseryn, J. de Rooij, and M.C. van den Toorn. Groningen: Wolters-Noordhoff; Leuven: Wolters, 1984.

Berg, B. van den. De zinsbouw in het Nederlands. *Nieuwe Taalgids.* 42.120-124, 1949.

Bolkestein, A.M., C. de Groot and J.L. Mackenzie, eds. *Syntax and Pragmatics in Functional Grammar.* Dordrecht: Foris (Functional Grammar Series #1), 1985.

Danes, Frantisek, ed. *Papers on Functional Sentence Perspective.* The Hague: Mouton (Janua Linguarum, Series Minor, 147), 1974.

Dik, C. *Functional Grammar.* Amsterdam: North-Holland (North-Holland Linguistic Series #37), 1978 (Third printing, 1981, Dordrecht: Foris).

----------. *Studies in Functional Grammar.* London: Academic Press, 1980.

----------. *Advances in Functional Grammar.* Dordrecht: Foris. 1983.

Firbas, Jan. *On Defining the Theme in Functional Sentence Analysis.* Travaux Linguistiques de Prague. 1.267-280, 1964.

Foley, William A. and Robert D. Van Valin Jr. *Functional Syntax and Universal Grammar.* Cambridge: Cambridge University Press, 1984.

Halliday, M.A.K. *Notes on Transitivity and Theme in English*, part 2. Journal of Linguistics. 3.199-244, 1967.

Hoek, Th. van den. Woordvolgorde en konstituentenstruktuur. *Spektator.* 1:125-135, 1972.

Koster, Jan. Het werkwoord als spiegelcentrum. *Spektator.* 3.8.601-618, 1974.

----------. Dutch as an SOV Language. *Linguistic Analysis.* 1.2.111-136, 1975.

Oosten, Jeanne van. Word Order in Dutch: *The Position of the Verb in Underlying Structure.* Ms., University of California, Berkeley, 1975.

----------. *The Nature of Subjects, Topics and agents: A cognitive Explanation.* Bloomington, Indiana: Indiana University Linguistics Club, 1986.

Schutter, Georges de. 1985. *Pragmatic and Syntactic Aspects of Word Order in Dutch.* In Bolkestein, De Groot, and Mackenzie, 137-154, 1985.

---------- and P. van Hauwermeiren. *De structuur van het Nederlands.* Taalbeschouwelijke grammatica. Malle: De Sikkel, 1983.

DUTCH ON THE EDGE THE LEXICOGRAPHICAL TREATMENT OF PERIPHERAL VOCABULARY

Roland Willemyns
Free University, Brussels

1985 has been an unusually prolific year for Dutch lexicography and all the credit is due to the Van Dale publishing company. Not only have they published bilingual dictionaries (E-D, F-D, G-D, D-F; D-E and D-G are forthcoming) but moreover an eleventh edition of the so-called *Grote Van Dale* (3 volumes) and on top of that the "contemporary Van Dale" (*Woordenboek van hedendaags Nederlands*, 1 volume). This mounts up to almost one yard of new lexicographical material, which is unusual enough to be widely mentioned and reviewed. Since this has already been done, time may have come to raise a few questions which are usually omited. One of them is the question of how so-called peripheral vocabulary is treated, which is the more interesting since a good many standardization issues come with it.

Large national dictionaries are supposed to present the vocabulary of the standard language at the not too informal, not too formal style level, plus usually some bonuses. These bonuses may comprise contemporary innovations, some jargon, some dialect words, some vulgar items and so on, but usually also some peripheral vocabulary, i.e. lexical items usually not considered to be part of the standard language yet more or less widely used in geographically determined areas where geographical dialects and a slightly diversing type of standard language are used. Peripheral vocabulary becomes the more interesting for the editor, the user and - lest we forget - the publisher, if these regions are situated outside the main country. Examples may be the Swiss or Austrian words not frequently used in German, Swiss, Walloon or in Quebec words hardly known in France, or Flemish words hardly occuring in the Netherlands. The latter case will be the main focus of this paper, while the others will be treated when looking for justifiable generalizations or as points of comparison as far as lexicographical practice is concerned. The main questions to be raised are:

1. What is peripheral Dutch?

2. How do modern dictionaries - and the HVD[1] in particular - treat peripheral vocabulary?

3. How should peripheral vocabulary be treated in Dutch dictionaries?

1. In an earlier paper (Willemyns 1985) I advocated the distinction between internal and external peripheral 'realizations' of the language. The centre of gravity of language standardization of Dutch is the so-called *Randstad* (the big cities in the West of the Netherlands). As compared to this centre all other parts of the language territory are to be considered

peripheral. The *internal periphery* then consists of the remaining territory within the Netherlands (e.g. Zeeland or Drenthe), the term *external periphery* referring to the Dutchspeaking territory outside the Netherlands, i.e. Flanders. A common characteristic of all peripheral territories is that language usage to a certain extent diverges from what it is in the centre, both on a geographical (e.g. Vienna, Zurich vs. Frankfurt, Berlin) and on a standard language level (the standard German of Austria differs from that of the Federal Republic).

The ANS defines Standard Dutch as the code which may be used in so-called secondary relations throughout the language territory, i.e. not linked to a special style, a particular region or a specific group of speakers.[2]

In other words Standard Language is unmarked, all other codes of the language being marked in one way or another. This paper will be concerned with the lexical elements of the codes used in a particular region. To all lexicographers the way in which to treat such lexical items is highly problematic since it implies

- determining the lexical norm of the standard language

- deciding on which non-standard lexical items will be nevertheless listed

- deciding on how these items are to be labeled

- trying to maintain a certain level of consistency.

The basic problem is that "there is no clear way of establishing a normative framework enabling the lexicographer to differentiate between items to be retained and items to be rejected" (Gendron 1983, 16),[3] whereas Macauly points out that "the basic problem in attempting to define a standard language is that the evidence lies at the intersection of two distinct areas of investigation. The first is the description of the language including all its varieties. The second is the study of the use of each variety in a speech community, to discover the norms of speech for that community, including the significance of the use of a particular variety in a specific situation" (Macauly 1973, 1331).

2. In order to find out to what extent the editors of the HVD have succeeded in coping with these problems I took a random sample from the *Zuidnederlands Woordenboek* (De Clerck 1981; i.e. the first and the last word of every tenth page) and examined how these words were treated in the HVD. It appears that :

    a.   82 words (= 60.7 % are not mentioned at all and consequently not considered to be part of the standard language.

    Examples: aanbelangen   beternis
                    effenaf   heenwedstrijd

	magistratuur	overjaars
	postman	stapelhuis
	uurrooster	zakencijfer

b. 31 words (= 23 %) are labeled AZN (= Algemeen Zuidnederlands; General Southern Dutch). The key to the abbreviations explains AZN- words as lexical elements "in use in the whole of the Southern territory, yet replaced by another variant in Standard Dutch."[4]

Examples: beenhouwer   betrachten
            schouw   kuisvrouw
            stofvod   vaststelling

c. 19 words (= 14 %) are mentioned without any label at all and are therefore considered to be part of Standard Dutch.

Examples: bedrijvig   eigenste
            living   part
            pensionaat   uurwerk (= horloge)
            verwikkeling verzwinden

d. 3 words are labeled in an alternative way, i.e. *regenscherm* and *vermits* as written language and *schouwen* als archaic.

This small test proves what was to be expected, i.e. that there is no consistency in the way peripheral vocabulary is treated (it should be stressed that De Clerck considers all the words mentioned in his dictionary to be peripheral).[5]

The remarkable thing, however, is that HVD does not mention any criteria at all as to the way peripheral vocabulary is or should be treated. No hint is to be found as to how the peripheral corpus was assembled nor on what grounds particular items were listed, rejected or labeled. This is certainly not meant to be a reproach since indeed lexicographers have very little to rely on. They may be expected, though, to at least establish some kind of theory or to establish some criteria.

3. Since I am neither a lexicographer nor a lexicologist I don't intend to prescribe to them the rules of their trade. Yet I can try to enter into a few matters the lexicographers should take into consideration, viz. (the mechanisms of) language standardization, norms, codification and style levels.

The paramount condition is to establish the style level (or register) one intends to describe. All dictionaries obviously list words from different style levels, yet it is absolutely vital that the unmarked level (or code, or register) be clearly defined since in a general way regional interference tends to increase dramatically the more the language shifts from H(igh) into the direction of L(ow). According to the HVD 4 style levels are distinguished :

formal (e.g. <u>wateren</u>)
unmarked (e.g. <u>plassen</u>)
informal (e.g. <u>pissen</u>)
vulgar (e.g. <u>zeiken</u>)

with the specific indication that the "casual written, and spoken language" represents the unmarked level. Simple and satisfactory as this may seem at first yet it is to be considered vague and unpractical. Not only is there the important and persistent difference between spoken and written language (and as a matter of fact most entries will be selected from written material) but moreover the social stratification of the language is completely overlooked. Let me stick to just one simple consideration : isn't the "casual" written and spoken language of the upper classes (or higher educational strata) supposed to be quite different from the equal "casual" written and spoken language of the lower classes (or lower educational strata)? Regional stratification left out as well and yet viewed from the centre, the casual language usage of the periphery (both internal and external) may be considered to display considerably more regional interference. Items considered to be marked in the centre may perfectly well be unmarked in the periphery (one single example : *vermits* is positively formal written language in the *center* yet casual spoken language in the South). From these and other considerations it follows that the unmarked level, the basis of all entries, should be defined as accurately as possible, more accurately anyway than is the case in the HVD (or any comparable dictionary for that matter). Proceeding this way one should bear in mind for whom the dictionary is intended, taking into consideration the wise words of Ernst Schüle saying : "A sociolinguistically paramount question is 'who am I addressing? Who is concerned if I adopt one word or another ?"[6]

4. Let us come now to the practical question of how peripheral vocabulary is to be treated in general Dutch dictionaries.

4.1. A possible standpoint may be that peripheral vocabulary is not to be considered at all in dictionaries of the Van Dale type. This would certainly save us a lot of trouble and solve a good many problems. Yet not only the lexicographer intending to do so would have to face the discontentment of his publisher but also such an attitude could never be justified from a scientific point of view. Since the Dutch language (as any language for that matter) is to be considered a diasystem (Goossens 1968) all of its components should theoretically be taken into consideration. Yet this is not a very practical procedure either, and therefore lexicographers mostly go for an intermediate solution leaving room for some peripheral items. The amount of "tolerance" thus displayed will mainly depend on two factors :

a. the tolerance towards variation and the attitudes towards "deviating" language usage in the language territory in general

b. the practical availability of lexicographic material from peripheral regions.

In both cases the situation in the Dutch language territory is not too bad. The attitudinal aspect may be the most unfavourable : although the Randstad nowadays tends to tolerate and even favour socially based domestic variation (Willemyns 1983) it still usually rejects variation from the periphery (Geerts,no date). On the other hand governmental attitudes in both countries (cf. *Taalunieverdrag*, Willemyns 1984) combined with favourable attitudes of larger parts of the Southern establishment towards the Northern norm (Willemyns 1983) account for a situation more resembling the centralizing policy of France (Al 1981) than the - at least at the lexicological level - more tolerance oriented policy in the German language territory (Beersmans 1981).

As to the second point, the situation should be rather favourable since the publication of De Clerck's *Zuidnederlands Woordenboek* provided us with a wealth of data, be it that they should be used rather cautiously.

4.2. Let us now turn to the practical side of the problem. A thorough study of North-South variation in the lexicon would be very useful to determine the amount of peripheral vocabulary to be incorporated in general dictionaries. Since no such study exists it may be helpful to draw up a list of lexicological subcategories to be taken into account. The following account, and the examples going with it, are intended to give lexicographers an idea of what their theoretical framework should be based on. The fact that some words may overlap or even get a wrong label is rather irrelevant.

1. Institutional terminology, i.e. words designating specific Belgian institutions:

    -   aanhoudingsmandaat (arrestatiebevel; warrant for arrest)
    -   assisenhof (rechtscollege met jury, belast met het vonnissen van zware misdrijven; criminal court)
    -   concordaat (gerechtelijk accoord; legal settlement)
    -   gouverneur (commissaris van de koningin; governor of a province; in G.B. : sheriff of a county)
    -   licentiaat (doctorandus; holder of a degree)
    -   observatiegraad (graad in het M.O.; grade in secondary school)
    -   onderzoeksrechter (rechter van instructie; examining magistrate)
    -   opcentiemen (opcenten; surtax)
    -   procureur (officier van justitie; public prosecutor, D.A.)
    -   regent (leraar met M.O. acte; non graduate holder of a teaching diploma)
    -   rijkswacht (rijkspolitie; constabulary)
    -   schepen (wethouder; alderman)

2. Archaisms, i.e. words having (almost) disappeared in Northern language usage, yet still very common in the South

- ajuin (ui; onion)
- draad (snoer; wire)
- heirkracht (overmacht; force majeur)
- kaak (wang; cheek)
- kleed (jurk; dress)
- kuisen (poetsen; to clean up)
- kwetsen (blesseren; to injure)
- manteljas; coat)
- nagel (spijker; nail)
- ouderling (bejaarde; old person)
- plots, adv. (plotseling; suddenly)
- verwittigen (waarschuwen; to warn)
- wenen (huilen; to cry)
- zetel (fauteuil; armchair)

3. Dialect interference, i.e. words existing in many Flemish dialects and therefore often used in Standard Language in the South

- afzien (pijn lijden; to suffer)
- beenhouwer (slager; butcher)
- doppen (stempelen, werkloos zijn; to be unemployed)
- hesp (ham; ham)
- nonkel (oom; uncle)
- pint (glas bier; glass of beer)
- pladijs (schol; plaice)
- schouw (schoorsteen; chimney)
- stoof (kachel; stove)
- taksplaat (nummerplaat; registration plate, licence number)
- verschieten (schrikken; to (be) startle(d)

4. Loanwords from other languages (mostly French), not used in Holland

- autostrade (autoweg; motorway, freeway)
- chauffage (centrale verwarming; central heating)
- living (woonkamer; living room)
- mazout (stookolie; fuel oil)
- mutualiteit (ziekenfonds; health insurance)
- occasie (tweedehands; second hand)
- parlementair, subst. (parlementslid; M.P.)
- pistolet (broodje; roll)
- praline (bonbon; chocolate)
- quotering (beoordelingscijfer; mark)
- reconversie (omschakeling; conversion)
- solden (koopjes; bargains, sales)
- syndicaat (vakbond; union)

5. Barbarisms (calques, mostly gallicisms)

- dagorde (agenda; agenda)
- droogkuis (stomerij; dry cleaner's)
- eraan houden (er prijs op stellen; to appreciate)
- hernemen (weer opnemen; to take up again)
- ordewoord (wachtwoord; slogan)
- overmaken (toesturen; to forward)
- overste (meerdere; superior)
- rondpunt (verkeersplein, rotonde; round-about, traffic circle)
- voorzien (bepalen, plannen; to stipulate)
- wapendracht (wapenbezit; (illegal) possession of arms)
- zakencijfer (omzetcijfer; annual turnover)
- zetelen (zitting hebben; hold office)

6. Hypercorrections

- bestemmeling (geadresseerde; addressee)
- betoelagen (subsidiëren; to subsidize)
- brieventas (portefeuille; wallet, pocket book)
- duimspijker (punaise; drawing-pin, thumb-tack)
- inkom(entree; entry)
- (kinder)kribbe (creche; day nursery)
- koetswerk (carrosserie; coach-work)
- regenscherm (paraplu; umbrella)
- vaststelling (constatering; to establish a fact)
- wisselstukken (reserveonderdelen; spare parts)
- zitpenning (presentiegeld; attendance fee)

7. Flemish neologisms, not having (yet) made their way North

- blokken (hard studeren; do one's revision, to study intensely)
- brugpensioen (V.U.T.; early retirement pension)
- buizen (zakken; to fail at exams)
- deelregering (deelstaat regering; state government)
- heenwedstrijd (eerste wedstrijd voor een return wedstrijd; first round in a return sports contest)
- kot (studentenkamer, kast; student room, digs)
- kousbroek (panty; tights, (panty) hose)
- langspeelfilm (avondvullende film; feature film)
- medepastoor (kapelaan; curate, chaplain)
- regeringsraad (kabinetsvergadering waar ook de staatssecretarissen aan deelnemen; meeting of the cabinet, including the deputy ministers)

4.3. It is quite obvious that at least some words from possibly all categories should be listed in the dictionary, yet it is equally obvious that no one dictionary comes up with valuable criteria to do so, other than the (relative) frequency of use, a criterion - all agree - that is not only vague and arbitrary, but also hard to define and to use in a general way.

De Clerck, for one, assumes another, no less problematic point of view when stating that since the lexicographer is not a referee, it is the language community itself which ultimately decides on the norm and the amount of tolerance towards deviating items.[7]

Obviously this is only partly the case. Not only will the lexicographer frequently have to decide for himself but moreover it is his job to *interpret* the so-called decisions of the language community. And it should be remembered that the lexicographer is no "neutral observer" but a member of the language community in his own right, a language user involved in linguistic processes of interaction yielding his personal views and attitudes towards the markedness of vocabulary items. The less a linguistic code is codified and standardized, the more the linguist and the lexicographer will have to decide for themselves. It would therefore be wrong to evade their responsibility, hiding behind the language user's back. The listing or rejecting of a word or meaning is ultimately part of the responsability of the interpreting lexicographer who, in order to do so, will have to come up with valid criteria, whether he likes it or not. The process is reciprocal anyway : the community influences the lexicographer who, in his turn influences the community. It is recommendable, therefore, to bear in mind that from a purely grammatical point of view even language use in the centre displays a considerable amount of variation compared to the hypothetical norm, which, anyway, is reproduced "correctly" by only a small portion of the population, be it in the centre or in the periphery. Yet, by a combination of social, economic, political and cultural factors the standard language usage of the central elite gains a *social surplus value* and whereas the deviating standard language use in the centre may profit from this social surplus value, the peripheral may not. This accounts for central variation not being perceived as variation anymore.

Consequently social surplus value is a self confirming phenomenon : the standard language use of the elite constitutes the frame of reference for grammars and dictionaries and in this way gains still more surplus value.

Unmarked dictionary entries are the surplus value ones, unlisted items obviously can claim no surplus value at all whereas marked entries are mortgaged. This clearly indicates the danger of apparently "reproducing" the "decisions" of the so-called speechmaking community. Also, it should be obvious that the position of the lexicographer within the community and the amount of social surplus value of his habitual code considerably influence the way in which he interprets the "signals" of the community.

4.4. Let me finally observe that language stratification plays a part lexicographers often fail to recognize. Relative frequency of peripheral words is a function of stylistic variation. The examples listed above are, to my knowledge, fairly well known all over the Flemish territory. Yet how frequently they are actually used will largely depend on the speaker's intentions. At the utmost level of formality, e.g. in the B.R.T. news broadcasts, they will be systematically avoided but their frequency will increase dramatically the less formal the style is. Whether or not they are *Algemeen Zuidnederlands*, as defined by the HVD, will therefore not only depend on how often they occur but mostly on the register they are supposed to be part of. The fact that the communicative competence of the majority of the population may be rather restricted may certainly obscure the lexicographer's view but should by no means influence his theoretical stand, the more so since the investigation of the standard language level is what he generally has in mind. Let me emphasize therefore that the treatment of peripheral vocabulary in general and of Southern Dutch in particular should be determined by factors which have, as yet, hardly been taken into consideration, viz. relative frequency, level of investigation and description and linguistic interaction. It will be the lexicographers task - and burden - to find ways to explore these fields of research in which obviously a great deal still remains to be done by linguists in general.

5. The actual way to proceed will depend largely on how familiar the lexicographer himself is with the peripheral code that is to provide his entries. If he is informed, he may want to rely on his personal (intuitive) knowledge; if he isn't he should ask for help !

5.1. In the French language territory specialists were requested to draw up a list of Swiss, Walloon, Quebec vocabulary, whose listing in the dictionary they would highly recommend (Schüle 1981, Doppagne 1981, Boulanger 1980). In the German speech community a similar system gives the Austrian and Swiss Duden committees the opportunity to propose the treatment of the peripheral vocabulary of their regions (Fenske 1973 proving that even then there is often a lack of consistency).

Although this way editors obtain a considerable amount of information not all problems meet with a satisfactory solution (Willemyns 1986) and then of course this procedure does not free them nor their collaborators of the urgent need to go into the methodological necessity of clearly establishing their criteria and pointing out the categories of peripheral vocabulary which ought to be represented in the dictionary. The persistant problems they encounter are determined by inherent structural difficulties. To name just a few :

    a.   in peripheral language usage the relationship between standard and non standard variants is considerably different from what it is in the center of gravity (in other words the sociolinguistic criteria determining standard language usage are fundamentally different);

    b.   peripheral language usage is less investigated than language usage in the center and even if satisfactory surveys do exist they may not always be very useful for lexicographical purposes;

    c.   attitudes towards standard language and variation in the periphery are rather particular and ambiguous since various extralinguistic considerations (e.g. language political ones) tend to obscure the attitude and view, even of so-called specialists, in a considerable way;

d. linguistic insecurity, a concomitant feature of peripheral language usage, is often responsible for overstressing the normative value of leading dictionaries.

5.2. I should like to end by formulating some personal considerations which may be helpful to clarify the lexicographer's mind.

Consideration 1: the lexicological material to be investigated has to be drawn from the linguistic production of those Flemings intending to speak Standard Dutch.

Comment: Since Flemings (or any other people for that matter) are not single style speakers, it is obvious that they may not always have this intention. The most practical and useful way to make sure is to refrain from using other than written sources (or equivalent spoken sources such as radio and television news broadcasts, formal interviews, lectures, etc.)

Consideration 2: The only codes yielding useful information are General Standard and Southern Standard, i.e. the codes labeled E and D in Willemyns 1983

Comment: Since any subdivision of the linguistic continuum is theoretical and arbitrary a practical problem may arise not only in drawing the line between E and D but mainly in separating both codes from the following one, the so-called Umgangssprache (C). Yet I think it is very important to take this theoretical stand anyway.

Consideration 3: There is no doubt whatever that non-general lexical items from E must find their place in the dictionary. An equal treatment should be reserved to some items from D; to what extent the latter is to happen will depend on the normative requests of the editor.

Comment: As far as the second point is concerned the lexicographer on the one side and the Southern dictionary user on the other may have diverging views. The latter may not be very enthusiastic about the descriptive principles generally hold by the former. It may even be assumed that most Flemings, influenced by both linguistic insecurity and language political motives, won't be prepared to acknowledge the need for information of the Northern dictionary user, eager to find an explanation of Southern words unfamiliar to him. Yet these Flemings may be the first victims of their attitude since most bilingual dictionaries tend to ignore peripheral vocabulary, even official Belgian terminology of the type *schepen, rijkswacht*, etc.[8]

Consideration 4: The average Southern dictionary user and most certainly the average Southern reviewer belong to what I called earlier the intellectual and cultural establishment, mostly concerned with integrational motives. Consequently they favour reduction rather than extension of Southern lexical items.

Comment: this paradoxical attitude is brought about by two paramount considerations easily exceeding all others, viz.

- the fact that one wants Southern vocabulary rather to be normed than described:

- the fact that many definitely want to avoid the impression (which would then be reinforced by the "official" Van Dale) that a Southern Standard Language differing even mildly from the Northern one, may exist.

Consideration 5: The absence of internal Southern standardization considerably limits the possible amount of so-called general Southern vocabulary

Comment: when considering peripheral vocabulary for general dictionaries one generally and naturally starts with items one is familiar with from one's own linguistic background, whereas items originating from other regions are often unknown. Since suggestions for acknowledgement are therefore most often rather disparate and hard to judge, the bulk of so-called general Southern vocabulary mostly consists of items belonging to the written language and hardly specific for any particular region.

6. Conclusions

The ideal solution to the problem at hand should be to carry out a vast research programme to make an inventory of peripheral vocabulary and to determine the frequency of use in various subregions and style levels. Yet, since the lexicographer can hardly be expected to patiently wait for such findings, an interim solution must be found. A practical suggestion may be to install some kind of committee of experts (i.e. a Belgian Van Dale committee on the example of the Duden committees) to which a corpus is handed over, consisting of the ZNW and the lists drawn up by the editors of both GVD and HVD.

Such a committee may then be expected :

    a.   to stablish criteria for acknowledgement, i.e. to establish on a theoretical basis which lexical categories are to be accepted and which style levels are to be taken into consideration

b. to advise as to the labeling of peripheral vocabulary; as far as I am concerned it seems obvious that one could limit the labels to only two :

- Belgian: official terminology, i.e. words from category 1 + occasionally from category 7

- peripheral: all other words considered for acknowledgement. These are, accidently, the labels already used in the GVD, be it that a lack of consistency is apparent; anyway one should refrain from applying the label *Belgian* to frequently used, yet not official lexical items.

Additionally I should like to point out that the introduction of a label *in Nederland* seems to be unavoidable. Since it is necessary to indicate that *rijkswacht, licentiaat, onderzoeksrechter* etc. are official terms only used in Belgium it is equally necessary to indicate that *marechaussee, tentamen, officier van justitie* are official terms only used in the Netherlands.

c. to fill in the categories on the basis of the corpus mentioned above, of the intuitive knowledge of the members and of all information gathered from previous reviews and papers on the subject. There should be no objection against completing the information yielded by the label by indications like archaic, written language or concerning the register the words are generally used in.

If a similar committee were installed, cooperating directly with the editors and having a permanent nature so as to be able to cope immediately with new materials and research findings, there is a reasonable chance that peripheral vocabulary in general dictionaries will at last be handled in a serious and scientifically acceptable way and may yield reliable and useful results.

NOTES

[1] Van Dale : Groot Woordenboek van hedendaags Nederlands, door P.G.J. van Sterkenburg en W.J.J. Pijnenburg. Utrecht/Antwerpen, Van Dale Lexicografie.

[2] Algemene Nederlandse Spraakkunst. Groningen (Wolters-Noordhoff)and Leuven (Wolters), p. 12.

[3] The original quotation reads : "il n'existe pas de doctrine claire... sur ce qui devrait servir de cadre normatif au departage des termes a recevoir et a proscrire."

[4]"Wel is een beperkt aantal woorden die men uitsluitend in het hele Zuidnederlandse gebied aantreft, maar waarmee een andere variant in de standaardtaal correspondeert, voorzien van het label AZN, dat de betekenis Algemeen Zuidnederlands heeft" (p. 25)

[5]cf. appendix for the varying and often opposing way the GVD, HVD and the F-D Van Dale label peripheral vocabulary.

[6]"C'est de la sociolinguistique a l'etat pur que de se demander : en face de qui suis-je ? En face de qui adopter ce mot-ci ou celui-la ?" (Schüle 1981, 188).

[7]"De lexicograaf is geen scheidsrechter die bepaalt wat al of niet tot het Zuidnederlands of tot de standaardtaal behoort. Dat beslist de taalgemeenschap zelf : zij bepaalt welke elementen in het 'systeem' van de taal kunnen functioneren, welke elementen als 'regionaal', 'gewestelijk', 'deftig', 'onconventioneel' enz. dienen opgevat te worden, kortom zij beslist over het leven van ieder element door het gebruik dat zij ervan maakt. Zij stelt zelf de 'norm' vast, d.i. wat algemeen gebruikelijk is en wat storend is voor de communicatie. Het is de taak van de lexicograaf in het woordenboek hiervan een weerspiegeling te geven" (De Clerck 1981, xii).

[8]The only bilingual Van Dale with Dutch on the left published so far (the D-F one) constitutes a commendable exception to this general rule (cf. appendix)

BIBLIOGRAPHY

Al, B. Norm en variatie in het Frans. *Lecture, Amsterdam* 19.09.1981 (forthcoming), 1981.

Baetens Beardsmore, H. *Le francais régional de Bruxelles*. Bruxelles, Presses Universitaires, 1971.

Beersmans, F. Norm en variatie in het Duits. *Lecture, Amsterdam* 19.09.1981 (forthcoming), 1981.

Boulanger, J.C. *Les francais régionaux : observations sur les recherches actuelles*. Montreal, Office de la langue francaise, 1980.

Clerck, W. de. *Nijhoffs Zuidnederlands Woordenboek*. 's-Gravenhage/Antwerpen, M. Nijhoff, 1981.

Coetsem, F. van. Het Zuidnederlands bij Van Dale. In *Leuvense Bijdragen*, 65-69, 1961.

Doppagne, A. Le francais régional de Belgique. In *Actes du colloque Les français régionaux* (Doc. du Conseil de la langue française no 9). Québec, Editeur officiel du Québec, 169-180, 1981.

Fenske, H. *Schweizerische und österreichische Besonderheiten in deutschen Wörterbuchern*. Mannheim, Institut für deutsche Sprache. Forschungsberichte 10, 1973.

Geerts, G. Het gezag van Van Dale. In *Dietsche Warande en Belfort*, 54-65, 1967.

_____ Wat betekent Vlaams in Nederland ? In *Opstellen aangeboden aan Dr. C.H.A. Kruyskamp*. 's-Gravenhage, M. Nijhoff 88-96, no date.

Gendron, J-D. La norme et les critéres de normalisation du language au Québec. In *Zeitschrift der Gesellschaft für Kanada-Studien*, 3. 5-24, 1983.

Goossens, J. *Wat zijn Nederlandse dialecten* ? Groningen, Wolters-Noordhoff 1968.

Macaulay, R. Double Standards. In *American Anthropologist* 75, 1324-1337, 1973.

Schüle, E. Le français régional de Suisse. In *Actes du colloque Les régionaux* (Doc. du Conseil de la langue française no 9). Quebec, Éditeur officiel du Québec, 181-193, 1981.

Willemyns, R. Taalvarianten en normbewustzijn. In *Achtste Colloquium van docenten in de Neerlandistiek aan buitenlandse universiteiten.* 's-Gravenhage/Hasselt, 79-96, 1983.

Willemyns, R. A Common Legal Framework for Language Unity in the Dutch Language Area. The Treaty of Linguistic Union (Taalunieverdrag). In *Multilingua* 3-4, 215-223, 1984.

Willemyns, R. Vlaanderen en Quebec. Standaardtaalontwikkeling in perifere gebieden. In *Ons Erfdeel* 28, 409-417, 1985.

Willemyns, R. Regionalismen in het Nederlands. In *Handelingen van de Kon.Academie voor Nederlandse Taal- en Letterkunde.* (forthcoming), 1986.

APPENDIX: LABELING OF THE EXAMPLES FROM 4.2. IN GVD, HVD AND D-F VAN DALE.

1. Institutional terminology

	GVD	HVD	D-F
aanhoudingsmandaat	Belg(gal)	-	-
assisenhof	Belg	Belg	Belg
concordaat	Belg	AZN	unlabeled
gouverneur	Belg	-	-
licentiaat	Belg	Belg	unlabeled
observatiegraad	-	-	-
onderzoeksrechter	Belg	-	-
opcentiemen	Belg	-	-
procureur	Belg	-	-
regent	Belg	Belg	Belg
rijkswacht	Belg	Belg	Belg
schepen	Belg	Belg	AZN

2. Archaisms

ajuin	regional	-	unlabeled
draad	-	-	-
heirkracht	unlabeled	-	-
kaak	unlabeled	unlabeled	unlabeled
kleed	regional	AZN	written/lang.
kuisen	regional	AZN	AZN
kwetsen	unlabeled	unlabeled	unlabeled
mantel	unlabeled	unlabeled	unlabeled
nagel	Belg	unlabeled	unlabeled
ouderling	regional	-	-
plots	unlabeled	AZN	AZN
verwittigen	Belg	unlabeled	unlabeled
wenen	formal	written lang	unlabeled
zetel	regional	AZN	AZN

3. Dialect Interference

afzien	regional	unlabeled	unlabeled
beenhouwer	not general	AZN	AZN
doppen	regional	AZN	AZN
hesp	regional	AZN AZN	
nonkel	regional	AZN	AZN
pint	Belg	unlabeled	unlabeled
pladijs	regional	AZN	AZN
schouw	archaic, reg.	AZN	AZN
stoof	regional	AZN	AZN
taksplaat	Belg	-	-
verschieten	regional	-	-

4. Loanwords

autostrade	regional	-	-
chauffage	-	-	-
living	Belg	unlabeled	unlabeled
mazout	archaic, reg.	AZN	AZN
mutualiteit	Belg	-	-
occasie	Belg	AZN	AZN
parlementair	-	-	unlabeled
pistolet	unlabeled	unlabeled	unlabeled
praline	regional	unlabeled	unlabeled
quotering	Belg-	-	-
reconversie	Belg	-	-
solden	Belg	AZN	AZN
syndicaat	Belg	unlabeled	unlabeled

5. Barbarisms

dagorde	unlabeled	unlabeled	unlabeled
droogkuis	-	-	-
eraan houden	Belg(gal)	-	-
hernemen	Belg(gal)	-	-
ordewoord	Belg(gal)	-	-
overmaken	unlabeled	-	-
overste	-	-	-
rondpunt	Belg(gal)	-	-
voorzien	regional	-	-
wapendracht	-	-	-
zakencijfer	-	-	-
zetelen	unlabeled	unlabeled	-

6. Hypercorrections

bestemmeling	Belg	AZN	AZN
betoelagen	Belg(pur)	-	-
brieventas	unlabeled	-	-
duimspijker	hyper-correction	-	unlabeled
inkom	regional	AZN	AZN
(kinder)kribbe	Belg(pur)	-	-
koetswerk	unlabeled	unlabeled	unlabeled
regenscherm	regional	writtenlang	written lang
vaststelling	Belg	AZN	unlabeled
wisselstukken	-	-	-
zitpenning	regional	-	-

7. Neologisms

blokken	unlabeled	unlabeled	Belg
brugpensioen	Belg	-	-
buizen	Belg	AZN	AZN

deelregering	Belg	-	-
heenwedstrijd	Belg	-	-
kot	not general	AZN	AZN
kous(e)broek	unusual	AZN	AZN
langspeelfilm	-	-	-
medepastoor	-	-	-
regeringsraad	Belg	-	-